Sand in Their Shoes

A CAPE COD READER

Sand in th

Our fathers were a good people, we
have been a free people and if you
will not let us remain so any longer
we shall be a great people.
— JAMES OTIS to the British Crown

ir Shoes

A Cape Cod Reader

EDITED BY EDITH SHAY
AND FRANK SHAY

Parnassus Imprints
21 Canal Road
Orleans, Mass, 02653

FOREWORD

A GREAT Cape Cod historian, finishing his monumental *Truro — Cape Cod: Landmarks and Seamarks,* in 1883, wrote of the people of the past he had lived with so long:

"As one by one these pages have been slowly gathered, one by one, and in little groups, these friends have also been gathered. I have found them delightful companions. Always the same: they have no new or changed faces. Our acquaintanceship has ripened into tender relationship and unchanging friendship that has repaid many times all my toil."

With reverence to Shebnah Rich, not dreaming of comparing their labors with his, these editors echo his words.

We have lived on Cape Cod for many years, reading everything we could get our hands on about the Cape, now and then writing about what we read and observed. Again and again we have found ourselves for reasons of space obliged to paraphrase or to quote briefly from far better writers than ourselves. "If we could only give it all!" we have said to each other ruefully. This book is a response to an old compulsion to give as much of it as possible.

In compiling it we felt privileged to call upon any and all of the people of Cape Cod and we can only say that they responded in the most gratifying manner. To thank all individually would be next to the impossible.

Particular gratitude is due to Miss Phyllis Duganne, of Truro, who opened the Cobb family archives; to Dr. Oliver L. Austin, Jr., of Eastham, who gave up valuable time to prepare for the book an authoritative article on Cape Cod bird life; to Mr. Donald G. Trayser, of Barnstable, historian and antiquarian of Cape Cod lore, for making available his fine collection of historical material.

To Mrs. Florence C. Lincoln, of Chatham, for permission to include material by her late husband, Joseph C. Lincoln; to Mrs. Dorothy Paine Collier, of Provincetown, for the use of the works of her aunt, Nancy W. Paine Smith; to Mrs. George Sargent Burgess, of Wellesley Hills, for an excerpt from the works of Katharine Lee Bates; to Mrs. Mary Heaton Vorse, of Provincetown, to Harry Kemp, of Provincetown, and to the heirs of the late Susan Glaspell, for valuable material.

To Walter Muir Whitehill, and the Peabody Museum, of Salem; to the Yale University Press; to Paul and Dorothy Lambert of *The Provincetown Advocate;* and to Jack Johnson, of *The Cape Codder.*

Cape Cod librarians have been universally helpful and we wish particularly to acknowledge the aid of Mrs. F. A. Ellis, of the Brewster Ladies' Library Association; Miss Ruth L. Barnard, of the Snow Library, Orleans; Mrs. Eleanor T. Rowland, of the Provincetown Public Library, and Mrs. Margaret E. Gilliatt, of the Wellfleet Public Library.

E. S. and F. S.

CONTENTS

INTRODUCTION

The sandy dunes and strands of Cape Cod are not suggestive
of high-standing corn-fields or rich rolling meadows. If her
crop of men is no better, there need be little said.
— SHEBNAH RICH

IN THE EARLY PAGES of this book we say Cape Cod was not really discovered, it was unveiled. We cannot quarrel with our own words nor do we want to eat them, but the true fact is that Cape Cod is the most discovered land in history. It is discovered, or rediscovered if you prefer, thousands of times each year. Wide-eyed and almost speechless at first, the latter-day Breretons finally manage to proclaim: "Here I stay!" But the most cursory examination of the census reports show that, save for the natural increase expected of a healthy people, abandonment jogs on the heels of discovery and adoption. To a very few the Cape is merely a network of highways entirely surrounded by sand.

The shock of recognition comes easiest to the city-choked American who, with a week or two, or even a month of freedom from the usual grind, finds himself propelled into the cleanliness, rather call it the purity, of early America. That he recognizes it so quickly is a tribute to his perspicacity, that he enjoys it so greatly is a credit to his nativity and that he finally returns to more familiar and profitable scenes is no reflection on his intelligence.

To the average American who works for his living this long, sandy spike is Hardscrabble. It is not by any means a land of opportunity, and enterprising Cape Cod boys and girls often demonstrate the quality of their enterprise by leaving it. As they go, their places are taken by outsiders: some have money to live on and simply like the Cape; many are workers in the arts who find here a congenial environment in which to work. But it isn't the Americans and English who make Paris and it isn't these displaced persons who make Cape Cod. Behind the sometimes rather Bohemian smoke screen laid down upon Cape Cod dunes and shores by the literary, artistic, income-bearing newcomers, move some of the most resourceful people in the world steering their old course. They have had more economic ups and downs than most people. At several points in their history they have been at the top of the heap, and just as often have they been in the doldrums. They are a hardy people, they are industrious and smart, they are amphibious.

In the early days they were seafarers: whalefishers, fishermen, traders. But when coal oil took the place of whale oil, the whalefisheries declined; when steam took the place of sail, owners no longer felt obliged to demand the experience of a Cape Cod master on the quarter-deck as guarantee of safety for passengers, ship and cargo. And there have always been times when the price of fish dropped so low it was folly to go after them. In such periods of stress Cape Cod people have always had — or found — an ace in the hole.

The first oysters of commerce came from the Cape, being taken from Wellfleet and hawked along the Fish Wharf in Boston. Cape Cod oystermen taught the world a trick right then: the boat brought the shellfish to the wharf and the crew erected a small hut for their cargo and left one of their number to sell it while they went back for more oysters. Go there today and look at the good Cape names over the modern oyster houses! But we're not through. When the Cape oysters were all but exhausted these same men went to the Chesapeake and brought back the southern bivalves on the same leap-frog plan. Go down there, too, and read the old Cape names on the oyster piers. When the Boston customers found fault with the flavor of the new oysters, the Cape shellfishermen came up with another cute trick: they brought the southern oysters to their home ports, let them lie in the cold, clean waters for a season, and then sold them as the old Cape Cod originals.

Cranberries, strawberries, spinach, asparagus, turnips, chickens, ducks, turkeys, it was found, do well on the Cape's sandy well-drained soil. When fish start running or prices rise, the Cape Cod farmer to this day is inclined to leave the farm work to the juniors and elders and women and go back to his lines and nets. But he has his farm to come home to.

Not all owned farms or cared for farming. Back in the last century Cape Cod discovered summer visitors, or perhaps it should be put the other way. And long before then, as now, the restless and ambitious sometimes moved away.

Perhaps those who stayed will be found to be a little set in their ways: after all, they've been here a long time and have become thoroughly acclimatized and such people do not easily give up old habits. A comparison of the signers of the Mayflower Compact with a 1950 directory shows that more than seventy-five per cent of the signers still have namesakes on Cape Cod. These seldom boast their ancestry and they seem to be in general agreement that if the Pilgrims didn't like the place well enough to stay, that was their business. As a seafaring people they agree that the famous passage of the Mayflower was probably one of the dullest voyages in history.

Those who left carried the Cape Cod tradition of enterprise and astuteness far afield. Among the earliest to leave was the young lawyer, James Otis of West Barnstable, who in 1761 struck the match that lighted the American Revolution. Isaac Rich, as a poor Wellfleet boy, hawked his town's oysters through the streets of Boston and, what with one thing and another, managed to amass a fortune which he dedicated to the founding of Boston University. Elisha Doane, also of Wellfleet, did so well on several sperm-whaling voyages that he decided to stay ashore and finance other ventures. Elisha was the richest man in all New England when he died.

Up Barnstable way another young man found the Cape economy cramping. He was Gustavus Swift who operated a small rolling butcher shop. Young Gus found too much competition in the easily available fish and looked for a scene where meat appetites were heartier and fish expensive. He found it in the new West where he built the meat-packing firm of Swift and Company. And there was Captain Lorenzo Dow Baker, a Wellfleet coastal freighting captain, who enjoyed so much the bananas he ate in Jamaica that he decided to share his delight with his fellow Americans. The fruit justified his confidence and he is remembered today as the man who laid the keel of the United Fruit Company's White Fleet.

A Truro boy had one of the most exciting careers of all. He was Edward Knight Collins, born to an old seafaring family. Instead of going to the quarter-deck through the hawse hole or with his gloves on, he stayed ashore and secured the ships and cargoes, at first for his many relatives. His wider career was launched in the Gulf ports with a small fleet of packets. In 1835 he returned to the north and established the famous Dramatic Line of New York and Liverpool packets. It was officially called the Collins Line but the owner named his vessels for Garrick, Siddons, Sheridan and others famous in the theatre and the people gave it the nickname. Collins was one of the first to recognize the importance of steam and in 1850 he founded the Collins Steam Mail Line, the first ocean liners in America. The *Atlantic, Pacific, Arctic, Baltic* and other vessels of the fleet were the fastest, largest, and best equipped vessels afloat.

It was in these years that the British Empire decided to exhibit its enormous and widespread resources to the world in a great exposition held in the Crystal Palace, London. They were great days for the British, but they were somewhat marred, first by the victory of the *America* in the yacht regatta and then constantly by the fact that the Collins liners beat the daylights out of the steamships operated by their own Samuel Cunard.

In the field of letters Falmouth gave Katharine Lee Bates to Wellesley and the world. Among the Cape Cod writers who have set down Cape Cod history with permanence are Shebnah Rich and Frederick Freeman of Truro, C. W. Swift of Yarmouthport, Elizabeth Reynard of Chatham, Henry C. Kittredge of Barnstable; not to mention the many genealogists, Amos Otis of Yarmouth outstanding. Brewster was the birthplace of Joseph C. Lincoln and Phyllis Duganne, Sandwich of Thornton Burgess, creator of "Peter Rabbit" and writer of many children's stories, Wellfleet of Phoebe Atwood Taylor of Asey Mayo fame. Which reminds us that Horatio Alger, Jr., the granddaddy of all American popular writers, once held the pulpit in a Brewster church. And, lest we forget, Dr. Pitcher, a Hyannis druggist, quieted the babies of generations with his famous soothing syrup so that their parents might read in bed.

Cape Cod has been, still is, and will always be good for America.

FRANK SHAY

Sand in Their Shoes

A CAPE COD READER

CAPE COD

BY GEORGE SANTAYANA

T HE LOW sandy beach and the thin scrub pine,
The wide reach of bay and the long sky line, —
  O, I am far from home!

The salt, salt smell of the thick sea air,
And the smooth round stones that the ebbtides wear, —
  When will the good ship come?

The wretched stumps all charred and burned,
And the deep soft rut where the cartwheel turned, —
  Why is the world so old?

The lapping wave, and the broad grey sky
Where the cawing crows and the slow gulls fly, —
  Where are the dead untold?

The thin, slant willows by the flooded bog,
The huge stranded hulk and the floating log, —
  Sorrow with life began!

And among the dark pines, and along the flat shore,
O the wind, and the wind, for evermore!
  What will become of man?

From POEMS

The First Comers

1602–1620

THE FIRST COMERS

*B*ART GOSNOLD *discovered Cape Cod, they'll tell you on the Cape where nearly every town has its Gosnold Street. This is scarcely true, but, as says Shebnah Rich,* "Whatever else did or did not this ancient mariner, everybody is agreed that he named Cape Cod; and so effectually, that blow high or low, cold or hot, thick or thin, fish or no fish, it has hung on like a lamper-eel from that day to this." *Gosnold did more than this. He brought with him in his ship's company two literate gentlemen, John Brereton and Gabriel Archer, who each wrote his "true relation" of all he'd seen and done upon the voyage and so, for the first time, established Cape Cod and the Islands as a widely recognized, always recognizable part of geography. But Cape Cod was never truly discovered. It was unveiled. Its unmistakable sickle shape appears and disappears and reappears through the swirling mists of European tale and legend for centuries before Gosnold sailed.*

You can fetch a vessel from Norway to Cape Cod by following sailing directions in ancient Scandinavian manuscripts, navigators say. If legend can be believed Thorwald, son of Eric the Red, visited the now vanished Isle of Nauset in 1003 and, in St. Malo, France, fishermen will tell you that for generations before Columbus their forefathers fished off a sandy hook of land now called Cape Cod. Cruising northward towards Maine from the Carolinas in 1524 — nearly a hundred years before the Mayflower came — John da Verrazano came ashore on Cape Cod and, in a letter to his patron, Francis I of France, described its "rude and barbarous" Indians. Sir Francis Drake was probably here in 1584. French, Dutch, Basque, Portuguese and British whalemen, fishermen and adventurers were coming and going all through the sixteenth century, but they were for the most part unlettered men who carried home only stories, not written accounts, of the teeming waters and the secure harbor at the Cape's end.

4

Bartholomew Gosnold and his company, arriving in the Cape's lovely, belated spring, believed they had wandered into an unknown Paradise.

℮≈◎

1602

CAPE COD AND THE ISLANDS

BY JOHN BRERETON

MAY IT PLEASE your Lordship [1] therefore to understand, that upon the sixth and twentieth of March *1602,* being Friday, we went from *Falmouth,* being in all, two and thirty persons, in a small bark of *Dartmouth,* called The *Concord,* holding a course for the North part of Virginia: and although by chance the wind favored us not at first as we wished, but inforced us so far to the Southward, as we fell in with *S. Marie,* one of the islands of the *Azores* (which was not much out of our way) yet holding our course directly from thence, we made our journey shorter (than hitherto accustomed) by the better part of a thousand leagues, [2] yet were we longer in our passage than we expected; which happened, for that our bark being weak, we were loath to press her with much sail; also, our sailors being few, and they none of the best, we bare (except in fair weather) but low sail; besides, our going upon an unknown coast, made us not over-bold to stand in with the shore, but in open weather; which caused us to be certain days in sounding, before we discovered the coast, the weather being by chance, somewhat foggy.

But on Friday the fourteenth of May, early in the morning, we made the land, being full of fair trees, the land somewhat low, certain hummocks or hills lying into the land, the shore full of white sand, but very stony or rocky. [3] And standing fair alongst by the shore, about twelve of the clock the same day, we came to an anchor,

---

[1] Brereton's account is addressed to Sir Walter Ralegh.
[2] Gosnold on this journey was the first Englishman to set his course directly across the Atlantic instead of following Columbus' passage by way of the Canaries.
[3] Cape Neddock, Maine.

where six Indians, in a bask-shallop with mast and sail, an iron grapple, and a kettle of copper, came boldly aboard us, one of them apparelled with a waistcoat and breeches of black serge, made after our sea-fashion, hose and shoes on his feet; all the rest (saving one that had a pair of breeches of blue cloth) were all naked. These people are of tall stature, broad and grim visage, of a black swart complexion, their eyebrows painted white; their weapons are bows and arrows; it seemed by some words and signs they made, that some Basques or of *S. John de Luz,* have fished or traded in this place, being in the latitude of 43 degrees.

But riding here, in no very good harbor, and withal, doubting the weather, about three of the clock the same day in the afternoon we weighed, & standing southerly off into sea the rest of that day and the night following, with a fresh gale of wind, in the morning we found ourselves embayed with a mighty headland; [4] but coming to an anchor about nine of the clock the same day, within a league of the shore, we hoised out the one half of our shallop, and captain *Bartholomew Gosnold,* myself, and three others, went ashore, being a white sandy and very bold shore; and marching all that afternoon with our muskets on our necks, on the highest hills which we saw (the weather very hot) at length we perceived this headland to be a parcel of the main, and sundry islands lying almost round about it: so returning (towards evening) to our shallop (for by that time the other part was brought ashore and set together) we espied an Indian, a young man, of proper stature, and of a pleasing countenance; and after some familiarity with him, we left him at the sea side, and returned to our ship, where in five or six hours absence, we had pestered our ship so with codfish, that we threw numbers of them overboard again; [5] and surely, I am persuaded that in the months of March, April, and May, there is upon this coast, better fishing, and in as great plenty, as in *Newfoundland:* for the skulls of mackerel, herrings, cod, and other fish, that we daily saw as we went and came from the shore, were wonderful. . . .

From this place, we sailed round about this headland, almost all

4 The cliffs of Truro.

5 "The fifteenth day we had again sight of the land, which made ahead, being as we thought an island, by reason of a large sound that appeared westward between it and the main, for coming to the West end thereof, we did perceive a large opening, we called it Shoal Hope. Near this cape we came to anchor in fifteen fathoms, where we took great store of codfish, for which we altered the name, and called it Cape Cod." — GABRIEL ARCHER.

the points of the compass, the shore very bold: but as no coast is free from dangers, so I am persuaded, this is as free as any; the land somewhat low, full of goodly woods, but in some places plain: at length we were come along many fair islands, which we had partly discerned at our first landing; all lying within a league or two one of another, and the outermost not above six or seven leagues from the main; but coming to anchor under one of them, which was about three or four leagues from the main, captain *Gosnold,* myself, and some others, went ashore, & going round about it, we found it to be four English miles in compass, without house or inhabitant, saving a little old house made of boughs, covered with bark, an old piece of a weir of the Indians, to catch fish, and one or two places, where they had made fires.

The chiefest trees of this island, are beeches and cedars; the outward parts all overgrown with low bushy trees, three or four feet in height, which bear some kind of fruits, as appeared by their blossoms; strawberries, red and white, as sweet and much bigger than ours in *England,* raspberries, gooseberries, hurtleberries, and such; an incredible store of vines, as well in the woody part of the island, where they run upon every tree, as on the outward parts, that we could not go for treading upon them: also, many springs of excellent sweet water, and a great standing lake of fresh water, near the sea side, an English mile in compass, which is maintained with the springs running exceeding pleasantly through the woody grounds which are very rocky.

Here are also in this island, great store of deer, which we saw, and other beasts, as appeared by their tracks; as also divers fowls, as cranes, hernshaws, bitterns, geese, mallards, teals, and other fowls, in great plenty; also, great store of peas, which grow in certain plots all the island over.

. . . . .

From hence we went to another island, to the northwest of this, and within a league or two of the main, which we found to be greater than before we imagined, being 16 English miles at least in compass [6] . . . in mid May we did sow in this island (as for a trial) in sundry places, wheat, barley, oats, and peas, which in fourteen days were sprung up nine inches and more: the soil is fat and lusty; the upper crust, of gray color; but a foot or less in depth, of the color of our hemp-lands in *England;* and being thus apt for these and

[6] Cuttyhunk.

the like grains; the sowing or setting (after the ground is cleansed) is no greater labor, than if you should set or sow in one of our best prepared gardens in England.

This island is full of high timbered oaks, their leaves thrice so broad as ours; cedars, straight and tall; beech, elm, holly, walnut trees in abundance, the fruit as big as ours, as appeared by those we found under the trees, which had lain all the year ungathered; hazelnut trees, cherry trees, the leaf, bark and bigness not differing from ours in *England,* but the stalk beareth the blossoms or fruit at the end thereof, like a cluster of grapes, forty or fifty in a bunch; sassafras trees great plenty all the island over, a tree of high price and profit; also divers other fruit trees, some of them with strange barks, or an orange color, in feeling soft and smooth like velvet: in the thickest part of these woods, you may see a furlong or more round about.

On the northwest side of this island, near to the sea side, is a standing lake of fresh water, almost three English miles in compass, in the middest whereof stands a plot of woody ground, an acre in quantity or not above: this lake is full of small tortoises, and exceedingly frequented with all sorts of fowls before rehearsed, which breed, some low on the banks, and others on low trees about this lake in great abundance, whose young ones of all sorts we took and eat at our pleasure: but all these fowls are much bigger than ours in *England.*

Also, in every island, and almost in every part of every island, are great store of ground nuts, forty together on a string, some of them as big as hen's eggs; they grow not two inches under ground: the which nuts we found to be as good as potatoes. Also, divers sorts of shellfish, as scallops, mussels, cockles, lobsters, crabs, oysters, and wilks, exceeding good and very great.

But not to cloy you with particular rehearsal of such things as God & nature hath bestowed on these places, in comparison whereof, the most fertile part of all *England* is (of itself) but barren; we went in our light-horseman from this island to the main, right against this island some two leagues off,[7] where coming ashore, we stood a while like men ravished at the beauty and delicacy of this sweet soil; for besides divers clear lakes of fresh water (whereof we saw no end) meadows very large and full of green grass; even the most woody places (I speak only of such as I saw) do grow so distinct and apart,

[7] Buzzard's Bay.

one tree from another, upon green grassy ground, somewhat higher than the plains, as if Nature would show herself above her power, artificial.

Hard by, we espied seven Indians; and coming up to them, at first they expressed some fear; but being emboldened by our courteous visage, and some trifles which we gave them, they followed us to a neck of land, which we imagined had been severed from the main; but finding it otherwise, we perceived a broad harbor or river's mouth, which ran up into the main: but because the day was far spent, we were forced to return to the island from whence we came, leaving the discovery of this harbor, for a time of better leisure. . . .

Now the next day, we determined to fortify ourselves in the little plot of ground in the midst of the lake above mentioned, where we built an house, and covered it with sedge, which grew about this lake in great abundance; in building whereof, we spent three weeks and more: but the second day after our coming from the main, we espied 9 canoes or boats, with fifty Indians in them, coming toward us from this part of the main, where we, two days before, landed.

And being loath they should discover our fortification, we went out on the sea side to meet them; and coming somewhat near them, they all sat down upon the stones, calling aloud to us (as we rightly guessed) to do the like, a little distance from them: having sat a while in this order, captain *Gosnold* willed me to go unto them, to see what countenance they would make; but as soon as I came up unto them, one of them, to whom I had given a knife two days before in the main, knew me (whom I also very well remembered) and smiling upon me, spake somewhat unto their lord or captain, which sat in the midst of them, who presently rose up and took a large beaver skin from one that stood about him, and gave it unto me, which I requited for that time the best I could: but I pointing towards captain *Gosnold,* made signs unto him, that he was our captain, and desirous to be his friend, and enter league with him, which (as I perceived) he understood, and made signs of joy.

Whereupon captain *Gosnold* with the rest of his company, being twenty in all, came up unto them; and after many signs of gratulations . . . we became very great friends, and sent for meat aboard our shallop, and gave them such meats as we had then ready dressed, whereof they misliked nothing but our mustard, whereat they made many a sour face.[8]

[8] "It was sport to behold their faces made being bitten therewith." Gabriel Archer.

So the rest of the day we spent in trading with them for furs, which are beavers, luzernes, martins, otters, wild-cat skins very large and deep fur, black foxes, coney skins, of the color of our hares, but somewhat less, deer skins very large, seal skins. and other beasts' skins, to us unknown.

Thus they continued with us three days, every night retiring themselves to the furthermost part of our island two or three miles from our fort: but the fourth day they returned to the main, pointing five or six times to the sun, and once to the main, which we understood, that within five or six days they would come from the main to us again: but being in their canoes a little from the shore, they made huge cries & shouts of joy unto us; and we with our trumpet and cornet, and casting up our caps into the air, made them the best farewell we could.

Yet six or seven of them remained with us behind, bearing us company every day into the woods, and helped us to cut and carry our sassafras, and some of them lay aboard our ship.

These people, as they are exceeding courteous, gentle of disposition, and well conditioned, excelling all others we have seen; so for shape of body and lovely favor, I think they excel all the people of *America;* of stature much higher than we; of complexion or color, much like a dark olive; their eye-brows and hair black, which they wear long, tied up behind in knots, whereupon they prick feathers of fowls, in fashion of a crownet: some of them are black thin bearded; they make beards of the hair of beasts: and one of them offered a beard of their making to one of our sailors, for his that grew on his face, which because it was of a red color, they judged to be none of his own.

They are quick eyed, and steadfast in their looks, fearless of others' harms, as intending none themselves; some of the meaner sort given to filching, which the very name of savages (not weighing their ignorance in good or evil) may easily excuse: their garments are of deer skins, and some of them wear furs round and close about their necks. They pronounce our language with great facility; for one of them sitting by me, upon occasion I spake smiling to him these words: *How now (sirha) are you so saucy with my tobacco:* which words (without any further repetition) he suddenly spake so plain and distinctly, as if he had been a long scholar in the language.

Many other such trials we had, which are here needless to repeat. Their women (such as we saw) which were but three in all, were but low ot stature, their eye-brows, hair, apparell, and manner of wearing, like to the men, fat, and very well favored, and much delighted in our company; the men very dutiful towards them. . . .

For the agreeing of this climate with us (I speak of myself, & so I may justly do for the rest of our company) that we found our health and strength all the while we remained there, so to renew and increase, as notwithstanding our diet and lodging was none of the best, yet not one of our company (God be thanked) felt the least grudging or inclination to any disease or sickness, but were much fatter and in better health than when we went out of *England*.

But after our bark had taken in so much sassafras, cedar, furs, skins, and other commodities, as were thought convenient; some of our company that had promised captain *Gosnold* to stay, having nothing but a saving voyage in their minds, made our company of inhabitants (which was small enough before) much smaller; so as captain *Gosnold* seeing his whole strength to consist but of twelve men, and they but meanly provided, determined to return for *England*, leaving this island (which he called *Elizabeth's Island*) with as many true sorrowful eyes, as were before desirous to see it. So the 18 of June, being Friday, we weighed, and with indifferent fair wind and weather came to anchor the 23 of July, being also Friday (in all, bare five weeks) before Exmouth.

— From A Brief and True Relation of the
Discovery of the North Part of Virginia

Brereton's Brief and True Relation, *the earliest English book relating to New England, was published in London in the year of the voyage, 1602. It made a mighty stir. Soon other adventurers were flying towards these shores, seeking mainly sassafras. This was the wonder drug of the times, "a plant," writes Martin Pring, "of sovereign virtue for the French pox, and as some of late have learnedly written good against the plague and many other maladies." (Also a cure for eating a surfeit of dogfish, Gabriel Archer relates.)*

Pring himself was here in 1603, after sassafras. Samuel Champlain accompanied two expeditions to Cape Cod, one in 1605 and one in 1606, seeking a warmer site for the French colony freezing at St. Croix and finally discouraged from settlement by trouble with the Indians. Henry Hudson came by in 1609.

In 1614 Captain John Smith inspired in part, he tells us, by Brereton's narrative, sailed with two ships from London and arrived in April at the "Ile of Monahiggan" *in Maine.* "Our plot was there to take whales and make trials of a mine of gold and copper. If those failed, fish and furs was then our refuge, to make ourselves savers howsoever." *The whalefishing proved* "a costly conclusion" *and there were no mines of gold but, exploring the coast from Penobscot to a little south of Cape Cod, Smith discovered fish to be far more than the mere refuge for which he had hoped.*

☙

1616
THE MAIN STAPLE

BY CAPTAIN JOHN SMITH

THE MAIN STAPLE, from hence to be extracted for the present to produce the rest, is fish; which however it may seem a mean and base commodity; yet who will but truly take the pains and consider the sequel, I think will allow it well worth the labour. It is strange to see what great adventures the hopes of setting forth men of war to rob the industrious innocent, would procure: or such massy promises in gross: though more are choked than well fed with such hasty hopes. But who doth not know that the poor Hollanders, chiefly by fishing, at a great charge and labor in all weathers in the open sea, are made a people so hardy, and industrious? and by venting this poor commodity to the Easterlings for as mean, which is wood, flax, pitch, tar, rosin, cordage, and such like (which they exchange again, to the French, Spaniards, Portugals, and English, &c. for what they want) are made so mighty, strong and rich, as no state but *Venice,* of twice their magnitude, is so well furnished with so many fair cities, goodly towns, strong fortresses, and that abundance of shipping and all sorts of merchandise, as well as of gold, silver, pearls, diamonds, precious stones, silks, velvets, and cloth of gold; as fish, pitch, wood, or such gross commodities? What voyages and discoveries, east and west, north and south, yea about the world, make they? What an army by sea and land, have they long maintained in despite of one of the greatest princes of the world? And

never could the Spaniard with all his mines of gold and silver, pay
his debts, his friends, and army, half so truly, as the Hollanders still
have done by this contemptible trade of fish. Divers (I know) may
allege, many other assistances: but this is their mine; and the sea the
source of those silvered streams of all their virtue; which hath made
them now the very miracle of industry, the pattern of perfection for
these affairs: and the benefit of fishing is that *Primum mobile* that
turns all their *Spheres* to this height of plenty, strength, honor and
admiration.

· · · · ·

In March, April, May, and half June, here is cod in abundance;
in May, June, July and August mullet and sturgeon; whose roes do
make caviar and puttargo. Herring, if any desire them, I have taken
many out of the bellies of cod, some in nets; but the savages compare
their store in the sea, to the hairs of their heads: and surely there are
an incredible abundance upon this coast. In the end of August, September, October, and November, you have cod again to make cor-
fish, or poor John: and each hundred is as good as two or three
hundred in the *New-found Land*. So that half the labour in hooking,
splitting, and turning, is saved: and you may have your fish at what
market you will, before they can have any in *New-found Land:* where
their fishing is chiefly but in June and July: whereas it is here in
March, April, May, September, October, and November, as is said.
So that by reason of this plantation, the merchants may have freight
both out and home: which yields an advantage worth consideration.

Your cod-fish you may in like manner transport as you see cause,
to serve the ports in *Portugal* (as *Lisbon, Avera, Porta port,* and
divers others, or what market you please) before your *Islanders*
return: They being tied to the season in the open sea; you having a
double season, and fishing before your doors, may every night sleep
quietly ashore with good cheer and what fires you will, or when you
please with your wives and family: they only, their ships in the main
ocean.

· · · · ·

Salt upon salt may assuredly be made; if not at first in the ponds,
yet till they be provided this may be used: then the ships may transport kine, horse, goats, coarse cloth, and such commodities as we
want; by whose arrival may be made that provision of fish to freight

the ships that they stay not: and then if the sailors go for wages, it matters not. It is hard if this return defray not the charge: but care must be had, they arrive in the spring, or else provision be made for them against the winter.

· · · · ·

Cape Cod is the next presents itself: which is only a headland of high hills of sand, overgrown with shrubby pines, hurts, and such trash; but an excellent harbor for all weathers. This *Cape* is made by the main sea on the one side and a great bay on the other in forme of a sickle: on it doth inhabit the people of *Pawmet:* and in the bottom of the bay, the people of *Chawum.* Towards the South and South west of this *Cape,* is found a long and dangerous shoal of sands and rocks. But so far as I encircled it, I found thirty fathom water aboard the shore and strong current: which makes me think there is a channel about this shoal; where is the best and greatest fish to be had, winter and summer, in all that country. But, the savages say there is no channel, but that the shoals begin from the main at *Pawmet,* to the isle of *Nauset;* and so extends beyond their knowledge into the sea.

— From A DESCRIPTION OF NEW ENGLAND

Like John Brereton's BRIEF AND TRUE RELATION, *John Smith's* A DESCRIPTION OF NEW ENGLAND *is a piece of pure promotional literature. Containing a surprisingly accurate map of the coast, it was published in London in 1616 and for the first time gave the name* NEW ENGLAND *to a large region which before had been known only as a part of the North Part of Virginia. Smith dedicated the work to Prince Charles, humbly suing him to change at his pleasure the names he had given to various points along the coast, "so that posterity might ever be able to say Prince Charles was their god-father." Some of the changes the young prince made remain to this day. Cape Tragabizanda, for instance, became and still is Cape Ann, but he failed when he tried to re-name Cape Cod for his royal father.*

Captain John Smith's vision far outran his times. He showed New England the way but it was to be many years before the minds of other men caught up with him.

☙

1620

THE MAYFLOWER VOYAGE

BY WILLIAM BRADFORD

SEPTr. 6. These troubles being blown over, and now all being compact together in one ship, they put to sea again with a prosperous wind, which continued divers days together, which was some encouragement unto them; yet according to the usual manner many were afflicted with sea-sickness. And I may not omit here a special work of God's providence. There was a proud and very profane young man, one of the seamen, of a lusty, able body, which made him the more haughty; he would always be contemning the poor people in their sickness, and cursing them daily with grievous execrations, and did not let to tell them, that he hoped to help cast half of them overboard before they came to their journey's end, and to make merry with what they had; and if he were by any gently reproved, he would curse and swear most bitterly. But it pleased God before they came half seas over, to smite this young man with a grievous disease, of which he died in a desperate manner, and so was himself the first that was thrown overboard. Thus his curses lit on his own head; and it was an astonishment to all his fellows, for they noted it to be the just hand of God upon him.

After they had enjoyed fair winds and weather for a season, they were encountered many times with crosswinds, and met with many fierce storms, with which the ship was shrewdly shaken, and her upper works made very leaky; and one of the main beams in the midships was bowed and cracked, which put them in some fear that the ship could not be able to perform the voyage. So some of the chief of the company, perceiving the mariners to fear the sufficiency of the ship, as appeared by their mutterings, they entered into serious consultation with the master and other officers of the ship, to consider in time of the danger; and rather to return than to cast themselves into a desperate and inevitable peril. And truly there was great distraction and difference of opinion amongst the mariners themselves; fain would they do what could be done for their wages' sake, (being now half the seas over,) and on the other hand they were loath to hazard their lives too desperately. But in examination of all opinions, the master and others affirmed they knew the ship to be strong and firm under water; and for the buckling of the main beam, there was a great iron screw the passengers brought out of Holland, which would raise the beam into its place; the which being done, the carpenter and master affirmed that with a post put under it, set firm in the lower deck, and otherways bound, he would make it sufficient. And as for the decks and the upper works they would caulk them as well as they could, and though with the working of the ship they would not long keep staunch, yet there would otherwise be no great danger, if they did not overpress her with sails. So they committed themselves to the will of God and resolved to proceed.

In sundry of these storms the winds were so fierce, and the seas so high, as they could not bear a knot of sail, but were forced to hull, for divers days together. And in one of them, as they thus lay at hull, in a mighty storm, a lusty young man (called John Howland) coming upon some occasion above the gratings, was, with a seele of the ship, thrown into the sea; but it pleased God that he caught hold of the topsail halyards, which hung overboard, and ran out at length; yet he held his hold (though he was sundry fathoms under water) till he was hauled up by the same rope to the brim of the water, and then with a boathook and other means got into the ship again, and his life saved; and though he was something ill with it, yet he lived many years after, and became a profitable member both in church and commonwealth.

In all this voyage there died but one of the passengers, which was William Butten, a youth, servant to Samuel Fuller, when they drew near the coast.

But to omit other things, (that I may be brief) after long beating at sea they fell with that land which is called Cape Cod; the which being made and certainly known to be it, they were not a little joyful. After some deliberation had amongst themselves and with the master of the ship, they tacked about and resolved to stand for the southward (the wind and weather being fair) to find some place about Hudson's river for their habitation. But after they had sailed that course about half the day, they fell amongst dangerous shoals and roaring breakers, and they were so far entangled therewith as they conceived themselves in great danger; and the wind shrinking upon them withal, they resolved to bear up again for the Cape, and thought themselves happy to get out of those dangers before night overtook them, as by God's providence they did. And the next day they got into the Cape-harbor where they rode in safety.

A word or two by the way of this cape; it was thus first named by Captain Gosnold and his company Ano: 1602, and after by Captain Smith was called Cape James; but it retains the former name amongst seamen. Also that point which first showed those dangerous shoals unto them, they called Point Care, and Tucker's Terror; but the French and Dutch to this day call it Mallebarre, by reason of those perilous shoals and the losses they have suffered there.

Being thus arrived in a good harbor and brought safe to land, they fell upon their knees and blessed the God of heaven, who had brought them over the vast and furious ocean, and delivered them from all the perils and miseries thereof, again to set their feet on the firm and stable earth, their proper element.... But here I cannot but stay and make a pause, and stand half amazed at this poor peoples' present condition; and so I think will the reader too, when he well considers the same. Being thus past the vast ocean, and a sea of troubles before in their preparation (as may be remembered by that which went before), they had now no friends to welcome them, nor inns to entertain or refresh their weatherbeaten bodies, no houses or much less towns to repair to, to seek for succor. . . . And for the season, it was winter, and they that know the winters of that country know them to be sharp and violent, and subject to cruel and fierce storms, dangerous to travel to known places, much more to search an unknown coast. Besides, what could they see but a hideous and desolate wilderness, full of wild beasts and wild men? and what multitude there might be of them they knew not. Neither could they, as it were, go up to the top of Pisgah, to view from this wilderness a more goodly country to feed their hopes; for which way soever they turned their eyes (save upward to the heavens) they could have little solace or content in respect of any outward objects. For summer being done, all things stand upon them with a weatherbeaten face; and the whole country, full of woods and thickets, represented a wild and savage hue.

If they looked behind them, there was the mighty ocean which they had passed, and was now as a main bar and gulf to separate them from all the civil parts of the world. If it be said they had a ship to succor them, it is true; but what heard they daily from the master and company? but that with speed they should look out a place with their shallop, where they would be at some near distance; for the season was such as he would not stir from thence till a safe harbor was discovered by them where they would be, and he might go without danger; and that victuals consumed apace, but he must and would keep sufficient for themselves and their return. Yea, it was muttered by some, that if they got not a place in time, they would turn them and their goods ashore and leave them. . . . What could now sustain them but the spirit of God and his grace? May not and ought not the children of these fathers rightly say: *Our fathers were Englishmen which came over this great ocean, and were ready to perish in this wilderness, but they cried unto the Lord, and he heard their voice and looked on their adversity, &c. . . . Let them confess before the Lord his loving kindness, and his wonderful works before the sons of men. . . .*

—From OF PLYMOUTH PLANTATION

· · · · ·

This book was rit by govener William bradford and given to his son mager William Bradford and by him to his son mager John Bradford. rit by me Samuel bradford mach 20, 1705.
—Annotation appearing on the original manuscript of OF PLYMOUTH PLANTATION

Governor William Bradford's OF PLYMOUTH PLANTATION *has had a curious history. Written in Plymouth during the years between 1630 and 1650, it came in about 1728 into the possession of Thomas Prince, the pastor of the Old South Church in Boston. Prince made excerpts from it for his* NEW ENGLAND CHRONOLOGY *and placed it with other ancient manuscripts in his library in the church. Governor Thomas Hutchinson and other historical writers are known to have consulted it there only a few years before the Revolution. Sometime between then and the British evacuation of Boston in 1776 it disappeared. For many years it was given up for lost. Then, in 1855, two American scholars simultaneously discovered in Samuel Wilberforce's* HISTORY OF THE PROTESTANT EPISCOPAL CHURCH IN AMERICA *passages which convinced them the author had made use of Bradford's history. This clue led to the library of the bishop's summer palace at Fulham on the outskirts of London where the missing manuscript was discovered, its 270 pages intact, having come there no one knew when nor how.*

The manuscript itself came home in 1897. On April 29, after forty-odd years of American agitation for its return, our ambassador received it for delivery to the Governor of Massachusetts from the hands of the Lord Bishop of London acting upon a decree of the Consistory Court of the Diocese of London.

In deciding to part with OF PLYMOUTH PLANTATION *this body recognized not American rights to an American document of great historic value, but, in their own words,* "the necessity of protecting the pecuniary interests of the families named in it, in tracing and establishing their rights to succession of property." *Today the manuscript is lodged in a glass case in the State House in Boston.*

∽

1620

THE PILGRIMS ON CAPE COD

BY "G. MOURT"

WEDNESDAY, the sixth of September, the wind coming east-north-east, a fine small gale, we loosed from Plymouth, having been kindly entertained and courteously used by divers friends there dwelling; and after many difficulties in boisterous storms, at length, by God's Providence, upon the ninth of November [1] following, by break of the day, we espied land, which we deemed to be Cape Cod, and so afterward it proved. And the appearance of it much comforted us, especially seeing so goodly a land, and wooded to the brink of the sea. It caused us to rejoice together, and praise God that had given us once again to see land. And thus we made our course south-south-west, proposing to go to a river seven leagues to the south of the Cape. But at night the wind being contrary, we put around again for the bay of Cape Cod; and upon the 11th of November we came to an anchor in the bay, which is a good harbor and pleasant bay, circled round, except in the entrance, which is about four miles over from land to land, compassed about to the very sea with oaks, pines, juniper, sassafras, and other sweet wood. It is a harbor wherein a thousand sail of ships may safely ride. There we relieved ourselves with wood and water, and refreshed our people, while our shallop was fitted to

[1] Old Style. November 19 by our calendar.

coast the bay to search for a habitation. There was the greatest store of fowl that ever we saw.

And every day we saw whales playing hard by us, of which in that place, if we had instruments and means to take them, we might have made a very rich return; which, to our great grief, we wanted. Our master and his mate, and others experienced in fishing, professed we might have made three or four thousand pounds worth of oil. They preferred it before Greenland whale-fishing, and purpose the next winter to fish for whale here. For cod we assayed, but found none; there is good store, no doubt, in their season. Neither got we any fish all the time we lay there, but some few little ones on the shore. We found great muscles, and very fat and full of sea-pearl; but we could not eat them, for they made us all sick that did eat, as well sailors as passengers. They caused to cast and scour; but they were soon well again.

The bay is so round and circling, that before we could come to anchor, we went round all the points of the compass. We could not come near the shore by three quarters of an English mile, because of shallow water, which was a great prejudice to us; for our people, going on shore, were forced to wade a bowshot or two in going a-land, which caused many to get colds and coughs; for it was many times freezing cold weather.

This day, before we came to harbor, observing some not well affected to unity and concord, but gave some appearance of faction, it was thought good there should be an association and agreement, that we should combine together in one body, and to submit to such government and governors as we should by common consent agree to make and choose, and set our hands to this that follows, word for word.

In the name of God, Amen. We, whose names are underwritten, the loyal subjects of our dread sovereign Lord King James, by the grace of God, of Great Britain, France, and Ireland king, defender of the faith, &c.

Having undertaken for the glory of God, and advancement of the Christian faith, and honor of our king and country, a voyage to plant the first colony in the northern parts of Virginia, do by these presents solemnly and mutually, in the presence of God and one of another, covenant and combine ourselves together into a civil body politic, for our better ordering and preservation, and furtherance of the ends aforesaid; and by virtue hereof to enact, constitute, and frame such just and equal laws, ordinances, acts, constitutions, and offices from time to time, as shall be thought most meet and convenient for the general good of the colony; unto which we promised all due submission and obedience. In witness whereof we have hereunder subscribed our names, at Cape Cod, 11th of November, in the year of the reign of our sovereign Lord King James of England, France, and Ireland the 18th, and of Scotland the 54th, Anno Domini 1620.

The same day, so soon as we could, we set ashore 15 or 16 men, well armed, with some to fetch wood, for we had none left; as also to see what the land was, and what inhabitants they could meet with. They found it to be a small neck of land; on this side where we lay, is the bay, and the further side the sea; the ground or earth, sand hills much like the downs in Holland, but much better; the crust of the earth, a spit's depth, excellent black earth; all wooded with oaks, pines, sassafras, juniper, birch, holly, vines, some ash, walnut; the wood for the most part open and without underwood, fit either to go or ride in. At night our people returned, but found not any person, nor habitation; and laded their boat with juniper, which smelled very sweet and strong, and of which we burnt the most part of the time we lay there.

Monday, the 13th of November, we unshipped our shallop and drew her on land, to mend and repair her, having been forced to cut her down in bestowing her betwixt the decks, and she was much opened with the people's lying in her; which kept us long there, for it was 16 or 17 days before the carpenter had finished her. Our people went on shore to refresh themselves, and our women to wash, as they had great need. But whilst we lay thus still, hoping our shallop would be ready in five or six days at the furthest, (but our carpenter made slow work of it, so that) some of our people, impatient of delay, desired for our better furtherance to travel by land into the country, (which was not without appearance of danger, not having the shallop with them, nor means to carry provisions but on their backs) to see whether it might be fit for us to seat in or no; and the rather, because, as we sailed into the harbor, there seemed to be a river opening itself into the main land. The willingness of the persons was liked, but the thing itself, in regard to the danger, was rather permitted than approved; and so with cautions, directions, and instructions, sixteen men were set out, with every man his musket, sword, and corslet, under the conduct of Captain Miles Standish; unto to whom was adjoined, for counsel and advice, William Bradford, Stephen Hopkins, and Edward Tilley.

Wednesday, the 15th of November, they were set ashore; and when they had ordered themselves in the order of a single file and marched about the space of a mile by the sea, they espied five or six people with a dog, coming towards them, who were savages; who, when they saw them ran into the wood, and whistled the dog after them, &c. First they supposed them to be Master Jones, the master, and some of his men, for they were ashore and knew of their coming; but after they knew them to be Indians, they marched after them into the woods, lest other of the Indians should lie in ambush. But when the Indians saw our men following them, they ran away with might and main; and our men turned out of the wood after them — for it was the way they intended to go — but they could not come near them. They followed them that night about ten miles by the trace of their footings, and saw how they had come the same way they went, and at a turning perceived how they ran up a hill, to see whether they followed them. At length night came upon them, and they were constrained to take up their lodging. So they set forth three sentinels, and the rest, some kindled a fire, and others fetched wood, and there held our rendezvous that night.

In the morning, so soon as we could see the trace, we proceeded on our journey, and had the track until we had compassed the head of a long creek; and there they took into another wood, and we after them, supposing to find some of their dwellings. But we marched through boughs and bushes, and under hills and valleys, which tore our very armor in pieces, and yet could meet with none of them, nor their houses, nor find any fresh water, which we greatly desired and stood in need of; for we brought neither beer nor water with us, and our victuals was only biscuit and Holland cheese, and a little bottle of aquavitae, so as we were sore athirst. About ten o'clock we came into a deep valley full of brush, wood-gaile, and long grass, through which we found little paths or tracts; and there we saw a deer, and found springs of fresh water, of which we were heartily glad, and sat us down and drunk our first New England water with as much delight as ever we drunk drink in all our lives.

When we had refreshed ourselves, we directed our course full south, that we might come to the shore, which within a short while after we did, and there made a fire, that they in the ship might see where we were, as we had direction; and so marched on towards this supposed river. Anl as we went, in another valley, we found a fine clear pond of fresh water, being about a musket-shot broad, and twice as long. There grew also many small vines, and fowl and deer haunted there. There grew much sassafras. From thence we went on, and found much plain ground, about fifty acres, fit for the plow, and some signs where the Indians had formerly planted their corn. After this some thought it best, for nearness of the river, to go down and travel on the sea sands, by which means some of our men were tired and lagged behind. So we stayed and gathered them up, and struck into the land again; where we found a little path to certain heaps of sand, one whereof was covered with old mats, and had a wooden thing like a mortar, whelmed on the top of it, and an earthen pot laid in a little hole at the end thereof. We, musing what it might be, digged and found a bow, and, as we thought, arrows, but they were rotten. We supposed there were many other things; but because we deemed them graves, we put in the bow again, and made it up as it was, and left the rest untouched, because we thought it would be odious unto them to ransack their sepulchres.

We went on further and found new stubble, of which they had gotten corn this year, and many walnut trees full of nuts, and great store of strawberries, and some vines. Passing thus a field or two, which were not great, we came to another, which had also been new gotten, and there we found where an house had been, and four or five old planks laid together. Also we found a great kettle, which had been some ship's kettle, and brought out of Europe. There was also an heap of sand, made like the former, — but it was newly done; we might see how they had paddled it with their hands, — which we digged up, and in it we found a little old basket full of fair Indian corn; and digged further, and found a great new basket full of very fair corn of this year, with some 36 goodly ears of corn, some yellow, and some red, and others mixed with blue, which was a very goodly sight. The basket was round, and narrow at the top. It held about three or four bushels, which was as much as two of us could lift up from the ground, and was very handsomely and cunningly made. But whilst we were busy about these things, we set our men sentinel in a round ring, all but two or three, which digged up the corn. We were in suspense what to do with it and the kettle, and at length after much consultation, we concluded to take the kettle, and as much of the corn as we could carry away with us; and when our shallop came, if we could find any of the people and come to parley with them, we would give them the kettle again and satisfy them for their corn. So we took all the ears, and put a good deal of the loose corn in the kettle for two men to bring away on a staff. Besides, they that could put any into their pockets, filled the same. The rest we buried again; for we were so laden with armor that we could carry no more.

Not far from this place we found the remainder of an old fort or palisado, which, as we conceived, had been made by some Christians. This was also hard by that place we thought had been a river; unto which we went and found it to so be, dividing itself into two arms by a high bank standing right by the cut or mouth, which came from the sea. That which was next unto us was the less. The other arm was more than twice as big, and not unlike to be an harbor for ships; but whether it be a fresh river, or only an indraught of the sea, we had no time to discover; for we had commandment to be out but two days. Here also we saw two canoes; the one on one side, the other on the other side. We could not believe it was a canoe, till we came near it. So we returned, leaving the further discovery hereof to our shallop, and came that night back again to the fresh water pond; and there we made our rendezvous that night, making a great fire, and a barricado to windward of us, and kept good watch with three sentinels all night, every one standing when his turn came, while five or six inches of match was burning. It proved a very rainy night.

In the morning, we took our kettle and sunk it in the pond, and trimmed our muskets, for few of them would go off because of the wet; and so coasted the wood again to come home, in which we were shrewdly puzzled, and lost our way. As we wandered we came to a tree, where a young sprit was bowed down over a bow, and some acorns strewed underneath. Stephen Hopkins said, it had been to catch some deer. So as we were looking at it, William Bradford being in the rear, when he came looked also upon it, and as he went about, it gave a sudden jerk up, and he was immediately caught by the leg. It was a very pretty device, made with a rope of their own making, and having a noose as artificially made as any roper in England can make, as like ours as can be; which we brought away with us. In the end we got out of the wood, and were fallen about a mile too high above the creek; where we saw three bucks, but we had rather have had one of them. We also did spring three couple of partridges; and as we came along by the creek, we saw great flocks of wild geese and ducks, but they were very fearful of us. So we marched some while in the woods, some while on the sands, and other while in water up to the knees; till at length we came near the ship; and then we shot off our pieces, and the long boat came to fetch us. Master Jones and Master Carver being on the shore, with many of our people, came to meet us. And thus we came both weary and welcome home; and delivered in our corn into the store to be kept for seed, for we knew not how to come by any, and therefore were very glad, purposing, so soon as we could meet with any inhabitants of that place, to make them large satisfaction. This was our first discovery, whilst our shallop was in repairing.

Our people did make things as fitting as they could, and time would, in seeking out wood, and helving of tools, and sawing of timber; to build a new shallop. But the discommodiousness of the harbor did much hinder us; for we could neither go to nor come from the shore but at high water; which was much to our hindrance and hurt; for oftentimes they waded to the middle of the thighs, and oft to the knees, to go and come from land. Some did it necessarily, and some for their own pleasure; but it brought to the most, if not to all, coughs and colds, (the weather proving suddenly cold and stormy), which afterwards turned to the scurvy, whereof many died.

When our shallop was fit, (indeed before she was fully fitted, for there was two days' work after bestowed on her), there was appointed some four and twenty men of our own, and armed, then to go and make a more full discovery of the rivers before mentioned. Master Jones was desirous to go with us, and took such of his sailors as he thought useful for us; so we were in all about four and thirty men. We made Master Jones our leader; for we thought it best herein to gratify his kindness and forwardness. When we were set forth, it proved rough weather and cross winds; so as we were constrained, some in the shallop, and others in the long boat, to row to the nearest shore the wind would suffer them to go unto, and then to wade out above the knees. The wind was so strong as the shallop could not keep the water, but was forced to harbor there that night. But we marched six or seven miles further, and appointed the shallop to come to us as soon as they could. It blowed and did snow all that day and night, and froze withal. Some of our people that are dead took the original of their death there.

The next day about eleven o'clock our shallop came to us, and we shipped ourselves; and the wind being good, we sailed to the river we formerly discovered, which we named *Cold Harbor;* to which when we came, we found it not navigable for ships; yet we thought it might be a good harbor for boats, for it flows there twelve foot at high water. We landed our men between the two creeks, and marched some four or five miles by the greater of them, and the shallop followed us. At length night grew on, and our men were tired with marching up and down the steep hills and deep valleys, which lay half a foot thick with snow. Master Jones, wearied with marching, was desirous we should take up our lodging, though some of us would have marched further. So we made there our rendezvous for that night under a few pine trees; and as it fell out, we got three fat geese, and six ducks to our supper, which we eat with soldiers' stomachs, for we had eaten little all that day. Our resolution was, next morning to go up to the head of this river, for we supposed it would prove fresh water.

But in the morning our resolution held not, because many liked not the hilliness of the soil and badness of the harbor. So we turned towards the other creek, that we might go over and look for the rest of the corn that we left behind when we were here before. When we came to the creek, we saw the canoe lie on the dry ground, and a flock of geese in the river, at which one made a shot and killed a couple of them; and we launched the canoe and fetched them, and when we had done, she carried us over by seven or eight at once. This done, we marched to the place where we had the corn formerly, which place we called *Cornhill;* and digged and found the rest, of which we were very glad. We also digged in a place a little further off, and found a bottle of oil. We went to another place which we had seen before, and digged and found more corn, viz. two or three baskets full of Indian wheat, and a bag of beans, with a good many of fair wheat ears. Whilst some of us were digging up this, some others found another heap of corn, which they digged up also; so as we had in all about ten bushels, which will serve us sufficiently for seed. And sure it was God's good providence that we found this corn, for else we know not how we should have done; for we knew not how we should find or meet with any of the Indians, except it be to do us a mischief. Also, we had never in all likelihood seen a grain of it, if we had not made our first journey; for the ground was now covered with snow, and so hard frozen that we were fain with our curtlaxes and short swords to hew and carve the ground a foot deep, and then wrest it up with levers, for we had forgot to bring other tools. Whilst we were in this employment, foul weather being towards, Master Jones was earnest to go aboard; but sundry of us desired to make further discovery and to find out the Indians' habitations. So we sent home with him our weakest people, and some that were sick, and all the corn; and eighteen of us stayed still, and lodged there that night, and desired that the shallop might return to us next day, and bring us some mattocks and spades with them.

The next morning we followed certain beaten paths and tracts of the Indians into the woods, supposing they would have led us into some town or houses. After we had gone a while, we light upon a very broad beaten path, well nigh two foot broad. Then we lighted all our matches, and prepared ourselves, concluding that we were near their dwellings. But in the end we found it to be only a path made to drive deer in, when the Indians hunt, as we supposed.

When we had marched five or six miles into the woods and could find no signs of any people, we returned again another way; and as we came into the plain ground, we found a place like a grave, but it was much bigger and longer than any we had yet seen. It was also covered with boards, so as we mused what it should be, and resolved to dig it up; where we found first a mat, and under that a fair bow, and then another mat, and under that a board about three quarters long, finely carved and painted, with three tines or broaches on the top like a crown; also between the mats we found bowls, trays, dishes, and such like trinkets. At length we came to a fair new mat, and under that two bundles, the one bigger, the other less. We opened the greater, and found in it a great quantity of fine and perfect red powder, and in it the bones and skull of a man. The skull had fine yellow hair still on it, and some of the flesh unconsumed. There was bound up with it a knife, a pack-needle, and two or three old iron things. It was bound up in a sailor's canvas cassock and a pair of cloth breeches. The red powder was a kind of embalmment, and yielded a strong, but no offensive smell; it was as fine as any flour. We opened the less bundle likewise, and found of the same powder in it, and the bones and head of a little child. About the legs and other parts of it was bound strings and bracelets of fine white beads. There was also by it a little bow, about three quarters long, and some other odd knacks. We brought sundry of the prettiest things away with us, and covered the corpse up again. After this we digged in sundry like places, but found no more corn, nor anything else but graves.

There was a variety of opinion amongst us about the embalmed person. Some thought it was an Indian lord and king. Others said, the Indians have all black hair, and never any was seen with brown or yellow hair. Some thought it was a Christian of some special note, which had died amongst them, and they thus buried him to honor him. Others thought they had killed him, and did it in triumph over them.

Whilst we were thus ranging and searching, two of the sailors which were newly come on the shore, by chance espied two houses, which had been lately dwelt in, but the people were gone. They having their pieces and hearing nobody, entered the houses, and took out some things, and durst not stay, but came again and told us. So some seven or eight of us went with them, and found how we had gone within a flight shot of them before. The houses were made with long young sapling trees bended and both ends stuck into the ground. They were made round like unto an arbor, and covered down to the ground with thick and well wrought mats; and the door was not over a yard high, made of a mat to open. The chimney was a wide open hole in the top, for which they had a mat to cover it close when they pleased. One might stand and go upright in them. In the midst of them were four little trunches knocked into the ground, and small sticks laid over, on which they hung their pots and what they had to seethe. Round about the fire they lay on mats, which are their beds. The houses were double matted; for as they were matted without, so were they within, with newer and fairer mats. In the houses we found wooden bowls, trays, and dishes, earthen pots, hand-baskets made of · crab-shells wrought together; also an English pail or bucket; it wanted a bail, but it had two iron ears; there was also baskets of sundry sorts, bigger and some lesser, finer and some coarser. Some were curiously wrought with black and white in pretty works, and sundry other of their household stuff. We found also two or three deer's heads, one whereof had been newly killed, for it was still fresh. There was also a company of deer's feet stuck up in the houses, harts' horns, and eagles' claws, and sundry such like things there was; also two or three baskets full of parched acorns, pieces of fish, and a piece of a broiled herring. We found also a little silk grass, and a little tobacco seed, with some other seeds which we knew not. Without was sundry bundles of flags, and sedge, bulrushes, and other stuff to make mats. There was thrust into an hollow tree two or three pieces of venison; but we thought it fitter for the dogs than for us. Some of the best things we took away with us, and left the houses standing still as they were.

So it growing towards night, and the tide almost spent, we hasted with our things down to the shallop, and got aboard that night, intending to have brought some beads and other things to have left in the house, in sign of peace, and that we meant to truck with them; but it was not done by means of our hasty coming away from Cape Cod.[1] But so soon as we meet conveniently with them, we will give them full satisfaction. Thus much for our second discovery.

Having thus discovered this place, it was controversial amongst us what to do touching our abode and settling there.

Some thought it best, for many reasons, to abide there. At first, that there was a convenient harbor for boats, though not for ships. Secondly, good corn-ground ready to our hands, as we saw by experience in the goodly corn it yielded, which would again agree with the ground and be natural seed for the same. Thirdly, Cape Cod was like to be a place of good fishing; for we saw daily great whales, of the best kind for oil and bone, come close aboard our ship, and, in fair weather, swim and play about us. There was once one, when the sun shone warm, came and lay above water as if she had been dead, for a good while together, within half a musket shot of the ship; at which two were prepared to shoot, to see whether she would stir or no. He that gave fire first, his musket flew in pieces, both stock and barrel; yet thanks be to God, neither he nor any man was hurt with it, though many were there about. But when the whale saw her time, she gave a snuff and away.

Fourthly, the place was likely to be healthful, secure, and defensible.

But the last and especial reason was, that now the heart of winter and unseasonable weather was come upon us, so that we could not go upon coasting and discovery without danger of losing men and boat, upon which would follow the overthrow of all, especially considering what variable winds and sudden storms do there arise. Also,

---

[1] The term Cape Cod in the early days described only the tip end of the Cape. The explorers here have advanced only to Truro but they consider they have left Cape Cod behind.

cold and wet lodging had so tainted our people, (for scarce any of us were free from vehement coughs,) as if they should continue long in that estate, it would endanger the lives of many, and breed diseases and infection amongst us. Again, we had yet some beer, butter, flesh, and other such victuals left, which would quickly be all gone; and then we should have nothing to comfort us in the great labor and toil we were like to undergo at the first. It was also conceived, whilst we had competent victuals, that the ship would stay with us; but when that grew low, they would be gone, and let us shift as we could.

Others, again, urged greatly the going to Anguum, or Angoum, a place twenty leagues off to the northwards, which they had heard to be an excellent harbor for ships, better ground, and better fishing. Secondly, for anything we knew, there might be hard by us a far better seat; and it should be a great hindrance to seat where we should remove again. Thirdly, the water was but in ponds; and it was thought there would be none in summer, or very little. Fourthly, the water must be fetched up a steep hill.

But to omit many reasons and replies used hereabouts, it was in the end concluded to make some discovery within the bay, but in no case so far as Angoum. Besides, Robert Coppin, our pilot, made relation of a great navigable river and good harbor in the other headland of the bay, almost right over against Cape Cod, being a right line, not much above eight leagues distant, in which he had been once; and because that one of the wild men with whom they had some trucking stole a harping iron from them, they called it *Thievish Harbor*. And beyond that place they were enjoined not to go. Whereupon a company was chosen to go out upon a third discovery. Whilst some were employed in this discovery, it pleased God that Mistress White was brought abed of a son, which was called Peregrine.

The 5th day we, through God's mercy, escaped a great danger by the foolishness of a boy, one of Francis Billington's sons, who, in his father's absence, had got gunpowder, and had shot off a piece or two, and made squibs; and there being a fowling-piece charged in his father's cabin, shot her off in the cabin, there being a little barrel of powder half full, scattered in and about the cabin, the fire being within four foot of the bed between the decks, and many flints and iron things about the cabin, and many people about the fire; and yet, by God's mercy, no harm done.

Wednesday, the sixth of December, it was resolved our discoverers should set forth, for the day before was too foul weather, — and so they did, though it was well o'er the day ere all things could be ready. So ten of our men were appointed who were of themselves willing to undertake it, to wit, Captain Standish, Master Carver, William Bradford, Edward Winsloe, John Tilley, Edward Tilley, John Houland, and three of London, Richard Warren, Steeven Hopkins, and Edward Dotte, and two of our seamen, John Alderton and Thomas English. Of the ship's company there went two of the master's mates, Master Clarke and Master Copin, the master gunner, and three sailors. The narration of which discovery follows, penned by one of the company.

Wednesday, the 6th of December, we set out, being very cold and hard weather. We were a long while, after we launched from the ship, before we could get clear of a sandy point, which lay within less than a furlong of the same.[2] In which time two were very sick, and Edward Tilley had like to have sounded with cold. The gunner also was sick unto death (but hope of trucking made him to go,) and so remained all that day and the next night. At length we got clear of the sandy point, and got up our sails, and within an hour or two we got under the weather shore, and then had smoother water and better sailing, but it was very cold; for the water froze on our clothes, and made them many times like coats of iron.

We sailed six or seven leagues by the shore, but saw neither river nor creek. At length we met with a tongue of land, being flat off from the shore, with a sandy point. We bore up to gain the point, and found there a fair income or road of a bay, being a league over at the narrowest, and some two or three in length;[3] but we made right over to the land before us, and left the discovery of this income till the next day. As we drew near to the shore, we espied some ten or twelve Indians very busy about a black thing — what it was we could not tell — till afterwards they saw us, and ran to and fro, as if they had been carrying something away. We landed a league or two from them, and had much ado to put ashore any where, it lay so full of flat sands. When we came to shore, we made us a barricado, and got firewood, and set out sentinels, and betook us to our lodging, such as it was. We saw the smoke of the fire which the savages made that night about four or five miles from us.

In the morning we divided our company, some eight in the shallop,

2 Long Point.   3 Wellfleet Bay.

and the rest on the shore went to discover this place. But we found it only to be a bay, without either river or creek coming into it. Yet we deemed it to be as good a harbor as Cape Cod; for they that sounded it found a ship might ride in five fathom water. We on the land found it to be a level soil, but none of the fruitfullest. We saw two becks of fresh water, which were the first running streams that we saw in the country; but one might stride over them. We found also a great fish, called a grampus, dead on the sands. They in the shallop found two of them also in the bottom of the bay, dead in like sort. They were cast up at high water, and could not get off for the frost and ice. They were some five or six paces long, and about two inches thick of fat, and fleshed like a swine. They would have yielded a great deal of oil, if there had been time and means to have taken it. So we finding nothing for our turn, both we and our shallop returned.

We then directed our course along the sea sands to the place where we first saw the Indians. When we were there, we saw it was also a grampus which they were cutting up. They cut it into long rands or pieces, about an ell long and two handfull broad. We found here and there a piece scattered by the way, as it seemed, for haste. This place the most were minded we should call the *Grampus Bay,* because we found so many of them there. We followed the track of the Indians' bare feet a good way on the sands. At length we saw where they struck into the woods by the side of a pond. As we went to view the place, one said he thought he saw an Indian house among the trees; so went up to see. And here we and the shallop lost sight one of another till night, it being now about nine or ten o'clock. So we light on a path, but saw no house, and followed a great way into the woods. At length we found where corn had been set, but not that year. Anon, we found a great burying place, one part whereof was encompassed with a large palisado, like a church-yard with young spires, four or five yards long, set as close one by another as they could, two or three foot in the ground. Within it was full of graves, some bigger and some less. Some were also paled about; and others had like an Indian house made over them, but not matted. Those graves were more sumptuous than those at *Cornhill;* yet we digged none of them up, but only viewed them and went our way. Without the palisado were graves also, but not so costly. From this place we went and found more corn-ground, but not of this year. As we ranged, we light on four or five Indian houses, which had been lately dwelt in;

but they were uncovered, and had no mats about them; else they were like those we found at *Cornhill,* but had not been so lately dwelt in. There was nothing left but two or three pieces of old mats, and a little sedge. Also a little further we found two baskets full of parched acorns hid in the ground, which we supposed had been corn when we began to dig the same; we cast earth thereon again, and went our way. All this while we saw no people.

We went ranging up and down till the sun began to draw low, and then we hasted out of the woods, that we might come to our shallop; which, when we were out of the woods, we espied a great way off, and called them to come unto us; the which they did as soon as they could, for it was not yet high water. They were exceedingly glad to see us, for they feared because they had not seen us in so long a time, thinking we would have kept by the shore side. So being both weary and faint, — for we had eaten nothing all that day, — we fell to make our rendezvous and get fire wood, which always cost us a great deal of labor.[4] By that time we had done and our shallop come to us, it was within night; and we fed upon such victuals as we had, and betook us to our rest, after we had set out our watch. About midnight we heard a great and hideous cry; and our sentinels called, *"Arm! Arm!"* So we bestirred ourselves, and shot off a couple of muskets, and the noise ceased. We concluded that it was a company of wolves or foxes; for one told us he had heard such a noise in Newfoundland.

About five o'clock in the morning we began to be stirring; and two or three, which doubted whether their pieces would go off or no, made trial of them and shot them off, but thought nothing at all. After prayer we prepared ourselves for breakfast, and for a journey; and it being now the twilight in the morning, it was thought meet to carry the things down to the shallop. Some said it was not best to carry the armor down. Others said, they would be readier. Two or three said, they would not carry theirs till they went themselves, but mistrusting nothing at all. As it fell out, the water not being high enough, they laid the things down upon the shore, and came up to breakfast. Anon, all upon a sudden, we heard a great and strange cry, which we knew to be the same voices, though they varied their notes. One of our company, being abroad, came running in, and cried, "They are men! Indians! Indians!" and withal their arrows came flying amongst us. Our men ran out with all speed to recover

4 At Eastham.

their arms; as by the good providence of God they did. In the mean time Captain Miles Standish, having a snapchance ready, made a shot; and after him another. After they two had shot, other two of us were ready; but he wished us not to shoot till we could take aim, for we knew not what need we should have; and there were four only of us which had their arms there ready, and stood before the open side of our barricado, which was first assaulted. They thought it best to defend it, lest the enemy should take it and our stuff, and so have the more vantage against us. Our care was no less for the shallop; but we hoped all the rest would defend it. We called unto to them to know how it was with them; and they answered "Well! Well!" every one, and "Be of good courage!" We heard three of their pieces go off, and the rest called for a firebrand to light their matches. One took a log out of the fire on his shoulder and went and carried it unto them; which was thought did not a little discourage our enemies. The cry of our enemies was dreadful, especially when our men ran out to recover their arms. Their note was after this manner, *"Woach, woach, ha ha, hach, woach."* Our men were no sooner come to their arms, but the enemy was ready to assault them.

There was a lusty man, and no whit less valiant, who was thought to be their captain, stood behind a tree within half a musket shot of us, and there let his arrows fly at us. He was seen to shoot three arrows, which were all avoided; for he at whom the first arrow was aimed, saw it, and stooped down, and it flew over him. The rest were avoided also. He stood three shots of a musket. At length, one took, as he said, full aim at him; after which he gave an extraordinary cry, and away they went all. We followed them bout a quarter of a mile; but we left six to keep our shallop, for we were careful of our business. Then we shouted all together two several times, and shot off a couple of muskets, and so returned. This we did that they might see we were not afraid of them, nor discouraged.

Thus it pleased God to vanquish our enemies and give us deliverance. By their noise we could not guess that they were less than thirty or forty, though some thought that they were many more. Yet, in the dark of the morning, we could not so well discern them among the trees, as they could see us by the fire-side. We took up eighteen of their arrows, which we have sent to England by Master Jones; some whereof were headed with brass, others with harts' horns, and others with eagles' claws. Many more no doubt were shot, for these we found were almost covered with leaves; yet, by the especial providence of God, none of them either hit or hurt us, though many came close by us and on every side of us, and some coats which hung up in our barricado were shot through and through.

So after we had given God thanks for our deliverance, we took our shallop and went on our journey, and called this place *The First Encounter.* From hence we intended to have sailed to the aforesaid *Thievish Harbor,* if we found no convenient harbor by the way. Having the wind good, we sailed all that day along the coast about fifteen leagues; but saw neither river or creek to put into. After we had sailed an hour or two, it began to snow and rain, and to be bad weather. About the midst of the afternoon the wind increased, and the seas began to be very rough; and the hinges of the rudder broke, so that we could steer no longer with it, but two men with much ado were fain to serve with a couple of oars. The seas were grown so great that we were much troubled and in great danger; and night grew on. Anon, Master Coppin bade us be of good cheer, he saw the harbor. As we drew near, the gale being stiff, and we bearing great sail to get in, split our mast in 3 pieces, and were like to have cast away our shallop. Yet, by God's mercy recovering ourselves, we had the flood with us, and struck into the harbor.

Now he that thought that had been the place, was deceived, it being a place where not any of us had been before; and coming into the harbor, he that was our pilot did bear up northward, which if we had continued, we had been cast away. Yet still the Lord kept us, and we bare up for an island before us; and recovering of that island, being compassed about with many rocks, and dark night growing upon us, it pleased the divine providence that we fell upon a place of sandy ground, where our shallop did ride safe and secure all that night; and coming upon a strange island, kept our watch all night in the rain upon that island. And in the morning we marched about it, and found no inhabitants at all; and here we made our rendezvous all that day, being Saturday, 10th of December. On the Sabbath day we rested; and on Monday we sounded the harbor, and found it a very good harbor for our shipping. We marched also into the land, and found divers cornfields, and little running brooks, a place very good for situation. So we returned to our ship again with good news to the rest of our people, which did much comfort their hearts.

On the 15th day we weighed anchor to go to the place we had discovered; and coming within two leagues of the land, we could not fetch the harbor, but were fain to put round again towards Cape Cod, our course lying west, and the wind was at northwest. But it pleased God that the next day, being Saturday the 16th day, the wind came fair, and we put to sea again, and came safely into a safe harbor; and within half an hour the wind changed, so as if we had been letted but a little, we had gone back to Cape Cod.

This harbor is a bay greater than Cape Cod, compassed with a goodly land; and in the bay 2 fine islands uninhabited, wherein are nothing but wood, oaks, pines, walnuts, beech, sassafras, vines and other trees we know not. This bay is a most hopeful place; innumerable store of fowl, and excellent good; and cannot but be of fish in their seasons; skate, cod, turbot, and herring, we have tasted of; abundance of muscles, the greatest and best that ever we saw; crabs and lobsters, in their time infinite. It is in fashion like a sickle, or fish-hook.

—From Mourt's Relation of the Beginning
and Proceeding of the English Plantation
Settled at Plymouth in New England

The book commonly called Mourt's Relations *was published in London in 1623, a bid for attention and succor, spicily baited with rosy prophecies for the future of the colony then suffering the hardships that came close to wiping it out. It is a book written by brave men who knew how to write. It was certainly not written by the mysterious G. Mourt who signed it. He is assumed to have been George Morton, the Pilgrims' agent in London, who in all likelihood had a hand in editing and preparing it for the press. Early writers generally ascribe it to William Bradford who later told much the same story in his* Of Plymouth Plantation *but it is unmistakably the work of more than one pen as variations in spelling and person constantly reveal. Scholars today concur in giving Edward Winslow equal credit. It is livelier reading than Bradford's history, richer in small sharply observed detail; man's relation to his Maker, so strongly emphasized in both works, is dealt with by "Mourt" in a less lofty, more matter-of-fact vein.*

⁘

MAUSHOPE

BY FRANK SHAY

LONG BEFORE the Pilgrims landed on Cape Cod the Indians of the long barren strand knew of the possibility of invasion by white men. Many strange canoes with sails had cruised along the coast, some had landed parties searching for water and to make surveys. These parties had been watched from behind trees and sand dunes and as long as they went about their own business they were not disturbed. Though the Indians wondered about these men who had other ways and habits than their own they feared neither them nor the thunder-death they dealt to their enemies. For always there was Maushope, the strongest of men, standing guard over their lodges. None had ever seen the great giant but they knew he was ever on the watch for their enemies.

Great were the tales of his anger and how when in a great rage he would tear up the cedars and the pines by the roots and toss huge rocks about like playthings. The Cummaquids, Nausets and Pamets could tell you that upon the approach of an unfriendly ship Maushope would wade out into Massachusetts harbor, or into the deep Atlantic for that matter, and tip over the invader's ship. They would tell you of his great kindliness and of the protective care he had for his people, how he would push his great forefinger into the sand and bring forth a geyser of fresh water. With his great foot he would plow out harbors and bays for the fishermens' canoes. They would tell you how he watched over the forlorn maiden who had fallen in love with the great trout, and how he dug Cotuit Creek so that the lover could come nearer to his beloved, and how, later, he induced the good gods to make her a trout that she might accompany her lover to his watery home.

And Maushope's great secret was their secret and they kept it buried in their hearts so that the hated and warlike Narragansetts should never hear of it. Maushope's great strength was seated in his crown and there too lay the point of his greatest weakness. The only weapon that could injure him was the blue cone of the fir tree. This was the secret they kept from Maushope's enemies.

Indian mothers, who never struck their men children for fear they might become cowards, would tell them whenever the tempest raged through the forest and the branches of the trees creaked and groaned and were split:

"Maushope is gathering his firewood."

He was taller than the tallest tree and larger around than the leaf spread of the young elms. When he was in a rage his voice drowned out the thunder of the skies and the pounding of the storm sea on the shore. Yet he could be tender and thoughtful of all his people. A widowed squaw with no one to bring her food would find a great heap of fish and grain before her lonely wigwam. A boy born of but small courage might pray his gods to be made strong and fearless and in the night Maushope would come, and drawing his forefinger along the sleeping lad's spine, give him those qualities by which the good warrior was measured.

He foretold storms saving many fishermen from watery graves; he could see great distances and direct his people to schools of whales and blackfish. All these things he did for them through signs and the manifestations of these signs were guarded as they guarded his secret. When the rain was slow to come and the crops seemed ready to turn over he reached up and brought the clouds together causing rain to fall and when too much had fallen he moved the clouds from over the land far out to sea. To the Cape Indians he was the Big Father.

It was to young lovers that Maushope was particularly kind. To older lovers he was the beacon that lighted their path to happiness. Only nagging wives and dissolute husbands brought down his tremendous wrath.

There lived at the upper end of the Cape the very rich and powerful sachem, Niwasse. His wealth was in ponds well-stocked with perch and pickerel, swamps full of terrapin and wild fowl, of harbors and bays rich in oysters and clams. Niwasse had a beautiful daughter, tall and slender quite unlike the women of her race, hair and eyes like a raven's wing. Her step was light and graceful and her father's lodge was full of suitors for her hand. She was doubly desirable inasmuch as she could follow a deer trail and draw a bow with the best of the young braves. She laughed at their presents made of eagle feathers and conch shells, dismissed those suiters who brought her presents of rare game. Could she not secure all these for herself and enjoy, too, the glory of the chase? She loved one, a young warrior of the Pamets, a tribe that lived far to the north of the Cape.

As none could persuade her father to consent to the match there was nothing to do but to go to Maushope and lay the whole matter before him. The two lovers arrived at a lucky hour. He had that morning caused a school of whales to founder on the shore and the fishermen had just presented him with some excellent tobacco. He listened to their story and agreed to help them.

He placed a few hundred pounds of tobacco in his pouch and set out upon his journey with the young brave on his shoulder and the maiden in the crook of his arm. He reached the sachem's lodge in a moment.

"Why cannot these charming people marry, O great chief?" he roared into the lodge.

The sachem stammered something about the young brave's poverty; he was without fame and wore but three scalp-locks at his belt.

"Is that all the trouble?" roared the giant. "What must this brave warrior have to win this maiden?"

"A great deal of land, he must have a whole island," answered the sachem.

"Good! Follow me," said Maushope, blowing great clouds of smoke through his nostrils. "Follow me, O chief of the Cummaquids."

The fat old sachem followed as fast as he could and a great crowd of people hurried after him to see what the giant would do.

Maushope never did things by halves. He went to the high land overlooking the south shore and sat down. He filled his pipe with fresh tobacco and kindled it with a bolt of lightning. He bowed once to the rising sun, twice to the north star and three times to the God of Thunder. Then he muttered some strange words and fell to smoking at a great rate.

Thunder rolled, lightning flashed and rain poured down. Voices of strange gods were heard puffing and blowing as if in terrific labor. The air was filled with a thick mist that even the strongest eyes could not penetrate. Then the watching and waiting crowd heard a tremendous hissing sound as if live coals were dropped into the sea. Maushope had emptied his pipe. Again he filled his pipe and smoked. For three long days he sat thus smoking and dropping the ashes into the ocean.

On the fourth day he reached up and cleared the mist away and let the sun shine down upon the pleasant land. The people looked and behold there was a beautiful island, the ashes from Maushope's pipe. The happy couple upon whom he bestowed this island named it Nantucket, which is the name it bears to this day.

Maushope's only reward was the great happiness he got from making others happy. He returned to his duties of keeping watch over his people of the Cape.

One day a great canoe with sails entered Massachusetts Harbor and dropped anchor. It was named the *Mayflower* and from his lofty perch Maushope decided these were a friendly people and did not molest them. Many years later when he saw his land overrun with white people and his own people driven to the strange lands of the West he fell ill. A small group of white men fed an Indian some firewater and when he was very drunk learned the secret of Maushope's weakness. Going to his lodge they found him asleep and pelted him with the blue cones of the fir tree until he was dead.

Even now, when the tempest rages through the forests and the branches of the trees creak and groan and split and the waves pound heavily on the shore, the old people of the Cape say:

"Maushope is gathering his firewood."

— From HERE'S AUDACITY! AMERICAN LEGENDARY HEROES

This god appears under several names in Indian mythology, Kwasind, Maushope, Hiawatha and others. To the Peruvian Indians he is Hurakan, whose name gave us the term hurricane.

Life in the Old Colony

LIFE IN THE OLD COLONY

*T*HE FIRST *four towns established on Cape Cod were Sandwich, Barnstable and Yarmouth, incorporated in 1639, and Eastham, settled in 1641, incorporated in 1644, and called Nauset until 1651. From a later division and subdivision of these towns all the other eleven towns upon the Cape have been derived. Harwich, for example, is an offshoot of Yarmouth, Brewster of Harwich; Truro was once a part of Eastham and Provincetown of Truro, Bourne of Sandwich. Eastham alone was founded directly and entirely by emigrants from Plymouth but all four towns were established under the jurisdiction of the General Court at Plymouth and continued under that jurisdiction until the union of the Plymouth Colony and the Massachusetts Bay Colony in 1692.*

The General Court was comprised of the Governor and his assistants and to this all-powerful body the towns were empowered to send two deputies to vote in their name for the Court officers. We see here an early step towards representative government but a very shaky one since the Court had the right to demand the replacement of any deputy of whom it did not approve. With the growth of the colony the Court began to find itself overworked. A Cape Cod tribunal was established in 1641 to judge cases involving not more than forty shillings and, in 1658, the towns were ordered to choose "three or fiue Celect men" for the better managing of their affairs. Plymouth still held the reins through the right of the Court to pass upon the merits of judges, selectmen, and voters.

There was little that was democratic about life in the Old Colony. Newcomers who tried to settle were warned out of town unless they had permission from the authorities; if allowed to remain, after careful screening, they were obliged to forego the rights of a proprietor in the common lands and to give bond to "save the town harmless" if their families became destitute. Even within the established group rigid caste and property distinctions were observed. Sober, industrious churchmembers in good standing whose estate was not less than twenty pounds alone were entitled to vote. It was a crime to call any man "mister" or his wife "mistress" unless he was a member of the government, a minister, an elder of the church, a schoolmaster, or a commissioned officer in the militia; exceptions were made for men of great wealth or men who in England were connected with the gentry or nobility. Yet something new was developing. A life of mutual dependence and mutual enterprise in the wilderness was gradually dissolving the matter-of-fact subserviency to the social customs of the Old World which the colonists had brought with them to the New.

⤬

1636
A DECLARATION OF RIGHTS

"WE, the associates of New Plymouth, coming hither as freeborn subjects of the state of England, and endowed with all and singular the privileges belonging to such, being assembled, do ordain that no act, imposition, law or ordinance, be made or imposed on us, at the present or to come, but shall be made or imposed by consent of the body of associates, or their representatives, legally assembled, — which is according to the liberties of the state of England."

This extraordinary statement of principles has been called the first American Declaration of Independence. It forms part of a constitution drawn up by the Court of Associates at Plymouth in November, 1636, to serve the growing colony. Matter-of-factly, even innocently uttered, it clearly foreshadows 1776 when we consider that it was upon men who thought in such terms that the long series of British oppressions, beginning with the usurpation of their government by Andros in 1686, was to be laid.

⤬

GOODMAN HALLETT'S HOUSE

BY AMOS OTIS

ANDREW HALLETT, JR., is the common ancestor of all families of the name in Barnstable and Yarmouth. He was one of the first settlers of the town of Sandwich, and at the division of the common meadows, April 16, 1640, he had seven and one-half acres assigned to him. The division of the common lands and meadows in Sandwich was made "according to each man's estate and condition," or "quality," a most aristocratic rule. . . .

The division was made by a committee of ten, five representing the aristocracy, and five the townsmen. The first five awarded to themselves, one hundred and fourteen acres, nearly one third of the whole. The other five were more modest in their demands, and took only forty and one-half acres — leaving to be divided to the other 56 inhabitants named, 214½ acres, less than four to each; 7½ acres being awarded to Andrew Hallett, it shows that he had at that time a good estate and was comparatively a wealthy man. . . .

From Sandwich Andrew Hallett removed to Yarmouth, of which town he continued to be an inhabitant till his death in 1684. In 1642 he bought the dwelling-house of Gyles Hopkins, the first built by the English in Yarmouth. . . . By subsequent purchases Andrew Hallett, Jr., became the largest landholder in Yarmouth, owning about 300 acres of the best lands and meadows in the town. . . . The house which he bought of Gyles Hopkins . . . stood on the eastern declivity of the hill. . . . An excavation was made into the side of the hill to level the ground, and the stone and cob work chimney was built against this bank, and outside the frame of the house. It probably contained at first only one room. The excavation into the hill, and the chimney, covered nearly the whole of the west side, and the other three sides were covered with hand-sawed or hewn planks, and the roof with thatch. The walls were not shingled on the outside, or plastered on the in. The seams in the boards were filled or "daubed" with clay. Oiled paper supplied the place of glass. The sills were hewn from large logs, and projected into the room, forming low seats on three sides. The floor was fastened to sleepers laid on the ground, and even with the lower edge of the sills. A ladder to the chamber and a cleat door with a wooden latch and string, completed the fixtures of the house.

In this rudely built shanty, two of the children of Gyles Hopkins, who came over in the Mayflower, were born, and here resided a number of years the most opulent man in Yarmouth. Nearly all the houses of our ancestors were of this description. . . . As late as 1717 it was not common to plaster the inside walls. The seams between the boards on the Meeting House built that year on Cobb's Hill were filled with mortar, or "daubed" precisely in the same manner as practiced by the first settlers. That boards were used in the construction of their dwellings, by the first settlers, is also shown by the agreement made June 19, 1641, between the inhabitants of Barnstable and the Indian chief Nepaiton, to build the latter a house. A part of the contract was that it should be built, "with a chamber floored with boards, with a chimney and an oven therein.". . .

Some writers on our early history speak of the "log cabins of ancestors." I find no evidence that they built a single log-house. The timber in the vicinity of the settlements was unfit for such buildings. . . . The fortification houses of our fathers were built, the lower story of stone, where it could be conveniently procured, and the second of wood. In a part of Yarmouth (now South Dennis) where no stone could be conveniently found, a block house was built for defense. This in its construction resembled a log-house, but no one calls such a structure by that name. Many common houses like that of John Crocker were surrounded by a palisade, and were intended as places of resort, should the Indians prove unfriendly.

Major Gookin in speaking of the wigwams, of the Indians, says some of them were large and convenient, and more comfortable than many houses built by the English. Mr. Lothrop[1] calls some of the houses of our ancestors, booths, indicating that they were most uncomfortable residences in the winter. Some he calls palisado, meaning I presume that the walls were built of two parallel rows of poles, and the space between them filled in with clay or other material. Others were frame houses not large or elegantly finished, but warm and comfortable. Dwellings of the latter description, only a few men who

[1] John Lothrop, the celebrated clergyman who with his congregation founded Barnstable.

were comparatively wealthy, had the means to build.

In such rude shelters from the piercing storms of the winter of 1639-40, the great mass of our ancestors resided more happily and more comfortably than do their descendants at this day,[2] in their well built and well furnished mansions. . . . In the summer of 1640 they had their lands to clear, fence and plant, to build roads, and do many things that are incident to the settlement of a new country, and they found little time, if they had the means, of improving their dwellings. Many of them resided all their days in the houses they first erected. Improvements were made from time to time. The thatched roof, the paper windows, and the cob work chimney disappeared, and shingled roofs, diamond glass windows and brick chimneys and ovens were substituted. As the family increased, the house was enlarged, first by adding a lean-to, and afterwards by adding another story. Some of the largest old houses now remaining . . . were built by adding one room at a time.

The second house in which Andrew Hallett, Jr., resided, in Yar-mouth . . . was built on a little knoll, and fronted due south, as all ancient dwellings did. By such a location, our fathers secured two objects which they considered essential: the rays of the sun at noon, or dinner-time, as they called that hour of the day, shone parallel with the side of the house, and their "great room" in which they lived, was on the sunny or warm side of the house. The chimney was uniformly built on the west side, and projected outside of the frame. The exact size of Andrew Hallett's new house cannot be stated accurately: it was about 22 feet by 26 on the ground, and was only one or one-half stories high. . . . The "great room," about 17 feet square, occupied the southeast corner. The fireplace was eight feet wide and four feet deep, and the mantle, which was of wood, was laid about five and a half feet high, so that the family could pass to the oven, which opened on the back of the fireplace near the south corner. There was a small kitchen or workroom at the northwest corner; at the northeast corner a small pantry, with a trap door leading to the cellar. Between the pantry and the great room was a bed-room, the floor of which was elevated about two feet, to give greater depth to the cellar. The bed occupied nearly all the space, and it was so low in the walls that a tall person could not stand upright therein. A ladder to the front entry led to the chamber, which was occupied

[2] 1861.

for weaving and lodging rooms. No part of the house was ever painted or any of the rooms papered. The windows were of small diamond shaped glass set in lead. No blinds or curtains were needed, and none were ever used.

The furniture of the house was for use, not for show. Half a dozen flag bottomed, one low and one large armed chair, a table, a large chest, and a cradle, all of domestic manufacture, was the furniture usually to be seen in the summer in the great room, and in the winter a bed occupied one corner and the looms another. On one side of the room there were usually two large "trencher shelves," on which the pewter ware of the family was displayed, an iron candlestick, an hour glass, a pen and ink horn, the bible, and hymn book.

A clock or timepiece was an article not to be found in the settlement. Time was reckoned thus, "daylight, sunrise, sun an hour, two hours and three hours high, and the reverse in the afternoon. When the sun shone, they could tell the precise apparent time of noon, and they had marks by which they judged very accurately of the time from 9 A.M. till 3 P.M. Sun dials were early introduced, and many had them fastened to posts set in front of their houses.

If we lay aside one consideration, the cost of fuel, it may be safely said that for comfort, convenience and health, nothing superior to the old fashioned fireplace has yet been invented. . . . Talk with the aged, they will uniformly tell you that the happiest hours of their lives were spent in the corner of an old fashioned kitchen fireplace. In the long winter evenings the younger members of the family occupied the low bench in the left chimney corner, the smaller one perhaps mounted on the dye-tub. Here they were warm and comfortable, and could read or play without molestation, or gaze up at the stars through the capacious chimney. In the other corner sat the mistress of the family in her low rocking-chair, and in front, the father in his round-about, or in an old fashioned arm chair.

In those days there was a social equality now unknown. There were no visits of ceremony, — no calls to leave a card; but neighbor called on neighbor, without previous invitation to spend a long evening. In such cases, all the children of the neighborhood assembled at the house left vacant by the parents. They parched corn, cracked nuts, and played blind man's buff, hunt the slipper, thread the needle through the eye, hull gull, and many other plays and games, which the boarding-school Miss now regards with horror, although she can witness with delight the indelicate gyrations of the ballet dancer, or unseemly pranks of a French waltz.

The old folks first discussed the English news, though it was four or five months old. Some one had had a letter from their relatives in the father land. This was passed around from family to family, and read and discussed by the whole vicinity. The ministry — the church — the acts of the Court — and the crops were subjects that passed in review, and often familism, pedo-baptism, quakerism, and witchcraft came in for a share of the conversation. . . .

The fire was never suffered to go out during the cool season, and very rarely in the summer. Every morning in the winter, the coals were raked forward, and a ponderous back-log put on, with two or three smaller ones, as riders. A large fore-stick, four feet in length, was laid on the andirons, and two or three smaller ones between that and the back-log forming a bed into which the coals raked forward were shovelled. Some dry sticks were laid on these, and in a few minutes a large fire was sparkling on the hearth. Wood cost nothing in those days, and our ancestors always enjoyed the luxury of a good fire in cold weather, and however cold the weather, the great room was warm and comfortable. They always provided themselves with pine knots, then abundant, and in the long winter evenings these were used instead of candles.

The kitchen or back room was small and little used, excepting for a store room. The tubs and pails, and the spinning wheels, when not in use, were kept there, and a pile of wood for the morning's fire.

All the clothing and bedding of the family was made in the house. The flax and the wool were spun and wove by the inmates. The cloth for the thick clothing of the men was sent to the clothier to be fulled, colored and pressed.

Goodman Hallett lived on the produce of his farms. Indian corn was his principal crop, though every family had rye, and most of them raised sufficient wheat for their own consumption. They also cultivated peas, of which many were sent to Boston and other places to sell; beans, pumpkins, squashes, cucumbers, melons, turnips, beets, carrots, parsnips, and onions. Potatoes were not raised by the first settlers, and it was many years before they were produced in large quantities. Cattle were scarce and of high price, and few were killed for beef by the first settlers; but in time they became abundant and cheap. Goats were kept, and their milk was used. Horses were early introduced; but the country did not become well stocked till fifty years after the settlement of Plymouth. Pigs multiplied rapidly, and were soon abundant in all the settlements. Poultry of all kinds were raised. Deer and other wild animals suitable for food then roamed in the forests, and the shores, at certain seasons, were covered with flocks of geese, ducks, plover and other birds.

Clams, quahogs and oysters, could be obtained at any season of the year, and codfish, mackerel, bass, eels, and other fish were then more easily taken than at the present time.

None but the idle and the dissolute complained. The first settlers, after securing their first crop in 1640, never suffered for food — they always had an abundance of what was wholesome and palatable. At first they were short of clothing. They had to patch up that which they brought out of England. The skins of the deer and other animals, dressed by the Indians, were soft and pliable. These supplied many of their wants and furnished them with warm and comfortable, though not elegant articles of dress.

The little money they obtained by the sale of peltry, oil and fish, was carefully husbanded and used to supply their most pressing wants. Tools, iron and some kinds of building materials, were indispensable, and it was many years before they were fully supplied. . . .

Goodman Hallett is called a husbandman. By honest industry, skilful management and economy, he accumulated a large estate. In 1676 his tax was equal to one twentieth of the whole assessment. . . . He may also have been engaged in the fisheries, and probably was, for nearly all the first settlers were at certain seasons of the year. . . . They were not sole owners of their vessels. Others who did not take an active part in these employments were interested as owners, and shared the profits.

His out of door arrangements were as rude as those within. On the east of his house was a fine spring of water, in which he placed a large hollow log for a curb. The supply was pure and abundant, and in times of drought was the resort of the neighborhood. His large wood-pile was in front of his house, not cut and piled, but standing on end, on each side of a large pole resting on crutches, settled into the ground. Forty cords he considered a year's supply, and it was cut up as wanted for the fire, into pieces three and four feet long. Some of the logs used were large, and required the strength of two men to roll them in, and adjust them in the fireplace for backlogs.

Goodman Hallett built his cribs as all in those times did, with slender poles. Posts were set at each corner having short branches left thereon, about three feet from the ground. On those branches two stout poles were laid, 12 or 15 feet long. Across these smaller ones, four feet in length, were closely laid. The sides were constructed with long poles, and the roof with boards overlapping each other. At each end there was a door or opening. He had several, in which he stored his large crops. Corn was then the measure of value. With it a man could pay his taxes or his debts, buy houses and lands; the necessaries or the luxuries of life. To have corn in the crib, in those times, was like having stocks and money in the Bank at the present time. To say of a man "he has plenty of corn in his cribs," was equivalent to saying he had money in his purse. Goodman Hallett was not proud but he delighted to exhibit to visitors his extensive granaries, his herds and flocks, and the breadth of his cultivated lands. Excepting for hominy or samp, he consumed very little of his corn till it was a year old.

His barns in the field on the east of the mill road, were as rudely constructed as those now seen on the western prairies. Large stacks of salt hay stood near, surrounded by a fence. The barn, or cow-house, as it was called, was for the protection of the stock, not for the storage of fodder. No English hay was then cut. All the fresh fodder which the first settlers had, was the stalks and husks of the Indian corn, and a poor quality of fresh hay cut on the high meadows.

In the field by his house and in his barn field he set orchards. The Kentish Cherry brought over by the Pilgrims, had rapidly multiplied by suckers, and were always set on the outer edges, to protect the less hardy trees within. The apple trees were raised from seeds, brought from England, and were generally of inferior quality. The pignose, however, was very productive and a good winter apple. The Foxwell, yet cultivated, is a Fall apple of fair quality. The pears were also seedlings, and many of them worthless sorts; but the trees were hardy and long-lived. A seedling planted by him is a good autumn fruit and yet propagated by grafts from the original tree. The French sugar, a very early pear, was introduced soon after the settlement and grafted into the poorer seedlings. The iron pear, now known as the Black Worcester, a winter fruit, was introduced early — and afterwards the Catherine from the vicinity of Boston, and the Orange, a pear of superior quality. . . .

However rude may have been his dwellings, and however inelegant may have been its surroundings, it was the home of a happy and a contented family. . . . He lived as his neighbors lived. No room in his house was made a sanctum sanctorum, nor had he any furniture that was too good or too costly for his family to use. "Nothing," he would say, "was valuable that was not useful." Again, "A large house makes a slave of the wife, and elegant furniture drouges of the daughters." He had Indian servants who assisted him in the labors of the field. They were not fed and clothed to do that which he could do better himself, for it was his common remark, "He that waits on himself, is well served." When asked why he lived in so small a house, he replied, "Comfort lives in a small house and needs no servants; care in a large one, and requires many." . . .

In his domestic arrangements Goodman Hallett reduced his theories to practice. "Daylight," he would say, "was cheaper than candle-light," and as soon as the day broke he was up and dressed. He kindled the fire, brought water from the spring, went to his barn, fed his cattle, his pigs and his poultry and milked his cows. On his return, he found all the members of his household up and dressed, and breakfast prepared. Sitting down in their accustomed places, the older daughter read a passage from the Bible, and a few stanzas from a favorite hymn. Goodman Hallett kneeling down, in a fervent prayer craved the blessing and protection of Heaven on his country, his church, his household, and his dear friends in England. . . .

The labors of the morning and the religious exercises, had prepared them to partake of their meal with thankful hearts. No cloth covered the well scoured table. A large wooden bowl graced the center, filled with savory broth, and hulled corn supplied the place of bread. Each had a pewter spoon, and all dipped from the same dish, as the Saviour and his disciples did on the eve of the crucifixion. . . . After the bowl was removed, bread or samp, milk, butter and honey, a slice or two of meat, or a plate of fish succeeded. Goody Hallett also had tea, made from some favorite herb, that she had brought from the garden. During breakfast Goodman Hallett told pleasant stories about home, as he called Old England, to which the children were never tired of listening. . . .

The school lasted only a few weeks in each year, and however deep the snow or hard the storm, the children never failed of attending. Goodman Hallett would remark, that "it was as great a sin to cheat children of their learning, as of their money." They were all provided with Indian moccasins and snow shoes, and however difficult it is to acquire the art of wearing the latter, the children of those days acquired it almost as naturally as young ducks learn to swim. . . . The roads were never cleared of snow in those days. Some were partially broken out with teams, but not so as to supercede the necessity of snow shoes, especially after a recent storm. It was a pretty sight to see the little ones trailing along on their snow shoes towards the school-house; but it was a common occurrence then, and excited no curiosity.

If there was no school, and the weather was stormy, the parlor was a scene of varied industry. When the breakfast table was cleared off, and preliminary arrangements made for the dinner, the looms, which in cold weather stood in a corner of the parlor, were in motion, and the girls were merrily turning their spinning wheels.

Meantime the master of the house, assisted by an Indian servant, had watered and fed his large stock, and chopped the wood for the daily fire. He was not lacking in mechanical ingenuity, and on stormy days did many little odd jobs which saved money. His wife frequently repeated the old adage, "A stitch in time saves nine," and Goodman Hallett acquiesced. Taking his awl, his leather, thread, wax and knife, he seated himself in the chimney corner, and successively examined the shoes of the family. If a tap or patch was wanted, he put it on, or if there was a seam that required stitching, it was not overlooked. The andirons were of wrought iron, and had hooks on the front in which the spit rested. Wild fowl and venison were then abundant, and for the family dinner a sirloin had perhaps been spitted. Goodman Hallett turned the spit, and from time to time basted the meat from the contents of the dripping pan. The vegetables, which had been prepared in the morning, were hung over the fire, and at precisely twelve o'clock, if a bright day, the dinner was ready.

Before partaking of the meal, a blessing was craved. The meat was cut on a wooden trencher, and served on pewter plates. Vegetables and bread, samp or hulled corn, was on the table, and at every meal "spoon victuals" of some kind formed a part of the repast. Beer, which was regularly brewed every week, was used as a substitute for tea or coffee, and by the workmen, in the place of strong drink.

It was a saying of Goody Hallett, that "the girl who did not know that the dish-water should be heating during meal-time, was unfit to be married." Abigail was in her teens, and remembered this saying. When the dinner was finished, the water was hot, and the table was soon cleared, the dishes washed and put in their places on the "trencher" or in the cup-board.

By three o'clock the tasks of the day were finished. Goody Hallett had woven her five yards, Abigail had spun six skeins of woolen yarn, and Dorcas four of flax. The wheels were put away, the parlor swept and dusted, and clean sand was "lumped" on the floor or the old "herren boned," an act in which the women of those days displayed their good taste. The girls had a small looking-glass, an article of luxury which few families in those days possessed, before which they arranged their toilet. The Halletts were never extravagant; but they always dressed neatly. The petticoat was the principal article of dress, on which the most labor was expended. It was made of cloth of domestic manufacture, sometimes colored, of two thicknesses, and quilted throughout. On the lower border and on the front, there was some ornamental needle work. Over this a "loose gown" was worn. This was of also domestic manufacture, sometimes white; but usually checked or colored. It was open in front and did not extend so low as the under garment. The sleeves extended about half way from the elbow to the wrist. They had long knit gloves or "sleeves" which they wore when they went out. The neck and breast were covered with a handkerchief ordinarily; on great occasions with a bodice or a stomacher. White worsted stockings and Indian mocassins completed the winter apparel. This was the common dress of the woman. For the Sabbath and great occasions, the wealthy had gayer and more costly garments of foreign manufacture. These were carefully preserved, and handed down from generation to generation. Dresses are yet preserved in which mother, daughter and grand-daughter were successively married. All had checked aprons which they wore when employed in household duties, and often a clean nice starched one was put on in the afternoon and evening.

When they went out they had bonnets, and cloaks of thick cloth with a hood or covering for the head attached. For many years a bright red or scarlet was the fashionable color for these garments.

The common dresses of the men were short clothes or breeches, a long vest with lappets covering the hips, a round about coat or jacket for every day, and for the Sabbath a long coat, cut a little cross-way, not "straight down" in front, with a standing collar. The wealthy indulged large in silver buttons; but for every day wear horn was used. The pilgrims all wore round hats, but in after times they adopted the cocked hat of the cavaliers. They wore long blue woolen stockings that extended above the knee, and were kept in place by a buckle and strap on the lower part of the breeches. Shoes fastened with large buckles completed their dress. . . .

At the evening meal, in addition to "spoon victuals," they usually had "short cake" baked before the fire on a pan or in a spider.

In the evening the women were employed in knitting or sewing, and occasionally in making a kind of bobinet lace, on board frames. . . . Goodman Hallett kept a good fire, and as his beer barrels were never empty, he rarely was without company . . . and though the use of tobacco was prohibited by the "honorable Court," yet smoke from the pipe often curled up the chimney on the long winter evenings.

Our ancestors were systematic in their domestic arrangements. Monday was washing-day, a custom which has survived to this day. On Tuesday the clothes were ironed. Wednesday in summer was baking-day, but not in the winter. Thursday and Friday were devoted to spinning and weaving, and Saturday was baking-day the year round. For dinner on that day the Pilgrims eat fish, perhaps because the Catholics, all of whose customs they abjured, dined thereon Fridays. Baked beans, and Indian puddings were always found on their tables on the Sabbath, a custom yet continued in many families.

Saturday at 4 o'clock in the afternoon all servile labor for the week had ended. Preparations for the Sabbath had been made — the wood cut and brought in — the Sunday meal had been prepared, and preparations made to keep the day holy to the end thereof. . . . The Sabbath was a day of rest — all went to church morning and evening. They never allowed the weather to interfere with their religious duties, it was never too wet, never too hot, never too cold to go to meeting. . . .

Goodman Hallett died in the spring of 1684. . . . In early times it was customary, in making the inventory of a man's estate, to apprise the furniture in each room of the house by itself. . . . These old inventories exhibit no evidence of prodigality — no squalid poverty — no traces of licentious life. They exhibit a rude social organization — but beneath that organization they portray a noble race — with hardy virtues — of honest lives — content to live on the fruits of their own unremitted toil.

Andrew Hallett, Jr.'s, estate was apprised by John Miller and John

Thacher May 19, 1684, and sworn to by his widow Ann Hallett on the 31st of the same month.

In the "parlour" or "great room."

"His purse and apparell,"	£90.10.6
Books in the parlor,	13.6
A cup-board,	3.10.0
The bed furniture — all,	10.05.0
The great table — forme and stools,	1.14.0
A chest and chairs,	1.00.0
The trundle-bed and furniture,	3.10.0
Pewter,	2.15.9
Brass mortar *bac,* iron scummer, dripping pan, tin pans — all,	15.2
A Tunnell, spoones, candlesticks, a warming pan — all,	10.10
An hour-glass, a brush, fier-slice and tongs — a brass skillett,	6.06
Trammells, beer barrels, iron skillett, trays — all,	17.00
Spoones, trenchers, rowling pin, looking-glass, bottles jugs,	8.01
All in the parlor	116.16.04
Deducting purse and apparel	90.10.06
The furniture including bed	25.05.10

Such was the furniture in the parlor of the most opulent man of his times. The list was taken by honest and honorable men, and sworn to by the surviving widow who certainly knew what she had in her house. The looms and cradle had disappeared. Goody Hallett was too old to weave, and she had done all her rocking many years before.[4]

From GENEALOGICAL NOTES OF BARNSTABLE FAMILIES

Amos Otis was born in Barnstable in 1801, grandson of an Amos Otis who was first cousin to James Otis, the patriot. Much of his life was spent in the vast accumulation of spirited and sometimes rather scandalous data about Barnstable's first families. His fascinating and voluminous Notes, written with great precision and

[4] Goodman Hallett left an estate valued at £1,180.13.09. Of this, 909.00.00 was "in housing, lands and meadows." All his personal possessions, including forty head of cattle and other livestock, are comprised in the remaining 271.13.09. In the inventory, the objects in the chamber, the lean-to, and the kitchen are listed with same particularity as those in the parlour, down to such items as "a bagg," "3 yards of cloth," and (in the chamber) "hunney bees and hives."

wit, were first published in THE BARNSTABLE PATRIOT *in 1861. After his death in 1875 they were revised and completed by C. F. Swift who published them as a book in Barnstable in 1888.*

ॐ

They named their children with strange names out of the Bible, Shearsjusbub, Achsah, Zoheth. They named them with names to celebrate the circumstances of their birth, Oceanus, Seaborn, Peregrine. They gave them admonitory names, as Patience, Temperance, Thankful, Love, Fear, Wrestling, Desire, Mercy, Emulous, Virtue, Humility, Remember. Their names have the feeling of destiny.

ॐ

Lines From a Sampler

Sarah Palfrey is my name
Cape Cod is my station;
Eastham is my dwelling place
And Christ is my salvation.

ॐ

MAN'S LAW

1638.   *The General Court ordered that* "any person denying the Scriptures to be a rule of life, shall suffer corporal punishment at the discretion of the magistrates, so as not to extend to life or limb."

Another edict stated: "Whereas divers persons, unfit for marriage both in regard to their years and also their weak estate, — some practicing the inveigling of other men's daughters and maids under guardianship . . . and of maid servants . . . therefore it is decreed, that if any man make motion of marriage to any man's daughter or maid without first obtaining leave of her parents, guardian or master, he shall be punished by fine not exceeding five pounds, or by corporal punishment, or both."

A few years after this law was enacted a young man of Barnstable was laid under bond by the court "not to attempt to gain the affections" *of Elizabeth, daughter of Governor Prince.*

1640. *The grand jurors in each town were authorized by the Court* "to take special view and notice of all persons, married or single, that have small means to maintain themselves, and are supposed to live idly and loosely, and require an account of them how they live."

1641. *John Bryant and Daniel Pryor of Barnstable were presented before the Court* "for drinking tobacco upon the heigh way. Witness, Henr. Bourne."

1642. *The Court took cognizance of many cases of licentious living in the Colony. One man,* "for having a child born six weeks before the ordinary time of women after marriage, fined for uncleanness, and whipt, and his wife set in the stocks." *Another,* "for abusing himself with his wife before marriage, sentenced to be whipt publicly at the post, she to stand by whilst the execution is performed. Done, and he fined five pounds, for the trouble."

1651. *The Court ordered that,* "if any lazy, slothful, or profane persons, in any of the towns, neglect to attend public worship, they shall pay for each offense ten shillings, or be publicly whipped."

1652. *Ralph Allen and Richard Kirby of Sandwich were presented before the Court for* "speaking deridingly against God's word and ordinances," *and the wife of Tristram Hull, of Barnstable,* "for interfering with the service of a domestic in Mr. Samuel Mayo's family."

1655. *Sandwich was presented for not being provided with stocks and a whipping post; also for not having a full complement of arms.*

1660.   " 'George Barlow, the marshal (of Sandwich) having accused John Newland of saying he (Newland) is holy as God
is holy and perfect as God is perfect,' the matter being inquired into, and the language used not appearing to bear
precisely that construction, Newland was discharged. . . .
Daniel Butler, 'for rescuing a strange Quaker from the
marshal, was publicly whipped.' Thomas Butler and wife,
'for turbulent conduct,' were fined forty shillings. . . . William
Newland, 'for entertaining a strange Quaker called Wenlock
Christopherson,' was fined five pounds; and said Christopherson was ordered 'to depart out of the government.' Not com-
plying, the said Christopherson was sent to prison, and afterwards was sentenced to 'lay neck and heels.' He was then
'whipped and sent away.' " — FREDERICK FREEMAN.

1665.   *The Court ordered that* "whosoever shall shoot off a gun on
any unnecessary occasion (within the towns) or at any game,
except a wolf or an Indian, shall forfeit five shillings for every
such offense."

   Eastham voted that "all persons who should stand out of
the meeting-house during the time of divine service, should
be set in the stocks."

1666.   "William Sutton, of Barnstable, for taking away a Bible
out of the meeting house att Barnstable, fined 1:00:00. And
for telling a lye about the same, fined 0:10:00."

1668.   *Francis, sachem of Nauset, was fined £10 by the Court*
"for uncivil and inhumane words to Captain Allen, at Cape
Cod, when cast away."

1673.   *The Court enacted that* "Indians may be worked for debt;
that drunken Indians shall be fined and whipped; that idle
Indians shall be bound out to labor; and that for any theft,
they shall restore fourfold."

1695.   *In Eastham,* "the town agreed that the order which was
passed in 1675, for the destruction of crows and blackbirds,
should be continued and that, in addition, every unmarried
man in the township should kill six blackbirds or three crows
while he remains single; — as a penalty of not doing it, should

not be married till he obeyed the order." — ENOCH PRATT.

1711.   "The town laid out for all the widows in Eastham four acres of land to each." — ENOCH PRATT.

1773.   *Voted by the town of Provincetown,* "that any person should be found getting cranberys before ye twentyeth of September exceeding one quart should be liable to pay one doler & have the berys taken away."

Voted also that "they who shall find such persons so gathering shall have them and the doler."

Capital offenses were treason, murder, diabolical converse, arson and rape.

These samples of Old Colony jurisprudence have been selected from the Plymouth Colony Records and various town records, from Enoch Pratt's A COMPREHENSIVE HISTORY ECCLESIASTICAL AND CIVIL OF EASTHAM, WELLFLEET AND ORLEANS, ETC., (1844) *and from Frederick Freeman's* HISTORY OF CAPE COD, (1858). "A rigid morality was the end desired," *Freeman remarks.* "The reader may reprehend the means sometimes employed to effect this but will, we doubt not, be charitably candid in regard to the motive."

༄

1672–1715
GOD'S WRATH

BY SAMUEL TREAT

LET THIS TRUTH be an awful and solemn word of awakening to thee, that art yet in thy sins, and has not truly repented of them. I have pressed thee to seriousness from the consideration of death, and that is solemn; but it may be that seems a little thing to thee, and thou countest it no such great matter to die; and were the Epicurean principle a truth, that man dies in all points like the beasts that perish, it were of little concernment. Well then, if thou canst see nothing in the grave to make thee serious, I beseech thee to look a little further, and see if thou canst find nothing in hell to startle and amaze thee. Remember thou art not only going to the grave, which it may be thou mayst look upon as an easer of many of the sorrows of this life, and so mayst have some abatement of the terrours of it, but thou art going to hell, the beginner of worse, unspeakably worse sorrows.

Thou must erelong go to the bottomless pit. Hell hath enlarged herself and is ready to receive thee. There is room enough for thy entertainment: and dost thou know what it is for a condemned sinner to go to hell? I have told thee in the explication: but let me apply it to thee now.

Consider thou are going to a place, prepared by God on purpose to exalt his justice in; a place made for no employment but torments. Hell is God's house of correction; and remember God doth all things like himself. When God would show his justice, and what is the weight of his wrath, he makes a hell, where it shall indeed appear to purpose. Consider but what a spark of his wrath hath done in this world, and by that, rate the utmost of his fury. Let Sodom, Pharoah, Korah, and multitudes of the like monuments witness to thee. Remember that mercy and justice are the two great attributes, which God intends the exaltation of by the creature. Then will that be verified, Who knows the power of thine anger? Wo to thy soul, when thou shalt be set up as a butt for the arrows of the Almighty; be made a brier that must burn in the fire of his jealousy forever, and not be consumed.

Consider, God himself shall be the principal agent in thy misery. He is that consuming fire: his breath is the bellows, which blows up the flame of hell forever: he is the devouring fire, the everlasting burning: and if he punish thee, if he meet thee in his fury, he will not meet thee as a man; he will give thee an omnipotent blow. Little dost thou know what it is to enter the lists of contention with the Almighty. If his wrath kindle but a little while, we wither before it. Now thou are afraid of the wrath of man: what wilt thou do, when God takes thee in hand?

Consider, God will take delight to execute vengeance on thee. God delights in justice, and in executing his own decrees. Now it was his eternal decree to destroy sinners forever. He purposed to show his power, and make his wrath known, upon the vessels of wrath fitted to destruction. But wo to that soul, whom God shall delight to punish.

Now thou laughest at the reproofs which God gives thee by his ministers and people: God will laugh at thee shortly. And how wilt thou bear, when he shall torment thee, and thou shalt roar under thy torments? Thou shalt cry for mercy, and he shall mock thee. Thou now rejoicest in sinning; he will erelong rejoice in thy calamity.

Consider the company thou must go to: Thou goest to a place prepared for the devil and his angels. These were thy tempters here; they shall be thy companions there. Here thou chosest communion with them rather than with God and Christ; thou must have enough of their company erelong. And thy fellows in sin, with whom thou wentest hand in hand here in the world, and delightest thyself in their sinful society, — some of them have gone before thee to the place of woes, and others will come after thee; and there shall you meet together, and there shall they curse thee for thy wicked counsels and persuasions, in drawing them to that place of misery.

Consider what must be thy employment there.

1. Sin. Some think sinning ends with this life, but it is a mistake. The creature is held under an everlasting law: the damned increase in sin in hell. Possibly the mention of this may please thee. But remember there shall be no pleasant sins there; no eating, drinking, singing, dancing, wanton dalliance, and drinking stolen waters; but damned sins, bitter hellish sins, sins exasperated by torments, cursing God, spite, rage and blasphemy.

2. Thou shalt be delivered up into the hands of the tormentors: then Satan will pay thee thy wages for thy servile slavery to him, and thou shalt know what a cruel master thou hast here served. What cruelty hath Satan sometime exercised to some here in this world, that have been possessed by him, and to others that have sold themselves to him! What amazing stories doth the world afford of such things! What dost thou think he will do when he hath unlimited commission and full possession? How wilt thou endure, when thou shalt have a thousand devils rending, and tearing, and macerating thee; when all the rage of hell shall fall upon thee without restraint?

3. The never-dying worm shall gnaw and eat out all the heart of thy comfort. Thou shalt become thy own executioner: thy conscience shall pursue thee in hell, always crying out against thee, and bringing bitter things to thy mind, making thee to wring thy hands, and howl out sad lamentations. Thou canst hardly sit under one of these lectures now coming from the mouth of a poor minister; but let me tell

thee, conscience in hell will read it after another manner than can now be conceived; every thought and consideration whereof will be a sharp dagger at thy heart, that will let out all joy and comfort out of thy soul.

Remember how universal all this torment shall be. Here usually our pain is but in one part of the body; and yet what a misery it is to all the rest by sympathy? But then, soul and body shall be filled brimful: the guilt of all thy sins shall be laid upon the soul; and be made so many heaps of fuel; when that tender and delicate body shall have all its beauty blasted and pride consumed; when the flames shall have no respect to its comeliness; when every member's pain shall be intolerable, and that insupportable misery shall spread itself through the whole man; when eyes, ears, hands, feet, heart, and all shall be tormented in that flame.

Consider how near the time hastens, when all this must come to pass upon thee. Time is almost gone with thee, and thou standest at the gate of eternity; and death is waiting upon thee, to transport thee away to the place of all thy miseries. Shortly thou must die, and it will be but a moment from thence to hell. When thou hast sinned away a few more days, watched and slept out a few more nights, away thou goest irrecoverably. It may be thou dreamest of many days to come; but, thou fool, how knowest though but thy soul may be called for this very night; and the day of judgment is not far off.

Sinner, I beseech thee, realize the truth of these things. Do not go about to dream that this is derogatory to God's mercy, and nothing but a vain fable to scare children out of their wits withal. God can be merciful, though he make thee miserable. He shall have monuments enough of that precious attribute, shining like stars in the place of glory, and singing eternal hallelujahs to the praise of him that redeemed them: though to exalt the power of his justice, he damn sinners heaps upon heaps.

— From a Sermon

Calvinist Samuel Treat shrieked damnation to his congregation at Eastham and ministered with tenderness and great good sense to the Indians of the lower Cape for nearly forty-five years. "His voice was so loud that it could be heard at a great distance from the meeting-house, even amidst the shrieks of hysterical women, and the winds that howled over the plains of Nauset." *He terrified his listeners literally into fits, yet in person he was mild, affable, and fond of a joke. (Never, it is recorded, a shady one.) He preached to the Indians in their own tongue. He translated* The Confession of Faith *for their use. He wrote sermons for Indian preachers to deliver and taught Indian teachers to take charge of and teach in Indian schools. Like Richard Bourne, the great missionary of the upper Cape, he believed firmly in the Indians' right to self-government and labored all his life to make good citizens as well as Christians out of them. And the Indians gave him their love and trust. When he died during the great spring blizzard of 1715, it was they who tunnelled a path through the six-foot drifts of snow to carry him to his grave.*

൙

INDIAN BEARERS

KATHARINE LEE BATES

*White was the world as a winding-sheet
The day we buried Parson Treat.*

. . . . .

Sunday it was as the new days go,
That there fell the first of the Great March Snow.

. . . . .

As far as the reach of an Indian's gaze
Shrouded were all the familiar ways;
New were the hillocks, the hollows were new;
Nor fox nor squirrel had ventured through;
Never a track nor a trace was there
Of the little feet that our wood-paths share;
But steadily on through that printless snow
We dug a road for our friend to go;
Through the deepest drifts we cut an arch
Six feet high for the burial march;
The upflung snow, as our rude spades ploughed,
Fanned out above us a shimmering cloud.
Whenever a gust would the pine groves thrash

Till the icycles, thick on their boughs, would clash,
Or snow-laden fir give a sudden crack,
We started as if his laugh came back;
For a merry heart had old Parson Treat,
Though his voice was rough as the blasts that meet
On the plains of Nauset; he laughed as he died,
As his soul went out on the ebb of the tide.

·   ·   ·   ·   ·

It was love of him that held us tame
When every leaf whispered King Philip's name.

·   ·   ·   ·   ·

Oft we have stood at the meeting-house door
When the Parson's voice would the seas outroar,
While the Cape children, lulled by the stormy sounds,
Would sleep till the tithing-man went his rounds.
'Twas a wonder to hear our father shout
As he hammered the White God's anger out.
Yet in every wigwam his voice was sweet;
The papooses nestled between his feet;
And ever he soothed the sullen brave,
And the railing squaw with a smile forgave;
As soon as he saw her black eyes flash,
He would tease for a taste of her succotash.

·   ·   ·   ·   ·

The villages blithened when he came;
We hung the kettle and fanned the flame.
Ten mile afoot through the deepening sand
Makes a hungry guest; then the hearty hand
He would strike in ours, while from chest so stout
Ever the big laugh rumbled out.
Reading and writing he taught our young,
While he learned of our elders the Nauset tongue.
In the meeting-house that was twenty feet square,
Thatched and loop-holed, he taught us prayer.
He would bring the wild grapes of Monomoyick
All the way to Truro's sick;
In Sawtucket he used to praise
First their faith and then their maize.
From Pochet down to Provincetown tip,

Where first was seen the great winged ship,
He would trudge to strengthen a soul for flight;
He loved the red as he loved the white.

.   .   .   .

But oft in our villages while we heard
Our father thunder the awful word,
Our hearts were stirred by a longing dim
That the fierce White God were like to him.
— From AMERICA THE DREAM

.   .   .   .

*Katharine Lee Bates was born in Falmouth on Cape Cod in 1859
and her ashes were brought back there after her death in 1929. She
is the author of the anthem AMERICA THE BEAUTIFUL which all
Americans know and love. INDIAN BEARERS, from which the few
lines given here are taken, is a long poem expressing the Indians'
hatred for most white men and their love for one.*

&

MR. BODFISH AND THE WOLVES

BY AMOS OTIS

WHEN HE WAS EIGHTEEN, Plymouth had been settled fifty years,
and though liberal bounties had been paid to English and Indians
for wolves' heads, yet these ravenous animals abounded in the Colony.
In 1654, the whole number killed was nineteen — of which three
were killed in Barnstable, and in 1655, thirty-one — nine in Barnstable. In 1690, the number killed was thirteen, and in 1691, nineteen. Jonathan Bodfish said his grandfather could set a trap as cunningly as the oldest Indians, and that the duck or the goose that ventured to come within gunshot of him, rarely escaped being shot.
Wolf Neck, so named because it was the resort of these animals,
was about half a mile from Joseph Bodfish's house, and there he set
his traps. Once he narrowly escaped losing his own life. Seeing a
large wolf in his trap, he incautiously approached with a rotten pine
pole in his hand. He struck — the pole broke in his hand, and the

enraged beast sprang at him with the trap and broken chain attached to his leg. Mr. Bodfish stepped suddenly one side, and the wolf passed by him. Before the wolf could recover, Mr. Bodfish was beyond his reach. This trap is preserved in his family as an heir-loom.

Some years after a wolf was followed by hunters from Wareham to Barnstable, and they wished Mr. Bodfish to join them, but he declined. Having studied the habits of the animal, he felt certain it would return on the same track. Taking his gun he went into the woods, concealed himself within gunshot of the leeward side of the track, and waited for the return of the wolf. He was not disappointed, the wolf at last appeared and was shot. He returned to his house, and soon after the Wareham hunters came in and reported that they had followed the wolf to the lower part of Yarmouth, and the dogs had there lost the track, and they gave up the pursuit. They felt a little chagrined when the dead body of the wolf was shown to them.

All his sons, excepting Benjamin, were good gunners. Wolf hunting, however, was not a sport in which they engaged. It is said that the last wolf killed in Barnstable was shot by Joseph Bodfish; but this story requires confirmation.

— From GENEALOGICAL NOTES OF BARNSTABLE FAMILIES

ॐ

1769–1775
THE INDIANS OF CAPE COD
AND THE ISLANDS

BY HECTOR ST. JOHN DE CRÈVECOEUR

THREE YEARS before the arrival of the Europeans at Cape Cod, a frightful distemper had swept away a great many along its coasts, which made the landing and intrusion of our forefathers much easier than it otherwise might have been. In the year 1763, above half of the Indians of this island[1] perished by a strange fever, which the Europeans who nursed them never caught; they appear to be a race

[1] Nantucket.

doomed to recede and disappear before the superior genius of the Europeans. The only ancient custom of these people that is remembered is, that in their mutual exchanges, forty sun-dried clams, strung on a string, passed for the value of what might be called a copper. They were strangers to the use and value of wampum so well known to those of the main. The few families now remaining are meek and harmless; their ancient ferocity is gone; they were early christianized by the New England missionaries, as well as those of the Vineyard, and of several other parts of Massachusetts; and to this day they remain strict observers of the laws and customs of that religion, being carefully taught while young. Their sedentary life has led them to this degree of civilisation much more effectually, than if they had still remained hunters. They are fond of the sea, and expert mariners. They have learned from the Quakers the art of catching both the cod and whale, in consequence of which, five of them always make part of the complement of men requisite to fit out a whaleboat. Many have removed hither from the vineyard on which account they are more numerous on Nantucket than anywhere else.

It is strange what revolution has happened among them in less than two hundred years! What is become of those numerous tribes which formerly inhabited the extensive shores of the great bay of Massachusetts? Even from Numkeag (*Salem*), Saugus (*Lynn*), Shawmut *(Boston)*, Pataxet, Napouset *(Milton)*, Matapan *(Dorchester)*, Winèsimèt *(Chelsea)*, Poïasset, Pokànoket *(New Plymouth)*, Suecanosset *(Falmouth)*, Titicut *(Chatham)*, Nobscusset *(Yarmouth)*, Naussit *(Eastham)*, Hyanneès *(Barnstable)*, etc., and many others who lived on sea-shores of above three hundred miles in length; without mentioning those powerful tribes which once dwelt between the rivers Hudson, Connecticut, Piskàtaquà, and Kènnebèck, the Mèhikaudret, Mohiguine, Pèquods, Narragansets, Nianticks, Massachusetts, Wamponougs, Nipnets, Tarranteens, etc. — They are gone, and every memorial of them is lost; no vestiges whatever are left of those swarms which once inhabited this country, and replenished both sides of the great peninsula of Cape Cod; not even one of the posterity of the famous Masconomèo is left (the sachem of Cape Ann); not one of the descendants of Massasoit, father of Mètacomèt *(Philip)*, and Wamsutta *(Alexander)*, he who first conveyed some lands to the Plymouth Company. They have all disappeared either in the wars which the Europeans carried on against them, or else they have mouldered away, gathered in some of their ancient towns, in contempt and oblivion; nothing remains of them all, but one extraordinary monument, and even this they owe to the industry and religious zeal of the Europeans. I mean the Bible translated into the Nattick tongue. Many of these tribes giving way to the superior power of the whites, retired to their ancient villages, collecting the scattered remains of nations once populous; and in their grant of lands reserved to themselves and posterity certain portions, which lay contiguous to them. There forgetting their ancient manners, they dwelt in peace; in a few years their territories were surrounded by the improvements of the Europeans; in consequence of which they grew lazy, inactive, unwilling, and unapt to imitate, or to follow any of our trades, and in a few generations, either totally perished or else came over to the Vineyard, or to this island, to reunite themselves with such societies of their countrymen as would receive them. Such has been the fate of many nations, once warlike and independent; what we see now on the main, or on those islands, may be justly considered as the only remains of those ancient tribes. Might I be permitted to pay perhaps a very useless compliment to *those* at least who inhabited the great peninsula of Namset, now Cape Cod, with whose names and ancient situation I am well acquainted. This peninsula was divided into two great regions; that on the side of the bay was known by the name of Nobscusset, from one of its towns; the capital was called Nausit (now *Eastham*); hence the Indians of that region were called Nausit Indians, though they dwelt in the villages of Pamet, Nosset, Pashèe, Potomaket, Soktoowoket, Nobscusset (*Yarmouth*).

The region on the Atlantic side was called Mashpèe, and contained the tribes of Hyannèes, Costowet, Waquoit, Scootin, Saconasset, Mashpèe, and Namset. Several of these Indian towns have been since converted into flourishing European settlements, known by different names; for as the natives were excellent judges of land, which they had fertilised besides with the shells of their fish, etc., the latter could not make a better choice; though in general this great peninsula is but a sandy pine track, a few good spots excepted. It is divided into seven townships, viz. Barnstable, Yarmouth, Harwich, Chatham, Eastham, Pamet, Namset, or Province Town, at the extremity of the Cape. Yet these are very populous, though I am at a loss to conceive on what the inhabitants live, besides clams, oysters, and fish; their piny lands being the most un-grateful soil in the world. The minister of Namset or Province Town, receives from the government of Massachusetts a salary of fifty pounds per annum; and such is the poverty of the inhabitants of that place, that, unable to pay him any money, each master of a family is obliged to allow him two hundred horse feet (*sea spin*) with which this primitive priest fertilises the land of his glebe, which he tills himself; for nothing will grow on these hungry soils without the assistance of this extraordinary manure, fourteen bushels of Indian corn being looked upon as a good crop. But it is time to return from a digression, which I hope you will pardon.

— From LETTERS FROM AN AMERICAN FARMER

LETTERS FROM AN AMERICAN FARMER *was first published in London in 1782 but, in a footnote added at that time to the Introductory Letter, the writer says,* "The troubles that now convulse the American colonies had not broken out when this and some of the following letters were written." *A Norman by birth, English by education, Crèvecoeur came to the New World as a young man to serve under Montcalm, fell in love with America, and, in 1764, took out naturalization papers in New York. He combined a passionate love for the natural world with great and practical interest in people and their institutions and, in his* LETTERS, *has left us one of the sunniest, most delightful accounts of American life in the late eighteenth century.*

The First to Rebel

THE BARNSTABLE PATRIOT

By William Tudor, with interpolations by John Adams

> If we are to be slaves, the living have only to
> envy the dead; for without liberty I desire not
> to exist here.
>
> — JAMES OTIS, 1766

*J*AMES OTIS, the eldest son of Colonel James Otis of Barnstable, descended in the fifth generation from John Otis, the first of the name in this country, was born in the family mansion at Great Marshes, in what is now called West Barnstable, the 5th day of February 1725. He was one of thirteen children, five sons and eight daughters, several of whom died in infancy.[1] His father, always having regretted his own want of a classical education, was the more anxious that his children should have every opportunity to secure all its advantages. His son therefore was prepared for college under the care of the Rev. Jonathan Russell, the clergyman of the parish, and entered Cambridge in June, 1739. During the first two years of his college life, his natural ardor and vivacity made his society much courted by the elder students, and engaged him more in amusement than in study; but he changed his course in his junior year, and though yet in his boyhood, began thenceforward to give indications of great talent and power of application. He took the degree of A.B. in 1743, and that of A.M. in due course, three years afterward.

In 1745 he began the study of law in the office of Mr. Jeremiah Gridley, at that time one of the most eminent lawyers in the Province. After completing his studies he went to Plymouth, was first admitted to the bar of that county, and entered there upon the practice. But the narrow range of country business could not long detain a character like his from appearing on a scene more suited to his powers. After two years residence at Plymouth, which were more

---

[1] Of the survivors Joseph became brigadier general in command of the Cape forces in the war for independence and later collector of the Port of Barnstable; Samuel Allyne became the first secretary of the United States Senate and continued in that office through all changes of administration until his death in 1814; Mercy married Gen. James Warren and proved herself a writer of unusual merit. Mary married John Gray; the others dying unmarried.

occupied in study than in practice, he removed to Boston and very soon rose to the first rank in his profession.

His business became very extensive, and his reputation was firmly established for learning, eloquence and the most high-minded integrity. He was soon generally known in many of the other colonies, and often consulted from a distance; at one time he yielded to the urgent solicitations that were made to proceed to Halifax in the middle of winter, to plead the cause of three men accused of piracy, whom he defended so ably as to procure their acquital. On this occasion he received a fee which was said to have been the largest that ever had been given to any advocate in the Province.

In the spring of the year 1755, he married Miss Ruth Cunningham, the daughter of a respectable merchant. The lady was very beautiful and was possessed of a dowry which in those times was considered very large. Few characters could be more unlike than those of Mr. Otis and his wife, yet they were attached to each other. Beautiful, placid and formal, she was suited to the calm and monotonous routine of a quiet existence, while his ardent mind, impetuous genius and energetic will, qualified him to direct the leading events in a great crisis of national affairs. Her feelings too were not in sympathy with his on political topics.

JOHN ADAMS: "He has often told me that his wife was a high Tory and read him the most unmerciful curtain lectures."

In 1761 came the matter of Writs of Assistance and, as Advocate General, Otis was supposed to plead for their acceptance. Instead he resigned the office and went before the court to question their legality and the authority of the court to grant them. Mr. Gridley, his old teacher, appeared for the Crown.

In addition to the deep anxiety, which such a question as that of Writs of Assistance, involving so extensively not only the pecuniary concerns, but political and civil rights, must inevitably have created; this trial was also accompanied with a peculiar interest, arising out of incidental circumstances of a personal nature, some of which have already been mentioned. Otis was the pupil of Gridley, for whose character he felt a high respect, and for whose instruction he was sincerely grateful: and he never lost sight of these feelings in the course of the trial.

JOHN ADAMS: "It was a moral spectacle more affecting to me than any I have ever seen upon the stage, to observe a pupil treating his master with all the deference, respect, esteem and affection of a son to a father, and that without the least affectation; while he baffled and confounded, all his authorities, confuted all his arguments, and reduced him to silence. . . . The crown, by its agents, accumulated construction upon construction, and inference upon inference, as the giants heaped Pelion upon Ossa. . . . He dashed the whole building to pieces, and scattered the pulverized atoms to the four winds; and no judge, lawyer, or crown officer dared to say, why do ye so?"

James Otis addressed the Court

"May it please your honours, I was desired by one of the Court to look into the books and consider the question now before them concerning Writs of Assistance. I have accordingly considered it, and now appear not only in obedience to your order, but likewise in behalf of the residents of this town, who have presented another petition, and out of regard to the liberties of the subject. And I take this opportunity to declare, that whether under a fee or not, (for in such a cause as this I despise a fee,) I will to my dying day oppose with all the powers and faculties God has given me, all such instruments of slavery on one hand, and villainy on the other, as this writ of assistance is.

"It appears to me the worst instrument of arbitrary power, the most destructive of English liberties and the fundamental principles of law, that ever was found in an English law book. I must therefore beg your honours' patience and attention to the whole range of an argument, that may perhaps appear uncommon in many things, as well as to pints of learning that are more remote and unusual: that the whole tendency of my design may the more easily be perceived, the conclusions better descend, and the force of them be better felt. I shall not think much of my pains in this cause, as I engaged in it from principle. I was solicited to argue this cause as Advocate General; and because I would not, I have been charged with desertion from my office. To this charge I can give a very sufficient answer. I renounced that office, and I argue this cause from the same principle; and I argue it with the greater pleasure, as it is in favour of British liberty, at a time when we hear the greatest monarch upon earth declaring from his throne that he glories in the name of Briton, and that the privileges of his people are dearer to him than the most valuable prerogatives of his crown; and it is in opposition to a kind of power, the exercise of which in former periods of English

history, cost one king of England his head, and another his throne.
I have taken more pains in this cause, than I ever will take again,
although my engaging in this and another popular cause has raised
much resentment. But I think I can sincerely declare, that I cheerfully submit myself to every odious name for conscience' sake; and
from my soul I despise all those, whose guilt, malice, or folly, has
made them my foes. Let the consequences be what they will, I am
determined to proceed. The only principles of public conduct that
are worthy of a gentleman or a man, are to sacrifice estate, ease,
health, and applause, and even life, to the sacred calls of his country.

"These manly sentiments, in private life, make the good citizen; in
public life, the patriot and the hero. I do not say, that when brought
to the test, I shall be invincible. I pray God I may never be brought
to the melancholy trial, but if ever I should, it will be then known
how far I can reduce to practice, principles, which I know to be
founded in truth. In the meantime I will proceed to the subject of
this writ.

"Your honours will find in the old books concerning the office of
a justice of the peace, precedents of general warrants to search suspected houses. But in more modern books, you will find only special
warrants to search such and such houses, specially named, in which the
complainant has before sworn that he suspects his goods are concealed; and will find it adjudged, that special warrants only, are legal.
In the same manner I rely on it, that the writ prayed for in this
petition, being general, is illegal. It is a power that places the liberty
of every man in the hands of every petty officer. I say I admit that
special writs of assistance, to search special places, may be granted to
certain persons on oath; but I deny that the writ now prayed for can
be granted, for I beg leave to make some observations on the writ
itself, before I proceed to other acts of Parliament. In the first place,
the writ is universal, to be directed 'to all and singular justices,
sheriffs, constables, and all other officers and subjects'; so that, in short,
it is directed to every subject in the king's dominions. Every one with
this writ may be a tyrant in a legal manner, also may control, im-
prison, or murder anyone within the realm. In the next place, it is
perpetual, there is no return. A man is accountable to no person for
his doings. Every man may reign secure in his petty tyranny, and
spread terror and desolation around him, until the trump of the
archangel shall excite different emotions in his soul. In the third

place, a person with this writ, in the day time, may enter all houses, shops, etc., at will, and command all to assist him. Fourthly, by this writ, not only deputies, etc., but even their menial servants are allowed to lord it over us. What is this but to have the curse of Canaan with a witness on us; to be the servant of servants, the most despicable of God's creation? Now one of the most essential branches of English liberty is the freedom of one's house. A man's house is his castle; and whilst he is quiet, he is as well guarded as a prince in his castle. This writ, if it should be declared legal, would totally annihilate this privilege. Custom-house officers may enter our houses when they please; we are commanded to permit their entry. Their menial servants may enter, may break locks, bars, and everything in their way: and whether they break through malice or revenge, no man, no court, can enquire. Bare suspicion without oath is sufficient. This wanton exercise of this power is not a chimerical suggestion of a heated brain. I will mention some facts. Mr. Pew had one of these writs, and when Mr. Ware succeeded him, he endorsed this writ over to Mr. Ware: so that, these writs are negotiable from one officer to another; and so your honours have no opportunity of judging the persons to who this vast power is delegated. Another instance is this: Mr. Justice Walley had called this same Mr. Ware before, by a constable, to answer for a breach of the sabbath-day acts, or that of profane swearing. As soon as he had finished, Mr. Ware asked him if he had done. He replied, 'Yes.' 'Well then,' said Mr. Ware, 'I will show you a little of my power. I command you to permit me to search your house for un-customed goods,' and went on to search the house from the garret to the cellar; and then served the constable in the same manner! But to show another absurdity in this writ, if it should be established, I in-sist upon it every person by the 14th Charles second, has this power as well as the custom-house officers. The words are, 'it shall be lawful for any person or persons authorized, etc.' What a scene does this open! Every man prompted by revenge, ill humour, or wantonness to inspect the inside of his neighbour's house, may get a writ of assist-ance. Others will ask it from self-defense; one arbitrary exertion will provoke another, until society be involved in tumult and in blood." [2]

[2] The fragments of this speech are taken from Minot's *History*, vol. 2. It seems from the letters of President Adams, that they were derived from some imperfect notes, taken by him at the time, which were afterwards carried off by some individual, who "interpolated them with some bombastic expressions of his own," and printed them in a newspaper. W.T.

JOHN ADAMS: "In plain English, by cool, patient comparison of the phraseology of these statutes, their several provisions, the dates of their enactments, the privileges of our charters, the merits of the Colonists, etc., he showed the pretensions to introduce the revenue acts and these arbitrary and mechanical writs of assistance, as an instrument for the execution of them, to be so irrational; by his wit he represented the attempt as ludicrous and ridiculous; and by his dignified reprobation of an impudent attempt to impose on the people of America, he raised such a storm of indignation, that even Hutchinson, who had been appointed on purpose to sanction this writ, dared not utter a word in it favor, and Mr. Gridley himself seemed to me to exult inwardly at the glory and triumph of his pupil.

"Otis was a flame of fire; with a promptitude of classical allusions, a depth of research, a rapid summary of historical events and dates, a profusion of legal authorities, a prophetic glance of his eyes into futurity, and a rapid torrent of impetuous eleoquence, he hurried away all before him. American Independence was then and there born . . . Every man of an immense crowded audience appeared to me to go away as I did, ready to take up arms against Writs of Assistance. Then and there, was the first scene of the first act of opposition, to the arbitrary claims of Great Britain. Then and there, the child Independence was born. In fifteen years, in 1776, he grew up to manhood and declared himself free . . . I do say in the most solemn manner, that Mr. Otis's oration against writs of assistance, breathed into this nation the breath of life."

After the close of his argument the court adjourned for consideration, and at the close of the term Chief Justice Hutchinson pronounced the opinion: "The Court has considered the subject of writs of assistance, and can see no foundation for such a writ; but as the practice in England is not known, it has been thought best to continue the question to the next term, that in the meantime opportunity may be given to know the result."

JOHN ADAMS: "When the next term came no judgment was pronounced, nothing was said about writs of assistance. But it was generally reported and understood that the court clandestinely granted them, and the custom house officers had them in their pockets, though I never knew that they dared to produce and execute them in any one instance."

Although Mr. Otis had never before interfered in public affairs, his exertions on this single occasion secured him a commanding popularity with the friends of their country, and the terror and vengeance of her enemies, neither of which ever deserted him.

Early in the nineteenth century when the old veterans were refighting the war for independence, partisans claimed that Virginians were the originators of the war, basing their claim on Patrick Henry's resolutions against the Stamp Act in 1765. John Adams rose to the defense of Otis: in a letter to William Wirt, the biographer of Henry, from Quincy, March 7, 1818, he wrote:

"In 1764 was published, in Boston, 'The Rights of the British Colonies Asserted and Proved,' by James Otis, Esq. This work was read in the House of Representatives of Massachusetts, in manuscript, in 1764, and, though not ordered by them to be published, it was printed with their knowledge. In it these propositions are asserted as fundamental.

1. That the supreme and subordinate powers of legislation should be free and sacred in the hands where the community have once rightfully placed them.

2. The supreme, national legislative cannot be altered justly till the commonwealth is dissolved, nor a subordinate legislative taken away without forfeiture or other good cause. Nor then can the subjects in the subordinate government be reduced to a state of slavery, and subject to the despotic rule of others.

3. No legislative, supreme or subordinate, has a right to make itself arbitrary.

4. The supreme legislative cannot justly assume a power of ruling by extempore arbitrary decrees, but is bound to dispense justice by known, settled rules, and by duly authorized, independent judges.

5. The supreme power cannot take from any man any part of his property, without his consent in person, or by representation.

6. The legislative cannot transfer the power of making laws to any other hands.

'These are their bounds which, by God and nature, are fixed; hitherto have they a right to come, and no further.'

1. To govern by stated laws.

2. Those laws should have no other end ultimately but the good of the people.

3. Taxes are not to be laid on the people; but by their consent in person, or by deputation.

4. Their whole power is not transferable.

'These are the first principles of law and justice, and the great barriers of a free state, and of the British Constitution in particular. I ask, I want no more.'

This work, which in 1764 was as familiar to me as my alphabet, I had not seen for fifty-four years. . . .

In an appendix to this work is a copy of instructions given by the city of Boston at their annual meeting, in May 1764, to their representatives, Royal Tyler, James Otis, Thomas Cushing, and Oxenbridge Thacher, Esqrs. These instructions were drawn by Samuel Adams, who was one of those appointed by the town for that purpose. These instructions are a sample of that simplicity, purity, and harmony of style which distinguished all the productions of Mr. Adam's pen. I wish I could transcribe the whole, but the paragraph most directly to the present purpose is the following.

'But what still heightens our apprehensions is that these unexpected proceedings may be preparatory to new taxations upon us. For, if our trade may be taxed, why not our lands? Why not the produce of our lands, and everything we possess or make use of? This, we apprehend, annihilates our charter right to govern and tax ourselves. It strikes at our British privileges, which, as we have never forfeited them, we hold in common with our fellow-subjects who are natives of Britain. If taxes are laid upon us in any shape without our having a legal representation where they are laid, are we not reduced from the character of free subjects to the miserable state of tributary slaves?'

The whole work was published more than a year before Mr. Henry's resolutions were moved."

— John Adams, WORKS, vol. X, 292–94

"I have been young and now am old, and I solemnly say, I have never known a man whose love of country was more ardent or sincere, never one who suffered so much, never one whose services for any ten years of his life were so important and essential to the cause of his country as those of Mr. Otis from 1760 to 1770."

— JOHN ADAMS

By 1769 Otis had long been so conspicuous as a leader of the patriotic party, his power of exciting public feeling was so irresistible, his opposition to the administration was so bold and vehement, his detestation against those who were bringing ruin on the country, was so open and mortifying, that secret representations had long been making to render him particularly obnoxious to the ministry, and to stimulate them to arrest and try him for treason. At length, in the course of the summer, copies of several of the letters of Governor Bernard, and of the commissioners, filled with insinuations, and even charges of a treasonable nature, were procured at the public offices in England, and transmitted to him; leaving no doubt, that if these persons had ventured on such a crimination in official letters, they had gone much further in their private correspondence.

He was stung to madness, by the discovery and proofs of these malignant calumnies, and this secret treachery. Agitated as he was by the actual and impending evils that threatened the whole country, and that were more especially directed against his own province, and his home town; penetrated with anxious responsibility for the expediency of those measures of opposition, of which he was one of the chief advisers and had long been the ostensible leader; these attempts to destroy his character, if not his life, excited the deepest indignation. In defending the cause of the colonies he had looked forward to the time when justice would be done them, and when he should derive advantage and honor for all his exertions and sacrifices. He was not acting as a demagogue, nor as a revolutionist. He was proud of his rank in society, and in opposing the ministerial schemes he still felt loyalty towards the sovereign, and affections for England; and longed for the period when he might give proofs of both, not in opposing but in supporting the views of government. While at this very time he found that the crown officers had been assiduously laboring to blast his reputation, and endeavoring to have him torn from his home, to undergo imprisonment and persecution in the mother country. With the proofs of their conduct in his possession, he could no longer restrain himself, but hurled his defiance and contempt in the following notice in the Boston *Gazette*, September 4, 1769:

Advertisement. Whereas I have full evidence, that *Henry Hutton, Charles Paxton, William Burch* and *John Robinson*,[3] Esquires, have frequently and lately, treated the characters of all true North Ameri-

[3] The commissioners of the customs.

cans in a manner that is not to be endured, by *privately* and publicly representing them as *traitors* and *rebels,* and in a general combination to revolt from Great Britain; and whereas the said *Henry, Charles, William* and *John,* without the least provocation or color, have represented me by name as inimical to the rights of the crown, and disaffected to his majesty, to whom I annually swear, and am determined at all events to bear true, and faithful allegiance: for all which general, as well as personal abuse and insult, satisfaction has been personally demanded, due warning given, but no sufficient answer obtained; these are humbly to desire the lords commissioners of his majesty's treasury, his principal Secretaries of State, particularly my lord Hillsborough, the Board of Trade, and all others whom it may concern, or who may condescend to read this, to pay no kind of regard to any of the abusive representations of me or my country, that may be transmitted by the said *Henry, Charles, William* and *John,* or their confederates; for they are no more worthy of credit than those of sir Francis Bernard, of Nettleham, Bart., or of any of his cabal; which cabal may be well known from the papers in the house of commons, and at every great office in England.

— JAMES OTIS

The next evening, about seven o'clock, Mr. Otis went to the British coffee-house where Mr. Robinson, one of the commissioners, was sitting, as also a number of army, navy and revenue officers. As soon as he came in an altercation took place, which soon terminated in Robinson's striking him with a cane, which was returned by a weapon of the same kind. Great confusion then ensued. The lights were extinguished, and Otis without a friend, was surrounded by the adherents of Robinson. A young man by the name of Gridley, passing by, very boldly entered the coffee-house to take the part of Otis against so many foes; but he was also assaulted, beaten and turned out of the house. After some time the combatants were separated, Robinson retreated by a back passage, and Otis was led home wounded and bleeding.

Various and contradictory statements were given in the newspapers respecting it. It was said that this intentional assault was the result of a meditated plan of assassination. Five or six bludgeons and one scabbard were found on the floor after the struggle. Otis received a deep wound on the head, which the surgeons, Doctor Perkins and

Lloyd, testified must have been given by a sharp instrument. The accusation of a preconcerted intention to murder is doubtless unfounded, but from all the evidence in the case, it is plain that it was a brutal and cowardly assault, in which several persons took part with a disposition, that in the fury of the moment, sought to disable this great patriot, whom they so rancorously hated. If such was their purpose, it to a considerable degree succeeded.

At the time Otis's faculties were perpetually agitated, and he did not sufficiently master and subdue his indignation against subaltern agents, though prime movers in this mischief, yet who were in reality deserving only of his contempt. It was an unfortunate yielding to his anger, the placing himself on a level with the commissioners of the customs, whom he ought merely have unmasked and left to public scorn without degrading himself to a personal encounter. The injuries he sustained in it, impaired his power of self control and contributed essentially to his subsequent derangement.

The public career of Otis may be said to have ended in 1769, for though in 1771 he was again in the legislature, his exertions were less arduous, and after that period, notwithstanding his occasional appearances in the courts of justice and in town meetings, yet he was little more than a majestic ruin. In his lucid intervals he was still powerful, but as these were liable to be interrupted, it was impossible to confide important business to him.

His youngest brother, Samuel Allyne Otis, was appointed his guardian and he returned to his home in West Barnstable. Upon the death of his father, in 1778, he took lodgings with a Mr. Osgood, in Andover, and there on Friday, May 23, 1783, he was struck by lightning and died in the arms of his host.

He was a man of powerful genius and ardent temper, with wit and humor that never failed: as an orator he was bold, argumentative, impetuous and commanding, with an eloquence that made his own excitement irresistibly contagious; as a lawyer, his knowledge and ability placed him at the head of his profession; as a scholar, he was rich in acquisition and governed by a classic taste; as a statesman and civilian, he was sound and just in his views; as a patriot, he resisted all allurements that might weaken the cause of that country to which he devoted his life and for which he sacrificed it. The future historian of the United States, in considering the foundations of American independence, will find that one of the corner stones must be inscribed with the name of JAMES OTIS.

James Otis imposed a severe hardship upon his future biographer when, in a period of aberration, he destroyed all his papers. The above excerpts are from The Life of James Otis, of Massachusetts, by William Tudor, Boston: 1823. The interpolations are from The Works of John Adams, edited by Charles Francis Adams, Boston: 1850–56.

Independency

1775–1782

INDEPENDENCY

THERE HAS EVER BEEN a disposition among historical writers to lose sight of the sparsely peopled and scattered settlements — the remoter towns, villages, and by-ways; and to concentrate all the interest of their pages on cities and their inhabitants . . . What were the city without the country? what the most flaming zeal without the yeomanry of the land? . . . what were even a WASHINGTON without a soldiery and the back-bone and cool determination and fervent love of liberty that made up the aggregate from a whole community?"
— FREDERICK FREEMAN

၆ഐ

APRIL, 1775

BY JOHN GORHAM PALFREY

ACCESS HAS KINDLY been furnished me to a little journal kept about the beginning of the revolutionary war, by Eli Phinney, a gentleman of distinction in the town, and frequently employed in municipal trusts. It was written solely for private use, and was principally employed about private transactions; but occasionally, amidst the details of such matters as the getting in of hay, the sorting out of winter fodder for cattle, the mending of a fence, sickness in the family and the remedies applied, a ride to one neighbor's, and an evening's visit from another, is a passing reference to what was going on in the larger world; and it may be supposed to be a fair specimen of a hundred such journals kept at the time, but which no care was taken to preserve. There are passages which carry us back to the heroic age of the nation, with a vivid impression of the reality of the passing scene. For a single example, there are a few lines relating to the stir made at this place by the first news of the Lexington fight; — Lexington being, as you know, some eighty miles from Barnstable, the means of communication being very different from what they now are, and great part of the people of the latter place having probably not so much as known of the existence of the former, until they heard that the blood of Massachusetts men had been shed there by British mercenaries. Here is the record I speak of.

"20th April, Thursday. Received the dreadful news of an engagement." The engagement did not terminate till Wednesday at evening; and yet, on Thursday, they knew of it on the Cape. There were then no railroads, nor so much as fast coaches; if there had been the news could not have waited for them; it flew through Massachusetts as if the indignant winds of Massachusetts had charge of it. "Received the dreadful news of an engagement between the Regulars and Provincials, at Lexington." "Dreadful," Deacon Phinney calls it on Thursday the 20th; and well he might, being a man of peace. But, how dreadful? Did he mean to say it was news to be frightened at? And were the people, on Friday, wondering what would come next, or sending up their submission to General Gage? Let us see.

"21st April, Friday. Soldiers mustered. Sent off nineteen men from our company." And I warrant, fellow-citizens and friends, those nineteen stout Barnstable frames reported themselves at General Ward's head-quarters at Cambridge as soon as nature's vehicles could bring them there.

But here was a spasm. Three days and nights passed, and they had time to sleep over their rage, and go to church too, and get calm. What were they about at the end of that time? In what mood did they begin the next week? Let us ask our concise chronicler.

"24th April, Monday. Training our company." They did not know what, by this time, might have become of the nineteen men, and they meant that, if need should be, there should be ten times nineteen to follow them. *Training our company!* There could hardly be a greater economy of words. But imagination easily fills up the picture. Friday, they had shaken hands with their nineteen friends, selected perhaps as readiest for the emergency, as having no wives or children to provide for. Saturday, the old muskets of the French war had been cleaned, the flints and cartridgeboxes looked to, and blankets folded in the compact knapsack by the loving care of trembling hands. Sunday, the favor of the God of justice and the God of hosts had been reverently sought; and nothing remained but to *train our company,* as our Deacon says, on Monday morning, and take such pains as might yet be taken, in order that the next party that went should be prepared to do its best measure of service. Yes, something, it seems, did remain in Barnstable, as was then found, towards the doing of New-England justice on outrageous oppression; but it was not suffered to remain long. This was Monday the 24th. Here is the record of the next day.

"Tuesday, 25th April. Town meeting." They had had no town meeting till they found there was something to be done at it; getting together to harangue and pass resolutions was not a thing in their way. But, when Monday showed that something was to be done, it did not take them long to circulate a warrant. Barnstable sands are faster travelled over, on occasion, than strangers would suppose.

"Tuesday 25th. Town meeting to raise money to buy guns, &c. Voted three hundred pounds for a chest of arms and some ammunition."

This despatched, the next entry is, "28th. Ploughed with three teams"; and so the Diary goes back again, for the present, to its usual quiet jog over the farm.

— From an Address delivered in Barnstable at the celebration of the Second Centennial Anniversary of the Settlement of Cape Cod, September 3, 1839

❦

FALMOUTH ATTACKED

BY FREDERICK FREEMAN

IN 1779, APRIL 2, a formidable fleet resolved on the destruction of this town. At a late hour the night previous, a marauding party from the fleet now lying at Tarpaulin Cove, eluding the vigilance of our watch, landed from their boats, having a refugee for their conductor, and proceeded from Woods Hole to the farms of Messrs. Ephraim and Manassah Swift, committing sundry depredations; but were soon surprised and compelled to put off with little of their booty.

They drove off 12 head of cattle, knocked them on the head at the beach, and were in the act of taking the carcasses on board when surprised. The refugees who acted as guides knew that the Swifts kept fine dairies; and the officers had determined on the possession of a good supply of fresh butter and rich cheeses; therefore, whilst the main body were robbing stalls, pigsties and hen-roosts, a party entered one of the houses. Mrs. Manassah Swift was alone with her children; but, meeting the soldiers at the door, she demanded if they had a commander? One stepping forward and claiming he had the honor to command, she replied, "My house is defended by no man, and I have the right to presume that you are a gentleman who will not molest a helpless woman and her children." The officer politely inquired if she had any cheese? "Yes," she replied; "but no more than for my own use." He professed a willingness to *buy,* but she had none to *sell.* A *refugee,* who made one of the party, then led two of the soldiers to her cheese-room, and each pierced a cheese with his bayonet, expecting to bear them off without further parley; but Mrs. S. confronted them at the door, grasped, and slipped from their impalement, her cheeses, and bestowed them in her blue-checked apron. "You're a valiant set of fellows, to be sure!" She was not resisted; the enemy cowed, and, under a properly directed volley of wholesome advice retreated to join their comrades on the beach who were beginning to load the boat with the carcasses of the good woman's milch cows.

Returning to the fleet, it was decided to move forward the next day and burn the town. Information of the intention soon reached the town, and, of course, the excitement was very great. Expresses were sent to the adjoining villages and towns, whilst the men on hand hastened to the work of perfecting the intrenchments.

It is said that the evening of the 2d was spent by several of the British officers in a frolic at the house of one John Slocomb on Pesque Island. Slocum was a well-known tory. He, of course, was possessed of all their plans. But as he reflected on their purpose, his tory sympathies gave way, and he secretely despatched his son down the islands to cross over to the Hole that night and give warning to the Falmouth people.

The expected fleet hove in sight early on the morning of the 3d, and came to anchor abreast the town at about 9 A.M. They had taken this position evidently to facilitate the landing of troops; and were soon, doubtless, somewhat perplexed by finding unmistakable indications of a very considerable force in waiting for them. Already had a portion of the troops disembarked; but, in attempting to make the shore in boats, although under the cover of heavy guns from the ships, they were soon brought to reflect on the hazardous nature of their undertaking. They lay upon their oars for a moment, as if for consultation, and then a signal from the flag-ship seemed to change their purpose. Returning toward the ships, and then reconnoitring in the direction of Nobsque, they soon abandoned all attempt to land, and again went on shipboard.

Recurring to the record of these proceedings as published at the time, and then reproduced in "Almon's American Remembrancer," published in London, we gain a better view than we can otherwise obtain:

"Boston, April 15, 1779. The following account of the attempt of the enemy upon Falmouth, in the County of Barnstable, and their repulse by the militia, is authentic: —

"Falmouth, 5th April, 1779.

"Friday, April 2, in the afternoon, Major Dimock, of this town, was informed that about 10 or 12 vessels were seen in the Sound, steering this way; supposed with a design of plundering and destroying this town. He immediately sent expresses to Sandwich and Barnstable for the militia to come to our assistance. Col. Freeman with Capts. Fish and Swift of Sandwich and their companies, arrived here that night and Saturday morning. It being then very foggy, part of the enemy's fleet appeared off Woods Hole, to which a party of the militia were ordered and posted there. Soon after, the fog cleared off and several of the vessels appeared against the town, near a low, level piece of ground that extends from the shore quite to the houses. There had been a small intrenchment made some years ago, upon the edge of the beach, which yet remained. Col. Freeman marched the remainder of the men down to the shore, posting about 50 in said intrenchment, and about 30 at about 130 rods distance, — being the most convenient place for the enemy to land. At about half past eleven, they formed their fleet, consisting of two schooners and eight sloops, into a line against the two posts, and commenced a very warm fire on our people, with cannon-ball, double-deaded shot, bars of iron, grape shot, and small arms, and manned their boats, — about ten in number, with about 220 men, — having, to appearance, nearly double that number on board, and made various attempts to land in several places, keeping up a constant fire upon our people from half past 11 A.M. till half past 5 P.M.

"Col. Freeman and Maj. Dimock, with about 50 men, defended the intrenchments, and repeatedly challenged them (being within call) to land, which they durst not attempt. Our people, till now, had generally reserved their fire, but being ordered to fire, they soon moved off into the Sound, where they remained quiet till next morning. A party of them, in their boats, attempted to land at Woods Hole, but about 30 of our men posted there gave them a warm fire which soon drove them off, and the boats went to Nonnamesit, an island near Woods Hole, where they landed and killed the few sheep, cows, and hogs the enemy had before left, and threatened to kill the family that lived there, because, they said, the d —— d rebels had been killing them. They had two wounded men with them. Our people being about to go upon the island, they retreated precipitately to their boats, carrying off only one hog and half a cow that calved the day before. They inquired of the island's people our numbers, and said the rebels fought like devils.

"The next day, April 4th, a little after sunrise, they fired again from the vessels to drive us from our intrenchment, and our people returned them a warm fire with their small-arms for a few minutes, upon which they put off for Holmes' Hole. This morning, Monday 5th, one armed vessel proceeded to Nonnamesit Island, and sent off a boat to get the provisions they had killed and left there; but a party of our people got there before them and prevented their landing, and some boats of ours had like to have cut them off from the sloop. Upon the boat's getting to the sloop, they hasted to join the fleet which then made sail, as they said, for Nantucket. . . . "

The weather was favorable to our cause, for although many buildings were struck by the fire of the assailants, the thaw prevented the rebounding of their missiles, and but little damage was done. Alarms, however, continued to be frequent. A large fleet came into the Sound, Sept. 9; but, after inducing much alarm and a general mustering of the militia in the several towns, they drew off in the direction of Chatham.

There is an amusing anecdote associated with this alarm that ought not to be lost; and, as a record of it can now effect no detriment, but is in itself instructive, we permit its insertion. The several companies of the regiment had, on receipt of the express sounding the alarm, been ordered to march forthwith for the relief of Falmouth, and report themselves for orders at or before daybreak the next morning, at the conjunction of the Sandwich and Barnstable roads, about two miles short of the expected scene of action. The several companies were represented on the ground punctually, and almost simultaneously. Almost at the same moment, a note from Maj. Dimmick reached the officer in command, saying that the enemy had left in the direction of Chatham, and that there was no longer any cause for alarm.

The Col., thinking the opportunity should be usefully employed, instead of communicating the intelligence at once, drew the companies around him in a hollow square, and, still holding the letter in his hand . . . proceeded to address the assembled military, first in briefly complimentary terms on their alacrity in answering to orders; and then on the importance of entire devotion to the country's cause. The foe, against which the sons of liberty contend is formidable; his well-disciplined forces are no strangers to the battle-field; so that, if called this day to meet the enemy, nothing less than hard fighting must be expected. Nevertheless, whilst we would regret to see our numbers diminished at such a moment as this, if there be any present whose heart fails him, whose resolution falters, who is not ready, if need be to shed the last drop of his blood in the cause, I am willing to assume the responsibility of absolving him from moving one step further toward the field of action. If any such are here, let them intimate their wishes by stepping forward from the ranks, and their discharge shall be granted. All, with one only solitary exception, and he a lieutenant, were animated by the same spirit of ardor in the cause and eagerness for the conflict. A lieut. ventured to plead a domestic avocation on account of which he would be excused; the alarm came so unexpectedly that, in the haste of departure, he had entirely forgotten to loosen from the stall the "sparked" heifer that was about to calve. He seemed, too, really affected by the urgency of the case, submitted, — his voice becoming almost womanly and his eye glistening with moisture. The request, as might be seen by a glance along the lines, moved the pitiful contempt of many a stout heart; but the commanding officer's promise was redeemed, "with regret that the country must on this occasion be deprived of the services of an officer so patriotic," and two soldiers were detailed to conduct him beyond the lines.

This being done, all present were complimented on their approved patriotism and valor; the despatch from Major Dimmick was read, and the military — with a cordial invitation to remain a few moments in social chat and in partaking of some refreshments, in which, after breaking ranks, they might mutually pledge their country — were dismissed. . . .

It is needless to say, the "sparked heifer" was remembered long years after. In fact, when, 35 years after, the burning of the Capitol at Washington by the British was announced, producing a feeling that quickly brought around a certain post-office an eager and excited crowd, and the Lt., tottering under the weight of years, came also, — his patriotism not a whit improved, vociferating "I'm glad of it!" — he was in return greeted with a reminder of "the sparked heifer."

> — From THE ANNALS OF THE THIRTEEN TOWNS OF BARNSTABLE COUNTY, published for the author in Boston in 1862

This book is a companion piece to Frederick Freeman's great HISTORY OF CAPE COD, *published in 1858. In presenting their selection, the editors of* SAND IN THEIR SHOES *have incorporated in the text several incidents which appeared as footnotes in the volume.*

ॐ

WAR–TIME INFLATION

BY DONALD G. TRAYSER

JANUARY 2 Prices high now it seems? They were high on Cape Cod in January, 1779, too, when Benjamin Percival of South Sandwich recorded in his diary, rye selling for $10 a bushel, corn at $12 to $14, flax seed at $1 per pound, and molasses at $8 per gallon. Currency had so depreciated that the Town of Barnstable voted a bonus of 700 pounds to each man enlisting to fight the Redcoats. Seven hundred pounds sounds like a lot of money, but the next action was: "Voted that the money Paid the men that Shall Inlist into the

aforesaid Service shall be Paid at the Rate of Sixty Papper Dollars
for 1 Hard Dollars." By 1780 the ratio was 72 "Papper Dollars" for
one hard dollar. Dr. Abner Hersey of Barnstable in the spring of
1779 sold a cow, the proceeds of which, that fall, were barely
enough to purchase a goose.

— From ONCE UPON A TIME ON CAPE COD

ONCE UPON A TIME ON CAPE COD, "being notes on awful storms,
distressing shipwrecks, distinguished men and women, and events
of interest from the past of Cape Cod, arranged for each day in the
year," *appeared weekly during 1948 in* The Cape Codder, *published
at Orleans on Cape Cod.*

❧

AN APPEAL FOR JUSTICE

A Statement of some of the principal facts
which took place in the Revolutionary War
in and about the County of Barnstable

BY WILLIAM HALL

FIRSTLY — The last Tuesday of June, year 1775. It was at the stopping of the Court and the rearing of the Liberty Pole — which probably [was] the first Court stopped, and the first Liberty Pole in the
State, if not in the United States.

SECONDLY — All the Boys, anxious in the cause, were organized
into Companies, through the County, (as I believe,) but in Barnstable they were well tutored, disciplined and officered, being drilled
two or three times a week. In the latter part of the ensuing summer,
on a Sabbath day an armed Schooner came into the Harbor, about
the middle of the day, in the time of Divine Service; in the afternoon
it was discovered that a number of people were driving cattle together
in the common fields about a mile from the meeting House. We left
the House, and ran for the shore, got some guns at different houses
which proved to be loaded. When the Enemy discover'd us they
ran for their boats, leaving a number of the best cattle haltered, from

about 6 to 10. There proved to be three boats from the schooner, they were fired on, they soon left the Harbor. Soon after, five fishing boats, out from Bass River, in Yarmouth, discovered a large sloop, came near them to a place called Butler's Hole. They hailed from the Sloop for a Pilot, all went on board, she proved to be loaded with Flour from the Southward, for Gen. Gage's Army at Boston. They rose on her, run her to the mouth of Bass River, unloaded the Flour, let the Captain go off with the vessel (he being the owner of her,) carted the whole Flour across the Cape, to a place called Bass Hole — from thence it was rowed in boats to Scituate, and Cohasset and carted to Cambridge to General Washington's Army, without allowing any diminution whatever of any of it, 350 barrels or thereabouts.

It being thought proper, that some principal character of Yarmouth should proceed on to see Gen. Washington on the business, and to attend to its safe delivery, Col. Hallett proceeded on, and waited on Gen. Washington at Cambridge, informed him of all the transaction, and what time he supposed the flour would be there, arrangements were immediately made for its safe conveyance through Roxbury. The Commissary was sent for, who informed the General, that there was not more than four days supply of bread stuff for the army. That should a disappointment take place, in not receiving a quantity expected from Albany, they would then be under the necessity of drawing the supplies from the neighboring towns, which would be very troublesome and uncertain, and that would be the only alternative, or the army would discharge itself. Gen. Washington expressed the strongest sensations of gladness at this providential occurrence, at such a critical juncture, at the patriotism of all who were engaged in its obtainment, and offered to give Col. Hallett a certificate thereof, which he declined in receiving. The General informed Col. Hallett that the officers and men, of whom he was acquainted, from his quarter, were amongst the best men of the army.

In the winter of 1776, the ship Summer a British 74 was cast ashore on the back side of Cape Cod, said to have on board 1150 men, 350 of which were said to have been lost, the rest were marched to Boston, which occasioned great confusion and distress through the whole country in which they passed. The next spring and summer, the county had to organize a shore watch at night, to keep off the small privateers from landing and robbing in different directions; which exertion was continued through the War, and every possible means used to ward off and baffle the enemy.

In the spring 1776, when the British left Boston for Halifax and thence to New York, we were continuously assailed one side or the other of the Cape, causing the most arduous watchfulness and laborious exertions, being on duty obliged to continue several days together.

In the spring of 1778 our family removed to Yarmouth on our Farm. About this time, it was discovered that four of the richest farmers in the county, living on Scorton neck, between Sandwich and Barnstable, had sold to the British, and taken away a vessel load of live stock. — Col. Hallett, the sheriff of the county, gave me an order to go off in a boat fishing, as often as I could get a crew, and to row off back of Scorton neck to see if I could discover any suspicious vessel after another load of live stock; I did so as often as I could, keeping a vigilant look out. — He had also ascertained, that a David Bangs, of Harwick, had entered on board a British man of War, as a Pilot, cruising from Halifax to New York, which very much distressed our commerce. The Ship used to run in close to Harwick flats, and at one time, privately got Bangs' wife and Eldest son off on board the ship. She stayed about six weeks, the son remained on board and enter'd himself. Col. Hallett consulted his deputies to devise some way, if possible, to take him. They concluded that they would be more mistrusted, than myself, gave me private instructions in the pursuit. I followed them, and found, that she, (the wife,) was landed down the Cape, with some valuable presents from the Capt. of the ship, and doubtless money from her husband. I also learned that the captain would not allow him off the ship's deck; I was at least a month at times on the business and times, for years afterward to catch him, considering that the heinousness of his doings required urgent apprehension.

In the spring of 1779 (as near as I can recollect,) it was found by Capt. Chapman and others, as from where I lived, it being two mi. one way, and six mi. the other, that there was no water on the road, to water our horses when on those excursions and alarms, that I was urged to get a large log, and make a trough to have a supply of water from a new well I had just dug 25 feet deep. I immediately complied with the request, went to my wood lot, with the expectation of getting help to load the log, but was disappointed, attempted to load it myself in which, after a great exertion, I succeeded, but with difficulty, that I strained myself and was very much injured by the effort, and carry the effects of it ever with me to this day. I was disabled from doing military duty, for two summers from my exertions in the public cause; but part of the time rode about to do what the Colonel required of me.

About this time the Vineyard Sound was thronged with privateers, among the rest, was an English eight gun Brig. Capt. Dimmick, of Falmouth, had a vessel, called Shaving Mill, rowed with 19 oars, mounting 2 Swivels on Pivot. This eight gun Brig, had succeeded in the obtaining of two loads of live stock, one from the Vineyard, under the pretense of paying for them, but when on board, they went off without paying one cent. The other from Woods Hole and Norshon, they being tory there, suppose they paid them. The Brig came the 3d trip, when Capt. Dimmick discover'd her, came to anchor, about the middle of the day, in the Sound, called his company together, selected 10 of his bravest men (sent others to give a general alarm,) provided him a crew for a fishing, went out and anchored 1½ miles from the Brig, she having all her airings spread. When light, the deck of the Brig was filled with men; the boat was hailed for fish, and showed only six men, he answered them that he had but a few, and that when he had caught enough for them, he would bring them on board; about 11 o'clock, it being calm and hot, he observed only a few on deck, as a centry, he went along side, 20 all leaped on deck, disarmed the centinel, barred the hatch ways, stopped the gang ways, and compelled them all to surrender; kept his own men on deck, and drew from out of the Brig's hole one by one, until he manned his barge at the oars, and placed his best men to stear, with a hawser, towed the Brig into Falmouth, she proved to be a privateer of 4-6 pounders, and 4-8 pounders, with eighty two men, all told. . . .

After many unsuccessful attempts, which I made to find a suspicious vessel, going to Scorton, to get live stock, the Colonel and his associates, resolved on a plan, which proved effectual. He went to Boston, found a man who proceeded to Scorton, and there entered into a written contract with a Cornelius and John Wing, quakers — and John and Simon Jones, for as many beef cattle, fat sheep, hogs, &c., with all the necessaries for them to live on, to carry to Hallifax: they so planned the business, that, when he was leaving for Boston with the people escorting him to Sandwich, the Col. and his associates fell in with them, took the man prisoner, found all the contracts with him, they took the four contractors down to Barnstable jail, kept them till next day, and after a legal trial of examination found the four guilty: paid the man honorably for his services in the project, and the four were kept in prison, until released by the proper authority, and paying what was demanded. Such was the patriotic spirit persued in Barnstable county in favor of our then precious cause!

It is thought proper to relate a particular circumstance which happened in Barnstable county, amidst the troubles and losses then sustained by the inhabitants. In the town of Yarmouth, where our family lived, the small pox broke out amongst a tribe of native Indians, at the south part of the town, it raged to that degree, that it was very difficult to obtain persons to take care of them. In the abject state, which those people were in. The selectmen of the town had to procure a number of nurses for their assistance, which occasioned a very heavy town tax upon its inhabitants. The number which died with the distemper, was over eighty, nearly extinguishing the whole tribe. The whole expense of their assistance, fell on the inhabitants of Yarmouth.

When General Washington used to send his orders for more men, the town of Yarmouth, instead of drafting them, came to the conclusion, to offer those who would enlist, eight dollars per month, and to pay their families according to the stipulated act, and for the soldiers to draw their wages, when they could get it, for their own comfort. So we paid them and their families, by a town tax, which was punctually done, to keep them and their families comfortable. From which measure, in addition to my own and brother's labor, exertions and services, in our devotion to the cause, with the expenses attending, a very considerable tax was borne by the family property, to defray expense. For all of which, not one single cent, directly or indirectly has ever been received. Though many have since been rewarded for similar services. I have never found any way of obtaining any compensation, from that time to this. Nor should I ever perhaps have endeavored to seek for it, had not the many losses and misfortunes, which I have met with, unavoidably in my latter life, become a strong inducement for me to make my appeal to the justice and honorable consideration of government authority, for a due consideration of what I have with many others both proper and equitable claims.

— From a statement sworn to before a justice of the peace by William Hall, June 16, 1831.

A Cape Cod Skipper

A CAPE COD SKIPPER

BY ELIJAH COBB

Hard Times

My FATHER persued a seafaring life for subsistance; was Master of a Brig, & died on his passage from Cadiz to Quebec, in the 33*d* year of his age — leaving my Mother with 6 infant children, the oldest but 10 years of age, and the youngest, born after Father left home, the last time, — For the support of this helplefs flock; was a small cape cod farm, a small house & barn, and one cow — I have heard my Mother say, that she never received 100$ for my Fathers effects —

Under such circonstances; it was not posible to keep the family together — to support and educate them, with the means in her power, was out of the question — some of us, must leave the perternal dwelling & seek subsistance among strangers — my Bro*r*., being the Elder, was tried first, but wou'd not stay, & came home crying — I was then, in my 6*th* year, & altho' too young to earn my living, a place was offered me, & I left my dear Mother for that subsistance among strangers which she could not procure for me.

I continued from my Mother, except at times visiting her, untill my 13*th* year, when by an imprudent attempt, to lift beyond my strength, I broke a vefsell in my stomack, which entirely disabled me; and I was sent home to my Mother, incapable of labour of any kind.

I remained with her; under the care of a skilfull Doctor, about a year, when he advised me, to be sent to sea, as the best method to regain my health.

Accordingly, in the fall of 1783, I was fitted out for Boston, to look for a voyage — My whole wardrobe, was packed in a gin case, for a trunk; a tow bedsack, filled with rye straw, & a pair of, home-made, blankets, for sleeping appuratis, with two bushels of corn, to pay my pafsage to Boston — and acquipted thus, I left the family circle, with buoyant sperits and in full confidence that I should work myself through life, with honour & credit — I embarked, at Skaket, in a small Schooner of only 25 tons, called the *Creture;* & after going into Provinctown, & laying there during a gale of wind, we reached Boston, in about three days.

At the time, I am speaking of, there were more men, than could readily find employ, & frequently, the best of seamen, were destitute of voyages — several of our neighbouring young men, had been to Boston, that fall, previous to my leaving home, & had returned without giting employ, they told my Mother, that I would only spend the two bushels of corn, & return to her without giting a voyage — but their predictions were set at naught; for the first time I went down the long wharf, & stood gazeing at a new vefsell, wondering, & admiring her monstrous size, her great cables & anchors &c — a gentleman stept from her deck and thus accosted me! My lad, do you want a voyage —. Yes Sir — will you go with me in this vefsell — where are you bound Sir — to Siranam — I am told, Sir, that all flesh die, that go there — well my boy, to prove, that you have not been told the truth, I have been there 13 voyages, & you see I'm alive yet — well Sir, I should like to go, what wages will you allow me — do you know how to cook — not much Sir, but I can soon learn — well my boy, if you think so, I presume you will, I like your candour & will take you, & give you the customary wages of a boy; half of Seamens wages $3.50 pr month, but you must go immediately on board, & git dinner for the men at work — & thus I commenced my duty as cook & cabin Boy.

When the men broke off work, at night, they all went away; and the Capt. then asked me, where my bed and cloaths were — I told him on board the creture, in town dock — well, you must go and git them, & I'll keep ship untill you return, you must sleep on board to night — who else will sleep on board — nobody, there is no one belongs to the vefsell, except you & myself — not liking the idea of sleeping on board alone, I took the liberty of asking him, where his mate was — he said, he had not got one yet — I told him, I *gessed,* I knew a good man, that would like to go — who is he — I

said, My Uncle, who came up, in the creture to look for a voyage —
has he ever been mate — Yes Sir, & prise mastre too, in the war —
well, you go after your things, & if you see your Uncle, ask him to
come down & see me, in the morning when I got on board the
creture, my Uncle was there, and by way of a reprimand, asked,
where I had been all day — why Uncle, said I, I have shipped myself,
& I believe I have got a voyage for you also.

To make a short story, my Uncle went down in the morning, &
shipped & went the voyage. — I then wrote to my Mother, that I
had got a voyage for myself & Uncle, & if those young men would
come to Boston before I sailed, I would ship them off, rather than
have them stay at home Idle, & upon expense all winter.

The vefsell was soon loaded, & we went to sea — my inexperienc,
& being very sea-sick, for a while, rendered my situation very unpleasant, but I soon surmounted those deficulties; & began to injoy
my new mode of life; after the opperation of David Jones's medecine
(sea-sicknefs) I felt my health improved, & by the time we arrived
in Surinam, I felt quite well, and I found I was able to give pritty
good satisfaction in my line of duty.

My perticular attention to the officers, procured me some presents,
by wh I was enabled to purchase a Barrel of molafses, & some fruit,
for an adventure back to Boston.

Nothing meterial took place, during the remainder of the voyage,
worth noting; we returned to Boston in the spring of 1784, discharged our cargo, mollases, was paid our wages & seperated, each
to home. My wages amounted to 21$, & by the sale of my bbl of
Molases, & some my fruit, I was enabled to git myself a new suit of
sailors cloaths, from the Slopshop, & carried home, & put into my
Mothers hands, 20 silver Dollars — probably, the largest sum of
money she had possessd since she had been a widow — & that, from
her poor little sick Boy — her tears flowed freely, upon the occasion, but they were tears of gratitude to our heavenly Father, for his
mercies to her child, in permitting his return home, in the injoy-
ment of so much better health, than he left it — my own feelings,
upon the occasion, can be better imagined than discribed. . . .

Ten Years Later

After making several voyages, to Virginia, & one to the West
Idies; in April 1793, I went to the cape, & got married; I was

then my 25*th*. year. — I continued in the employ of the Mess*rs*. Reynolds's; principally in the virginia trade, about two years longer, when they concluded to send me, on a voyage to Europe — their object was, to cadiz; but at that time, the algerines were at war with America; & it was reported, that their cruisers were outside of the streights of Gibaraltar — in consequence, it was recommended that I should clear my vessell for Curruna, a northern port in spain, and there essertain, whether it would be safe, to proceed to Cadiz — I was however, spared the trouble of enquirry, by falling in, with a French frigate, who captur*ed*, & sent me to France xxxx & here commences my first trouble & anxiety, as a ship Master — having under my charge, a valuable vefsell & cargo, inexperienced in business — carried into a foreign port, unacquainted with the language, no American consel, or merchant to advise with — and my reputation, as a ship master, depending upon the measures I persued &c &c.

That time, that I arrived in France, was during the french Revolution, and in the *bloody* reign of Robertspeire — all was arnachy & confusion — the galliotine, in continual operation, & their streets and publick squars, drenched with human blood — I minuted down, 1000 persons, that I saw beheaded, by that *infernal* machine; and probably saw, as many more, that I did not note down, men, women, preists & laymen, of all ages — and finally, before I left the country; I saw Robertspeirs head taken off, by the same Machine — But, to return to my induvidual, and embarised affairs — all my papers, relative to my ship & voyage, had been taken from me, on board the Frigate, at sea; I concluded they were put in possession of the prise Master, who brought me in, but he, was not to be found; neither could I find any clue to my papers, and without them, I could not prove, any demand for redrefs upon the government, for their violation of our neutrality — it was true, my vefsel was there; but her cargo, Flour & Rice, was taken out, & was daily made into bread, soups, &c &c, for the half starved, populace — and without papers, I could not, even substanciate my claim to an empty ship — they meerly condecended, to send me to a Hotell, to board; & those of my ships crew, that were sent in with me, were also, provided for.

In this very unpleasant perdicerment I remained about six weeks — I had, however, in that time, written to the american charge des affairs at Paris, & received an answer, but it contained nothing definite, he regreted my situation, & that of my countrymen generally, in

France, & that it was owing to the disorganized state of affairs in the country; and that, I must exercise patiance, & the government wd. do what was right in time.

In about six weeks, as before observed, I was called upon, at my lodgings, by an officer, of the tribunal of commerce, bringing, a copy of the judgment, of said tribunal, upon my vefsel and cargo, & a linguister to explain it to me.

Thus, had they tried me, & passed sentance without my hearing, or even knowing that I was on trial — but, in that way, all businefs was managed in France at that time.

The decision of the tribunal, was, however, so favourable, that it gave a spring to my feelings, & a sensation that gave new life.

They declared, my vefsell & cargo, to be newtrial property; & that, as the cargo was at *my* disposition, I should be paid for it, by the government, at the prices that might be fixed upon, by myself & the agent of the government, and an adequate endemnification, for my capture, detention, expenditures, &c &c

I was then waited upon, to the agent of marine, to sell my cargo; when it is presumed, there was not a pound, of the flour, or rice in existance — and after battleing, in words, three days in succefsion, we fixed the prices, as follows, viz — Flour $16.50, & Rice $5.50 — this, was a good beginning, being over 200 pr cent on the invoice.

but a long altercation now insue'd, relative to the payment — money, was out of the question, for if they had it, to pay, there was a law against bringing it away from the country — goods, also, were out of the question, as well as bills on England or America — finally, I agreed to take, government Bills of exchange, on Hamburg, payable 60 days after date, and was promised, by the Agent; that I should have my bills, in 12 or 14 days — I waited patiently a month, but no bills came; & finding that no confidence could be placed in their promises, & feeling doubtful, as to obtaing any thing for my Cargo; I thought it advisable to send my vefsell home, under charge of the mate — consequently, I ballased her, & sent her away; writing to my owners, that I was determd to preserve, untill I obtained satisfaction.

My mind being releived, from seeing my vefsell laying Idle, & at great expense; I came to the determination of going to head quarters, Paris — but many deficulties were to be surmounted, in order to attain this object — 1st. the road was dangerous to travail; the adherents of royalty, were reduced to mere scurmaging parties, that committed their depradations under cover of the night, in solitary places, upon travellers, & the peaceble inhabitants — and as all horses were taken into requisition by the government, except those that convey*d*. the national dispatches; there was no other mode of travelling; and it was conterary to law, for them to take a pafsengers —but my mind was fixed upon going, as the only chance of ever accomplishing my businefs with the French government. I therefore called upon the Minister of Marine, & got an official copy, of my demands on the government, and had them ecorded (a precautionary measure) as I had lea(r)ned, that loseing a mans papers, was one of their methods of procrastination, to keep far off a settlement.

After this, I procured an interpreter, & waited upon Jean Con. S*t*. Andre, a man, holding high offices under the Government, & reported to be, favourably disposed to Americans — to him I made known my situation — the treatment I had received, the praplexity I was in — & the necessity of going to Paris — & praying him, not only to grant me a pasport, but to grant a special permitt, to one of the Coureirs, to carry me there — after a long demur, with himself, & repeatedly feeling of his neck, to see how it would bear the knife; he returned a favourable reply — viz. that I must call upon him the next day, when he would make the necessary arrangements &c.

Accordingly, in two days, I was underway for Paris, in one of the national coureirs with government dispatches, the Master of which, did not speak one word of English, & myself, but a few words of French, of course we were not *very* sociable — we were furnished, each with a pair of pistols, with a blunderbus, loaded, in front, our carriage, was musquet shot proof, except in front; drove, by a postilion outside with from 5, to 9 horses, according to the road, which at best, was very indifferent.

And thus we drove on, Jehu like, without stoping, except to exchange horses, & mail; taking occasionally, as we run, a mouthfull of bread, and washing it down, with some low prised, red Burgendy wine — as to sleep, I did not git one wink during the journey of 684 miles. But *la maitre de les despach,* would sleep, during the day, pitching about the carriage, for the roads were very rough, to my very great anoyance — but, during the night, his anxiety kept *him* awake, through fear, altho' we had a guard, of, from 12 to 24, mouted horsemen each night, from sunset, to sunrise, to proceed,

& follow — and as a demonstration, that the precaution was necessary, on the 2d morning, after leaving Brewst, just before our guards
left us, we witnefsed a scene, that filled us with horrow. — the remains, of a Coreir, laying in the road, the Master, the Postilion, &
5 horses laying dead, and mangled by it, & the mail mutalated and
scatered in all directions. We were informed, afterwards, that the
Coureir, was without an guard, that the evening previous; there was
an alarm in the visinity, that had called out, all their fources to
suprefs, consequently, at the last stage, there was none to supply;
& it was death by law, for national despatches to stop, therefore, the
Master proceeded, without a guard, and met the fate, as described.

The next night, at about sun-setting we came to a stage, where
we expected to receive our guard, & there was none for us, however,
the next stage, was only five miles, & not considered very dangerous;
we therefore proceeded on, altho" not without great anxiety; &
preparation of our fire arms, in case of an attact.

In the very neat village of Alancón, in Normondy, I had the first,
& only, word of English, sporken to me, during the journey, we
stopped to exchange horses & mail, when the *Maître,* as usual, was
called to an account for having a passenger, & a foreigner too, in the
Coureir; and while he was making his justification, shewing pas-
ports, &c; a man in a tattered uniform, came up to the door of the
Carriage, & reaching out his hand, said in quite good english; for
the love of God, my dear Sir, do permitt me to shake hands, with one,
who comes from that country where, the *great,* and beloved Washington resides — he only had time to say, 'that he went to America
with, La Fayettee, and had the honour of having served under the
best man God ever made, even the great Washington.

Nothing interesting took place untill we reached Paris. It was
at 4 o'clock, of a beautifull June morning, that the Carriage stopped
before the gate of Hotel de Boston, & the bell rung, having been
just 74 hours from the gates of Brest — during which time, I had
not lost myself in sleep, taken nothing warm upon my stomack,
nor used water, upon either hands or face — thus covered with dust,
& exhausted with fateague; I was received by the Porter, conveyed
to a chamber, providd. with washing apparatus, where I soon freed
myself from dust, applied clean linnen, and enscons'd myself in an
excellent Bed, saying to myself, *soul take thine ease in sleep* — but,
it appeared, that sleep had departed from me, I laid untill the clock
struck 10, without being able to obtain a doze, & then rose, & at-

tended, thro" the day, to finding out a train of my businefs, through the American Consul &c, retired to Bed again at 9 o Clock, heard the Clock strike 12, and knew nothing after, untill 11 o Clk the next day; when awoke, feeling like myself again; although I slept very sound the next night, for 9 hours without awaking.

After essertaining where to apply, my first object of attention was, to search for my Accounts, sent on from Brest — the result was, they denied, at all the offices, ever having received them, or heard of such a Brig, as the Jane, nor of her commander, Capt. Cobb — well, "as I before observed, I prepared for this event, before I left Brewst; by procuring a copy of my Accounts &c &c, accordingly I laid an official set before them, and thus introducing the *Jane,* & her commander — I was told, to call the next day, & they would let me know, when my Bills wou'd be ready. I therefore, was obliged to exercise patiance & wait; but when I called the next day, my papers were not to be found in the office — no one had put them away, no one could tell any thing about them — and finally, after a long French jabber, it was concluded, that they must have been left upon the counter, brushed off, & burned, among the lose papers.

This was too much, for my already perplexed, agitated, mind. I knew of no way, but to write back to Brest, for another set — & they, probably, would. meet the same fate, as the two preseeding ones had. I was now fully conveinced, that the whole was designed, for the purpose of procrastination & putting off pay day as long as possible — but it was a severe trial for me, in my inexperienced state. I consulted with our consul; & with our Minister at the court of France, but the only satisfaction was; git another set of papers, & we will guard against another lofs —

While seting, with writing meterials before me in my chamber, in the act of writing for another set of papers — a French gentleman, who occopied the next room, & who spoke good English, passed my door; I asked him in, & related to him my greivances — after he had thought for a few moments; he advised me, to endevour to obtain an interview with Roberspeire, & make known to him my greivances; assuring me that he was partial to Americans, & had no doubt, but he would give me such advice as would be servicable to me — But, I asked, will he, the leader of this nation, condescend to listen to a private induvidual, & interpose, in meely, a commercial transaction — yes, if the businefs is managed right, I am confident he will. But how shall I obtain an interview — simply by writing him a billet yourself, in the republican stile, an American cetizen, to citizen Roberspeire, & send it by a servant of the Hotel, requesting an interview upon businefs.

After duly considering upon the subject, I wrote the following, & sent it by servant.

An American citizen, captured by a French Frigate on the high seas, requests, a personal interview: & to lay his greivances before citizens Roberspeire.

Very respectfully
E. Cobb.

In about an hour, I received the following note, in his own hand writing.

I will grant Citizen Cobb an interview to morrow at 10 A.M.

Roberspeire.

This, gave a spring to my feelings, and banished that deprefsion which had held me in chains, for some days previous. I was puntual to the time — sent my name up, & was admitted into the presence of the great man. He pointed me to a seat without speaking; there was one man, only, in the Hall, an enterpreter, who told me that, Citizen Roberspeire whished me, to commince my relation, at the time of my capture, and to tell the whole, up to this time — I accordingly proceeded; and, thro" the interpreter, related my Capture & treatment, up to that time — upon my closing the detail; with a waive of Roberspeires hand, the interpreter left the Hall, and he, R—e, began conversing with me, in very good English, questioning me, upon some perticcular points, of the former conversation; but more perticurly, about the lofs of my papers, since I arrived in Paris — finally, he told me to call at an office, in Rue S*t*. Honorie, called the office of the *2d* department, & *demand* my papers, I told him, that I had been there repeatedly, & that I was forbid to enter the office again. upon my telling him that, he exclaimed. *Sacra coquin* — go, said he, to that office, & tell cetizen F. T., that you come from R——e, and if he does not produce your papers, & finish your business *immediately,* he will hear from me again, in a way not so pleasing to him. Observing at the same time, that he regreted that *his name* should be made use of, in a mercantile transaction, but that my case, absolutely demanded it.

I tendered my gratefull thanks for his services, & left him; after receiving his injunctions, to call & let him know how I succeeded — I went direct to the aforesd. office; and, by the previledge of making use of Roberspeirs name, I was kindly rec*d*. an opology made, for former abuses, and my businefs compleated the next day — but as my exchanges were drawn, payable sixty days after date, & the tribunal had decred, demurage &c, untill I received my Bills, I refused to receive them in Paris, as my pay wou'd then stop, but insisted on their being sent to the agent in Brest agreable to my contract — my object was, not to receive them untill 12 or 15 days before they were due, consequently I remained in Paris about 3 weeks after my bills were sent to Brest. and during that time, the great man, who had so assentially befriended me, was beheaded by the Galliotine.

· · · · ·

The fortunate close of this tedious voyage, and my return; being the first instance of the kind, under the then state of things in France, produced, no small, excitement among the merchants of Boston, who had property in France; and applications was continually made to me, for all the whys & wherefores, relative to the fortunate result of my businfs; and the consequence was, it added greatly to my fame, as a ship master.

Another voyage was immediately planned, by my owners, for France, & I was only allowed a very few days, to visit my family, — although, our first child (now Aunt Sampson) was but 24 hours old when I left home — when I return'd, could say *my par*. But short, endeed, was the time allotted me, for injoying the objects of my affection, I must leave them; and persue the road marked out, for obtaining that subsistance for myself & family, which nature required, and reason dictated.

After staying at home 4 days only, I returned to Boston, fitted out my vefsel, & sailed for Alexandria, & there purchased a cargo of Flour & sail'd for France. . . .

On my return home, I found that my pertner, in lifes voyage, had run me in debt, for a cape Cod farm; and as the place was distitute of a suitable building, for the accommodation of our little family, it was thought advisable to proceed to erect one, the following season; I consequently, felt myself under the necessity of declining businefs, in the sea-faring line, and attend to that of a more domestic nature, for a while — I remained at home, from August 1798 — untill Sep*t*. 1799 — and, as the events of this year, are something remarkable, I will name a few of them.

This year 1799, the beloved Washington, the Father of our

Country died, — this year our first son was born — this year I took possession of the farm, built my house, and the family moved into it on new years day 1800.

In Octo*r*. 1799 I took charge of the Brig Mary, went to Savannah, in Georgia, from that to Lisbon, from thence to London, to Rotterdam, Copenhagen, S*t*. Petersburg, and back to Boston — and performed the voyage, in 8 months & 4 days —

.   .   .   .   .

After discharging my cargo, in Boston, I visited my dear family, at the cape; where I found an aditional pledge of affection, in a little black-eye'd daughter, which we call'd Mary P, then 69 days old — it being in the night, & no light in the house, I hawl'd her out of Bed, and held her up to the window to look at her by moonlight. . . .

Elijah Cobb was born in Brewster in 1768 and died there in 1848, a wealthy, public-spirited, useful citizen whose memory is still green upon the Cape. In his autobiography written, he tells us, for "the gratification and amusement" of his grandchildren, he tells a thrilling story, depicts his times with an artful eye for detail, and paints the self-portrait of an extraordinary man: extraordinary because of the heights to which he raised his qualities, typical in them of a long line of shipmasters who were to follow him. He was ambitious, brave, stubborn, energetic, resourceful; an earnest Christian, a warm friend, a devoted son, brother, husband, father; a smuggler, a rum-runner, an almost light-hearted adventurer at times, not above taking a dubious advantage, bribing his way out of trouble, cozening his enemies. We find him flying the first American flag in Lubec ever floated in that city and taking a patriotic pride in it, and we find him in Norfolk, Virginia, in 1807, performing prodigies of hasty preparation in order to get his vessel to sea before Mr. Madison's Embargo came down upon him. "Cheating the embargo," he calls it, and none of his many triumphs seem to have gratified him more.

He is said to have been a very handsome man.

His autobiography appeared first in the YARMOUTH REGISTER *in 1878. In 1925, under the title* ELIJAH COBB, A CAPE COD SKIPPER, *with a foreword and notes by Ralph D. Paine, it was published by the Yale University Press.*

"The Present Ruinous
and Unhappy War"

1811–1814
"THE PRESENT RUINOUS AND UNHAPPY WAR"

V OTED UNANIMOUSLY, that as this town have ever expressed their decided disapprobation of the present ruinous and unhappy war, and have hitherto refrained from engaging in the same; we are still determined not to engage in, encourage or support it any further than we are compelled to do, by the laws of the country of which we are citizens.

— From the records of a Yarmouth town meeting in 1814

Similar resolutions were passed in other town meetings on Cape Cod.

❦

WAR OF THE EMBARGO

BY SHEBNAH RICH

THE EMBARGO, such a calamity, and so much referred to by the old people of our younger days, was alleged as a necessary measure to protect our tonnage from British seizure. By the North, it was regarded as a Southern measure and was especially unpopular. It was another time of trial in New England, particularly in the coast towns. Upon the Cape it fell with most disastrous effect, causing much embarrassment and distress. The ocean fisheries were abandoned, the dismantled vessels rotted at the grassy wharves. Gloomy, indeed, was the prospect. The men cultivated their little farms,

112

taxing the light soil to the utmost, and fished in boats from the shore when possible. The women toiled hard at the wheel and loom; every house was a little factory. By joint labors and strict economy, the wolf was kept from the door. Our vessels were worse than captured when the Embargo went into effect. Cartloads of petitions bearing the names of all the active people of the North, poured in upon President Jefferson, but he stubbornly persisted in his destructive policy.

After two years of Embargo came the Non-intercourse Act, interdicting all trade with Great Britain and France. . . . The next turn of Great Britain was her "assumed Right of Search" and impressment of American seamen, whereby her ships were manned with thousands of our brave seamen who were forced on board by press gangs at the point of the sword.

These heaped-up and overbearing demands led to a formal declaration of war, June 18, 1811. . . . The Declaration of War opened lively privateering under Letters of Marque. Under the severity of the preceding years, our men had become restive and ready for any changes and hot for retaliation. The fishermen crowded the privateers and volunteered in the naval service. Our young navy achieved high honors, and acquired wide renown in this war that gave our history such names as Decatur, and Hull, and Perry, and Paul Jones. For a generation, the songs commemorating these naval victories were sung in the forecastle of every American ship on the ocean. If open to criticism, they stirred the old patriotic fire and were regarded as a tribute of honor to the brave sailor.

We quote a verse from one or two of the most popular:—

> You thought our frigates were but few,
>   And Yankees could not fight,
> Until bold Hull the *Guerriere* took,
>   And banished her from sight.

> Then next your *Macedonian*,
>   No finer ship could swim,
> Decatur took her gilt-work off,
>   And then he took her in.

·　　·　　·　　.　　·

Ye Parliaments of England, ye Lords and Commons too,
Consider well what you are about and what you mean
    to do;
You are now at war with Yankee boys, and soon you'll
    rue the day,
You roused the sons of Liberty in North America.

The Yankee privateers fully maintained the reputation acquired during the Revolutionary War, that nearly stripped English ships from the ocean and vexed English commerce from sea to sea. Considerable money was made privateering. The most noticeable instances in our community was that of Captain Rueben Rich, who with two others fitted out a vessel under Letters of Marque. The first day out they took an English East Indiaman, brought her to Boston, and Captain Rich sold out his interest for $17,000 and had his money in his pocket all within twenty-four hours.

The English men-of-war were as thick around the Cape as flies in summer, making Provincetown headquarters. The *Majestic* was the Admiral's ship. She used to lie at anchor between Truro and Provincetown, and used the old mill that then stood on Mill Hill, as a target during artillery practice. While this was going on, the people preferred the eastern side of the hill. . . .

The officers often landed, visited the houses, were always very civil, and became well acquainted with a good many families. They purchased butter, milk, eggs, chickens, and other supplies, and secured small repairs as needed, paying for them quite liberally in British gold. The officers made no efforts to conceal their well-filled purses of dazzling guineas which in those hard times quite dazzled the eyes of the poor people.

But the jingling of the guinea helps the hurt that honor feels.

If reports are true, the officers were sometimes equally dazzled by eyes bright as their guineas, and coy glances, withal. Provincetown received no small benefit from the English vessels, and some of the fortunes acquired, had their beginning from this source. Some timid people kept their cattle in the woods, for fear they would be carried off by the bargemen; but as dastardly as some of the Britishers' doings were reported on the water, I have heard of nothing dishonorable among the people.

The landing of the barges was watched with much interest; an old lady told me they (the girls) thought it good fun to see them land. Another lady said, that returning from school with her young companions, and meeting a party of Britishers on the road, they turned a little up the hill. The jaunty lieutenant said pleasantly, touching his gold braided cap. "Don't turn out of the road, young ladies, we won't harm you."

As it was impossible to carry fish to Boston market, it became a custom with the fishermen to load their boats, and, keeping well under the shore, and under cover of night or fog, work their way to Sandwich, where boat and cargo were carted over to Buzzard's Bay, and so sail on to New York, and steal back the same way.

The boats were sometimes overhauled by the barges and searched. I have heard of only one or two cases where they were stripped of their stores; but what were the provocations, if any, in these exceptional cases, I cannot tell. It is quite possible that the fishermen smarting under the sense of injustice, and with the old hatred toward the English, inherited from their fathers, often aggravated them, and it is quite probable that the young officers in charge of the barges often transcended the orders of their superiors. It is said that the boys after one or two trips to New York were ready to embark on a privateer as their only way of revenge.

Commander Ragget, of H.B.M. *Spencer,* made a demand upon Brewster for £250, which was paid. A demand was also made upon Orleans, which was refused, and the valiant captain paid in his own coin.[1] In a few instances they seized boats and held their crews prisoner till the demand was paid.

One day the great barge of the *Majestic* was out on a foraging expedition to Wellfleet. Being in need of a pilot, and finding two boys in a whaleboat catching mackerel off Truro, the lieutenant demanded that the oldest, a lad of fifteen, should go as their pilot; the boy said he was not a pilot, and could not leave his brother, a little fellow of nine years, alone in the boat. At the lieutenant's

[1] During an attempt to collect the ransom, a British barge entered Orleans harbor and took possession of a schooner and three sloops. The captors credulously placed a captured Cape Cod skipper on board the chief prize, the schooner, to pilot her to Boston. He promptly ran her aground and took her crew prisoner. Meantime landing parties were being repelled by Orleans militiamen in the Battle of Rock Harbor, for which the United States Government sixty years later indemnified the town.

glittering sword held over his head, and threat to cut his head off, he concluded to go, and let his brother get home as best he could. The boy rigged a Spanish windlass and weighed his anchor and managed to get ashore. The barge set the pilot boy ashore at Wellfleet, and he walked home without jacket, shoes or hat. . . .

In all the vicissitudes, losses and discomforts growing out of all these years of Embargo and war, Truro shared fully, and furnished more than an average number of men for all emergencies. The welcome news of peace was at last proclaimed. How it reached the Cape is related by a Provincetown man to his neighbor in the following story: "They say peace has got down as far as Truro, but it's hard telling, Billy D — 's boys lie so like fury."

— From TRURO — CAPE COD OR LAND MARKS AND SEA MARKS

Shebnah Rich was born in Truro in 1824 and published his history of the town in Boston in 1883. He was a man of erudition, and wide study forms the basis of his work but, whenever possible, he depended upon eyewitness accounts of past events. Cape Cod people generally enjoy long lives — there's a saying that if you're tough enough to grow up on Cape Cod, you're tough enough to live forever, — and Rich talked in his time not only to veterans of the War of 1812 but to men and women who remembered the Revolution; and from these elders he heard lively secondhand reports of even earlier days. His superbly written history has a gossipy quality rare in such chronicles. It is a Cape Cod classic.

☙

1814
CAPE COD BLOCKADED

BY HENRY EDWARD NAPIER[1]

ON SUNDAY, 24 April, again took our departure from Halifax, with the prayers and good wishes of all the *female* part at least of the

[1] Lieutenant in *H.M.S. Nymphe.*

inhabitants. The ladies are very pretty, excessively good humoured, not well educated, and like their mothers constantly on the watch for husbands. The navy much more than the army are their favourites, probably from being much more easily taken. On the whole the Haligonians (as they call themselves) have improved considerably on a nearer acquaintance, but then when we see nothing else, we could fancy an ourang-outang a pleasant companion. I'm afraid many matches and acquaintances are formed in a colony that afterwards lose all their attractions and would willingly be dissolved. Saw the *Rifleman* and sent her in. She had not taken the privateer.

The weather very cold on the twenty-fifth. . . . At half past four saw a schooner to the southeast. Bore up immediately and made all sail in chase going ten knots with moon sails set; the wind having abated considerably at sunset found we had gained considerably on the chase, whose waterline we could now see. She appeared to be a private schooner. Saw a brig to the westward in full chase of the same schooner; exchanged signals and found her to be the *Manly*. Coming on dark we were all very anxiously endeavoring to keep sight of the privateer, but notwithstanding all our pains, night glasses to help us and the moon, to wit, we suddenly lost sight of her. She must, on seeing us near her so fast, have lowered down her sails (a very common expedient with Yankees) and let us pass. These "clipper schooners," as they call them, are so very low and have so little rigging that it requires a remarkable quick eye to see them in the night when they decide to lower their sails and wait the event.

· · · · ·

May Day was ushered in as is usual on this coast by thick damp fogs and rain, complete suicide weather if one was inclined. I cannot say I am in the least tired of life. Ship standing to the westward. Barometer stationary at 29.9. Thermometer from 40° to 50°.

· · · · ·

Arrived in Boston Bay on the sixth. The weather unsettled and foggy. Wind round the compass. Barometer at 29.8. Thermometer 44°. Employed the people fishing, caught plenty of cod and being towards evening, the fog cleared away. Chased a vessel, apparently a clipper brig, close into Plymouth Lights. At eight o'clock finding we could not come up with the chase before she got within the Lights hauled our wind for the night.

. . . . .

22 May. Heavy rain and fogs, thunder and lightning. In the afternoon the weather cleared up with the wind to the westward. Stood in towards Cape Anne. Thermometer 50°. H.M.S. *Ramillies* joined company. All America blockaded. *Epervier* captured by the *Peacock* after an action of forty-five minutes. Lead the squadron into Cape Cod Bay, which is an excellent anchorage. Stiff clay bottom, secure from all winds except north, with which there can be very little sea, as it is off the shore, and even this may be avoided by going into the inner harbour, where there is an excellent anchorage in eleven fathoms, mud, if you, after having rounded the Race Point, bring the lighthouse to bear east by north.

On the twenty-third remarkably fine weather. *Ramillies* and *Junon* outsail us. Thermometer 52°.

On the twenty-fourth fine summer weather. Thermometer 60° to 62°. Sent the boat man'd and armed to cruise during the night alongshore. Search several schooners and sloops with oysters, scull and notions, as the Yankees call vegetables and small parcels of dry goods &c. The lobsters are remarkably large in Cape Cod Bay, and vessels come in numbers from New York and the southward. They fetch a good market. There is also a very extraordinary shell fish called the king crab. It abounds throughout almost the whole coast of America. It is in shape like a horseshoe (which name it also goes by), has claws like a crab, and a long horn about eight inches, sticking out of the sand with which its body is covered.

25 May. Weighed and made sail in company with squadron. Captured while at anchor four sloops and a schooner, took the cargoes out and restored the vessels.

Nothing material happened from the twenty-fifth to the twenty-seventh, when Sir Thomas Hardy came on board for the purpose of reconnoitring the coast, particularly Portsmouth, preparatory to an expedition being sent there.

On the twenty-eighth fine weather. *Ramillies* to keep in the offing. At nine thirty close in with Cape Anne town. Tacked to the eastward about a mile and a half from shore. By midnight hove off to Portsmouth.

. . . . .

On May 30, thick unpleasant weather from the southward. . . . Sent the *Junon's* boat in chase of a schooner, which she run on shore near Rye Beach, a little to the southward of Portsmouth. They attempted to take possession of her, but the militia assembled in rather formidable numbers, and concealing themselves behind a wall and in a wood which extended itself close to the beach, kept up a sharp and well-directed fire, which wounded two men. The boat had only a few muskets in it and no carronade, or it would soon have cleared the wood. No ship's boat ought to be sent singly away on an enemy coast without a gun in it, and if possible, no boat should be sent from the ship alone, as an unlucky shot may sink her and all her men without possibility of being saved. This particularly applies to the American coast, which is very rocky or excessively woody, both of which circumstances the Yankees make good use of by allowing boats to go in close, and then opening a fire with musketry and frequently field-pieces. They are not very good shots yet, or very enterprising, but they no doubt will improve.

Made a few signals with guns to alarm the coast by way of a frolic, which succeeded. They, conceiving the British Fleet to be off the port, assembled all their militia and regulars to repel the invasion.

31 May. The *Ramillies* joined, and Sir Thomas Hardy left us, to the regret of all the officers on board for various reasons. Ship running for Cape Cod. Thermometer 60°. Barometer 29.6. Made Cape Cod and anchored well up with the squadron. Sent the boats to examine every vessel in the inner harbour. Took one of our own and one of the *Junon's* boats to cruise for the night to the eastward of Cape Cod. Saw nothing worth making a prize of. Sent a flag of truce round Wellfleet Bay to collect stock, which the inhabitants were very willing to supply us with, being very well paid. It is our intention to oblige the Yankees to supply us with stock and vegetables at the market price. This is very reasonable; we leave all fishermen unmolested.

Nothing of consequence till the third when the *Ramillies* sailed for Bermuda.

On June 4 weighed and made sail towards Boston to reconnoitre the *Constitution,* who, we heard, was ready for sea. *Junon* in company.

Burned the *Tartar* schooner of Boston, disguised as a fisherman but having iron shackles on board. News of peace on the continent of Europe and the abdication of Napoleon. What astonishing events! Has he, or has he not, acted like a great man? I certainly thought he would not have survived his dethronement. Perhaps he may be reserved for more extraordinary events, for this is an age of wonders! . . .

. . . . .

Shannon, privateer, again out. Must drive her off, as she spoils our cruising ground. . . .

. . . . .

On June 16 fine summer weather. Standing towards Chatham. Ransomed the *Welcome Return* for $3500. Constant firing yesterday afternoon. The people of Boston celebrating the peace in Europe, much against the inclination of the Democrats who call them Englishmen.

On the seventeenth so foggy that we were unable to send the boats on a particular service between Brace's Cove and Thatcher's Island. Captured the *Polly* with government stores. This is another proof of the depravity of Americans. The master of the *Polly* has in his vessel a freight of government stores, which for the value of a few dollars, he, in conjunction with a rich merchant of Boston, forfeit their honour as men, their fidelity to their country and morality as Christians. Not only this but he assured us he had a rich uncle who would give him freight to a large amount and with whom he was a great favourite; that as soon as he got it he would immediately run down to us and thus fill his pocket by the basest ingratitude. My hope and prophecy is that he will be hung before his next birthday.

. . . . .

On the twenty-first stood close in to Gloucester. . . . Having information of a ship being off or rather in Chatham with a valuable cargo of quicksilver, made all sail with both tenders in company to attack her and the town, where we understood there were some large stores full of merchandise. Read *The Corsair,* Lord Byron's last work, and think it extremely interesting and well written but perhaps the poetry is not so fine as that of *The Giaour.* I could not help thinking our late depredations on this coast had a great of

The Corsair in them, particularly the one we are now going on.

On the twenty-second very foggy. Nothing particular happened.

23 June. After an unpleasant passage with fogs and other Yankee comforts, anchored off Chatham Lighthouse. East southeast in seven fathoms. Loose sandy bottoms. The golden or rather silver fleece which we came here for, proved to be a Spanish ship, so our trouble is needless. Could not send our boats in on account of a gale coming on, which we took for a short summer gale but it has every appearance of lasting. Towards evening the wind continuing to blow and coming round to north northwest with a heavy sea setting in, and no shelter, Captain Epworth conceived it better to cut our cable, which was accordingly done at a little after eight o'clock, standing to the eastward under storm staysail, it blowing very hard and a tremendous sea. Sound frequently from ten to thirty-seven fathoms. The tenders and prize brig in an awkward situation.

On the twenty-fourth the gale continued with unabated violence, though the ship was now clear of all shoals, should the wind shift. Barometer 30. Thermometer 40° to 50°. Weather cold and raw.

25 June. The same summer gale still continuing and the ship very uneasy. Thermometer 48°. Barometer 29.9.90. Our starboard quarter boat beat to pieces by a heavy sea and lee lurch. Split the main staysail. Blowing very hard.

On 26 June the gale abated considerably and totally exhausted itself toward the evening. Thick, hazy and unpleasant weather. . . .

.   .   .   .   .

29 June. The fog cleared away and we saw the land about Chatham. . . . Had the good fortune to recover our anchor. Thunder and lightning towards evening.

30 June. Very anxious for our tenders. Heavy, thick fogs and sultry weathers. The *Bulwark's* land company joined, have not seen ours since the gale. Yesterday we chased the *Ida,* letter of marque, but could not catch her. Barometer has deceived us lately. The weather sultry, foggy, oppressive and unpleasant. Thermometer 70° to 76°. The people much alarmed at Boston lest we should burn the *Independence,* gunboats, booms, and the *Constitution* all defending her, besides the batteries. By the way, I think these batteries might have been taken by the ship's boats with very trifling loss a short time ago and even now it would not be very difficult. They

certainly ought to have been destroyed before this. A young enterprising officer much wanted on this station.

. . . . .

On the seventh fine weather. On board one of the vessels taken
by the tender the crew, consisting of three men, rose on the two who
were sent to take charge,[2] when off their guard; knocked one overboard with a handspike, when heaving up the anchor. While in the
water, he heard the other calling out for mercy, and as there was a
great deal of blood on deck, when the tender's boat came and took
him up, they suppose he had been murdered. In another prize, which
she took and sent the surgeon's assistant in, they also rose and made
him prisoner, were going to murder him, but he with great presence
of mind told them that the tender was close by and if they did not
allow him to go, every man of them would be killed! In this manner
he actually bullied them into letting him go, giving him a boat for
the purpose! Misfortune attended him still, for scarce had he got
clear of the schooner when two armed boats came out from Chatham
and brought him in like a stray pig. As putting a bold face on had
served him before, he determined to try it again and accordingly
assured them that if they presumed to keep him prisoner, the *Nymphe*
would come and blow the town down, destroy all the inhabitants
and lay the whole country under contribution. They, knowing that
this was as easily done as said, immediately sent him off to the tender,
which he reached in safety. The *David Porter* got out, after having
been chased by the boats.

8 July. Anchored in Cape Cod Bay, where we found our prizes,
which we ransomed for $100 each. Detained all Wellfleet boats.
From them we learned that the man who we supposed to have been
kill'd was badly wounded only, and taken on shore. We instantly
threatened to burn their town unless he was immediately sent off.
I was much provoked by hearing that a fishing pleasure boat which
I saw when in Boston Harbour the other day (and which I would
not take on account of discovering we were armed and thereby
defeat our purpose, which was to take an armed vessel we expected
out) contained Mr. Gerry, a violent Democrat and *Vice President*
of the *United States.*

On the ninth fine summer weather. The selectmen of Truro, Well-

---

[2] This was always happening.

fleet, and Provincetown came on board. These selectmen, as Rochford says of all the Yankee towns, are certainly *very select*. Purchased beef at the rate of 7 *d* a pound. Fitted out the *Mariner* as a tender for a cruise off Nantucket, gave her seventeen men. Took the *Rambler* in tow. On the tenth fine summer weather. Weigh'd from Cape Cod. Several Boston gentlemen came on board to see the ship. Among others, the editor of the *Boston Centinel,* a very moderate paper. Among the party was a Dutch dancing-master, a great oddity. Fine weather. Thermometer 60° to 64°.

· · · · ·

On the fourteenth and fifteenth fine summer weather. The selectmen from Chatham and Wellfleet came off, the latter bringing with them our lost sheep, who we thought had been killed. Sent our lean sheep on shore to Thatcher's Island and brought off some fat ones in return. "Exchange is not robbery!" Released a prisoner, called George Washington, this day. Our seamen paid the amount of two days' pay for the relief of the widows and orphans of those who were killed in the *Shannon.*

On the sixteenth sent the barge to cruise off Cape Cod without success. . . .

· · · · ·

On the nineteenth stood into Boston Bay and observed the *Constitution* ready for sea. There are various reports concerning her and none to be depended on. Thermometer 70° to 74°.

· · · · ·

On the twenty-third our tender joined, looking very pretty. She has brought us $800. Sent her, the *Spencer's* boat, and our boat into Plymouth.

On the twenty-fourth saw *Tenedos* to leeward. She has captured a fine prize. *Leander* gone to the northward. Thermometer 70°. Barometer 29.7. Sent a sloop to Halifax with provisions.

The tender returned with the *Spencer's* boat and our pinnace-men. In chasing into Plymouth she unfortunately went too close in to the battery, a shot from which sunk her without hurting a single man, although there were nineteen men in the boat. They first hauled their colours down and hoisted them Union downward, when finding they did not cease firing, they were rehoisted Union upwards, and the boat immediately went down with flying colours. The Yankees in a most infamous manner continued still a well-directed fire at the people when in the water, but fortunately did not touch one, although the shot fell within two or three feet of some, and passed between the masts of the *Spencer's* boats in picking them up, which she succeeded in doing. The tender fired several shots at the battery. We were all excessively sorry about this poor boat. She was so beautiful, sailed and pulled so well and was almost built on board. She came up after having the gun disengaged, and was picked up by a fisherman and towed in. We ought to take the battery immediately and get the boat, which might easily be accomplished. In the evening anchored in Cape Cod Bay and sent a flag of truce on shore. Commenced watering.

On the twenty-fifth watered the ship at Provincetown. We were obliged to raft the casks off to some large schooners laying in the harbour and bring it off to the ship. The tide rises here from twelve to fourteen feet.

On the twenty-sixth in the morning finished watering and in the evening joined H.M.S. *Spencer* and *Leander* outside. They had been joined during the day by the *Alban,* schooner commanded by a commander. The boats were towed in towards Barnstable by her. Our tender went towards Boston.

27 July. The weather still continuing fine; indeed we have been highly favoured lately. Mr. Foster and the three men who were sent in with the *Bee* returned, also two supernumeraries for the ship. Made sail towards Cape Cod Bay to procure bullocks for the squadron.

Made the unfortunate master of a fishing boat, who formerly had permission to fish and came out, trusting to that protection, pay $200 for a ransom. The poor creature has a wife and seven children, no money, and was in debt for his salt and fishing lines even. He with great difficulty scraped up by sixpences and shillings the amount of the money at Provincetown and came on board with tears in his eyes. This is an ungenerous war against the poor and unworthy of Englishmen. I am ashamed of Captain Epworth's conduct.

> "When self the wavering ballance hold,
>   Its rarely right adjusted."

is a true saying, I see it more and more every day. Mr. Bertram, the officer who has suspended me, is very gentlemanlike. He is related to poor Sir Charles Ross.

Provincetown, formerly famous for whaling, now completely cut off from all trade and at the mercy of any person.

Weather still fine but cloudy.

· · · · ·

Friday, 29 July. Strong summer gales and rainy weather, towards the afternoon the wind shifted to the northwest with clear weather. Made sail towards Cape Cod intending to anchor there to take bullocks. At five-thirty anchored. Towards night blowing fresh and the weather sultry.

Saturday, 30 July. Weather excessive hot. Sent the boats armed to procure oxen. Arms are put in to save appearances for the people are willing enough to supply us with whatever we want, indeed a deputation of Quakers off to beg we would go a little further to the southward and we should be supplied with much fatter and better cattle. Thermometer 70° in the morning. The tender returned with a sloop prize, loaded with iron and sundries. She was to have been ransomed for $800 but from some misunderstanding between Captain Epworth and his officers, in which the latter are, in my opinion, perfectly correct; indeed they would not act honourable to the *Bulwark's* officers if they allowed the sharing of any other ship besides and without their consent.

Sunday, 31 July. Thermometer 70°, and weather excessive sultry. Weighed from Cape Cod and stood to the northward — *Spencer* in sight. No particular occurrence this day.

— From THE JOURNAL OF HENRY EDWARD NAPIER

Henry Edward Napier, born in 1789, was the son of Colonel the Hon. George Napier and his second wife, Lady Sarah Lennox, a great-granddaughter of Charles II and early flame of George III. General Sir Charles James Napier, General Sir Charles Thomas Napier, and General Sir William Francis Patrick Napier were his brothers. The lieutenant early chose the sea. His character and mind were in many ways typical of the best of his class and time. War was his profession, matter-of-factly accepted. He felt sympathy for its victims, some indignation against the enemy, apparently no hatred. Like Captain Elijah Cobb of Brewster, a contemporary in a very different walk of life whose memoir appears elsewhere in this book, he thoroughly enjoyed living. In August, 1814, he left the Nymphe *to command the* Gorée, *a prison ship at Bermuda and shortly afterwards was appointed Captain of* H.M. Brig Rifleman.

His journal of life aboard the Nymphe, *edited by Walter Muir Whitehill, was published in Salem in 1939 by the Peabody Museum under the title* NEW ENGLAND BLOCKADED IN 1814. *Only that part of it touching upon Cape Cod is reprinted here.*

ᘒᔍᕲ

The Glory Years

1814–1861
THE GLORY YEARS

Great years; great events; great men. — THOMAS HALL

*T*HESE *were the years between the War of 1812 and the Civil War. They were the years when fleets of Cape Cod whaleships and Grand Bankers and mackerel-fishers ranged the seas; when the packets sailing between Cape Cod and Boston were always carrying some Cape Cod merchant-captain to the beginning or end of his long voyage; when harbors and river mouths were jammed with sail and crowded, bustling, lively towns rang with industry. Almost everyone who wasn't going to sea was engaged in making something for those who were: salt, rope, sails, harpoons, cutting-spades, boats, at one time even ships. Mansions rose where cottages had stood. Life became cosmopolitan. And the keel of many and many snug long-lived fortune was laid.*

Cape Cod had known great years before. Times had been flourishing before the Revolution but when the war ended and men looked at their vessels rotting at their wharves and at the empty seas, stripped of sail by the enemy, they had feared such days might never come again. The War of 1812 struck the reviving industries down once more. But with that unpleasant episode out of the way, with the United States a firmly established nation, and with all maritime New England booming, Cape Cod embarked on such a lucky, "greasy," fishy voyage to ports of gold as had never been known before.

The sea was the business of Cape Cod, the source of all, but Cape Cod men had never been inclined to put all their fish in one basket. They still farmed and they still sniffed the wind for opportunity of whatever kind.

Before the Revolution Cape Cod people had made the salt required for their fisheries by the slow process of boiling sea-water in iron kettles. By the 1830's Cape Cod beaches were lined with elaborate series of huge vats of pine into which sea-water was pumped by windmills to be evaporated by the sun and the "salt upon salt" Captain John Smith had envisaged had become a reality. The vastly profitable industry was a development of crude experiments made by

128

Captain John Sears of Dennis — "Sears' Folly," they were called — in 1776 when war had sent the price of salt skyhigh.

Cranberries grow wild on Cape Cod and were once called bear-berries because bears ate them or craneberries because the blossom and stem resembled the head and neck of a crane. The uncultivated berries are called hog-cranberries today. In 1816 Henry Hall of Dennis cutting brush accidentally precipitated a sand-slide on his cranberry swamp and the next year discovered that far from damaging them the sandy blanket had improved the plants. Word got around and other farmers began to experiment with "the little waif of the swamps" with astonishing results. By the middle of the century everybody on the Cape had gone hog-cranberry-wild and there was a scramble to buy the swamps.

After the Civil War when men came home to face the long sunset of their sea-going life, cranberries saved Cape Cod economy. They are of enormous importance today. In 1947 Massachusetts grew more than half the cranberries sold to the world and a large proportion of these were raised on the Cape.

A few shirt and shoe-factories were built in the booming days but they were not of great importance to Cape Cod life. The one manufacturing establishment to make history was the Boston and Sandwich Glass Factory which achieved world-wide fame and in sixty-three years of existence poured more than $30,000,000 into Sandwich. It was founded by Deming Jarves in 1825 and closed forever by a strike in 1888. Cape Cod people will tell you that when the smoke of the great stacks died away owners, glassworkers, and townspeople wept.

℘

1851
BARTHOLOMEW GOSNOLD'S VISION

BY BENJAMIN DREW

There sailed an ancient mariner,
Bart. Gosnold was he hight —
The Cape was all a wilderness
When Gosnold hove in sight.

He saw canoes and wigwams rude,—
    By ruder builders made,—
Squaws pounded samp about the doors,
    And dark papooses played.

The hills were bold and fair to view,
    And covered o'er with trees,
Said Gosnold "bring a fishing-line
    While lulls the evening breeze:

I'll christen that there sandy shore
    From the first fish I take: —
Tautog or toadfish, cusk or cod,
    Horse mackerel or hake,

Hard head or haddock, sculpin, squid,
    Goose-fish, pipe-fish or cunner —
No matter what, shall with its name
    Yon promontory honor."

Old Neptune heard the promise made,
    Down dove the water god —
He scared the meaner fish away,
    And hooked the MAMMOTH COD.

Quick, Gosnold hauled — "Cape-Cape-Cape-Cod!"
    "Cape Cod!" the crew cried louder:
"Here, steward! take the fish along,
    And give the boys a chowder."

Then Gosnold took his telescope,
    And swept the hilly shore:
A second sight was in the lens —
    A thing unknown before.

For tangled swamp and forest dense,
    Cleared fields and gardens prim
Now met his view: for wigwam rude
    The cottage neat and trim.

He saw the busy salt-mills whirl,
    The packets anchored near,
Acres of flakes on which were spread
    The fortunes of a year.

Three spires or more in every town,
  Wild meetings of come-outers,
Men of a hundred varying creeds
  From Catholics to doubters.

He saw great gatherings in a grove,
  A grove near Pamet Bay,
Where thousands heard the preacher's word,
  And dozens kneeled to pray.

Aghast he stands in sudden fright,
  His hair! behold it bristle!
The lens has brought a train so near,
  He hears the horrid whistle!

And peering into further years, —
  Not far from this, our day, —
He saw the happy era when
  The Cape Cod Branch will *pay*.

Still as he looked, the wondrous lens
  Revealed the future ages, —
He saw the Naushon run away
  From Higgins and the stages!

Unwonted wealth in Barnstable,
  Gold, silver, Yarmouth notes:
For *Barker's dyke* had changed the crops
  From thatch to rye and oats.

From Plymouth line to High-Pole hill
  He saw the vigorous Saxon,
Bold, enterprising, hardy, brave,
  "Born to command," like Jackson.

Captains were they of every craft,
  Of clippers, yachts and whalers:
Ah! Gosnold thought — these go ahead
  Of even our English sailors.

Anon he looks with gaze intense, —
  The fair ones pass in view —
Chaste, pious, prudent, helpmeets wise,
  With loving hearts and true.

> A flag he spies — the stars and stripes
> On Scargo's beacon land —
> Then mournfully he dropped the glass,
> And saw — but woods and sand.

The Cape Cod Association of Boston, organized in February, 1851, celebrated its first "anniversary" at a meeting held at Assembly Hall on November 11 of that year. This day was chosen to commemorate the signing of the Mayflower Compact in Provincetown harbor on November 11 in 1620. Speeches were delivered, toasts proposed, songs sung. BARTHOLOMEW GOSNOLD'S VISION, *composed for the occasion, was read by Benjamin Drew who in a few preliminary remarks referred to himself facetiously as the author of certain other articles in rhyme which had given him "an immortality of near a week." He could not have foreseen that the verses he read that night would still be highly relished on Cape Cod after a hundred years.*

ᘯ

1830
THE POST–BOY

BY SHEBNAH RICH

GOING TO BOSTON by land was less common than a voyage to China. It must be the king's business that demanded such an outlay of time and capital. Excepting the mails, carriage by water was the only recognized connection with Boston. Hence the "packet" early became almost a personality. My history would be imperfect without some reference thereto. I cannot learn that any one vessel was engaged in this traffic till after the War of 1812. Yet I have no reasonable doubt that there was some periodical connection many years before. The first regularly established packet of which I have authentic information, was the pinkey *Comet,* Captain Zoheth Rich. In about 1830, Captain Rich and his friends determined to build a first-class packet. The result was the schooner *Post-boy,* the finest specimen of naval architecture, and of passenger accommodation, in the Bay waters. Her cabin and furniture were finished in solid mahogany and bird's eye, and silk draperies. She was the admiration of the travelling public; all that had been promised in a first-class packet, and was often crowded to overflowing with passengers. Captain Rich, better known at home as Captain Zoheth, knew the way to Boston in the darkest night, and could keep his passengers good-natured with a head wind. He could laugh as heartily at an old story as a new one, and was always a good listener. Good listeners have many secrets. . . . The captain of the *Post-boy* was not a fluent man, nor of a vivid imagination. His vocabulary was limited to the fewest monosyllabic words, which he used with miserly economy, cutting them short in a quick, hurried, inimical style; then as if impressed that he had not done full justice to his subject, he would repeat his first words still quicker, and with more marked emphasis.

The first day from Boston was always a busy one, and the captain was on the alert. People would soon begin to inquire, "Captain Zoheth, when do you go to Boston again?" "I think we'll go Wens'dy, wind and weather permit'n; yes, go to Bost'n about Wens'dy." They knew well enough that the *Post-boy* never went to Boston on that declaration; none expected it. The next day the same question would be asked, with this answer, "Goin' to-morrer, if can get out the harbor; go to-morrer." "To-morrer" was sure to being a scant tide, and the packet would not move.

Somebody was now sure to ask, "Why, Capt'n, you didn't go to Boston today." "No, didn't get out; *divilish* low tide, and head wind." "Well, when *are* you going?" The last said, perhaps, with a slight impatience. "The *Piz-by* will go to Bost'n to-morrer; yes, *sir,* the *Piz-by* will go to Bost'n to-morrer, wind or no wind, tide or no tide, by·gracious!" Now it was well understood the packet would go to Boston tomorrow. Early the next morning the captain would be seen coming with his little black-leather trunk that always meant business; long before highwater the colors floated at the topmast head, the signal for Boston; and the *Post-boy* went to Boston, just about the time the captain intended, and when from the first it was understood she would go. I do not mean to say this was the captain's rule, by no means; when business was good he made quick trips and never stood on the order of going or coming; but there are scores now living,* who well remember the *Post-boy,* Captain Zoheth, and his nervous Anglo-Saxon.

* 1883.

Never were travellers more happy or content than on the *Post-boy*. Never since *Canterbury Tales* was social freedom and story-telling better practised or enjoyed. She sailed on no time-table. Passengers well understood at the start, that a few hours, or a few days, might be required, and that the stock of stores and stories would hold out. They knew that the interest and pleasure of the trip depended upon the good-feeling and comfort of their fellow-passengers, who, when at home, were most neighbors and townsmen. Here was sure to be some Marco Polo captain, who had killed elephants in India or seen the Brahma's great white bull. Some Western adventurer, who discoursed of steamboat races, herds of buffalo, and Indians. Here were the home-traders, discussing the price of sugar, eggs, and palm-leaf hats. Skippers talked of mackerel and codfish. If the sail flapped idly against the mast, somebody had been becalmed in the Indian Ocean for weeks, without a cat's-paw on the face of the water, or had run down the trade winds from the Windward Islands to the Equator, without starting his topgallant studding-sail brace; or, like the flying Dutchman, had beaten for weeks off Cape Horn. There was no monopoly or obtrusiveness in all this freedom of conversation. Each told their experience, or listened with interest and pleasure to the rest, and all sought with unaffected good-nature to please and profit.

The few travellers, visiting the Cape for health, pleasure or profit, for the first time, were drawn towards these people. Social conventionalities, wealth, birth and education melted their narrow partitions in this genial atmosphere, and, not unfrequently, those who met as strangers separated as life-long friends.

Captain Rich retired from packeting at the decline of the business, and spent the remainder of his days, till threescore and ten, in his snug little home, which for nice keeping was a gem. No grass was greener, no garden cleaner, no grapes larger, and no horse or cow fatter than his. For many years he shared the fellowship of the Church, died in her faith, and was gathered unto his fathers.

— From TRURO — CAPE COD

ESTEEMED GIRL

A Brewster Courtship

BY PHYLLIS DUGANNE

SOME YEARS AGO my aunt, Inez Haynes Irwin, said to me: "Ask questions of old people. Ask them all the time. When I remember how few questions I asked, as a child, and how bored I was with my elders' reminiscences, I am consumed by regret. My father, as a little boy, listened to the conversations of men who had fought in the American Revolution, but I never inquired a word of what they said. Now I shall never know."

Even as she spoke, I realized that for myself, too, it was too late. Personal links with the past break so swiftly, and are irrevocably gone. I could have asked questions, a short time before, and heard the answers, about Caroline Snow and the second Elijah Cobb. I had known two of their daughters, Annette Theresa and Emily Cunningham Cobb. I suppose that I was a little afraid of my great-aunts; certainly I was awed by them. They were tall, imposing women, who wore long black dresses with high boned collars, and they lived, not in the old General's house where a child could feel at ease, but in a mansard-roofed mansion nearby, with ceilings and French windows so high and furnishings of such richness that a small girl was silenced by sheer elegance.

My father's sister, named Caroline after the Esteemed Girl of these letters, told me what things I know. I did at least listen long enough to learn that great-aunt Netty had her middle name from "the Spanish girl Theresa" who nursed my great-great-uncle Albert Cobb through a fatal illness in Spain, and perhaps loved him. In any case, she cared enough to write the details of his death to his mother on Cape Cod, through the shaded, spiralling penmanship of a professional letter-writer. But even while Aunt Caro talked, I would become restive. It was more exciting to climb up to General Cobb's attic and dress myself in hoopskirts and basques, the pumpkin-hoods and coal-hod bonnets which may have belonged to Caroline Snow, than to hear about her.

The young should certainly ask more questions, but the old should not so jealously guard family records and letters until they die. If I had been allowed to read these love-letters while Caroline's daughters and granddaughter lived, I am sure that I would have been voluble with questions which now must remain unanswered.

Why was their early correspondence clandestine? Did Elijah's family object to Miss Snow? She came straight down from Stephen Hopkins and the *Mayflower;* as a matter of fact so did he. So, even, did my mother, a stranger to Cape Cod until her marriage. Perhaps that was not important, a century ago. Fine Cape Cod names are in Caroline's lineage, Bangs and Berry, Dillingham and Freeman. Her mother took for a second husband Kenelm Winslow, a man of property and character. Surely there was no reason for social disapproval.

Did Caroline's mother, who had lost her two other children, feel that the young Elijah was not good enough for her one remaining daughter? The first Elijah, his father, seems a stalwart as well as glamorous figure, the young captain who at twenty-five was captured by a French frigate and sailed, chaperoned by a "prise-master" straight into the heart of the French Revolution. A romantic, satisfying ancestor to have — but did Mrs. Olive Bangs Snow Winslow possibly see in him a sharp sea-captain who, we know of his own admission, smuggled rum into Ireland, and who is not wholly unsuspected of some traffic in Black Ivory? Or did their respective families think them too young? Caroline was sixteen, Elijah twenty-one, when their romance began.

In an unfinished, undated fragment of autobiography which Caroline wrote, she makes no mention of family disapproval. They were, she writes, engaged in her fifteenth year, though the date of their first exchange of letters contradicts her own words by twelve months, and married in her twenty-first. "Taken for better or worse, and I believe proved much the worse for that gent ever after," she records, with a flippancy one comes to know well from her letters. Elijah's words to her, as a husband, give the lie to her statement. On May 8th, 1833, he writes to her: — "Yes, eight years ago since mutual love (never was this stronger) was Cemented in holy bonds which I can truly say time has indiminishable strengthend — yes, all union that I anticipated has been realized — and shall we not be grateful?"

It was obviously a happy marriage, thirty-six years of it, bles't by seven children. In her thwarted attempt at autobiography, she says of herself: — "She possessed neither wit nor beauty, but nature endowed her with a tolerable good disposition and a moderate share of common sense." Again, I suspect my great-grandmother of being deliberately — to use a word she must have invented, in one of her early letters to her suitor — "funnical."

Elijah may have had humor; if he did, his epistolary style is well fitted to conceal it. Nothing could conceal Caroline's. In her first letter to him, she may or may not have been teasing; it is difficult to pierce through the measured formality of her young-girl's etiquette. Her second letter is unquestionably coy, coquettish, and in my opinion not without sarcasm, even though her sixteen year old emotions have been stirred and flattered by the young man's solemnity. By her fourth letter, of December, 1820, she has abandoned etiquette, and the exquisite, steel-engraving penmanship which must have been many times copied is abandoned with it. She is her own unvarnished, mocking, teasing self. After much news, she remarks that she gives him this particular account of the "transactions" of the last week, "not because I think them interesting, but because you requested it." One reads between the lines that E. Cobb, Jr. was more than a little jealous of the Esteemed Girl who later describes herself: — "She was rather below the common stature, with a considerable stoop to her figure, rather small, with a sallow complexion, brown hair, blue eyes, long peaked nose, great mouth and large teeth." One reads, too, that for all that "*he* was a tall and manly figure, with black hair and eyes and a very white and prominent forehead, oval face and good features"; she was not so impressed by her good luck that she could not make fun of him. When he writes, concerning her slight indisposition, "I am unwilling to think your cold, Caroline, was caus'd by imprudence on your part," she waits until the last half-inch of her letter-paper to report, "Oh, by the bye, I forgot to thank Doc Cobb for his advice respecting my health which is quite *good* excepting a cold which I caught I don't know where or when."

In their four letters each, during their courtship, he addresses her with three salutations, Esteemed Girl, My Esteemed Friend, and finally My Dear Friend. Her first and second letters to him commence with copy-book correctness, Sir; her third and fourth have no beginning whatever, though in her fourth letter, she slips in a casual "Elijah," setting in parentheses after it — "or Mr. Cobb which you please."

Almost five and a half years elapse between their first exchange of letters and their marriage. We know that they saw one another often. In her sixteenth year, Caroline attended school in Boston, where Elijah frequently visited her, and their roots were in Brewster, where they must have met often.

Of the nine letters written after their marriage, only three are from her, but they remain characteristically individual and colored by her own personality. Elijah falls easily into the frequent and somewhat unconvincing reverence and humility of his period, with constant allusions to the kindness and beneficence of their Heavenly Father. Caroline, at forty-five, objects with spirit to the sermon of one of their Heavenly Father's servants. She writes, from Brewster, to her husband: "The subject [of the sermon] was education. I think he spoke too slightingly of the accomplishments and gave domestic education too exalted a place. He said he did not know but I think he meant me or mine in speaking of young ladies playing the pianno after much arguing I told him I had seen more happiness marred for the want of accomplishments and education than for want of knowledge on domestic affairs, that I thought when circumstances permitted it was better that youth should be spent in acquirment of knowledge and accomplishments than the drudgery of cleaning and cooking, that when necessary, with good sense a lady might soon learn the use of the broom and to make bread, this was in reference to something he said about painting a flower but ignorant of the use of the flour from the barrel, and hands that could strike the keys of the Pianno, but unused to handle the broom."

Her last letter, when she is forty-eight years old, to "My dearest friend" from "Your loving Caroline" is a brisk, housewifely account of the preparations for their daughter's wedding, which is to be a small affair, since, "if we ask others, we shall not know when to stop." Of the five girls, only Helen and Annette Therese married, and I am glad that Helen did, since had she not, Caroline Snow Cobb would not have been my great-grandmother.

· · · · ·

Boston, Jany. 10. 1820

Esteemed Girl,

I am fully aware that in thus addressing you I may be deemed presumptious, yet excuse this liberty — I can conceive of no sufficient motive why I should restrain my feelings — *neither will I,* — but will frankly and candidly tell you, Caroline, that I feel a deep interest and particular regard for you — which do me the justice to believe is sincere, when I assure you that is the case. No hasty motive has induced me to write you, neither have I similar intentions in view — all I ask is an acknowledgement of feelings, similar to my own on your part, which you may rest assured would be most congenial to my feelings as well as happiness.

These feelings are not entirely new, Caroline — I should have esteemed it a favor to have had, *and to now have,* opportunity for personally evincing them — but that has in a measure been, and is now, impracticable — distance is the separating line, and I have recourse to this method. I must earnestly request so much of your attention to this, Caroline, as will ensure me a line from you — which you can hand to my sister, Mrs. Sampson,[1] and I shall receive it. — my sister will hand you this, in whom only have I confided.

The discontinuance of the packets, in coming to Boston, connected with our present embargoed situation, which winter restricts upon us serves to increase the dullness which we naturally feel in separation from friends — I think I could well enjoy the winter at Brewster, but am necessitated to deprive myself of that pleasure. I must again solicit a line from you and

I am with due respect and regard Yrs. E. Cobb Jr.
Miss Caroline Snow
Brewster

· · · · ·

Brewster Jan' 28th, 1820
Sir,

I was much surprised at the reception of your letter, its contents were so entirely unexpected to me, that I must confess I hardly know how to answer it, yet am sensible that a reply is requisite. You say that "all you ask is an acknowledgement of feelings on my part simillar to your own" this I cannot *at present* express, but can only say that perhaps you are not entirely indifferent to me. I will not be so uncharitable as to accuse you of insincerity in your profession of regard for me, but you are young, and I fear have not sufficiently considered the subject. It is an important one, and requires deep reflection, for by fancying we feel an attachment, when in reality we do not, or rather do not feel *that attachment* which will become *per-*

[1] Deborah R. Cobb — b. 1794, m. Dr. Joseph Sampson in 1815.

manent, we lay the foundation for much future unhappiness. But time, which will reveal the secret purposes of every heart, will show, whether what *you think* you feel for me, is really affection, or only the semblance of it. However it is my sincere wish that whatever may be our lot in life, we may ever feel that friendship, which will be as lasting as our lives.

Accept the best wishes for your happiness, of

Your friend C. Snow

· · · · ·

Boston Feby 25, 1820

Esteemed Girl,

Your favor of 28th Jany, I have rec*d* and perused with much interest. your observations I most readily acknowledge are with strict propriety, and deserve particular attention — that the subject upon which I before addressed you, is of a most important nature, and should be seriously and duly reflected upon, I hope I am not unmindful of — an attachment of this nature to be form'd for life, certainly should demand our most serious consideration. I am unwilling to think you so uncharitable, as to suppose my former letter was written without any consideration of reflection, although you have just grounds for fears. I must request your belief, when I tell you, that the real and sincere feelings of my heart, was my dictator. — believe me, *Caroline,* none but sincere motives would have prompted me, to have thus declared to you my feelings and wishes. I am fully aware, that in this early stage of life, we are more liable to adopt measures which would hereafter appear inconsistent, or imbibe feelings which are transient, — yet I conceive the most permanent attachments may be thus formed, if pure motives and affections are rightly affix'd. I shall esteem it a peculiar favor to hear from you soon, as I feel much interest to understand your feelings on this subject —

Your friend E. Cobb Jr.

· · · · ·

Brewster March 11*th* 1820

Sir,

I received your letter of the 25th and thank you for the sentiments you there expressed toward me. You say "you are anxious to understand my feelings upon the subject," and I hope I am ingenuous enough to wish that you should, for I consider it as much a duty to use candour in *such* a case, as in almost any other instance in life.

I thought that in my former letter, I said as much as I then could with propriety, but if I failed in my attempt to shew you the true state of my mind, I trust I may now add without appearing too forward that should you retain the sentiments which you have professed, they may receive a reciprocal return. I will be sincere enough to acknowledge that tho' I felt no particular prefference for any one, previous to my receiving your first letter, if I now do, it is to you. But there are bounds which a female should not pass, if I have now surpassed them, I must trust to your goodness to overlook it, and to reccollect that I am but a novice in conversing upon the subject. Wishing you health and happiness,

I must subscribe myself, your friend,

C. Snow

.   .   .   .   .

Boston May 2. 1820

My esteemed friend

I will not hesitate to acknowledge that I have indulged myself not a little in the pleasing anticipation of seeing you in one of the packets, but our anticipations to often prove delusive — I will not appologize for the intrusion of a few scrawls at this time, trusting very soon to a personal interview. We had an agreeable passage down, and arrived the next evening after leaving you — My stay at home was rather short yet I very often with sweet remembrance recal the pleasure and satisfaction I enjoyed, even in that short period — the review is a source of much satisfaction to me and I fondly hope in some degree to you — I cannot but indulge myself in the pleasure of thinking so *at least.* I can only sincerely hope, *Caroline,* that I may not be so unfortunate as to be unworthy of your friendship and I am not unconscious but it may even now be the case, nevertheless I am most generally willing to anticipate the favourable part, especcially where my feelings and wishes cooperate — Contrary to my expectations, I have not heard a syllable uttered respecting my visit home, *or rather occurrences at home,* since my return. I am inclined to think reports have not yet been transported across the mighty deep — or I sh*d* have rec*d* some intimations from same, either by sour looks, or in some way, but that has not been the case — I expect you will relate a different story, or I shall not think it characteristic of the inhabitants of Brewster, if you do not — — I

shall expect my father in the return of the Fame, and conclude you
will also take passage in her, as it perhaps would be rather more
agreeable than to come with those with whom you are not acquainted
— should any occurence prevent your coming, you will not fail to
adopt my mode of communication.

Your sincere friend — E. Cobb Jr.

·   ·   ·   ·   ·

Brewster Oct' 13*th* 1820

Yours by the last packet, I received almost a week after its arrival,
and in compliance with your request of writing *soon* have seated myself to answer your letter that recommenses a correspondence, which
I will not *deny* affords me pleasure. I am happy to hear that you
are getting reconcil'd for the loss of your Brewster friends, I shall
advise you to visit them *but* seldom, *since* a visit to the Cape makes
you *un*happy for so long a *time* after it. *Un*happy you cannot be,
but discontented with the situation in which you are placed. You have
taken an effectual method for banishing unpleasant reflections, and
I hope before I hear from you again, you will not only be *almost,*
but *quite reinstated.*

Visiting, which *raged so violently* when you were here, has sub-
sided. There has been but one party, or at least a large party, since
you left, that was at Uncle Snow's. I was not there, but understand
they had a very pleasant time.

I spent last even at Aunt Clark's, have not been there before
since you accompanied me, and complained *so bitterly* of the *way,*
or *rather walking.* I *there* heard of your brothers safe arrival in
Boston, think him quite fortunate in meeting your Mother. We anticipate the pleasure of a visit from your Sister this afternoon. She was
here last week with your Mother, and I *believe* came purposely to
deliver your letter. We ought to be grateful to her for her kindness,
for I'm *sure* we could not correspond without it.

Capt' & Mrs. Gray, Mr. and Mrs. Thatcher spent that very unpleasant Tuesday, on which you left home and returned again, with
us. Mr. & Mrs. H. and Mr. & Mrs. T. & all called as they were returning. I was very much surprised that they should leave home
in such disagreeable weather. I have received but one letter from
Eliza since then — in that she expressed her Mother's intention of
visiting Boston this season and her wish, that I should be with her,
during her absence. I think it quite improbable that I shall visit

Y. so soon, tho' I imagine we should have a *fine time, almost equal to the wedding.*

Last Thursday eve I went to see Elizabeth expecting that she was alone — *contra* to my expectations, the packet had not sailed, and I found her playing backgammon with John. My *gallant* was *no other but* Mr. Joseph Winslow. Do not *stare* and I will relate the circumstance as it happened. know then that Miss P. Winslow, had a small party, and as I had previously engaged to be with E. that night, I refused to spend the evening with them unless Nathaniel, her brother would promise to ride down town with me — to this he consented but when the time arrived for me to take my leave N. appeared unwilling to go. Joseph then offer'd *his services* very politely and was accepted. It was the first time that we have met since — but I believe former transactions were forgotten, for he was very sociable & agreeable. It was not J. but his brother that you saw the day you left Brewster. I should not tell you of your mistake, only I thought it would *serve to impress upon your mind* that *silence* is the best way of passing off such triffling insults.

I am much obliged to you for the notes you sent; and for your generosity accept my thanks & be assured that the gift in every way pleased and was acceptable.

to your friend Caroline.

·   ·   ·   ·   ·

Boston October 31, 1820

My dear friend

Your valued favor of the 13th Ulto came duly to hand and I have delayed an answer only because I believe it your policy or you think it best at *least* not to write too often — I however must say a frequent correspondence best comports with my wishes — I had this morning the very unpleasant news of your illness — how fickle and uncertain is health, and every other blessing we enjoy — have rec'd since a letter from home, written last evening — and, I need not tell you, I was happy to hear you was more comfortable — the gratification w'd be great, *my dear* girl, to be with you and did I think your illness of continuance or more severe — that pleasure should not be deny'd me — but I anticipate, when again I hear — to hear your health *the first of all blessings* in a great measure reestablish'd. Colds are prevalent — I was attacked severely but by prudent measures avoided a fever — I am unwilling to think your cold *Caroline* was caus'd by imprudence on your part — I w'd beg you as a friend to be cautious of your health — but you have at hand an ever constant friend, for advice and instruction — *a mother.* — I am compel'd to be brief Caroline in this letter — tho, I would not deny myself the pleasure of writing now. Mr. Haven was down in the packet for Chatham on special business — and the packet going unexpected, is the cause of my briefness — she arriv'd this morning — I make this apology because I am an advocate for long letters — I will write you Caroline next packet and sh'd be truly grateful to have you write as soon as you get better — in the meantime accept my renewed assurances of sincere affection and friendship

In haste your friend E. Cobb Jr.

.   .   .   .   .

Yours I received yesterday and will assure you I perused its contents with pleasure. I was happy to hear of your safe arrival at last. You had waited so long for a fair wind that I was afraid Capt' L. would venture before there was a prospect of a pleasant passage. I presume you was absent from Boston a sufficient length of time to make your friends in that place glad to see you and indeed, you ought for it would be a *hard case* to *part* with friends in one place not to *find any* in an other to *welcome* us.

You left us about 7 oclock Sunday evening. The idea that my best friends were to be absent so long, struck me so forcibly, that I was glad of any excuse to leave the company therefore complained of a headache and retired I fancy before you reached your *home.* The next day I finished reading 'Rob Roy' which you will recollect I commenced the week before, and my Mother would not allow me to read more than five minutes at once. Tuesday I wrote to Eliza Thatcher. O. Bangs spent the evening with me. Wednesday Doct' Sampson spent an hour or two with us and beat me most unmercifully both in checkers and gammon. Thursday I *rode* out, called on Mrs. Susan Seers. She is keeping house for her father S. who is a very unsteady man, his family consists only of a boy, you observed who has a most ungovernable temper. How Susan can content herself I can't conceive and indeed she could not had she not been blest with a remarkable happy disposition.

Saturday. I can think. Oh! I have got before my story. I believe I have not yet returned from Dennis. Well, then, I did not return home from there, but stopped at Aunt Clark's where I spent the night and the most part of the next day. *Well* now I have arrived to Saturday but can think of nothing that occurred worthy of mentioning. I have not given you this particular account of the *transactions* of last week because I thought them interesting, but because you requested it. Yesterday morning I attended meeting, as I was returning observed an *expressive* look from your Sister, which convinced me she had a letter. She had not the oppertunity of giving it to me then and I was apprehensive that I should not receive before night however by the help of good *friends* it reached me before I arrived home. I have no prospect of a conveyance of this to your Sister, but trust there will be one before the packet sails, if not the *consciousness of haveing done my duty* will compensate me for my trouble. I always write from selfish motives, but you wrote at a time when you could not reasonably expect an answer and are thereby deserving praise. My thanks you have had, therefore I will not repeat them.

Wednesday. I was interrupted Monday morn by *callers* and was prevented writing you in the afternoon by company. I will confess that I was glad of an excuse to lay aside my pen, as I was afflicted with my *old enemy* the head ache. This you must consider as an apology for some of the numerous errors with which the foregoing is filled. I believe every word was begun with the last letter but imagine it will be excused. Doct' Sampson called yesterday and delivered the cage you were so kind as to send, for which accept my sincere thanks. *Poll* appears to be pleased with her new habitation and I dare say feels grateful to the donor.

P. Clark a cousin of mine is to be married tomorrow afternoon. I go not, for the want thereof of an invitation. The intended's name is Eldridge, his place of residence Chatham. To my parents Elijah (or Mr. Cobb which you please) no apology is necessary. I cannot say that our neighbours, or the world *at large* (Town, I mean), have let your 'frequent visits' pass unobserved, or mine to your friends either, and they have given me credit for more than my *due*. I heard at Dennis that I had dined at Gen. Cobb's Thanksgiving. You always appeared not to mind such reports, and have taught me in a *measure* to *soar above* them. Your horse I presume did not think it subject of laughter to stand upon this *mount* that cold night, nor did you I fancy while he was reminding you that you had *wronged* him. I think you might have *lent* him your great coat since it was your will that he should not be *housed*. It would have been quite a serious affair if he had lodg'd you in the pond and a little *funnical* too I think. I hope for the future you will have more compassion upon your *humble servant.* A frequent correspondence Elijah by mail, I think would be giving *a little too much* trouble to your friends, however since they are your friends you are at liberty to *trouble* them as much as you please. This is my only objection for I will assure nothing affords me more pleasure than to receive letters from absent friends therefore write as often as you think *propper* and I will endeavour to answer you. I find a considerable inconvenience in conveying my letters to your sister's and greatly fear I shall not be able to send this to her, and it would be a pity for you must know that it has been written in about every room in the house and with pretty cold fingers too. When I hear one door open I march out of the other and it seems as if they were never open'd oftener.

Had Doct' S. given me a hint or an oppertunity I should have given this *said* letter to him yesterday but he gave me neither, and now I leave you trusting that you will be satisfied as to the length of my epistle and will favour me with a reply by the return of the packet. Oh by the way, I forgot to thank Doc Cobb for his advice respecting my health which is quite good excepting a cold which I caught I don't know when or how.

C.S.

ELIJAH'S LINE: *Elder Henry Cobb, came to Plymouth 1629; Samuel, 1654; Jonathan, 1694; Jonathan, 1718; Gen. Elijah Cobb, 1768; Elijah, Jr. 1799.*

CAROLINE'S LINE: *Nicholas Snow, 1600 came to Plymouth 1624, and settled in Eastham, 1644; Jabez, 1645; Edward, 1672; moved to Brewster; Joseph, 1718; Joseph, 1740; Sylvanus, 1774; Caroline, 1804.*

On May 8, 1825 Elijah Cobb, Jr. and Caroline Snow were married. Their children were, Caroline Olivia, 1826; Elijah Winslow, 1827; Helen, 1829; Mary Louisa, 1833; Alfred Sylvanus, 1836; Annette Theresa, 1838; Emily Cunningham, 1840

Elijah Cobb, Jr. died, September 2, 1861

Caroline Snow Cobb, died August 20, 1871

෧∾෨

The Rev. Daniel Greenleaf, was minister at Yarmouth between 1707 and 1727 when he moved to Boston with his wife and thirteen children. He died aged eighty-two. For two years before his death he was in bed in consequence of a severe injury, received in a fall. When an old friend sympathized, "God has laid his hand heavily upon you," Mr. Greenleaf replied, "True, but the Almighty's arm is underneath me."

℀

"There is a Cape Codder of eighty-two here in Barnstable who, when I say, 'What do you know, John?' every day, answers 'I know that my Redeemer liveth.'"

D.G.T.

℀

CAPE COD AUTUMN

BY J. MILTON MACKIE

THERE IS ALWAYS a second summer in the American year. When the September gales have swept over the woods, and shaken the first leaves of autumn to the ground; when from the gardens the more delicate buds and fragrant blossoms have passed away; when the earlier fruits have ripened and been gathered; when evening begins sooner to draw the curtains of the day, and the sun's horses start later on their morning courses; when the pleasure parties of the season are breaking up, and words of farewell are being said, and over the most buoyant mind a certain pensiveness steals, and regrets fall upon it as from out the autumnal air, then the year, which had begun to withdraw its face, turns again with a parting smile, and kisses its hand to us. Then comes a succession of golden days, when the air is still, and the heavens, slightly veiled with purple haze, are without a cloud. The autumnal flowers are arrayed in all their glory. The orchards yield up their red-sided, gold-colored apples for the winter's store. The grapes are turned to purple. The latest pears melt upon the devouring lips, and the last drops of sweetness are being distilled into the yet unplucked peaches. Now the diligent housewife gathers from out the leaves, still green, the yellow, shining quince, and, correcting its tart juices with melted sugar, lays it by for winter tea drinkings. The farmer husks his corn, making the greensward shine with the long, broad line of glittering ears. He piles up, also, the yellow pumpkins, or hangs the squashes against the wall, by their necks. His boys bring home at night the cows from still green and thickly matted meadows, with udders wide distended. The poultry yards are full of cackling, and youthful attempts at chanticleering. Fleets of geese and ducks float down the brooks, or lie moored on the ponds; and the half-grown turkey cocks gabble, and spread their tails over vast spaces of yard and pasture. This season is the mellowing of the year. In sunny European lands, and beneath sacred Oriental skies, the grapes are now trodden in the winepress; and even in our own New Jersey, the bounty of nature runs to sweet cider. The earth has put forth her great productive power, and rejoices as a woman after childbearing; the sun has done his year's work, and ripened all seeds and grains; there is food garnered up for man and beast; and the great God seems to look down out of heaven upon what He hath wrought, and pronounce it good.

It is a season to be enjoyed as one does old wine. As we bring this out of the cellar on high festal occasions, to celebrate the rite matrimonial, or to honor the anniversary of a birthday, to greet the coming of long-absent friends, and freshen the memories which run far back to days of "auld lang syne;" so this brief second summer of the year should be filled up with unusual joys. Then make a holiday. Then telegraph to your best friend to come with wife and child. Let boys and girls be loose from school, that they may go a-nutting. Let there be picnics in the glens and on the hillsides. Climb the mountains. Coast the shores. 'Tis the hunter's moon, and you may follow the path of the buck and the doe, or hey on pointer or setter. You see the breaking of day as you go on your way to lie for wild fowl, which, when it gets dark, fly overhead with whistling wings; while far off is heard the scream of the coming wild geese. Now let the reel hiss, as the line is cast from the rocks for tautog. It is the season, also, for bass fishing. Now let the lover of nature and mushrooms prevent the sun, and gather his breakfast with the dew on it. Let all men — all Yankees — eat pumpkin pie. The full moon favors husking by night; and he who finds brindled ears may kiss his partner, though he may no longer drink milk punch, for it is contrary to law. Now is "training" time; and there will be cakes at the muster for old and young — and, surely, pop beer. Now pack into country wagons, three on a seat. At morning, wind the horn, and let the hounds bay. At night, draw the bow, dance, sing, and make merry, giving God thanks; for this glorious second summer, called Indian, is given us but for seven days, or it may be ten. Then get quickly out of doors — be off — and caps in the air!

Happy harvest days! and happily did I spend them, ankle deep in thy golden sands, Cape Cod!

Perhaps I should have done better still to have gone in rough weather. The scene here, doubtless, is more characteristic when nature frowns, than when she smiles. For the Cape is decidedly tragic. Its great mood is when nature is angry, and all her elements are at war. . . . But, at the period of my visit, the stormy Cape was lying as calm and placid in the midst of the sea, as, in midsummer, rise the round tops of the Alleghanies in the untroubled southern heavens . . . by day my eyes feasted, through all the hours, on the richly colored autumnal landscape. Here stretch, for miles beyond miles, the salt meadows of Barnstable, watered not by rains and dews only, but by the monthly flowing of the tides; and these level tracts are now as tawny as the lion's skin. This, likewise, being the season when the pine trees shed their needles, the earth beneath them is no less tawny than the open marshes. And everywhere the sand of the shore is as yellow as the breast of a robin. In the warm rays of the sun it even shines like beaten gold, making the whole Cape gilt-edged. But on the uplands, the yellow runs into a russet, a richly tinted brown, and forms a background which is covered with a glory of autumnal tints, the purple of oaks and whortleberry bushes, the orange and scarlet of maples, the green of pines and cedars. There is color everywhere — on the fields and trees; on the meadows and the shores; in the hollows and around the edge of pools. Not a bush but glows, not a stone but shines. The very particles of sand, if closely inspected, flash like diamonds by candle-light; and though held in your hand, seem almost as far off and glittering as the stars in the blue twilight of the night. And these colors are all dashed together — a beautiful variety in unity — making a kaleidoscope in the eyes of every man. Still, it must be acknowledged that, as one proceeds farther upon the Cape, he notices a gradual falling off in the tone of nature's coloring, as old pictures in travelling down the course of time lose, during each century, more and more of their first blush and gorgeousness. The brilliancy of the reds and purples fades, and the browns grow duller. Even the fine gold of the pumpkins becomes tarnished; the color of animals runs to sorrel; and the habitations of man, partaking of the tendency of nature, show only the unpainted gray, or the stains of the original red and green, or the blank white of modern fashion, which makes the pupils of the eye instinctively contract to look at it. There is evidently a deficiency of coloring matter on the great painter's easel; and, at last, whether the power of nature be diminished, or this part of her work be yet raw and unfinished, there remain only the green of the pines and the yellow of the sands, wherein is no harmony.

And yet there is a notable exception to this law of gradual fading. There is more red in the faces of the Cape Codders, all the way down to Provincetown, than of any other people in the States. It is the old English red — blood-red. Though the skin be generally pretty thoroughly sunburnt, bronzed often by the glare from the salt water, yet the vermilion shines through, giving evidence of good blood and vigorous arteries. The race is, indeed, purely British. For the inhabitants are all descendants of the Puritans, or, at least, of early emigrants from Great Britain. There has been no mixture of races here. While the Cape has always been a fruitful womb of men, sending her sons out into all the broad American earth, there has, on the contrary, been no reflex tide of immigration. The Cape, therefore, is all of one blood, of one face, of one speech, of one homogeneous heart. True, there are Indians still in Marshpee; but are they not also red men? Their faces are, indeed, not a little smutted by a dash of negro blood in them; but some, fortunately still show the reddish glitter of the original copper. At least, they are not pale faced, but high colored, and come not without a degree of grace into the autumnal landscape.

And this red-facedness of the people is a great point in the description of Cape Cod. For, while the earth gradually loses its color and all its signs of vigor, as we travel toward the end of his path in the sands, we see that the lord of nature, on the contrary, remains ruddy and strong featured. Neither the weakness of the land, nor the extraordinary strength of the circumambient waters and winds had been able to produce degeneracy of the race of man. He has buffeted the waves, and overmastered them. He has sailed in the very eyes and teeth of the winds. He has fixed the floating sands, by planting them with beach grass; has sown the pine trees in furrows; has set oaks on the hilltops, that when the winds, rising in their might, threaten to tear him from the land, he may have something to hold on to; has planted the barren shore with Indian corn, putting a dead "horse foot" in every hill; has grown potatoes from seaward down to the very line of highwater mark; has turned the mud of flats to oysters; has dried the cod from the great deep into codfish; and, has manufactured the sea itself into salt. Thus has man made himself master; and though in struggling with the earth to till it, he has sometimes come upon his hip, like Jacob wrestling with the angel, and though he has often been pinched by the wind, and jammed against the leeward shore, yet, after all, he has fought the lifelong battle with the natural elements triumphantly, and still hangs out his flag of victory in the red of his face.

The Cape Codder is hardy and vigorous, and may emphatically be said to be a self-made man — external nature having done so little for him. If the bone of this young country may be considered as yet somewhat in the gristle, it is not so with that of this Cape. Its bone is mature, and its muscle, also, is as hard as rope's end and bowline. Oft pelted by storms and riddled by gales; now buried in snow banks, and never quite sure of his footing in the sands; now petrified by east winds fresh from Greenland and the ice islands, and then, in hot summer days, when there is not a breath of air to break the glazed surface of the surrounding ocean, baked as if he were an ostrich egg; obliged constantly to harass the surface of the earth, in order to extort from it even a niggardly increase; and, finally, driven in despair to the wall of the sea, and in straits compelled to sound the depths of the ocean with line, hook, and sinker, and to vex its surface with his keels, the Cape Cod man has to fight his way through existence as a gladiator his way out the ring. Of course, the feebler children die early; but the grown man is all thews and sinews. His nerves are of whalebone, and his skin will keep out water like oakum.

But while this hardness of nature seems only to develop a superior hardness in the frame of man, all lower animals are ground down in the face against it. I saw but few of them anywhere, and these mostly stunted. Scarcely a dog yelped at me from one end of the Cape to the other; for dogs do not thrive well on fish; and, besides, the waves are there to do the barking. But one would suppose it a very paradise for cats; yet, as there are no mice but water rats, so all the cats are catfish. And, accordingly, in all my lying awake to listen to the vespers which the waves on the beaches chanted through the livelong hours of the night, I heard not a single charivari. Sailors, too, are notoriously hard on horses; and drift sand, like Jordan, makes a hard road to travel. Shanghae fowls do not thrive well here. Their tails do not grow, and they become so stupid as scarcely to know how to set one foot before the other; making awkward, uncertain movements, as if they were on stilts, or even walking on their own eggs. At the cattle show in the county town where I happened to be present, the native breeds were all inferior. Whatever was big and fat was foreign born, or, at least, of blood not strictly Capish. Such was their great Ayrshire bull — as huge a monster as the Trojan horse, or the whale which, in attempting to jump the Cape, landed himself, with all his tusks and blubber, high and dry on the sands. All the fat pigs were Lady Suffolks; all the battering rams were Southdowns; and all the hens that laid golden eggs were born Poles. In fact, the only native animals at all worth the showing were the men themselves. One in particular there was at the ploughing match, who reminded me of that Triptolemus of Eleusis, to whom, first of mortals, Ceres taught the use of the plough. Cincinnatus himself could not have bent over the tails with broader shoulders, nor a nose more truly Roman. Between his legs and the length of his furrows there was a certain correspondence. When standing upright, he cast a shadow over half the scene, and dwarfed the oxen before him till they looked scarcely bigger than rats.

The inhabitants of this ridge of drift sand are remarkably thrifty . . . But the thrift of Cape Cod is not of that kind which follows fawning. Here dwells evidently an independent race of men, and all living at arm's length of each other. Even in the towns the houses do not touch, but stand apart. Every one has its separate enclosure, with plot of greensward, orchard, and garden patch. House and grounds form a distinct and independent establishment, leaning on no other for its support; and though, unfortunately, there are no plank roads in these sands, yet every front door is approached from the street by a planked pathway. . . .

And no Spaniard goes to bed earlier. He does his work by daylight, and economizes candles. All his habits are simple and natural. He dines on the stroke of noon. He takes his tea — rather weak —

at the hour when the merchant in the city sits down to dinner; and he gets up in the morning just as the town snob is going to bed. His fare, too, is simple: at breakfast, fish; at dinner, fish — fish fried, broiled, boiled, baked and chowdered! Though, probably, there is not one housewife in ten that has not a pie, or a loaf of cake, stowed away somewhere. And you shall nowhere eat such delectable "apple slump;" nowhere such doughnuts, scarcely even in Connecticut; nowhere such baked clams, out of Rhode Island and Providence Plantations. There is, also, a love of junketing and tea drinking, when neighbors come together in winter evenings, and when lassies assemble of an afternoon at a "quilting," making the bridal bedspread with innumerable stitches, and squares of white calico, upon each of which is written, in indelible ink, the name of the fair sempstress who presented it. On these occasions the number of hot biscuits and sweet cakes served up is almost incredible; and, the next morning after one, I have seen with my own eyes a small Cape boy make a hearty breakfast of pound cake with plums in it.

After all, life on the Cape is more like holiday than one might suppose who had never been there. For the men, being mostly seafaring, they do their work in all parts of the world rather than at home. The Cape Codder is omnipresent. He casts his line wherever there are codfish. If there is a school of bass or mackerel on any coast, he is after them with his seine. He chases whales from the southern frozen zone to the northern; and will, some day, throw his harpoon in the open sea at the pole. In all the steamers, liners, packets, he is captain and first mate. On the high seas, or the coast, there is no better man to handle a ship. You find him in all the crack clippers; and if a fore-and-after schooner runs her nose into any strange place, ten to one there is at her helm a Cape Codder. He has also been in his day a fighting man. Some of our proudest frigates have been sailed by him. He was on the lakes in the last war with England, and threw up his cap there; and as for privateering, it is that one among all the trades of which he is Jack that he likes best to turn his hand to. Though not much of a fist at marching on land, the Cape Codder, nevertheless, was at Bunker Hill and Saratoga, besides having fought the French and Indians in the old wars, and shouldered arms at Quebec.

But when, having sailed all the seas, and roved the world over, he comes back to his cot in the sands, the short season he spends at home is a holiday. Then give him a fast horse, and his good wife or sweetheart by his side. He must go to see all his cousins. Nor does any man have so many uncles and aunts, and kindred of various degrees. In fact, nearly all the inhabitants are first cousins, or call themselves such. Therefore, when the mariner comes home, there must necessarily be a good deal of shaking of hands and merry making. Everybody must tell him the news; and he, in return, must tell everybody of his adventures on sea and shore. He has probably seen the sea serpent — at least a mermaid, a whale, the elephant in his own country, or the Grand Mogul. Undoubtedly the longest yarns are spun on Cape Cod which are spun anywhere in this country. And be it observed, that the Cape Cod man, let him go to whatever part of the world he may, is sure to come back. His local tastes never die out; and where'er he roams, at every step away he drags a lengthening cable. If he run a packet between Boston and some other of our principal seaport cities, he does not remove his family to town; but, the moment he gets on shore, hies away to the Cape. He does not like the air of great cities, and cannot really feel at home anywhere that there is not sand under his feet, or even a little of it running over his shoe quarters. . . .

— From FROM CAPE COD TO DIXIE AND THE TROPICS

J. Milton Mackie tells us in a preface dated 1864: "These sketches of travel were written before the breaking out of the present rebellion in the Southern States; but as, on the occurrence of this event, letters very properly yielded to arms, they were withheld from publication." *The book appeared that same year.*

౿ఌౖ

1849
ANOTHER VIEW

BY N. PARKER WILLIS

ON THE RAISED LEG of New England, (which Cape, or Barnstable county, looks to be, on the map,) the proposed *ship canal* from Buzzard's Bay to Massachusetts Bay, would be the well-placed *garter*. Mr. Everett, by-the-way, very felicitously called this peninsular Cape, the outstretched arm which Providence held forth, to enclose, with protecting welcome, the Pilgrims of the Mayflower; but I insist, notwithstanding, that it resembles more a *raised leg, clad with the spurred boot of a cavalier* — Falmouth, at the spacious opening of its top, the long island off Chatham forming the long rowel of its spur, and the Elizabeth cluster, from Naushon to Kutiyhunk, furnishing its appropriate edging of lace.

The railroad, extending only to Sandwich, barely crosses the line of this proposed garter canal. My companion and guide intended to lodge ten miles further down, at Yarmouth. We found an old-fashioned stage, waiting for passengers "bound down," and, rejoicing in it as a long missed and pleasant friend, I mounted to the top for one of the pleasantest summer-evening rides that I remember. With a full moon rising before us, a delicious southern breeze laden with the breath of sweet-briar and new hay, and a consequent mood rather sentimental than otherwise, I commenced acquaintance with Cape Cod — a country, the mention of which does not (usually, at least,) call up associations of so tender a complexion.

We were fourteen passengers, but the carrying of us and our baggage seemed to be a secondary part of the driver's vocation. He was apparently the agent, parcel-carrier, commission-broker, apologist, and bearer of special intelligence for the whole population. His hat was the "way-mail," and, with his whip and the reins of four horses in his hands, he uncovered, and transacted business constantly and expeditiously. The presence of fourteen detained listeners was no barrier to the delivery of confidential messages. We pulled up before one of the most respectable-looking houses on the road, and a gentleman came out, evidently prepared to receive something he had expected.

"Mr. B——," said the driver, "told me to tell yer he couldn't send yer that money today."

"Why not?" said the expectant, clearly disappointed.

" 'Cause he had to go to Court."

"Wal!" said the gentleman, putting his hands in his pockets and giving the driver a sly look as he turned on his heel, "you hain't pocketed it yourself, have yer?"

"Tluck, tluck!" and along we went again, pulling up, a mile further on, to receive a parcel from a man in an apron.

"Seventy-five cents to be paid on that!" said the mechanic, holding out his hand to receive from the driver what his customer was to pay on delivery — an advance, or loan on security, of course, which the driver handed over without objection.

Presently we were stopped by a man with a letter in his hand. The driver was a minute or two deciphering the address, and, after some delay, to which none of the fourteen passengers made any objection, he discovered that it was directed to Boston, and he was to drop it into the office at Yarmouth.

"Anything to pay on't?" asked the man.

"No. Tluck, tluck!" and away we went again.

These, and slighter errands, made a difference of perhaps half an hour in our time of arrival — a tax upon transient passengers for the benefit of regular customers on the road, but which, like most other arrangements of the Cape, was indicative of the primitive simplicity of old time.

.   .   .   .   .

The small village of Hyannis, which is five miles south of the usual line of travel, is upon a bank of sand, which affords only a scanty hold to vegetation, and it looks like a settlement of Socialists, or like the ideal of Pitcairn's island — so all alike are its houses, and so tidy, thrifty, homely, and after one pattern, are all the surroundings of each. There seems to be but one idea of the structure of a dwelling — to have nothing superfluous and to paint the remainder white. The garden fences are made of close boards, to keep out the sand in windy weather, and every house stands in a white box, accordingly. These are, almost without exception, the residences of the families of seafaring men, and we were told that we should be safe in calling any man "Captain" whom we might meet in Hyannis. They raise better captains than trees, here. The stunted pine, with its bald roots, looks scrofulous and pinched, and the only shade-tree which seems to thrive is the silver-leaved poplar, of which we saw, here and there one, in the boxed up gardens.

.   .   .   .   .

Wherever we chanced to be, at about the dinner hour, we were kept to dine — losing time for me, as our entertainers were of a class that is the same all over the world, and, delightful as was their hospitality, it furnished of course, neither material nor liberty of description. . . . I must mention the introduction to a centenarian, whom I noticed that every one called "the old *gentleman*," though he enjoys a celebrity as having been *servant to the father* of James Otis the patriot. It was a curious confusion of dates, to hear a patriot, who has gone down to history, spoken of, by a living person, as "young Jem" — the name by which the old man invariably designates James Otis.

· · · · ·

The houses in this intermediate region, are of a most curiously inelegant plainness — the roof all painted red, the sides of rusty white if painted at all, and the model invariably the same, and such as a carpenter would build who thought only of the cheapest shelter. Ornament of any kind seems as unknown as beggary. The portion of a house, which in every foreign country is decently concealed, — and unobserved access to which, is contrived, at the humblest cottage of Europe, in some way or other, — is here the most conspicuous and unsheltered of the appendages to a dwelling-house — an insensibility to delicacy, the more strange, as the females of this part of the country are proverbially and fastidiously modest. The next two most conspicuous things are the school-house and the graveyard — life's beginning and its ending — the latter a tree-less collection of white stones occupying, everywhere, the summit of the highest ground.

· · · · ·

Whether the sandy soil, which seems so unfavorable to ostentation, is also the enemy which the climate seems to contain, as well, for the proportions of the female bust, I can scarce venture to say; but flatness of chest in the forms of the feminine population of Cape Cod, is curiously universal. Those to whom I spoke on the subject, attributed it partly to the fact that the mothers of most of them had been obliged, in the absence of husbands and sons at sea, to do much of the labor of the farm, and all superfluities had of course been worked into muscle. This is somewhat verified by the manly robustness of the well-limbed sons of these spartan mothers, but still it is unfortunate that the daughters, (as far as I could judge by their arms and shoulders,) seem to have inherited the loss without the elsewhere equivalent.

— From HURRY-GRAPHS; OR, SKETCHES OF SCENERY, CELEBRITIES AND SOCIETY, TAKEN FROM LIFE. Second Edition. New York: 1851.

☙

1848–1873
THE RAILROAD COMES TO CAPE COD

BY DONALD G. TRAYSER

MAY 26   Today in 1848 marked the beginning of the railroad service to Cape Cod. It was noted with an enthusiastic celebration. The line extending down from Agawam was complete. The depot built by the Boston and Sandwich Glass Company was ready, gaily decorated with greenery and bouquets, and set with tables for luncheon, with cut and colored Sandwich glassware bearing sandwiches on each plate. The first train left the Old Colony depot at Boston at 9. A.M. with a large party of notables. It arrived at Sandwich at 1 P.M., a train of fourteen cars, festively decorated. The engine was "the noble Cape Codder" hung with flags, evergreens, bouquets, and suspended above it a "life size" neatly carved wooden cod. As this rare sight puffed down the rails into Sandwich a waiting throng of nearly 800 Cape Codders broke into a long, loud shout of greeting. After the luncheon there were addresses by many distinguished citizens, including J. H. Page of New Bedford, one of the Old Colony directors, President E. H. Derby of the Old Colony, and Josiah Quincy, Mayor of Boston. The train left Sandwich at 4, and arrived at Boston at 9. It was a great day.

But the arrival of the railway was not warmly greeted by all. One old Cape Cod mariner, after seeing his first train, remarked: "Why, there's nought manly about it. Watch a ship now, with her sails bellying out, laying down to it just enough to show she feels the breeze, tossing the spray from her bows, and lifting her head over the seas as if she stepped 'em. There's something like life there. There's something about a horse; he steps as if he knew he was going and fond of his duty, and able to do it. But that lubber — bah — comes insinivating, sneaking along, crawling on his belly like a thundering long snake with a pipe in his mouth."

.   .   .   .   .

July 8   Flags flew, bells rang, and a "huge throng" of some three thousand persons greeted, in the early evening of this day in 1854, the arrival of the first railroad train in Hyannis. The extension from Sandwich to Hyannis had taken nearly six years to build. On the great day when the first train rolled down, many Hyannis people drove over to Barnstable, to ride with the first train into their village. So many crowded into the four cars that only a few more could be squeezed in at Yarmouth. An "elegant" new depot was ready, with "a large spacious room, richly carpeted and as elegantly furnished as a gentleman's parlor. Sofas of luxurious laces, chairs, rockers, and a table of costly style and structure, a mirror in which you can see yourself in full as others see you, what nots, yes, even what nots . . . Another saloon so richly and luxuriously furnished cannot be found in any depot on the Cape." So the contemporary account related. The elegant new depot of 1854 is still the Hyannis depot — one of the few pre-Civil War buildings still standing on the main street of this busy village.

· · · · ·

July 22   On this day in 1873 the first railroad train rolled into Provincetown, and a gay celebration marked the occasion. The railroad had reached Wellfleet in 1870, in 1872 the Cape Cod Railroad was merged with the Old Colony, and in '73 the fourteen-mile link from Wellfleet to Provincetown was opened to travel. Perhaps the story which will last longest about the Provincetown end of the railroad is that of the visitor who kept at the conductor to let her know when the train reached Provincetown. She varied her reminder once by asking if he was sure the train would stop at Provincetown. He replied, the old story goes, "Lady, if it doesn't, there will be a dem big splash."

— From ONCE UPON A TIME ON CAPE COD

⤪

The great Atlantic Railroad for old Cape Cod; all hail!
Bring on the locomotive, lay down the iron rail;
Across the Eastham prairies, by steam we're bound to go,
The railroad cars are coming, let's all get up and crow.
The little dogs in Dogtown will wag their little tails,
They'll think that something's coming, a-riding on the rails.
      — By the Reverend A. J. Church from verses composed for
         a celebration held to welcome the railroad to Wellfleet.

For a long time after the coming of the railroad, the Cape Cod stockholders in the company, who comprised almost everyone of any means, were offered a free round trip to Boston once every year on what was known as Stockholders' Day. The train on that day carried vast numbers of Cape Cod men, women, and children, including always one old lady who had no business to transact in the city and was terrified of it. She would take her knitting and sit all day in the Boston station until time to return.

౿∿౿

1825–1888
SANDWICH GLASS

BY FRANK W. CHIPMAN

WHILE MR. JARVES ESTABLISHED his Sandwich Factory, in 1825, as a glass blowing plant, in conformity with the universal method of commercial glass-making at that time, it is important to keep in mind the fact that the Sandwich Glass which became famous and distinctive was the pressed ware. This, in a large measure, superseded the blown glass after 1830.

In the Sandwich Factory the glass was pressed in metal moulds with the figures cut in the plunger. The blown-in-the-mould method was tried with wooden moulds and was unsuccessful because the molten glass ignited the moulds. It is said that a carpenter originated this idea of the wooden mould and Mr. Jarves gave it a fair trial. Necessity fathered the introduction later of moulds of steel, iron and brass. These were made in sets, the lower dish having a pattern traced upon its surface. Into this receptacle was poured the molten glass and a second steel dish or plunger was pressed down upon it.

The earlier patterns were of old Irish and English designs, as the first workmen came from those countries, but, later, designs of a distinctly American tendency were originated, equally lovely in beauty of sentiment and form.

Lace glass was originated in the Boston and Sandwich Glass Factory about 1835. This lace glass is superior to any pressed glass ever made, not only in the excellence of quality of the metal but also in the marvelous construction of the moulds. Some compound was used in mixing the metal which brought a silvery sheen to the glass which was never equalled in any other factory. The designs were of extreme fineness and very beautiful, giving the pattern a frosted, lacy appearance. These lace articles are easily the aristocrats of the Glass Kingdom.

The moulds in which Sandwich Lace Glass and other intricate designs were pressed were not made in a day or a week. Months were required for a single mould, as can be attested with authority. In one instance, as revealed in the letter of Deming Jarves to Daniel Webster, the mould that produced the famous "Union Bowl" required the constant services of two men for a period of six months.

· · · · ·

Patterns of Old Sandwich Glass were indeed numerous and varied. I have been able to authenticate no less than 158. It is necessary to study and become familiar with a wide range of standard designs made in this Factory if one is desirous of identifying Old Sandwich. In the first place let it be known that not all the designs of Sandwich origin were used on all the different glass articles made.

The cup plate designs of George Washington, Bunker Hill, Henry Clay, Cadmus, Constitution, Heart, Fort Meigs, Butterfly, Chancellor Livingstone, Lafayette, Victoria, Prince of Wales, and Benjamin Franklin are not found on other articles. The Eagle dated 1831 was confined to cup plates, although an Eagle pattern not dated is occasionally found on larger plates and dishes. The Lyre pattern is found in mugs and salts as well as in cup plates. Dolphin stems were particularly applied to candlesticks but compotes and whale oil lamps were sometimes supported by Dolphin standards. The Bee Hive and Thistle pattern on glass plates is not to be found on goblets or other tableware.

Old Sandwich goblets exceed all other articles in number of patterns and variety of design. There are about 150 variations of size and patterns in goblets. These are found in fruit, floral, animal, scenic and conventional designs.

Standard designations in table ware, which always included goblets, are Bell Flower (five variations), Chrysanthemum Leaf, Fern, Double Fern, Inverted Fern, Daisy, Moss Rose, Ivy, Dewdrop or Pinpoint, Tulip, Primrose, Cat-o-Ninetail, Hairpin, Bleeding Heart, Acanthus, Morning Glory, Fuchsia, Acorn, Pineapple, Holly, Holly and Blue Jay, Peacock, Mulberry, Peacock Feather, Grape (five variations), Blackberry, Strawberry, Cherry, Oak Leaf, Lion, Deer, Polar Bear and Seal, Squirrel, Dog, Cat, Frog, Bear, Westward Ho, Owl, Buckle, Loop, Loop and Jewel (stippled), Shell, Fence, Lincoln, Drape, Curtain, Raised Diamond or Diamond Point, Grant, Thumbprint, Block, Waffle, Cable, Bull's Eye or Thousand Eyes, Parthenon, Huber, Utica, Hamilton, Hob Nail, Sandwich or Cane Seat, Grecian Border, Centennial, Horn of Plenty (two varieties), Mitchell, Ashburton, Star and Punty or Star and Bull's Eye, Star and Feather, Shield, Fleur de Lis, Snake Skin and other conventional designs. A number of these patterns were made with stippled surface.

The Hairpin and Fleur de Lis pattern, limited to lace cup plates and cake plates, is one of the most charming creations in all pressed glass.

· · · · ·

Salts were made in shapes, sizes and designs of wide range. There was the Lafayette Boat Salt for one. It has the name of Lafayette on the stern and Sandwich in the bottom. This was the only glass article made in the Factory that was marked with such distinction.

Some very fine lace-glass salts were produced in Boat, Sleigh, Sofa and Cradle types. Heavy plain glass Colonial salts in oval and rectangular shape, some footed, were early products. Bird salts, Barrel salts with metal tops (some of these in color), salts with three faces and acid finish, and the little oval kind with small flutings complete the group. Cruets for both metal and glass castors, with engraved vinegars, salts and peppers were plentifully produced.

Tumblers, both plain and fluted, were turned out in abundance. Some of these were beautifully engraved. Cream pitchers, sugar bowls, compotes, butter dishes, spoonholders and celery holders (upright), as well as decanters, were constant and standard productions in the floral, fruit, animal and conventional patterns. Nappies, frequently called sauce dishes, many of which were footed, were supplied with every set of table ware.

Sandwich finger bowls in beautiful ruby, cobalt blue, magenta, purple and canary colors were unsurpassed. Some of these were richly engraved but most of them were without pattern.

· · · · ·

Large flint glass plates were a standard production. The Sheaf of Wheat, Liberty Bell, Grant, Garfield and the "Give Us This Day Our Daily Bread" were the predominating designs in this line.

Flower vases in flint and colored glass with floral decorations were among the easily marketed articles of Sandwich make.

Lace glass dishes with covers, a few cup plates and miniature sets of table ware, in purple and sapphire blue, were choice articles of Sandwich origin.

.   .   .   .   .

Lapidary and blow glass toppers of all sizes and shapes were turned out by the thousand.

Glass pens with their vari-colored threads of glass and bird ornaments seemed ever to attract the attention of glass buyers. Making threaded ware required more skill than most of the other methods of production. Wines, goblets, bottles and flasks were the articles selected for this decoration. The article to be threaded was attached to a revolving rod and kept whirling. The glassmaker gathered a slim rod of colored glass, usually ruby, sometimes blue, shaped it to a fine point and at red heat carefully made a contact with the revolving piece, thus depositing those tiny rings of red or blue around the article.

Glass bears, usually black, sometimes white, blue, or purple, and made for match holders, had a place on the kitchen mantel of every Sandwich home.

Toothpick holders were never omitted from the Sandwich stock of glass articles. Pin trays also served their purpose in most households at that day.

Punch bowls, beer tumblers, wines, whiskey glasses and egg cups were frequently included in filling an order.

Prominent in the Sandwich list was the Lion pattern. The king of beasts posed on the foot and stem and also on the cover of compotes, sugars and butters. The Lion was made in acid finish.

Pickle dishes, honey dishes and ink wells were turned out daily by the glassmakers in Sandwich. Mirror knobs in opalescent hue, curtain pulls in amber, blue and purple, plain and opalescent knobs for bureau and table drawers comprised an important branch of the industry.

Small glass mugs with animal designs and A B C plates for youngsters had a fixed place in the regular catalogue.

Sandwich bottles were largely of the perfume, wine and smelling salt varieties. Colored and plain, the crucifix was another Factory special. Colored pint flasks, single and double with both straight and crooked necks, were a striking specialty. Cut glass bibles for paper weight use supplied many gift orders.

Beaded edges characterized a large proportion of flat ware.

· · · · ·

Studded glass table ware, commonly designated a Pin Point pattern, makes strong appeal to the glass collector. Marble or slag glass with its irregular coloring, and splash glass, also colored in disorderly fashion, have a niche in the glass hall of fame of Sandwich origin.

Glass hats in amber, yellow, purple and blue; sleighs and stoves were among the novelties of Sandwich make.

A very rare specimen of Old Sandwich is the Peacock plate. This plate was made in four and six-inch sizes. The Peacock occupies the centre of the plate and its tail, at full spread, covers the rest of the inner surface.

It can readily be understood that during the early days of the Factory the variety of patterns, as well as the diversity of articles made, was limited. This was especially true until after 1830 when the process of moulding was discovered and adopted.

Whale oil lamps, petticoat and squash lamps, candlesticks and some tableware, such as tumblers, goblets, salts, nappies, sugar bowls and pitchers, were turned out during the first few years and these were more varied in shape and size than in design. In fact, all early blown glass was somewhat plain.

· · · · ·

In determining the patterns, colors and periods of Old Sandwich Glass, I have been guided by, and informed through, the following sources of knowledge: Contacts with the glassmakers, handling the moulds, watching the operations, searching the early records, examining specimens of the glass and the fragments that have always been available in the Factory Yard and which furnish unimpeachable proof of color and design.

Many pieces of Old Sandwich Glass have a brilliant sheen, a bell-like ring and a soft, smooth texture but these are contributing features and not determining.

Many patterns of Old Sandwich Glass had a stippled surface,

others a snake skin surface and still others were heavily figured on the outside. All three types thus described produce no ring.

Concerning the pontil mark or punty mark, as it was termed in the Factory, I would inform my readers that while this is usually to be relied upon as an evidence of early glass, it must be distinguished from the imitation which is to be found in reproductions.

The footed ware, except goblets, made previous to 1850, old paper weights, vases and bottles can be identified by a rough uneven pontil, but the reproduction, if examined with due care, will reveal numerous chippings and less bulge.

My father, Thomas H. Chipman, was a puntier and by the use of a revolving emery wheel he smoothed the rough pontil and polished the mark with a cork wheel. It frequently happened that Sandwich people who owned early glass articles with a rough pontil that caused an uneven position on the table or mantel, would bring these pieces back to the Factory (perhaps twenty years after their manufacture) and in spare time my father would grind off the pontil and smooth up the article. Thus it can be understood that some of the old specimens found in Sandwich, or even elsewhere, without pontil, might well be of an earlier period than the collector could establish.

·   ·   ·   ·   ·

Snake Skin and Lace glass are not at all alike yet collectors frequently confuse them. Usually the confusion arises from the fact that they never have compared the two types. Essentially the difference is this: Snake Skin has a very dull, rough surface. It imitates the scaly skin of the snake very realistically and the design is always in irregular, rounding lines resembling those on the skin of a snake.

Snake Skin glass is the one striking example of Old Sandwich Glass that does not have that clear bell-like ring. Glass surfaced in this manner, or stippled, will not permit resonance.

Lace glass, on the other hand, has a brilliant silvery sheen, in contrast to the dull rough surface of Snake Skin glass. The fine pinpoint effect unmistakably resembles delicate lace work.

It is not an uncommon occurrence for me to receive communications which seek information that will enable the enquirer to distinguish the late reproductions of lace glass from the genuine old Sandwich lace ware.

It requires but a moment to determine the difference. The reproduction is never as bright, plainly lacks the texture, depth, and perfection of design, and weighs decidedly less than the genuine. The ring also is missing.

. . . . .

The processes of engraving and etching glass are too often confused though the methods are entirely different. The engraving of glass was really a process of cutting by means of a sharp steel or copper wheel disk with which the designs were engraved upon the article. Real skill was required in this operation. A trained eye and steady hand were the requisites.

Narrow glass panes, which were installed on each side of the front doors in the old wood and brick houses of a century ago, were produced extensively at Sandwich. These glass panels were of acid finish, with scroll engraving. One need only to visit the South End of Boston, where the well-to-do of those days resided, to find these windows still adorning the old doorways. Frequently, too, they may be observed in the rural communities of New England where the old country house has not been re-modeled. This holds true also in New York and in the Middle West.

. . . . .

Golden Ruby! These are magic words when glass is mentioned in Sandwich. Why — since the method of making ruby glass was discovered by Johann Knuckel in Berlin in the Seventeenth Century? The answer is obvious: Because the perfection attained in ruby glass at the Sandwich Factory has never been excelled before or since.

The Sandwich Ruby Glass is like solidified flame. It has the indescribable character of a red and gold sunset. There is an elusiveness of tone in its living red that not even the opal glass of Sandwich, with its lovely changing colors, possesses. It causes one to add mentally those touches of changing blue and purple, of sulphur yellow, that characterize a November sky at daylight's end. One wonders why, because to actual vision there is nothing observable but shifting depths of ruby red. Therein lies the marvel of this glass that Sandwich workmen created — it lures the fancy of the beholder, even as it tempted and fired the imagination of its creators.

During the later years of the Factory's operation milk white glass, plain, with openwork edges, figured and in basket weave, was turned out in abundance . . . all through these years, from 1831 on, an abundance of beautiful colored glass [was] made and sold.

Here again the Sandwich Factory led all rivals. It is freely admitted that the Golden Ruby, Sapphire Blue, Opalescent, Jade, Amber, Purple, Magenta, Yellow, Salmon, Pink and Green shades evolved in Sandwich were not paralleled in the glass industry.

The beautiful overlay lamps, jade salts, tinted toilet sets, vases and vari-colored tableware manufactured in Sandwich were unequalled in the pressed glass field. In no other factory was the overlay work done in three colors.

·　·　·　·　·

The Sandwich Historical Society has in its rooms some very fine specimens donated by the families of old glassworkers and the exhibition is open for public inspection during the summer months.

An outstanding article in the Society's treasure group is an old ruby glass lantern made for the Lincoln presidential campaign. This square beacon bears the engraved name of the martyred President and was carried through the streets of Sandwich by the Lincoln paraders. The inscription reads "Lincoln and Hamlin."

Worthy of mention in unique design, also, are:

A tall, gracefully-shaped glass goblet with a tiny china doll inserted in the stem and richly engraved with this inscription: "To Rebecca Newcomb, our beloved teacher, from her pupils of the Class of 1860." This memento, in all its original beauty, is now owned by Miss Martha Newcomb, of Sandwich, niece of the deceased recipient.

A shapely, well proportioned lamp with a china doll standing erect in the stem is the property of Miss Ella Briggs.

An overlay ruby jug intricately cut, with stopper to match, and the designations "Whiskey" and "Rum" engraved on the sides; a marvelous lamp with frosted and engraved dome, prism danglers, bronze stem in Corinthian style with bust of Washington in bas-relief encircled by a wreath and surmounted by a spread Eagle — these prize pieces are owned by Mrs. George S. Wing, of Sandwich, and were the gifts from the Company to her grandfather, William Boyden.

Some fifty years back, Angus R. Pope, the local ice dealer, when delivering ice in the vicinity of the Glass Factory, was occasionally asked to leave a cake on the window sill of the Packing Room. A package of glass was usually left on the same sill which Mr. Pope accepted as his recompense for the ice. Most of this uniquely-acquired collection is still in Mr. Pope's possession.

— From THE ROMANCE OF OLD SANDWICH GLASS

Frank W. Chipman's book, published in Sandwich in 1932, is dedicated "To The Memory Of My Father and Mother Sandwich Glassworkers Who Took Pride In Their Craftsmanship."

இ∾௦

A TALE THAT IS TOLD

BY NANCY W. PAINE SMITH

OLD CAPTAIN NEWCOMB was dead. "Like as a shock of corn cometh in in his season." A long line walked in slow procession from the front door of Captain Newcomb's: first the widow, as was decent, then the grandchildren from Chicago, after them the nephews and nieces, followed by the cousins, and finally the neighbors and the members of the church and the lodge. Down the front walk bordered by box, through the front gate flanked by lilacs, they carried their burden. They passed the boathouse with the old captain's dory and its killick dry and clean, with ropes neatly coiled and with nets and sails in order along the side. Toward the tolling bell they bore him, as if he would still obey the summons he had never disregarded. They turned away from the harbor and from the tide, for ninety years the dial of his days, and moved up to the Newcomb lot in the graveyard on the hill. There they laid him down near the stones of "Samuel Newcomb, Jr., died at Port au Prince, aged twenty-five," and "Jonathan Newcomb, lost at sea, aged nineteen," and "Delia, infant daughter of Samuel and Rebecca," and "Lydia, aged four years." They laid him very near Rebecca, beloved consort of Samuel Newcomb, aged fifty-five years and months and days.

All these were in a row with a little space at the end of the row for Myra, the widow, when her turn should come. At the other side of the lot lay the old captain's father and mother whom nobody in the world remembered, now the old captain was dead, and in the far end of the lot Grandsir Newcomb, "A Revolutionary Soldier."

. . . . .

When all was done, part of the group at the grave walked back to the house with Myra, part lingered talking of the old captain and telling over again the tale of his life. Great-aunt Jerusha spoke the epilogue, "What will Myra put on the cap'n's stone to tell what he was? Will she write, 'His works do follow him'?" And all who heard Great-aunt Jerusha speak knew of what she was speaking.

. . . . .

The old house, substantial without, set-in-order within, made plain its story to all who would read it.

For a hundred years it had stood by the shore, handy to the boats and the fishing, but not so close to the water as to be swept by a spring tide in a northeaster; not too near the howling in the rigging of a stormy night, but just up from the rising. It stood low and four-square, facing the south, shielded from the northers by a little hill behind. Its shingled roof and sides easily repaired, its frame braced against the big chimney and held together by oak pins which neither moth nor rust could corrupt, the old house proclaimed permanence and thrift.

Myra, the widow, received her guests with a dignity that forbade questions, though the conversation was reminiscent and personal. The old captain had often said of her, "Myra Miller, Myra Miller, the smartest woman alive."

Nobody ever contradicted the old captain on that, for he knew whereof he spoke, and the neighborhood knew and recalled now how the old captain had courted Myra when she was a young girl, and he was an old bachelor, and how he had courted her too long and had not made her an offer, and how one night when he complimented her, "Myra Miller, Myra Miller, smartest girl alive," she bade him good-night with, "Smart enough to send you kiting. You need not call again." And Samuel did not dare go again, and he married Rebecca, who was a good housekeeper and always pleasant, and never made him walk a crack.

Now, when Rebecca had scrubbed away her days and Samuel had

retired from sea, and his boys were dead and his daughter married in Chicago, he went again to Myra, and on the first call he said:

"Myra Miller, Myra Miller, smartest woman alive, will you have me now? I have twenty-five thousand dollars in savings banks, High Toss and a pew in the meeting-house."

And Myra answered, "Samuel, I will marry you next Sunday after the sermon, but when I go to High Toss, Aunt Hitty goes with me. I must provide for Aunt Hitty."

And Samuel said, "Aunt Hitty is welcome in my house and at my board."

So, after the sermon, Samuel rose from his pew and Myra rose from hers, and they stood together before the minister and made their age-old vows, and Myra went home to High Toss with Samuel, and that was fourteen years ago. All this the neighbors knew and, after the funeral, repeated.

* * * * *

The oldest man in town is dead, and those who knew him talked of him, one with another. They did not make mention of his honesty, of his thrift, of his loyalty and neighborly kindness, known to all: these were accepted as we accept the light of day. God alone marked the day when it was light and said it was good. But there had been one revealing incident in the life of the old man that told his story. As the words on the old slate,

"Samuel Newcomb 1756-1840
A Revolutionary Soldier"

identified and distinguished him from the long line of that name, so "Aunt Hitty's Board Money" is the old captain's own story.

They told it the Sunday after the funeral. They repeated it Thanksgiving Day afternoon. They wove it into their nets as they sat on the sand and mended them. They quilted it into the quilts at sewing circle.

"The old cap'n left no will," they said, "and that is right. The widow will get her thirds and that will pay her well, and there will be something for all the grandchildren, (no doubt some of them need it,) and Myra has put the five-dollar bill into the contribution box at last."

"Fifty-two times for fourteen years," they reckoned, "she has handled that money. Ten times fifty-two is five hundred and twenty; four times fifty is two hundred and four times two is eight; seven hundred and twenty-eight times Myra has passed the board money to Aunt Hitty and Aunt Hitty has passed it back to the cap'n, and the old cap'n has passed it back to Myra, the same identical five-dollar bill."

"You see," they explained, "Myra would not marry the old cap'n unless she could bring Hitty with her to High Toss. Samuel agreed, but, when Myra and Aunt Hitty got there, he said, 'Of course Aunt Hitty is welcome, but she must pay her board.' When he saw Myra's black eyes aflashing, he said, 'Jes'so, jes'so, Myra, you may have the board money for spending money.' So nigh a thousand times the old five-dollar bill has traveled from Aunt Hitty to Samuel, from Samuel to Myra, from Myra to Aunt Hitty, and swing your partners round the circle. Samuel, close as he was, never caught on."

— From OUR HERITAGE, privately printed, 1930

．　　．　　．　　．　　．

A Cape man's recipe for a happy marriage: "I luff and bear away when she riles, she luffs and bears away when I rile."

The Business of the Sea

THE BUSINESS OF THE SEA

WE'VE RODE the wave, in storm and calm,
    From boyhood's days till now;
Still let us guide our swift-winged craft,
    And not the snail-paced plow.

We leave to you your verdant fields,
    Your crops on hill and lea,
Our home is still 'mid Cape Cod sands,
    Our farms, *the broad blue sea.*

We lift the Pilgrims' war-cry still,
    "For Freedom and for God,"
And wear as proudest title yet,
    "The sons of old Cape Cod."

                    —T. N. STONE, 1868

❧

I might here recreate your wearied eyes with a hunting spectacle of the greatest chase that nature yieldeth; I mean the killing of a whale.

                    — PURCHAS

In view of Cape Cod's great whalefishing and fishing history, it is strange to reflect that the first settlers were drawn here by no vision of the enormous future wealth that was to be speared with harpoons and hauled up in nets such as had dazzled Captain John Smith twenty-odd years before. They were seeking what pioneers have sought on so many American frontiers, food for cattle, and the salt-hay marshes around Sandwich and Barnstable and Yarmouth were the Cape's attraction. Their first concern was to clear and plant their farms. But the endless schools of darkly moving cod and flashing mackerel charging the Cape Cod coast and the great herds of whales sporting in the Bay and sometimes floundering ashore to die could not for long fail to suggest thoughts of profit; particularly, at first, the stranded whales.

God sent them, so in some places a part of the booty was always set aside to pay the minister. Very early towns were quarreling over their rights to whales in trouble on debatable beaches. It began to seem that God was not casting them away fast enough. Taking a leaf from the Indians' book, Cape Cod men and boys started going out in small boats to frighten them ashore or, failing that, to kill them in the water and tow them in.

൙

1605
INDIAN WHALERS

BY GEORGE WEYMOUTH

ONE ESPECIAL THING is their manner of killing the whale, which they call Powdawe; and will describe his form; how he bloweth up the water; and that he is 12 fathoms long; and that they go in company of their King with a multitude of their boats, and strike him with a bone made in fashion of a harping iron fastened to a rope, which they make great and strong of the bark of trees, which they veere out after him; then all their boats come about him, and as he riseth above the water, with their arrows they shoot him to death; when they have killed him & dragged him to shore, they call all their chief lords together, & sing a song of joy; and those chief lords, whom they call Sagamos, divide the spoil, and give to every man a share, which pieces so distributed they hang up about their houses for provision: and when they boil them, they blow off the fat, and put to their peas, maise, and other pulse, which they eat.

— From his JOURNAL

The Indians taught Cape Cod to whale, and Cape Cod taught the world. Men had hunted the whale, of course, long before America was discovered, but the art — in the old accounts it is always called an "art" — of whalefishery as it was known in the great whaling days was developed on the Cape. In 1690 Ichabod Paddock of Yarmouth was called to Nantucket "to instruct the people in the art of killing whales in boats from the shore." Late in the next century Captain Jesse Holbrook of Wellfleet, famous for having taken fifty-four Sperm Whales, was employed for twelve years teaching whalefishery in a school in London.

Nantucket very early, New Bedford later, pulled ahead of their teacher in the number of men and vessels employed but, until the Revolution, Wellfleet, Cape Cod's "greasiest" town, ranked third among the whaling ports of Massachusetts. The war destroyed the fleet and the people were too poor to rebuild it.

Provincetown later became Cape Cod's great whaling port.

ᏨᏯ

1706
"ALL OR MOST OF US"

ALL OR MOST of us are concerned in fitting out Boats to catch and take Whales when ye Season of ye Year serves ... when we have taken any whale or whales, our Custom is to Cutt them up and take away ye Fat and ye Bone of such Whales as are brought in, and afterwards to let ye Body of ye Lean of whales Lye on Shoar in lowe water to be washt away by yea sea, being of noe value nor worth anything to us. ...
— From a petition made by some citizens of
Eastham to the General Court

Lookout stations lined the Bay coast and, in some towns, every citizen was required by law to serve his turn in watching for whales. When a school hove in sight, the lookout shouting "Towner!" brought the people running. "Towner" is an Indian word meaning that the whales have been sighted twice.

This cry on a Sabbath more than once emptied a meeting-house of worshippers before you could say Amen. But it rang out less often as time went by and whales grew scarce. The whalemen, obliged to build bigger boats and sail greater distances to fish, now began cutting in the whales at sea — an important step towards deep-sea whaling — and bringing the blubber back in casks to the tryworks on the shore.

Their common prey were the midget Blackfish, the "gamesome and light-hearted" Humpback and the huge Right Whale. The profits were great, the voyages short, the hazards slight. Greenhorn whalemen, it is said, were sometimes prevented from gazing into the gaping jaws of the Right Whale lest the awful sight scare them witless, but this monster is less formidable than it appears. The jaws are toothless and the cavernous red mouth is latticed closely with pendant strips of baleen or whalebone through which it sieves the tiny sea-life it feeds upon. There is considerable danger from its flukes, for the Right Whale, peaceable by nature, will attack a whaleboat when roused and with these mighty weapons can knock men overboard or stove a boat. But if the whale was agile, so were the whalemen, and timing was of the essence of their art. Death or injury to the shore-whalefishers from enemy action was almost unknown.

In the mid-eighteenth century this story changed.

Gambolling in tropic or semi-tropic seas swam a different kind of whale, far more valuable, inexpressibly more dangerous. No other true whale has teeth. This whale's tremendous underslung jaw is lined with tusks. It has a mean disposition, and it fights, as the whalemen said, "at both ends;" that is, with its flukes and with its jaws and head.

❦

THE BATTERING–RAM

BY HERMAN MELVILLE

ERE QUITTING, for the nonce, the Sperm Whale's head, I would have you, as a sensible physiologist, simply — particularly remark its front aspect, in all its compacted collectedness. I would have you investigate it now with the sole view of forming to yourself some un-exaggerated, intelligent estimate of whatever battering-ram power may be lodged there. Here is a vital point; for you must either satis-factorily settle this matter with yourself, or for ever remain an in-fidel as to one of the most appalling, but not the less true events, per-haps anywhere to be found in all recorded history.

You observe that in the ordinary swimming position of the Sperm Whale, the front of his head presents an almost wholly vertical plane to the water; you observe that the lower part of that front slopes considerably backwards, so as to furnish more of a retreat for the long socket which receives the boom-like lower jaw; you observe that the mouth is entirely under the head, much in the same way, indeed, as though your mouth were entirely under your chin. More-over you observe that the whale has no external nose; and that what nose he had — his spout hole — is on the top of his head; you observe that his eyes and ears are at the sides of his head, nearly one third of his entire length from the front. Wherefore, you must now have perceived that the front of the Sperm Whale's head is a dead, blind wall, without a single organ or tender prominence of any sort whatsoever. Furthermore, you are now to consider that only in the extreme, lower, backward sloping part of the front of the head, is there the slightest vestige of bone; and not until you get nearly twenty feet from the forehead do you come to the full cranial development. So that this whole enormous boneless mass is as one wad. Finally, though, as will soon be revealed, its contents partly comprise the most delicate oil; yet, you are now to be apprised of the nature of the substance which so impregnably invests all that apparent effeminacy. In some previous place I have described to you how the blubber wraps the body of the whale, as the rind wraps an orange. Just so with the head; but with this difference: about the head this envelope, though not so thick, is of a boneless toughness, inestimable by any man who has not handled it. The severest pointed harpoon, the sharpest lance darted by the strongest human arm, impotently rebounds from it. It is as though the fore-head of the Sperm Whale were paved with horses' hoofs. I do not think that any sensation lurks in it.

Bethink yourself also of another thing. When two large, loaded Indiamen chance to crowd and crush towards each other in the docks, what do the sailors do? They do not suspend between them, at the point of coming contact, any merely hard susbstance, like iron or wood. No, they hold there a large, round wad of tow and cork, enveloped in the thickest and toughest of ox-hide. That bravely and uninjured takes the jam which would have snapped all their oaken handspikes and iron crow-bars. By itself this sufficiently illustrates the obvious fact I drive at. But supplementary to this, it has hypothetically occurred to me, that as ordinary fish possess what is called a swimming bladder in them, capable, at will, of distension or contraction; and as the Sperm Whale, as far as I know, has no such provision in him; considering, too, the otherwise inexplicable manner in which he now depresses his head altogether beneath the surface, and anon swims with it high elevated out of the water; considering the unobstructed elasticity of its envelop; considering the unique interior of his head; it has hypothetically occurred to me, I say, that those mystical lung-celled honeycombs there may possibly have some hitherto unknown and unsuspected connexion with the outer air, so as to be susceptible to atmospheric distension and contraction. If this be so, fancy the irresistibleness of that might, to which the most impalpable and destructive of all elements contributes.

Now, mark. Unerringly impelling this dead, impregnable, uninjurable wall, and this most buoyant thing within; there swims behind it all a mass of tremendous life, only to be adequately estimated as piled wood us — by the cord; and all obedient to one volition, as the smallest insect. So that when I shall hereafter detail to you all the specialties and concentrations of potency everywhere lurking in this expansive monster; when I shall show you some of his more inconsiderable braining feats; I trust you will have renounced all ignorant incredulity, and be ready to abide by this; that though the Sperm Whale stove a passage through the Isthmus of Darien, and mixed the Atlantic with the Pacific, you would not elevate one hair of your eye-brow. For unless you own the whale, you are but a provincial and sentimentalist in Truth. Truth is a thing for salamander giants only to encounter; how small the chance for the provincials then? What befel the weakling youth lifting the dread goddess's veil at Lais?

— From MOBY-DICK

This fearful head is about one-third the creature's length.
Sperm Whales were not unknown to the shore-whalefishers of the Cape and the Islands, for the life in their waters, like the birds in their air and the flora and fauna of their land, partook of the

character of both north and south. In 1712 Captain Christopher Hussey of Nantucket blown out to sea in winter in command of an open boat took a Sperm Whale off Georges Banks and brought it in, the slick from its carcass calming the raging seas — or so the story goes. His adventure made whaling history and the shore-whalemen afterwards kept a sharp eye out for "sparmecity." By 1740 and Right and Humpback Whales had very nearly disappeared from Cape Cod waters and the serious chase of the Sperm Whale began.

The industry was still largely seasonal and, to get along, a Cape Cod whaleman was obliged to be a jack of all trades and a master of many.

☙

1742–1744

"SOME TRANSACTIONS AND MOST REMARKABLES"

BY BENJAMIN BANGS

A MEMORANDUM or short acct. of ye Life of Benj. Bangs, containing some Transactions and most Remarkables for my own Satisfaction.

Begun at Harwich in ye 22nd year of my age. Lived with my father in ye house that my grandfather lived in. We removed here in June, 1741, and uncles Ebenezer and Doctr. moved to his house. Father built a new end to this house in ye summer of ye year 1742. In Oct., 1742, our Harwich people killed 4 or 5 hundred black-fish at Mulford's clefts, and cleared £79, single share. Our old boat had one share.

Jan., 1742, O.S.

1. Went to visit my sister at Yarmouth.
8. I am keeping school at uncle Ebenezer Bangs'.
9. I had Seth Mirick at school, and sundry other young boys.
17. I am exceedingly perplext with toothache. Had the tooth

pulled at 12 times by 3 men. It broke 6 times and they could not get it out. I got cold in my face and lay by till ye 27th day. Got out to school again.

Feb.
13. I was at uncle Collins', at Truro.
14. We got as far as ye ponds.
15. We got to ye cape,[1] and catch but 3 codfish.

March.
10. Moses Mayo married. I was at the wedding.
18. This day I broke up keeping school.
22. I began to learn navigation of Mr. Selew at Mr. Foster's.
24. Public Fast in ye province.
28, 29. These two days I learnt 5 cases in plain sailing.

April.
13. This day I finisht learning navigation. Gave £5, and was part of 12 days in learning.
21. Thomas Joyce of Yarmouth hanged himself 20th day.

May.
1. Sam'l Paddock got home from ye Spaniards where he was taken some time ago and carried to Cuba
   War was proclaimed between ye English & Spaniards in ye Spring of ye year 1739.
7. I shipt to go with Sam'l Paddock whaling in a bumpkin ·sloop, fitted out by Esq. Paine.
9. This day we set out from Harwich to go whaling.
10. We got to Cape Cod harbor. N. E. storm of rain.
14. We came out around ye Cape — met several vessels.
24. This day we got among ye spermacetis in Lat. 36–45. We killed one ye first stroke. See 3 sloops more cutting up fish.[2]
30. See a sloop. We are among ye fish as thick as bees and as wild, for we could strike none, in lat. 36–15.

[1] Bangs means Provincetown. For many years only the tip end of the Cape was called "Cape Cod" or "the Cape."
[2] The whaleman's common term for whales.

June.

1. Sperm cetes very plenty — killed two Lat. 36–30. See three sloops.
2. We set out for home N. N. E. course, got 4 sperm cetes on board.
5. We made ye west end of Nantucket.
6. We run round ye Cape — catch plenty of mackerel.
14. We came over to Harwich for stores and set out again for another trip. Paid my way to Dick Sears at store.

15–17. Southerly wind. We are turning round ye cape. We catch fine parcel of cod and mackerel.

24. We met a brig from West Indies. This is my birthday, 22 years old.
30. Found a fine school sperma cetes. Struck two but killed only one. We got 6 sperma cetes in strips — made 73 bls. oil. Cleared 23–15 to a man's share. Oil is £100 per ton. There are great voyages made this year in general.

July.

1–3. We see a few sperm whales, but could not strike any, and were forced to set out for home to carry Eben Burgess, sick.
11. I began work at home. Capt. Paddock sailed out again.
31. Father went to ye eastward, and I at work am at home.

August

24. I am getting hay. Father came home 19th day.
25. Joshua Freeman went with his family to Casco Bay, to live there. I sent Clark Lincoln and Isaac Jeams with Freeman to work on our sloop that's building there by Snow.
30. Father and Davis Welts went to Boston to carry stores to ye eastward for ye sloop. Esq. Sturges and Prince and a great gang more were here on a frolick.

September.

28. Our sloop was launched at Casco ye 22nd of this month.

October.

1–3. We are husking our corn; a good harvest.
7. Went to Barnstable with J. Hatch. Came home

8. and put up our corn. Had 177 bushels from 6 acres of land.

13. A thanksgiving day for ye success of ye king in a battle in Germany. We had a chorus at night.

18. J. Hatch and I came to Yarmouth to go to Boston with Miller.

19, 20. We came out and got to Boston, and hid in ye oats for fear of ye press, which is very hot.

22. This day is a very remarkable storm of wind and rain. Great damage is done in Boston and all over ye country.

November.

24. A public thanksgiving. Clark Lincoln came home for me to go to Boston.

28. Clark and I set out by land for Boston. Got to Ellis's at night, wet as drowned rats. It rains hard.

29. We got to Sylvester Hanover's.

30. We got to Boston, almost tired.

December

1. I agreed to go to No. Carolina for Mr. Sherburn. Our sloop is a pretty vessel named Rebecca. Father went home. I entered the sloop out.

7. We got to High Annus and came home to Harwich.

8. Mr. Singleton is passenger. We came up to High Annus again.

15. This day we made Cape Henry and run close into it.

16. Fine gale of north wind. We run from Cape Henry to Cape Hatteras in about 10 hours.

18. We came through ye swash in company with Capt. Lot Chase. Got to Pamlico at night.

19. We both turned up ye river and got to Bathtown.

20, 21. I entered ye sloop. Daniel Freeman came down ye river to town. I am consigned to him.

30. We came up to Woodstock. Left Freeman at Slade's creek with his sloop.

January, 1743, O.S.

5. We came down ye river and met Freeman

6. and lay lashed-sides too. We began to take in tar. We

have for a time seen a blazing star in ye west; very remarkable.

18, 19. Lay at Meeart's Creek, taking in tar. Chase and Capt. Atkins and Freeman are all together here, carousing.

20. We came to Pantego, drank our rum all out, and

24. came to Foscue's creek; got more rum — all got boozed.

February.

15. Came to Woodstock. Ye peach trees are blossomed.

16, 17. We are loading tar, and have no rum to drink, nor

19, 20. haven't had any for a week, and so keep sober. Freeman came here. We got 2 deers to carry home.

24. We came to Pungo and finished loading — high time for it. We had about 600 bbls. on board.

28. We came away to go home.

April.

1–8. I am fixing up our sloop and conclude to go a whaling. We have news of a fight between ye English and French.

8. Mathews won ye battle. Destroyed near 20 French ships.

19. Came out to go a whaling — got as far as Chatham, and then sprang a leak. We were forced to put back into Cape Cod harbor.

24, 25. We came out of ye Cape in company with Saml. Paddock — came through ye sound together.

27, 28. We run out S.S.W. from Noman's land. We found 2 spermacetes and were chasing them when there came a sloop down up on us and chased us 4 hours. They could not come up to us and so left us at night.

May

1. We are running westward in company with 2 or 3 Nantucket men and a large ship. We got one black-fish on the 4th day. We leak very much and find no whales.

6. We are in lat. 36–20 and spermacetes are thick enough and vessels plenty. Spoke John Smalley and J. Swain.

8–9. Violent storm.

10. We came out of ye gulph. Our leak increases and we broke both our pump-spears, and agreed to go home. Met several vessels Lat. 37–36.

18. We got into Nantucket. 45 spermacetes are brought in here this day.

19. We have found our leak. It is an auger hole through her keel.

23. We have got ready to go again with much difficulty, for our Irishmen got by ye ears and made terrible work, so that Eb. Nickerson was forced to leave us.

June.

3. In Lat 39–36. Abundance of whalemen in sight.

6. We found a dead spermacete and cabled her.

7. We cut ye fish. She filled 12 hh good bluber.

23. We came out through Butler Hole and brought Collins and 2 boats. They were cast away at Cape Poge.

24. We got to Harwich. It is my birthday. Lay at point Vox. Our fare made 48½ bbls. oil. Got our oil to Boston and broke up. We have a Fast Day on account of ye enemy who are very plenty on our coast, so that we dare not stir.

30. We have a great tumult in town with ye New-Lights. We hear that war was proclaimed against France ye 2nd day of June in Boston. Next day an Earthquake was heard all over New England. War was proclaimed against Spain in ye spring of ye year 1739. On ye 22nd a French Privateer took Hascal Laden with oil off ye table; ye men came away in their boat. On ye 23rd, early in ye morning, Captain Thwing in ye country Galley, met with ye privateer and took her off ye back of our Cape. She is a sloop with 94 men and 8 carriage guns. They carried her to Boston. Ye widow Hopkins had a son injured. He tore his guts out with a plough and died. Whaling voyages are not so good this year as last year. Ye noise of ye war spoils us all; and we have civil war at home about a set of people called *New Lights,* who have been growing this year or two, and now make a deal of disturbance all over New England. Some of them act very strangely.

July

From ye 1st to ye 10th we lay at Point Rocks, with our sloop not much in a hurry, for we are afraid to go out. They are beating up for volunteers to secure Annapolis Royal.

11. Father went to Boston with the sloop. I stay at home. I am harvesting. Tom Doane, David Sears, and Ed Taylor got home from ye Spaniards. We have news from Rhode Island. There has been carried in there two Spanish prizes, very rich; and many are taken on both sides. Our sloop is
31. gone to Casco Bay.

August
9. A gang of us went to Bass Ponds watermeloning.
14. We are moving Judah Berry's house.
17. I am sowing wheat by J. Davis's.
22. I am getting hay at Skaket.
29. I got 7 pigeons.
— From the HISTORY AND GENEALOGY OF THE BANGS FAMILY IN AMERICA, by Dean Dudley, 1896

While "the King of the Sea" led whalemen ever further south, some turned to the hunt of the Arctic or Greenland Whale. With the final development of a whaleship carrying tryworks on the deck, voyages lengthened from months to years. In 1774 Captains David Smith and Gamaliel Collins of Truro were fishing off the Falkland Islands, the first known whalemen to approach that archipelago. Cape Cod people like to believe that a great British statesman's celebrated eulogy of the American whalemen was inspired by their exploit.

ॐ

1775

THE WHALEFISHERS OF NEW ENGLAND

BY EDMUND BURKE

WHILST WE FOLLOW THEM among the tumbling mountains of ice, and behold them penetrating into the deepest frozen recesses of Hudson's Bay and Davis's Straits, whilst we are looking for them beneath the arctic circle, we hear that they have pierced into the op-

posite region of polar cold, that they are at the antipodes, and engaged under the frozen serpent of the south. Falkland Island, which
seemed too remote and romantic an object for the grasp of national
ambition, is but a stage and resting-place in the progress of their
victorious industry. Nor is the equinoctial heat more discouraging to
them than the accumulated winter of both the poles. We know that,
whilst some of them draw the line and strike the harpoon on the
coast of Africa, others run the longitude and pursue the gigantic
game along the coast of Brazil. No sea but what is vexed by their
fisheries. No climate that is not witness to their toils. Neither the
perserverance of Holland, nor the activity of France, nor the dexterous
and firm sagacity of English enterprise, ever carried this most perilous
mode of hard industry to the extent to which it has been pushed by
this recent people, a people who are still, as it were, but in the gristle,
and not yet hardened into the bone of manhood.

— From his speech in Parliament urging conciliation
with the American Colonies

*A common Sperm Whale measures from forty to fifty feet in length
and yields about forty-five barrels of oil but giants far exceeding this
in size were fairly common in the early days. Takes of over a hundred and fifty barrels of oil have been recorded, derived from bulls
probably eighty feet long or more. The cow is only one-fifth to one-
fourth the size of her mate. The forehead or "case" of the whale —
called by Melville "the great Heidelburgh Tun" — is largely filled
with pure spermaceti. "It has a slight rose tint, and looks like ice
cream or white butter half churned," Cheever tells us, describing the
cutting-in of a giant Sperm; men dip it up in buckets from the half-
hoisted head and pass it by bucket-brigade to the tubs. Cheever's
whale yielded sixteen barrels of the precious stuff and about seventy
barrels more of oil. While the crew were cutting-in, the water that
side the ship was white with spermaceti and blubber and boys provided with big scoops were out in boats dipping up this waste under
a cloud of feasting albatrosses, gulls and haglets amid the rush of
prowling pick-nose sharks. In the pursuit of such whales as this,
whalefishing profits soared; and with them, casualties.*

*"Killed by a Whale" becomes for the first time a common entry
in logs and in town and family records. The motto engraved on a
monument to her whalemen in New Bedford was coined in the*

Sperm-whalefishing days: "A Dead Whale or a Stove Boat." *Not even a whaleship was proof against the battering-ram.*

❧

A STRANGE, EVENTFUL STORY

BY HENRY T. CHEEVER

BUT THE MOST DREADFUL DISPLAY of the whale's strength and prowess yet authentically recorded was that made upon the American whale ship Essex, Captain Pollard, which sailed from Nantucket for the Pacific Ocean in August, 1819. Late in the fall of the same year, when in latitude forty of the South Pacific, a school of sperm whales were discovered, and three boats were manned and sent in pursuit. The mate's boat was struck by one of them, and he was obliged to return to the ship in order to repair the damage.

While he was engaged in that work, a sperm whale, judged to be eighty-five feet long, broke water about twenty rods from the ship, on her weather bow. He was going at the rate of about three knots an hour, and the ship at nearly the same rate, when he struck the bows of the vessel just forward of her chains.

At the shock produced by the collision of two such mighty masses of matter in motion, the ship shook like a leaf. The seemingly malicious whale dove and passed under the ship, grating her keel, and then appeared at about the distance of a ship's length, lashing the sea with fins and tail, as if suffering the most horrible agony. He was evidently hurt by the collision, and blindly frantic with instinctive rage.

In a few minutes he seemed to recover himself, and started with great speed directly across the vessel's course to the windward. Mean time the hands on board discovered the ship to be gradually settling down at the bows, and the pumps were to be rigged. While working at them one of the men cried out, "God have mercy! he comes again!"

The whale had turned at about one hundred rods from the ship, and was making for her with double his former speed, his pathway white with foam. Rushing head on, he struck her again at the bow, and the tremendous blow stove her in. The whale dived under again and disappeared, and the ship foundered in ten minutes from the first collision.

After incredible hardships and sufferings in their open boats, on the 20th of December the survivors of this catastrophe reached the low island called Ducies, in latitude twenty-four degrees forty minutes south, longitude one hundred and twenty-four degrees forty minutes west. It was a mere sandbank, nearly barren, which supplied them only with water and sea-fowl. On this uninhabited island, dreary as it was, three of the men chose to remain, rather than again commit themselves to the uncertainties of the sea. They have never since been heard from, the island being seldom visited.

On the 27th of December, the three boats, with the remainder of the men, put away together for the Island of Juan Fernandez, at a distance of two thousand miles. The mate's boat was taken up by the Indian, of London, on the 19th of February, ninety-three days from the time of the catastrophe, with only three living survivors.

The captain's boat was fallen in with by the Dauphin, of Nantucket, on the 23d of the same month, having only two men living, whose lives had been eked out only through that last resort of hunger in the wretched, which words shudder to relate! Out of a crew of twenty, five only survived to make the ear of the world tingle at their strange, eventful story.

— From THE WHALE AND HIS CAPTORS, 1849

Two of the three members of the crew who chose to stay on Ducie's Island were Cape Cod boys. Cheever is mistaken in saying they were never heard of again. Donald G. Trayser in his BARNSTABLE: THREE CENTURIES OF A CAPE COD TOWN *tells us that in 1822 Seth Weeks and William Wright came home to Barnstable. Ducie's Island is a rocky barren waste. They had subsisted there for 102 days on birds' eggs, shellfish, and water from a spring that could be approached only at low tide. They had discovered in a cave eight skeletons of other shipwrecked men and found the name of the other lost vessel carved in a tree:* Elizabeth. *They had given themselves up for lost. But Captain Pollard, rescued by the* Dauphin *and taken into Valparaiso, was seeking help for them and, on April 8, 1821, they were picked up by the English ship* Surrey *and carried to London. William Wright's subsequent history is unknown. Seth Weeks con-*

tinued to chase the whale. Twenty-five years later we find him as master bringing home a fine cargo of sperm oil in the brig March, *one of the last whaleships listed from Barnstable. He died in Oster-ville in 1887, aged eighty-four, the last survivor of the* Essex *disaster.*

Henry T. Cheever's THE WHALE AND HIS CAPTORS *was published by Harper & Brothers in New York in 1855.*

e∾o

THE WHALE'S MALICE

BY OWEN CHASE

I TURNED AROUND and saw him about a hundred rods directly ahead of us coming down with apparently twice his ordinary speed, and to me it appeared with tenfold fury and vengeance in his aspect. The surf flew in all directions and his course toward us was marked by a white foam of a rod in width, which he made with continual violent thrashing of his tail. His head was about half out of water, and in that way he came upon and again struck the ship. I called out to the helmsman, "Hard up!" but she had not fallen off more than a point when we took the second shock. I should judge the speed of the ship to have been at this time about three knots and that of the whale about six. He struck her to windward, directly under the cathead, and completely stove in her bows. He passed under the ship again, went off to leeward, and we saw no more of him.

Every fact seemed to warrant me in concluding that it was anything but chance which directed his operations; he made two attacks upon the ship at short interval between them, both of which, according to their direction, were calculated to do us the most injury, by being made ahead and thereby combining the speed of two objects for the shock; to effect which the exact manoeuvres which he made were necessary. His aspect was most horrible and such as indicated re-sentment and fury. He came directly from the school, which we had just before entered, and in which we had struck three of his com-panions, as if fired with revenge for their sufferings. . . .

— From his account of the ESSEX disaster

Owen Chase, first mate of the Essex, *horrified the world with his explicit description of the cannibalism ultimately practiced in the boats. Stories about it preceded the survivors to America and Captain Pollard, it is said, on his return walked to his Nantucket home through streets lined "with a silent, awestruck crowd." In his boat his nephew, Owen Coffin, had been chosen by lot to die to sustain the life of the others. Pollard had begged to take the boy's place but the executioner, Charles Ramsdell, chosen also by lot, refused to kill him. Pollard abstained from the flesh of his young kinsman but when another man died, leaving in the boat only himself and Ramsdell, he turned with his companion to "the last resort of hunger."*

Cape Cod men and boys not only manned Cape Cod whaleships, but turned up in numbers in the crews of vessels from whaling ports everywhere.

༜

A CAPE–COD–MAN

BY HERMAN MELVILLE

STUBBS WAS the second mate. He was a native of Cape Cod; and hence, according to local usage, was called a Cape-Cod-man. A happy-go-lucky; neither craven nor valiant; taking perils as they came with an indifferent air; and while engaged in the most imminent crisis of the chase, toiling away, calm and collected as a journeyman joiner engaged for the year. Good-humored, easy, and careless, he presided over his whale-boat as if the most deadly encounter were but a dinner, and his crew all invited guests. He was as particular about the comfortable arrangement of his part of the boat, as an old stage-driver is about the snugness of his box. When close to the whale, in the very death-lock of the fight, he handled his un-pitying lance cooly and off-handedly, as a whistling tinker his hammer. He would hum over his old rigadig tunes while flank and flank with the most exasperated monster. Long usage had, for this Stubb, converted the jaws of death into an easy chair. What he thought of death itself, there is no telling. Whether he ever thought of it at all, might be a question; but, if he ever did chance to cast his mind that way after a comfortable dinner, no doubt like a good sailor, he took it to be a sort of call of the watch to tumble aloft, and bestir themselves there, about something which he would find out when he obeyed the order, and not sooner.

What, perhaps with other things, made Stubb such an easy-going, unfearing man, so cheerily trudging off with the burden of life in a world full of grave peddlers, all bowed to the ground with their packs; what helped to bring about that almost impious good-humor of his; that thing must have been his pipe. For, like his nose, his short, black little pipe was one of the regular features of his face. You would almost as soon expected him to turn out of his bunk without his nose as without his pipe. He kept a whole row of pipes there ready loaded, stuck in a rack, within easy reach of his hand; and, whenever he turned in, he smoked them all out in succession, lighting one from the other to the end of the chapter; then loading them again to be in readiness anew. For, when Stubb dressed, instead of first putting his legs into his trowsers, he put his pipe into his mouth.

I say this continual smoking must have been one cause, at least, of his peculiar disposition; for everyone knows that this earthly air, whether ashore or afloat, is terribly infected with the nameless miseries of the numberless mortals who have died exhaling it; and as in time of the cholera, some people go about with a camphorated handkerchief to their mouths; so, likewise, against all mortal tribulations, Stubb's tobacco smoke might have operated as a sort of disinfecting agent.

.   .   .   .   .

Of all the wondrous devices and dexterities, the sleights of hand and countless subtleties, to which the veteran whaleman is so often forced, none exceed that fine manoeuvre with the lance called pitchpoling. Small sword, or broad sword, in all its exercises boasts nothing like it. It is indispensable only with an inveterate running whale; its grand fact and feature is the wonderful distance to which the long lance is accurately darted from a violently rocking, jerking boat, under extreme headway. Steel and wood included, the entire spear is some ten or twelve feet in length; the staff is much slighter than that of the harpoon, and also of a lighter material — pine. It is furnished with a small rope called a warp, of considerable length, by which it can be hauled back to the hand after darting.

But before going further, it is important to mention here, that though the harpoon may be pitchpoled in the same way with the lance, yet it is seldom done; and when done, is still less frequently successful, on account of the greater weight and inferior length of the harpoon as compared with the lance, which in effect become serious drawbacks. As a general thing, therefore, you must first get fast to a whale, before any pitchpoling comes into play.

Look now at Stubb; a man who from his humorous, deliberate coolness and equanimity in the direst emergencies, was specially qualified to excel in pitchpoling. Look at him; he stands upright in the tossed bow of the flying boat; wrapt in fleecy foam, the towing whale is forty feet ahead. Handling the long lance lightly, glancing twice or thrice along its length to see if it be exactly straight, Stubb whistlingly gathers up the coil of the warp in one hand, so as to secure its free end in his grasp, leaving the rest unobstructed. Then holding the lance full before his waistband's middle, he levels it at the whale; when, covering him with it, he steadily depresses the butt-end in his hand, thereby elevating the point till the weapon stands fairly balanced upon his palm, fifteen feet in the air. He minds you somewhat of a juggler, balancing a long staff on his chin. Next moment with a rapid, nameless impulse, in a superb lofty arch the bright steel spans the foaming distance, and quivers in the life spot of the whale. Instead of sparkling water, he now spouts red blood.

"That drove the spigot out of him!" cries Stubb. "'Tis July's immortal Fourth; all fountains must run wine to-day! Would now, it were old Orleans whiskey, or old Ohio, or unspeakable old Monongahela! Then, Tashtego, lad, I'd have ye hold a canakin to the jet, and we'd drink round it! Yea, verily, hearts alive, we'd brew choice punch in the spread of his spout-hole there, and from the live punch-bowl quaff the living stuff!"

Again and again to such gamesome talk, the dexterous dart is repeated, the spear returning to its master like a greyhound held in skilful leash. The agonized whale goes into his flurry; the towline is slackened, and the pitchpoler dropping astern, folds his hands, and mutely watches the monster die.

— From MOBY-DICK

꩜

The South Seas held other perils than storm and the Sperm Whale as poor Captain Prince Coffin of Falmouth learned too late. He saw his crew put to flight and his vessel taken by a party of apparently friendly natives from the Marshall Islands he had received aboard his whaleship the Awashonks *in 1835. She was later recaptured but without her captain for he had been beheaded with one of his own blubber-spades.*

Not all savages were so unamiable. A Provincetown captain's wife when an old lady loved to tell the story of how her husband had taken her as a bride to visit a chieftain on the coast of South Africa. She took with her the offering — as she might have done to a neighbor at home — of a pan of doughnuts freshly fried by her own hands. Apparently they were a success for the next day the chief with two lieutenants repaid the call informally. They had received the Americans the day before clad in ceremonial robes but they came aboard the whaleship entirely unclothed. There was a great scurrying around while the captain secured from his wife three Mother Hubbards in which to drape them before he called her on deck to receive their guests.

In all the annals of whalefishing there are no stories so deeply tragic as those which came out of the North Pacific where in the last decades of the whaling era men chased the Bowhead Whale. Because of the vast distances and the short fishing season whalemen were obliged to make voyages lasting three, four, even five years to fill their ships. Vessels were imprisoned in the ice for months out of every year. Men froze to death, died of hunger and scurvy, went mad from the long dark and lonely monotony. Mutiny became a commonplace. And, because their husbands were to be gone so long, more captain's wives sailed in whaleships to the western Arctic than to any other whaling ground. A demented woman, flitting along Provincetown streets kicking at cats and cursing — "I'll teach that God damned black bastard to cross my bows!" — was a familiar pathetic figure not many years ago. She had lost her reason, the whisper ran, when her husband broke a promise he had made to bring her home at the end of a given year, full ship or no. Eugene O'Neill's one-act horror play, ILE, *was suggested by her story.*

A retired captain occasionally wrote his memoirs, but it is in the day-by-day record of old logs we see the whaleman as he was. The first mate usually kept the log, now and then the captain. You'll often see pictures of whales sketched or stamped in the margins. A whole whale means a whale that was taken; flukes only, a whale that got away. Conventionally, the entries for each date closed with the words:

"SO ENDS THIS DAY"

FEBRUARY 2, 1843. Things has got so now when you tel a man to doo anything they will doo as thar have a mind too and iff I try to macke them doo as I want then to thay up and smack me down iff they are alowed to go on this way they will soon have charge off the ship but they shall never hav charge of me as long as thare is A drop of bleed that floes thru my vanes.

· · · · ·

January 14, 1845. This day I got a cussing up the boat because my boat hit the Captain's Boat when we was fas to a whale.

February 6. . . . This day I got a cussing when I brought the whale alongside.

· · · · ·

January 1, 1848. Sixteen months gone and no word from home yet. Oh, those good old winter evenings I spent there two years ago. I fear they will not return for me. So much older, wiser and more discreet. I am almost thirty. Time to settle down for life with some-one. Who, pray?

· · · · ·

January 12, 1852. This day begins with light airs and calms and worm enough to roast a monkey and no mistake about it.

· · · · ·

October 27, 1852. Wind N E clear of the stream jibs for-top gallant sail all furled. The moon shines silver bright and the weather is getting very pleasant the sea water was warm as new milk and the lookout is as blue as indigo.

· · · · ·

November 28, 1858. Middle part, saw whales, Lowered. Struck. And the Larboard Boat got stove. The whale struck Mr. Tripp. He lived until he got on board the ship, but died almost as soon as we got him on board. God knows what I am going to do now, for we have lost one of our best men. We brought the whale alongside and cut him in.

November 30. Latter part put the remains of Mr. Tripp in a cask and filled it with New Rum. I want to carry it to the Islands and send him home if I can.

·   ·   ·   ·   ·

December 5, 1860. One of the Mens Berths Caught fire this forenoon from putting a pipe in it that he had been smoking after breakfast at Least we spose so & think so. Exrected a tooth for the carpenter.

January 20, 1861. . . . no whales, O Deer

February 4, 1861. Spoke an English Bark called the "Brendelburn" of Auckland went on board got some papers heard Abe Lincoln was President.

·   ·   ·   ·   ·

January 14, 1864. Daylight saw a shoal of sperm whales. Lowered three boats. Waist and bow Boats struck each a large whale. Bow boats Whale turned about and eat his boat entirely up. Larboard boat picked up the crew and took them aboard. 3rd mate took another boat. got a bomb lance in him. set him spouting blood. The Villain would chase a boat as soon as he could get sight of one. Waist boats Whale came near Eating up the boat that was fast to him. Stove her in three places with his jaws. Day ends with the loss of a boat with all gear. Waist boats iron broke. lost the whale.

·   ·   ·   ·   ·

October 25, 1868. Had some talk about standing mastheads and whaling on Sunday. Have agreed not to stand mastheads or look for fish Sunday, but, if they should be so unfortunate as to come to the ship we shall pitch in.

·   ·   ·   ·   ·

June 30, 1868. The wind dead ahead and ruged under double reefed topsails blowing against this unfortunate "Minnesota" and all concerned. impossible to go Eastward. Five days out and cannot get away from home —

July 1. No signs of L I F E here. Nothing for us. June has passed & we get Now wheir. No chance for us this season I fear. three seasons in the North Atlantic to get One Whale in this Unfortunate Vessel — Barren Water. Nothing to be seen.

July 2nd. . . . lowered boats to practice crews. they are very awkward indeed. Will the Lord ever favour us to get One Whale. I fear not very soon.

July 4. Comes in with a Head Wind. Fresh Breeze from ESE Heading about N E. Will the Wind even change. . . . This is the Fourth of July, a day of rejoicing with People at home: but a sad day with us. No Whales in the Ocean that we can find (A Head Wind). No chance to do anything or to ever get One Whale. The LORDS Hand appears to be against the Poor Old "Minnesota" and all concerned in her. Will the Lord in his infinite Mercy ever suffer us to get One Whale. . . .

July 8. . . . Some lucky Ship I fear has Boiled out the last Whale in the Atlantic. Captain Howland of the "Comm. Morris" I suppose.[1]

July 16. . . . I am discouraged this voyage. The Hand of Providence is against us: I do not fine any Whales (I do not expect to get One Whale this season. The Hand of Fortune is against us. It is too late to go to the "Morris" ground Now (nothing for us I fear).

October 28. I am about discouraged. I think the Ocean contains nothing that we can ever get. I go to Masthead & look untill I am allmost Blind. Not a Whale can I see. . . [2]

.   .   .   .   .

February 8, 1869. black Frank, the boatsteerer that we broke is off duty sick with the astmer. Ship leaking about sixteen hundred strokes in twenty-four hours.

May 2. sighted sperm whales going to windward. Lowered three boats but never saw them again — luck. They knew it was the "Herald."

September 19. Land Ho. Coast of Arabia.

October 3. employed in cutting and boiling. Found about thirty pounds of ambergris in the last whale.

.   .   .   .   .

June 10, 1872. 11 AM the Capt with his family came off got the ship underway.

June 20. . . . 5 P.M. one of the "Sailors" gave the Captain a letter Which had the signature of 4 men Viz. "W. H. Robinson, H. Loyd, E. W. Dunn & H. M. Davenport." Said letter stated that they had been greatly deceived by the Shipping Agents as they had been told

[1] The Commodore Morris was a famous ship built at Wood's Hole.
[2] The captain, Clothier Peirce, was the writer of this log. He didn't take a whale till until the following January and then only a small one, but he records in the log he was thankful to get that.

by them that their living would equal that of a first class restaurant or nearly so. They were disappointed in their fare & demanded better, & refused to do more work until said better fare came to hand. the Captain told them that they were having just such Provisions as was put on the ship for them & that he had & would give them all they required.

June 21. . . . let out men who are in durance Vile up three times today to eat.

Sept. 4. This morning we tied "Loyd" in the main rigging with his hands above his Head His feet standing on the Spar or rail as he chose. Said "Loyd" is a riotous & disorderly fellow. last night he quarreled and had a fight with the "Blacksmith." the Captain scolded him & told him to go forward. When in the forecastle he said in presence of several of the Crew, the Cook, Peter, Jose & Blacksmith that he would Desert the Ship & if it could be done not other way He would set F I R E to her. Tonight he takes lodging in the House with "Darbies" on his wrists.

April 11, 1875. . . . 1 P.M. Larboard boat struck with the noise & confusion the Poor little Whale yielded up the ghost.

July 4. (BOUND HOME) Centennial . . . all hands celebrating the King of all 4th of Julys in various ways. Some "scrimshawing" some washing & drying their Old clothes, while others are lying about the decks idle. 7 o'clock watch turned in. all hands religiously Sober.

.   .   .   .   .

July 27, 1846. Pitcarians Island — at sunset boats returned with 5 bbls of yam and 4 of the Islanders whitch spoke very good English and quite inteligent people.

August 10. off and on getting off recruits at 3 PM bade adue to the Islanders and come on board the island contains 135 soles including 3 Englishmen one of the first settlers still living.

.   .   .   .   .

December 25, 1867. This is what is called Christmas, Sarah. I have been at work all day as hard as I could put in — and the second mate sitting on his behind Looking at me. I say God damn a Provincetown 2nd mate. They go once a claming and then become capt.[3]

January 3, 1868. . . . Let me see. today Susie is Eleven Months old.

[3] This entry is from the log of the first mate of the Wellfleet schooner *Edith May*. Wellfleet was a great whaling port long before Provincetown.

Oh God Bless her. I hope she will Live to see her One Hundredth birthday. Kiss Susie Eleven times for me. Good night Sarah.

January 22. This has been a windy day Sarah and very thick. I have not been to the mast head today. Last night I had a nice Dream Oh Sarah I dreampt I had got home, that is as far as the depot, and as I was walking up to Deborahs (for you were there) as I got out by Capt. Mayhews I saw a little girl coming towards me and when she got up to me I asked her where she was going and she said to the depot. I asked her what she was going there for and she said to meet her Father. I asked her whose little girl she was said Mrs. Keiths then I asked her who sent her to the depot and she said her mother. I told her to take me by the hand and we would go and see her mother. so off we went and you may believe I felt proud to have such a girl. I must ask you to kiss Susie and bid her Good night for me. Dear Companion, sweet Sarah Good night.

· · · · ·

July 1, 1899. Sometimes Captain feels bad. I suppose he take cold going on deck with under ware I tell him Captain put your pants on and shirt because you are maybe get relaps and you are old man So he sais that guest make him feels good. Boiling very little blober —thru the night calm.

July 19. Commence gloomy and threatening accompanied with a fresh S W wind.

Buried the Captain. . . . So Ends This Day.

— From SHIPS LOGS AND CAPTAINS
DIARIES OF OLD CAPE COD

This pamphlet edited by Elisabeth Shoemaker was published by the Cape Cod Chamber of Commerce in 1937 in Hyannis. The logs it contains were chosen from over three thousand furnished to research workers of the Federal Writers Project of Massachusetts by Cape Cod people, libraries and historical societies.

၀ၘၐ

The peak years of the Whalefishing industry in general lay between 1833 and 1863. The decline, scarcely noticeable at first, began with the discovery of petroleum in 1859 and was accelerated by years of War when many whale fleets were lost. Cape Cod men, the first to whale, began to forsake the chase earlier than many others as the profits from cod and mackerel-fishing rose, but they never wholly abandoned it until Captain John Cook of Provincetown retired from the sea in 1916. As the demand for whale oil waned, more and more whalefishers turned to hunting Right Whales and Bowhead Whales for their bone. The discovery of satisfactory substitutes for whalebone in industry and women's rejection of whalebone-stayed corsets in this century sent whalefishing into its flurry.

The whales are coming back. In the spring the cold air above Cape Cod bays and harbors glitters with their blowing as they follow the spawning herring in. Schools of Blackfish yearly flounder ashore to die and when this happens men race for the beaches as they did three hundred years ago, for the head of the small whale contains a valuable very delicate oil much prized by watchmakers.

∽

THE WHALEMAN'S SPEECH

AWAY: *whaleboats lowered from whaleships to chase whales are said to be away.*

BLOWS: *a whale blows when in the act of breathing it emits a cloud of moist air, and this spout is called its blow. It reveals the presence of whales not otherwise visible. "Thar she blows!"*

BOATSTEERER: *the man who pulls the harpoon oar in the whaleboat, darts the harpoon, and steers while the man in command of the boat, usually a mate, dispatches the whale with his lance. He is sometimes called the harponier or harpooneer. "Harpooner" is a landsman's word.*

Although not officers, boatsteerers enjoyed high wages, special privileges and great prestige.

BOILING: *a whaleship is described as boiling when her tryworks are in use.*

BREACH: *a whale's leap clear of the water. In making the leap, the whale breaches. "Thar she blows! Thar she white-waters! Thar she breaches!"*

CLEAN SHIP: *a ship without oil.*

CUT IN: *whales are cut in, not up.*

DART: *harpoons and lances are darted, sometimes pitched, tossed, heaved; never thrown.*

FAST: *a whaleboat attached to a harpooned whale by means of the line is fast to the whale.*

FISH: *whales, to whalemen.*

FLUKES: *the whale's horizontal tail.*

GALLY: *to startle or frighten whales. For fear of gallying their prey whalemen often put their oars aside as they approached it and took up paddles which disturbed the water less. A whole herd might be gallied in an instant, and this was catastrophe, for there was then no hope of taking them.*

GAM: *a social visit paid by the company of one whaleship upon another at sea. There was living not long ago in Provincetown the wife of a captain who had spent more than twenty years of her young life a-whaling. She had known hurricanes and mutiny and shipwreck but she always said her most painful experience occurred on a day when, after they had been at sea for more than two years, her husband took her on a gam to a whaleship just out of New Bedford. The other captain's wife was resplendent in striped leg-o-mutton sleeves, a fashion of which the Provincetown lady had never even heard.*

GONEY: *albatross.*

GREASY: *whale-oily, hence lucky; as a greasy voyage, a greasy ship, a greasy captain.*

HARPOON: *A barbed iron or steel weapon mounted on a pole and attached to a line many fathoms long coiled in tubs. The object of the man who wields it is not to kill the whale but to secure it.*

IRON, OR HARPING-IRON: *common term for harpoon.*

LANCE: *the long, flat-headed, sharp-edged instrument used to kill the whale. It is mounted in a socket on a pole and attached to a line by which the whaleman can snatch it back.*

LIFE: *any vital part of the whale, as the lungs. To pierce the whale's life, is to kill it.*

LOBTAIL: *a Sperm Whale is lobtailing when it beats the surface of the water violently with its flukes.*

MELON: *the part of the head of the Blackfish containing oil.*

PITCH-POLE: *to pitch-pole is to dart the lance up and out and down in an arc covering a considerable distance. It is a supreme test of the whaleman's nerve and art, called for most often when the boat was fast to a still vigorous fleeing whale. See* A CAPE-COD-MAN *by Herman Melville in this book.*

PLUM-PUDDING VOYAGE: *a short summer whalefishing voyage to the Atlantic Arctic. It was so called, it is said, because the whaleman could rise from eating the last plum-pudding of one season and return in time to eat the first of the next. Slightly derisive.*

POD: *a herd of whales.*

SCHOOLMASTER: *the largest bull whale in the pod.*

SCRIMSHAW: *The whaleman's art of carving decorated and often useful objects from whale teeth and bone. Sometimes called Skrimshander.*

SLICK: *a smooth, oily spot left in the sea by a sounding whale.*

SOUND: *to plunge for the bottom of the sea, headfirst and headlong; said of whales.*

TAKE: *a whaleman takes a whale, he doesn't catch or capture it.*

WAIF: *a small flag with which whalemen marked a dead whale as their own. To plant the flag is to waif the whale.*

WATERBONED: *a whale unable to extricate itself from shoal water is waterboned.*

WHALEBOATS: *the open boats in which whalemen came to grips with whales. They are double-enders and admirably designed for launching and riding in the heaviest surf. At first propelled only with oars, they were later often equipped with sail, sloop-rigged.*

Fleets of Cape Cod whaleboats carrying troops up rivers and along broken coasts where the British Navy could not penetrate were active in King William's War in 1690, under Lieutenant Colonel John Gorham of Barnstable; in Queen Anne's War in 1703, and at the capture of Louisburg in 1745.

WHALER: *never a whaleman's word. A man might go a-whaling but neither he nor his vessel was a whaler. He was a whaleman or a whalefisher and she was a whaleboat or a whaleship.*

WHALESHIP: *any vessel engaged in whalefishing which carries try-works and whaleboats. Here is one of the few instances in which the word "ship" is loosely used by sea-going people. A whaleship might be almost anything. The ample bark came to be preferred in time but many Cape Cod ports, particularly Provincetown, clung to their fleet schooners.*

It didn't matter much whether you sailed fast on whaling grounds or not; it mattered a great deal if a sudden disappearance of the fish obliged you to leave one region for another perhaps half a world away.

☙

OLD SONG

Cape Cod girls
They have no combs.
They comb their hair
With codfish bones.

Cape Cod boys
They have no sleds.
They slide down dunes
On codfish heads.

Cape Cod cats
They have no tails.
They lost them all
In sou'east gales.

❦

"FOR THOUGH our Bay and Creekes were full of Basse, and other fish, yet by want of fit and strong Saynes, and other netting, they for the most part brake thorow and carried all away before them. And though the sea were full of Cod, yet we had neither tackling nor harseis for our Shalops. And indeede, had we not been in a place where divers sorts of Shel-fish are that may be taken with the hand, we must have perished, unless God had raised some unknowne or extraordinary meanes for our preservation," *wrote Edward Winslow in* GOOD NEWS FROM NEW ENGLAND *in 1622. William Bradford in the first years of Plymouth Colony said fishing was* "always a thing fatal to us" *and complained vehemently when now and again his planters took time off from their proper work to try their hands at it.*

But fish and fishermen could not be denied forever.

The Cape Cod fishermen-farmers changed the psychology and the economy of Plymouth Colony and unwittingly fathered the first public schools in America. "The Providence of God hath made Cape Cod convenient to us for fishing with seines," *piously announced the General Court in 1671, and decreed that the annual profit accruing to the Colony from such fishing be devoted to a free school* "in some town of this jurisdiction for the training up of youth in literature, for the good and benefit of posterity." *The town, naturally enough, turned out to be Plymouth, but in 1687 every town in the Colony consisting of fifty families or more was ordered to maintain a free grammar school to be supported in part by the townspeople and in part by the Cape Cod fisheries.*

The whaleman came a little before the fisher, but only a little. Often a man was both, cheerfully fishing when whales were scarce; in later days often carrying seines for fishing in his whaleship to hedge against an unlucky voyage. As early as 1730 codfishermen were making voyages to the Grand Banks. The Revolution destroyed the fishing fleets as it destroyed the whale fleets and when peace came the impoverished people, obliged to build smaller vessels, turned towards the coast of Labrador and the Bay of Chaleur. Here they ran into trouble with the British who were trying to close Canadian waters to Yankee fishermen. Seeking fishing grounds even closer to home, they found them off the Georges Banks.

These waters had long been known but held in dread, indeed, in superstitious awe, because of the violent currents, uncharted shoals and fierce sudden storms. It was an intrepid Gloucester fisherman who first demonstrated the practicability of fishing off the Georges, the Cape Cod fishermen swiftly followed his suit.

After the War of 1812 the tide of prosperity rose fast, sweeping fine new vessels to the Grand Banks again, washing tons of oysters and lobsters and clams and quahaugs to New York and Boston markets, floating fleets of mackerel-schooners.

❧

THE BARNSTABLE BOY

BY JOHN GORHAM PALFREY

WHEREVER, OVER THE WORLD, you see the stars and stripes floating, you may have good hope, that, beneath them, some one will be found, who can tell you the soundings of Barnstable, or Wellfleet, or

Chatham harbour. . . . The duck does not take to the water with a surer instinct than the Barnstable boy. He leaps from his leading-strings into the shrouds. It is but a bound from the mother's lap to the mast-head. He boxes the compass in his infant soliloquies. He can hand, reef, and steer, by the time he flies a kite. The ambition of his youth is, to "witch the world with noble *seamanship*"; and his manly "march is on the mountain wave, his home" — no, no! I am too fast, — his "home is *not* upon the deep," and, in his widest wanderings, he never forgets that it is not. . . . The first sign, from which the neighbours gather that the lad has been prospering, is, that the old people's house puts on a new coat of shingles, and another cow, if there needs one, is seen cropping their pasture; his second lucky adventure makes his younger brothers and sisters happy the next time they go abroad, not so much for the gayer figure it has enabled them to make, as because it betokens how kindly they were thought of by one so far away; and the third, — the third, is very apt to serve as an occasion for whispering in some not reluctant ear, that it is almost time he had a snug home of his own, where he could be made more comfortable after these tedious voyages.

— From his BARNSTABLE ADDRESS, 1839

This was the time when the beaches of Cape Cod began to be lined with rows of whirring salt-mills and with fishflakes, racks on which the fish were placed to dry in the sun; it was then that Provincetown, the town that is all beach, came into its own and secured the pre-eminence in fishing it has held ever since.

☙

SMYRA

BY CHARLES NORDHOFF

SCHOONER SAILING was somewhat strange to me. But the people, Cape Cod men all, were kind to me and bore with what must have seemed to them the rather gruff and odd ways of an old salt. Our crew consisted of five: captain, mate, two hands, and the cook. The latter was a little boy of ten years, the captain's son. All hands lived in the cabin, and the officers, although a little reserved in their conversation, as is the manner of Cape men, were kind-hearted, hard-working people.

They were plainly unused to the company of such an outlandish fellow as I had by this time grown to be. Every article of my clothing seemed a curiosity to them. My old sea chest was an object of mysterious interest to the little cook, who evidently connected it in his mind with numberless romantic adventures. The shrewd little fellow lost no time in finding my weak side, and having once, as he judged, established himself in my good graces, straightaway importuned me for a yarn; and I soon found out that Smyra — that was his singular name — faithfully repeated my tough yarns to his father, who used to smile good-naturedly at his childish enthusiasm, and at my, to him, queer ways.

For myself, the company of the child was grateful to my feelings. I liked his unsophisticated ways and ingenuous talk. And so I tried, and successfully, to win his regards. These little Cape boys start early into active life. Smyra had been cook since his eighth year, and now at ten, with all of the child about him yet, was as self-reliant and shrewd, in matters appertaining to his peculiar life, as many a young man at twenty-one.

Our crew had their homes in a little village on the Cape. It was the captain's custom to lay by here for a day or two, on each trip. Accordingly, when we were through the Vineyard Sound, our course was shaped toward Harwich, and by noon of the second day after we left New York, the little craft was safely moored at "Deep Hole" — the name of the particular anchorage chosen for her. We found there a number of schooners at anchor.

"What are those vessels, Smyra?" asked I, as we two were stowing the jib.

"Some coasters, and some fishermen."

With a quickness peculiar, I believe, to fishermen and coasters, the boy now began telling over the names of the various vessels. Many lay a mile off; but he knew them all. This was a coaster, that a fisherman; this is a Harwich vessel, that one from Barnstable.

"And yonder in the offing is a Down-Easter."

"How do you know that? Have you seen her before?"

"No; but I know by her rig. No Cape man would have such a clumsy masthead to his vessel."

When the sails were furled, and all was made snug, our crew departed shoreward in the boat, leaving me alone on board, as "ship-keeper."

"There's plenty of eggs, and everything else you want, in the cabin, Charley; you must cook *lots* for yourself," said Smyra, as he gaily jumped into the stern sheets.

"And there are some good books in the cabin, too, Charles," said the skipper, "you can take whatever you please."

So they went ashore to their pleasant homes, while I, poor fellow, remained on board in solitude. It was a solitude I very much enjoyed. A Sabbath stillness reigned over the little bay in which we were anchored. Most of the vessels at anchor were entirely deserted; a few had a solitary ship-keeper, like myself a stranger to the Cape. . . .

On the third morning our crew returned on board and we set sail for Boston. As we sailed past the Cape, we met numbers of fishing vessels returning to their port of discharge, laden with mackerel. Smyra, who had made several trips "mackereling," was loud in his praise of fishing, and unceasing in his fish stories.

"Have you never been fishing?" said he. "You ought to go. It's great fun; and besides, I believe one can make more there than at coasting."

I paid little attention at first to his remarks; but his continued laudation of fishing life at last induced me to ask the captain if "mackerel catching" was indeed a money-making business. He owned that in good seasons there was money made at it, but thought that steady wages were much preferable. I considered on the matter. Somehow, shortly, the old desire for novelty took possession of me, and I determined that after completing the return trip to New York, I would make a trial of "mackereling."

— From WHALING AND FISHING

Charles Nordhoff met Smyra on a schooner-packet bound from New York to Cape Cod on which he shipped as a hand after landing in New York, 1851, broke and discouraged after five years of various adventures at sea. WHALING AND FISHING, *a book of reminiscences, was published in 1856. In 1857 he joined the house of Harper & Brothers and settled down to devote the rest of his life to letters and to writing. He was the grandfather of Charles Nordhoff who with James Norman Hall wrote* MUTINY ON THE BOUNTY *and other books.*

ॐ

THE MACKEREL FISHERY

BY SHEBNAH RICH

THE HISTORIC MACKEREL made his best flip in America with his insatious friend, the conservative codfish, to the great delight of the Pilgrims and Puritans, in their exceeding time of need; a kind service their sons and daughters are not soon inclined to forget. Consequently the mackerel needs no introduction to a Boston audience. Physically, they are not unworthy your attention or criticism, independent of a scientific description.

Look at the mackerel as it drops from the fisherman's hook. See how it quivers with fear, and struggles in its new element for liberty. Mark the harmony and perfection of every line. A perfect model, according to the most approved rules of modern naval architecture. Sharp ends fore and aft, good floor, not too much dead rise, a clean run, carries no dead water, steers easy, fine sea-boat, and sails like a fish.

Behold nature's rich endowment and profusion of painting. Satin-silver to the lateral lines, then flashing to sapphire, emerald and cerulean. But the mackerel was made for food, as well as beauty and fast sailing. Perhaps you have never eaten a mackerel. Not the limpy, pale-eyed fish, matriculated at Commercial Wharf or Fulton Market and graduated uptown after a course on ice, and sold for mackerel.

I mean a plump, muscular, number one, of the old-fashioned cull; caught in the sunrise spurt, dressed and corned shipshape, and fisherman-fashion; curled up on the taffrail, just right for supper, and in full flavor. That's food fit for Jupiter. 'There's eating for you,' as the Indian said to the Frenchman whose brother he had eaten for breakfast.

Of all the finny tribes that roam or sport in the ocean, the mackerel is the most beautiful, eatable and valuable. While fresh, it is found upon the table of the rich and poor, many months in the year; affording always a healthy and desirable, sometimes a delicious, and often for months, an exceedingly cheap kind of food. Fresh mackerel have been sold in London Market, as high as seven shillings each and as low as 60 for one shilling.

In 1833, 16 boats carried into the London Market, mackerel valued at $25,000, caught in a single day. In 1864, a boat carried in one night, mackerel that sold for over $500.

. . . . .

It is almost incredible how fast mackerel can be caught by a trained crew. The mackerel sometimes go up so fast that the whole side of the vessel shines like silver. In July, 1842, a crew of 11 men and boys 'struck a school' of biting mackerel on Georges Banks. In 25 minutes they caught 30 strike-barrels (a barrel so full that the live mackerel jump out.) . . .

Among leading fishermen, Skipper Richard Rich, of Truro was a celebrity in his day. For many years he was 'high line' in the country. On account of sailing many years in the schooner Osceola, he became widely known as 'Osceola Dick'; some thought that mackerel knew him as well and came to his hook.

One hundred and fifty wash-barrels was not a great deck for Osceola Dick. He has taken 190 wash-barrels in a single day, all saved in good order, and without feeling very fishy. I would not contract to make one of these old 'lucky skippers' believe Mr. Cushing's doctrine that one man knew just as well as another how to find mackerel. They knew better. In the old hooking days, there used to be skippers that always found fish and never missed a comfortable income, however hard the season. Possibly — probably — they were not all scholars or statesmen — perhaps not all saints, but they knew where to find fish and how to catch them.

The art in fishing may be learned, but uniform success is genius and must be inborn or in technical phraseology, a lucky skipper must be 'fishy.'

— From THE MACKEREL FISHERY OF NORTH AMERICA —
ITS PERIL AND ITS RESCUE, read before the Massachusetts Fish and Game Association and published in 1879

❧

I GO MACKERELING

BY CHARLES NORDHOFF

I SAILED BACK to Harwich in a little schooner bound that way. On the vessel's arrival, I proceeded ashore, in company with the crew. By the kindness of one, I was introduced to a good widow lady, who consented to board me while on shore, and care somewhat for my effects while away. Thus a kind of home was provided for me, where at very little cost to myself, I could spend a few days after each cruise, in comfortable though rather solitary enjoyment. Solitary, because on the Cape a "stranger" is looked upon with some degree of distrust. The Cape people are tolerably clannish; and although universally kind-hearted, never fail to remind a new comer that he is not one of them. In this, they are not indeed far wrong, for many of the strangers who temporarily sojourn in the fishing villages, and find employment as mackerel and cod fishermen, are not too trust-worthy; while most of them come only on the rather selfish errand of making a little money for themselves, to carry to some more congenial place than the Cape, to spend.

I remained a few days on shore, while the vessel in which I had secured a berth was being made ready for her first cruise. In these days, I saw sufficient of the Cape to convince me that it is not the most pleasant spot on the surface of our globe. The face of the country affords a not over agreeable diversity of views, consisting of sandhills and salt water marshes, scrub oaks and stunted pines; the ground work and filling up of the picture being sand, the abundance of which amply entitles the country to the euphonious name of "the Great Desert of Cape Cod."

The outlook seaward is scarcely more dreary than that from the sea landward. The stunted vegetation, the snug but lonely looking little houses, the great, barn-like structures called fish houses, each with the wooden image of a codfish or mackerel swinging from its steep roof, the absence of grass or aught of green near the shores, and above all and mixed with all, the everlasting glare of the sand, all united to give the shores of the Cape a most desolate appearance.

Where a country is poor the people are generally thriving and — in their way — happy. So it is here. I don't know that a fisherman's life exactly fills my ideal of a happy existence. But the people are universally frugal, industrious and intelligent — their wants are few, their tastes the reverse of luxurious, and the labor of their hands suffices to make them a competence — so that after all, making due allowance for the many hardships of their peculiar life, they are very happy.

The widow lady with whom I had made my home on my arrival on shore, was kind enough to provide me with many little articles, necessary only on such a trip as I was about to make. She set apart for my use, during my stay on shore, a neat little room, in which — for the first time since starting to sea — I made myself perfectly at home. Here I enjoyed once more, to some degree, a freedom from exciting care, which seldom falls to the sailor's lot. The quiet of the country — how much and often I had longed for it! — did my soul good, and I found myself in a condition of mind to sit down and reason with myself on the folly of the life which I had so long been leading. Here was strengthened my previously formed determination to leave the sea, and make myself a place "on shore" — that mystery to a sailor, whose visits to the land are just sufficiently long to make the *shore life* a marvel to him.

A little clipper schooner, the Mary Hawes, was just fitting out for a mackerel cruise. She had made two trips to "the banks" that year, had been successful in both, and her captain was now about to complete the year's work by a couple of months mackereling. Captain Jonathan Young had the name of being a smart fisherman; a "very fishy man," as those who knew him best called him. He was bred to the business, and was supposed to know the haunts and motions of cod fish and mackerel as any one in that part of the country. It was a natural consequence that such a man should gather about him an able crew. Some of his men were not to be beaten; several had at different times been "high line" from Harwich; and all were good fishermen. I was fortunate in securing a berth in her, as there I enjoyed the advantage of all their experience to enlighten my ignorance.

Fishermen do not of course labor at regular wages. The business is carried on on shares. The vessel has a certain share of the general catch. The captain has a share for his additional trouble and responsibility. An account is kept of provisions and fish-bait used, and this is fairly averaged among the crew. Each man keeps his fish separate, and when they are "packed" (that is to say, inspected and sorted), he receives either his net share of the fish, or their equivalent in money at the highest market price.

Sometimes, young men make a different arrangement, which is called "fishing for halves." They agree with some one ashore, generally a packer or inspector, to give him all their catch, he paying them in return one half its value, in cash, and taking the risk of making a clear profit from the balance. If the season is favorable and the fisherman has good fortune, the shoresman makes money by this, while if the catch is small, he loses — the provisions and other incidental expenses averaging as high in one case as in the other.

Through the kindness of a friend, I was introduced to a gentleman who, in consideration that I was to go in the Mary Hawes, agreed to let me fish for him at "half-line." This arrangement gave me great satisfaction, as it reduced my chances more to a certainty; and I felt just then a strong desire to make them as *certain* as possible.

Fancy me then on board. Oiled clothes, a barvel (an oiled cloth apron), hooks and lines, a bait knife, fishing mittens, and divers other matters needed to make up a perfect fishing outfit, are procured; two suits of clothes, and an indefinite quantity of rags (for sores, my landlady says) are snugly stowed away in a white clothes bag. A stock of "Vineyard" stockings, and a few interesting books are duly placed under the mattress of my narrow berth; and so with a good breeze we get under way.

"The fleet," as the collection of mackerel fishermen is called, is known to be off Portland. Thither then we wend our way — slowly enough — with light winds and calms. The first two or three days out, all hands are busied in preparing fish gear. "Jigs," as the peculiar hooks used to catch mackerel are called, are cast and burnished up; lines are stretched, measured and coiled away; beckets and cleats are placed opposite each man's place at the rail; and these places are fairly portioned off and marked, in order that no confusion may arise when fish are "along side." All these matters duly attended, and there is room to look about us, and occasion to express impatience at our slow progress toward the fleet.

I presume I ought to describe as nearly as may be, the appearance of the craft in which I now found myself. She was schooner-rigged — that is, had two masts, and fore and aft sails. She was a neatly built, sharp little craft of about one hundred and fifty tons burthen. Our crew numbered twelve men besides the cook. The galley, or cooking stove and kitchen generally, was in the forecastle, a narrow and dark little hole, about six by eight feet, exclusive of the berths — which berths, I may add, were all occupied.

One half the crew slept in the forecastle. The other and older half found their sleeping accommodations in the cabin. This was another contracted den, about six by ten feet. Its center was completely occupied by a table, from which all hands partook of their food. Locker-seats ranged along the side, fitted to this table. A row of shelves and a box compass and quadrant fill one end; a small stove and the hatch ladder, the other. A sky-light overhead gives necessary light. The whole smells villainously of decayed fish.

The hold is filled with barrels, some empty, some full of water, used as ballast. The deck contains naught but a bait-mill, a barrel of bait, and some strike-barrels which it is hoped we shall shortly fill with mackerel.

The crew were a set of genuine Cape men. I was the only "stranger" on board. The rest were all born and bred fishermen: quick moving, nervous men in fact, although they seemed, when unexcited, slow enough to please the most lymphatic Hollander. Our captain was a tall, portly man, blue eyed but dark complexioned, and of a fair presence. He was reputed — as he afterward proved himself — the most skillful fisherman on board. His lines and jigs were fitted with the most scrupulous nicety. He had a set for every kind of weather we were likely to experience, from the large line and heavy jig to be used only on fish-days or rough weather, to the most delicate fly-lines, with minute hooks and jigs, with which to tempt the daintiest of mackerel on smooth days.

He was a man of infinite patience. In a calm he would lean over the rail for hours at a time, once in a while hauling in a huge mackerel, while the others were lounging idly about decks, or if at the rail at all, were inattentive to their lines. His exhortations to others to attend to the fish, were ceaseless, while fish were alongside.

"Now they bite, boys; here's a spirt!" he would cry whenever, by unusual wariness, he succeeded in capturing a mackerel. Then would follow a rush to the rail, a few minutes of breathless attention, and finally, "now they don't bite, boys," from some disappointed lounger, as he fell back upon the deck or hatchway. Such was "the skipper," and a better man could not be found to command a fishing vessel. . . .

It was on the fifth night after our leaving port, that we came into "the fleet." During the day an occasional homeward bounder, steering off with all sail set, had passed us. Toward evening, white sails were visible in many directions. At sunset we were already near the outsiders, the videttes of the fleet. And before retiring to rest we were in the midst of a vast collection of vessels, their innumerable lights glistening upon the smooth expanse of ocean, and dancing solemnly up and down on the great swell which the Atlantic ever keeps up, much more resembling the vessels in a vast naval panorama, than a scene of real life.

There is something solemn and thought-inspiring in a scene like this, at all events to a thinking person who for the first time witnesses it. The entire stillness which reigns by night over this vast aquatic town, the absence of all noise except the continual faint roar of the swell, the sorrowful creaking of the rigging, and the solitary "sug" of the vessel's bow, as she falls into the trough of the sea; the bare poles of the distant vessels thrown in vivid, almost unnatural relief against the sky; the crazy motion of the little barks, as they are tossed about at the mercy of the waves, having scarce steerage way; the lonely-looking light on the mast, seeming to be the spirit which has entire charge of the hull beneath; the absence of all life where but a short time ago all was life and bustle; all this contrasted so strangely with the lively appearance of the vessels by day, as they skim rapidly over the waters, their great piles of snow-white canvas gleaming gayly in the sun, and their crews moving merrily about the decks, as to make me almost doubt that there were in fact in the shapeless masses drifting past us, hither and thither, at the mercy of wind and wave, men stout and able, who had often battled for their lives with the same old Ocean upon whose bosom they were now so placidly reposing.

But here comes one, rolling towards us,

"As silent as a painted ship, upon a painted ocean," and seemingly just as likely to hit us as not. We hail him.

"Schooner ahoy!"

"Hillo!" is answered by a tall figure which starts up from a reclining posture on the companion hatch.

"How many mackerel did you get today?"

"About twenty wash-barrels, mostly large."

"Did the fleet do anything?"

"Some of them lay still a good while, and I guess had pretty good fishing."

Here some of our crew mutter out a weak imprecation upon the weather, which has prevented us from joining the fleet before. Our friend hails us —

"Are you just from home?"

"Yes; all well there."— And the faint sound of the waves as they surge under his bows tells us that we are too wide apart for speaking purposes.

Standing a little farther on, into the thickest of the fleet, we too, about nine o'clock, hauled down our mainsail and jibs, and leaving one man on deck as a lookout, went below to prepare by a sound sleep for the labors of the morrow.

At early dawn we turned out to make sail. Although yet too dark to distinguish the numerous fleet in whose midst we had taken our place, our ears were saluted on all sides by the rattle of ropes, the creak of blocks, and the rustling of canvas, and we were conscious that ten thousand men were actively employed around us, at the same moment, in the same work, and preparing for similiar duties and labors.

As the day breaks, a grand spectacle bursts upon our view. The sky is clear, and the sun, as he rises above the eastern horizon, gilds with his rays the sails of a thousand vessels, as they lie spread out upon the mirror-like surface of the sea. And now our crew begin looking for acquaintances among the vessels. My astonishment is unbounded at hearing them name vessels distant from a quarter of a mile to six or seven miles, and that with perfect certainty of their correctness. To such perfection has practice trained the vision of these men that notwithstanding mackerel catchers are scrupulously rigged alike, the crew would point out not only schooners with which they were acquainted, but also tell the *hailing-places* of many which they had never seen before.

As an old salt, I prided myself not a little on my expertness in detecting differences in rig or build, but was obliged here to give up my art as completely beaten. For where I could not detect the slightest distinguishing characteristic, the experienced eyes of one of my companions would at a glance reveal the whole history of the vessel in question, and would enable him to tell, with a certainty which scarcely ever failed, the place where she was built, where rigged, and where at present owned. This wonderful faculty is the result of keen eyes and long experience, and is found nowhere in such perfection as among American fishermen.

Lying to for a little while, to try for fish, we shortly got under way, and stood on with the rest of the fleet. The wind was from northwest and every one of the nine or ten hundred vessels composing the fleet, are tacked to the northward. It was curious to watch their motions. They have no head, no organization of any kind; yet do they move as much in concert as would the best organized naval fleet, working by the signals of their commodore.

See, the headmost vessel of the fleet is in stays.[1] There the next one tacks. Little squads of half a dozen follow suit; and in fifteen minutes the whole fleet is on the other tack, standing to the westward. And so we go all day, working to the windward as fast as the light breeze will bear us along. Every once in a while some one heaves to and tries for mackerel. But mackerel won't bite well, in general, on such a day as this; and this day we don't see a live one at all.

Mackerel go in large schools, one of which contains fish enough, if all caught, to fill up every vessel in a fleet. But, vast as such a body is, it occupies but a very small space in the ocean which supports it. A school of fish, therefore, is to be searched out as one would look for a needle in a haystack — unwearying patience and determination being qualifications as necessary to constitute a successful fisherman as to make one a fortunate searcher for needles.

The fishery is pursued in small vessels, of from thirty to one hundred and twenty tons, and invariably of the "schooner" rig, that is, having two masts and "fore and aft" sails. The business commences in the latter part of March, when the mackerel first return to our coasts from their winter's absence in more southern waters, and lasts until the end of November. At that time the fish — and of course their pursuers also — have made the entire circuit of our eastern coast, from the capes of Delaware, off which they are first seen in early spring, to the extreme borders of Maine and the bays of British America, and back again as far as the headland of Cape Cod. Thence the fish — about Thanksgiving Day — take their final departure for their as yet undiscovered winter quarters.

All attempts made by enterprising fishermen to follow the mackerel, after they leave "the Cape," have hitherto proved utterly futile,

[1] A vessel is in stays when heading into the wind in tacking.

every trace of the vast school which annually congregates there being invariably lost within fifty miles of the south shoals of Nantucket. Many different surmises have been offered to account for their sudden disappearance, and various theories started by those curious in such matters, to explain the why and wherefore of the eccentric motions of a school of mackerel. But the matter is apparently just as much in the dark as ever, and their disappearance about Thanksgiving time remains as much a subject for speculation as the similar annual disappearance of swallows. Many, wise in such matters, think that the fish, after leaving our coast, lie at the bottom of the sea, in comparatively shoal water, in a state of stupefaction until the return of warm weather; others suppose that they emigrate to warmer latitudes, where they swim deep beneath the surface, in order to keep themselves in a temperature suited to their nature; and many old fishermen devoutly believe that after leaving us they are, somehow, changed into fish of an entirely different species, and are met with in tropical seas as albicores, bonita, etc. All that is *known* on the subject is, that those which leave the coast at the beginning of the winter are of moderate size, but very fat; while those which return in the spring are large, extremely poor, and ravenously hungry.

The vessels in which the fish are pursued and caught, are small, but strongly built, formed to resist some degree of bad weather, and having, almost invariably, excellent sailing qualities. The latter, indeed, is a necessary qualification of a vessel intended for this business, as the success of a voyage, in many instances, depends on a vessel getting to a certain place, where fish have been discovered, an hour sooner or later.

Thus, it once happened that the entire fleet took shelter in Cape Ann harbor, on occasion of a storm. After lying in port two days the weather moderated. Early the following morning the fleet got under way. The first little squad of about a dozen vessels, manned probably by the most eager fishermen, but consisting also of the fastest sailing schooners, had about forty minutes start of the balance. It was a beautiful morning. A very light breeze prevailed, before which none but the sharpest vessels could make headway. These had hardly gotten clear of the land, when they "struck" mackerel. They at once "hove to," and did not again get under way until their decks were filled — the fish biting all this time as fast as they could be hauled in. Meantime, the slower moving portion of the fleet had just time to reach the harbor's mouth when the little breeze which had carried them thus far died away, and it fell a dead calm; and they were actually forced to lie there, within four or five miles of a vast school of fish, and in plain sight of their more fortunate companions, without feeling a bite.

"The fleet" is an aggregate of all the vessels engaged in the mackerel fishery. Experience has taught fishermen that the surest way to find mackerel is to cruise in one vast body, whose line of search will then extend over an area of many miles. When, as sometimes, a single vessel falls in with a large school, the catch is of course much greater. But vessels cruising separately or in small squads are much less likely to fall in with fish than is the large fleet. "The fleet" is therefore the aim of every mackerel fisherman. The best vessels generally maintain a position to the windward. Mackerel mostly work to the windward slowly, and those vessels farthest to the windward in the fleet are therefore most likely to fall in with the fish first; while from their position they can quickly run down, should mackerel be raised to the leeward.

Thus in a collection of from six hundred to a thousand vessels, cruising in one vast body, and spreading over many miles of water, is kept up a constant although silent and imperceptible communication, by means of incessant watching with good spyglasses. This is so thorough that a vessel at one end of the fleet can not have mackerel alongside, technically speaking, five minutes before every vessel in a circle, the diameter of which may be ten miles, will be aware of the fact, and every man of the ten thousand composing their crews will be engaged in spreading to the wind every available stitch of canvas to force each little bark as quickly as possible into close proximity to the coveted prize. And then commences the trail of speed. Then the best helmsman is called to steer; every eye watches the sails, to see that they draw well, and every hand is ready to jump to remedy any defect. Then is the anxious moment for fishermen; for they see spread out before them a vast school of fish, in the midst of which lie the few favored vessels which have succeeded in raising them, and are now reaping a golden harvest. This is indeed the most exciting scene in the experience of a mackerel catcher.

The fish are caught with hook and line, each fisherman using two lines. When hauled on board, they are struck off by a peculiarly quick motion of the right hand and arm, into a strike-barrel standing behind and a little to the right of its proprietor. The same motion which leaves the mackerel in the barrel also suffices to project the hook (which has a little pewter run on its shank) back into the water, and the fisherman immediately catches up his other line, going through the same maneuver with it. So ravenously do the fish bite, that a barrel full is sometimes caught in fifteen minutes by a single man.

The bait used to entice them alongside, and keep them there afterward, consists of a mixture of clams and a little fish known by the euphonious name of "porgies." The last are seined in great quantities every summer in the mouth of the Connecticut River, and the adjacent waters, and are used by farmers as manure for their land, as well as by mackerel catchers as bait. This bait is ground up fine in a mill provided on board for the purpose, and is then thrown out on the water. It sinks to the depth at which the fish lie, when they, in their eagerness for it, follow it up until they get alongside the vessel. Once alongside, they bite indiscriminately at bait or naked hook.

Life on board a mackerel catcher is very monotonous. There is literally nothing to do. One man who can steer can work the craft all day. The sails are so arranged that in tacking they work themselves. The hands do therefore what they please. Some sleep, some read, some talk over old times, and a few old fishermen sit upon the quarter, hour after hour, spyglass in hand, watching the fleet and wishing for fish.

Some days we catch a few mackerel; some days we do not see a live one, but tack and tack to the windward all day long, glad when the setting sun proclaims the time for heaving to and going below to sleep. After more than a week of this kind of life, there comes a day when fishermen begin to prophecy the approach of a "regular fish day."

All day the wind is light and baffling, while a swell comes rolling in from the eastward, which makes our little vessel tumble about strangely — sails slatting, and blocks creaking mournfully in the calm.

Toward evening the wind goes down, the sky is overcast by white clouds, and the weather becomes a pea-jacket colder. Having found no fish all day, we take in sail early, see everything clear for a fish-day tomorrow, and all but the watch (one man), turn in about eight o'clock.

At midnight, when I am called up out of my warm bed to stand an hour's watch, I find the vessel pitching uneasily, and hear the breeze blowing fitfully through the naked rigging. Going on deck I perceive that both wind and sea have "got up" since we retired to rest. The sky looks lowering, and the clouds are evidently surcharged with rain. In fine the weather, as my predecessor on watch informs me, bears every sign of an excellent fish-day on the morrow. I accordingly grind some bait, sharpen up my hooks once more, see my lines clear, and my heaviest jig . . . on the rail ready for use, and at one o'clock return to my comfortable bunk. I am soon again asleep, and dreaming of hearing fire-bells ringing, and seeing men rush to the fire; and just as I see "the machine" round the corner of the street, am startled out of my propriety, my dream, sleep, and all, by the loud cry of "Fish ho!"

I started up desperately in my narrow bunk, bringing my cranium in violent contact with a beam overhead, which has the effect of knocking me flat down in my berth again. After recovering as much consciousness as is necessary to appreciate my position, I roll out of bed, jerk savagely at my boots, and snatching up my cap and peajacket, make a rush at the companion way, up which I manage to fall in my haste, and then spring into the hold for a strike-barrel.

And now the mainsail is up, the jib down, and the captain is throwing bait. It is not yet quite light, but we hear other mainsails going up all round us. A cool drizzle makes the morning unmistakably uncomfortable, and we stand half asleep, with our sore hands in our pockets, wishing we were at home. The skipper, however, is holding his lines over the rail with an air which clearly intimates that the slightest kind of a nibble will be quite sufficient this morning to seal the doom of a mackerel.

There, by Jove! the captain hauls back — there, I told you so! skipper's got him — ho — aha, captain, you haul back too savagely!

With the first movement of the captain's arm indicating the presence of fish, everybody rushes madly to the rail. Jigs are heard on all sides plashing into the water, and eager hands and arms are stretched their full length over the side, feeling anxiously for a nibble.

"Sh — hish — there's something just passed my fly — I felt him," says an old man standing alongside of me.

"Yes, and I've got him," triumphantly shouts out the next man on the other side of him, hauling in as he speaks, a fine mackerel, and striking him off into his barrel in the most approved style.

Z-z-zip goes my line through and deep into my poor fingers, as a huge mackerel rushes savagely away with what he finds is not so great a prize as he thought it. I get confoundedly flurried, miss stroke half a dozen times in hauling in as many fathoms of line, and at length succeed in landing my first fish in my barrel, where he flounders away "most melodiously" as my neighbor says.

And now it is fairly daylight, and the rain, which has been threatening all night, begins to pour down in right earnest. As the heavy drops patter on the sea the fish begin to bite fast and furiously.

"Shorten up," says the skipper, and we shorten in our lines to about eight feet from the rail to the hooks, when we can jerk them in just as fast as we can move our hands and arms. "Keep your lines clear," is now the word, as the doomed fish flip faster and faster into the barrels standing to receive them. Here is one greedy fellow already casting furtive glances behind him, and calculating in his mind how many fish he will have to lose in the operation of getting his second strike-barrel.

Now you hear no sound except the steady flip of fish into the barrels. Every face wears an expression of anxious determination; every body moves as though by springs; every heart beats loud with excitement, and every hand hauls in fish and throws out hooks with a methodical precision, a kind of slow haste, which unites the greatest speed with the utmost security against fouling lines.

And now the rain increases. We hear jibs rattling down; and glancing up hastily, I am surprised to find our vessel surrounded on all sides by the fleet, which has already become aware that we have got fish alongside. Meantime the wind rises, and the sea struggles against the rain, which is endeavoring with its steady patter to subdue the turmoil of old Ocean. We are already on our third barrel each, and still the fish come in as fast as ever, and the business (sport it has ceased to be some time since), continues with vigor undiminished. Thick beads of perspiration chase each other down our faces. Jackets, caps, and even over-shirts, are thrown off, to give more freedom to limbs that are worked to their utmost.

"Hillo! where are the fish?" All gone, every line is felt eagerly for a bite, but not the faintest nibble is perceptible. The mackerel, which but a moment ago were fairly rushing on board, have in that moment disappeared so completely that not a sign of one is left. The vessel next under our lee holds them a little longer than we, but they finally also disappear from her side. And so on all around us.

And now we have time to look about us — to compare notes on each other's successes — to straighten our back bones, nearly broken and aching horribly with the constant reaching over; to examine our fingers, cut to pieces and grown sensationless with the perpetual dragging of small lines across them — to — "There, the skipper's got a bite! here they are again, boys, and big fellows too!" Everybody rushes once more to the rail, and business commences again, but not at so fast a rate as before. By-and-by there is another cessation, and we hoist our jib and run off a little way, into a new berth.

While running across, I take the first good look at the state of affairs in general. We lie, as before said, nearly in the center of the whole fleet, which from originally covering an area of perhaps fifteen miles each way, has knotted up into a little space, not above two miles square. In many places, although the sea is tolerably rough, the vessels lie so closely together that one could almost jump from one to the other. The greatest skill and care are necessary on such occasions to keep them apart, and prevent the inevitable consequences of a collision, a general smash-up of masts, booms, bulwarks, etc. Yet a great fish-day like this rarely passes off without some vessels sustaining serious damage. We thread our way among the vessels with as much care, and as daintily as a man would walk over ground covered with eggs; and finally get a berth under lee of a vessel which seems to hold the fish pretty well. Here we fish away by spells, for they have become "spirty," that is, they are capricious, and appear and disappear suddenly.

Meanwhile the rain continues pouring out of the leaden sky, which looks as though about to fall on us, and overwhelm us in a second deluge. The wind is getting high; and the old hands are debating among themselves as to the most judicious port to be made tonight. At ten we get breakfast, consisting of coffee, hot cakes, bread and butter, fish, beef, sweet cakes, and apple sauce. The morning's exercise has given us all a ravenous appetite, and the celerity with which the various comestibles spread out for us by the cook are made to disappear, would astonish a dyspeptic.

After breakfast, we begin to clear up the decks a little, preparatory to experiencing some part of the rough weather which is brewing. Oil clothes are in great demand, but the rain somehow contrives to soak through them, and they form but little protection. We secure our mackerel barrels to the bulwarks, lash up various loose objects about decks, and put on the hatches. The fish still bite, but more moderately, and by spirts, and in the half liquid state in which we all find ourselves, we mechanically hold our lines over the rail and haul in fish with as little motion to our bodies as possible; for the skin in such weather gets marvelously tender, and is apt to rub off on very slight provocation.

At one o'clock "Seat ye, one half," from the cook, proclaims dinner on the table, and one half accordingly go down to "finish their breakfast," as a facetious shipmate remarks. The cabin of a fisherman be it known is too confined to accommodate an entire fishing crew with seats around the table, and accordingly it is customary for the oldest hands to eat first, leaving the young men and boys to follow at second table.

After dinner we make preparations for dressing our fish. Gibtubs, split-knives, barrels, wash-barrels, buckets, mittens, and seaboots, are hunted up, and water begins to flow about the decks more plentifully than ever. Mackerel are dressed by splitting them down the back, taking out their entrails (called in fishermen's parlance "gibs"), clearing them of blood by immersion in salt water, and then salting them down in layers, in the barrels prepared for that purpose.

Two persons compose a "gang" for dressing. One of them splits the fish and throws them to the other, who by a dexterous twist of his thumbs and the fingers of his right hand, extracts the entrails and throws the cleaned fish into a barrel of salt water at hand. Dressing fish is disagreeable work in itself, but generally passes off lively enough, as it is the concluding scene in what fishermen call "a day's work." One now learns how much he has in reality caught, and miser-like plunges up to the armpits in the riches he has that day won. Then too, dressing is enlivened by many a jest, and anecdote, and song, everybody feeling joyful at the events of the day, and hopeful for the success of the voyage. And while the operation of catching fish is followed with an intensity and ardor which does not admit of the slightest flagging of attention, dressing is the very reverse, and may be made as lively as possible without detriment to the work.

Soon after commencing to dress, the whole fleet gets under way, and steers toward the land, which is faintly visible under our lee, the wind being from the northeast. Going square before it, we are soon near the land, and as we do so, both wind and sea increase. We have a grand chance to try the sailing qualities of our little boat — a chance which a mackerel man never neglects; for next to getting a good share of fish, a man is considered most fortunate if he has a smart sailing vessel. We overhaul a good many, and are badly beaten by a few of the vessels, as might be expected in so large a fleet. And as we have come into competition with some new vessel, our crew tell at once her name, if she is known to them, or if entirely unknown, at any rate her hailing place.

After dressing, we salt our catch. This is sorry work for sore fingers, hands, and arms, of which, after a day's work like the present, there is always a plentiful supply, mackereling being under any circumstances a business in which sores of all kinds on hands and feet are singularly plenty and hard to get rid of. But salting does not last forever, and the few preparations for going into harbor being already completed, we gather together, as dusk comes on, in little knots about the deck, discuss the day's work, point out familiar vessels, and argue on their various sailing qualities, and once in a while slily peep down the companion-way into the snug little cabin, where the "ram-cat" (the sailors' name for a cabin stove) glows so brightly, and everything looks so comfortable, and in particular *so dry,* that our hearts yearn for a place by the fire. Landsmen, poor fellows, have no idea how great an amount of real, unmistakable comfort may be contained in a little box eight feet by twelve, with a table in the middle, seats and berths at the sides, a stove and hatchway at one end, a row of shelves and a box-compass at the other, and a skylight over head, the whole smelling villainously of decayed fish and bilge-water. Happily for mankind, all happiness is comparative, else would not the dirty, confined cabin of a fisherman ever be considered a very Elysium of comfort, and a seat by its fire regarded as a luxury, than which the conqueror of the world can wish for nothing better.

We are fast nearing our haven. And glad enough we all are of it, for the wind has risen until it already blows a gale, and the great waves roll after us savagely, trying to overtake us, and looking as though if they did, they would inevitably smother our little craft. And then too, as the excitement of the day dies out, and we stand inactively about, the rain seems colder, and our wet clothes adhere clammily to our bodies, and make moving about a misery. Yonder is East Point Light shining brightly on our beam. The headmost of our companions have already shot around the point, and are running up to their anchorage.

"Man your sheets now, boys, and stand by to trim aft!" sings out our skipper. As we string along the ropes the helm goes down. She comes into the wind, shaking like a dog just come out of the water, and at the same time the sails are trimmed flat, and we gayly round the point. In less than fifteen minutes we are in smooth water.

Two tacks take us nearly up to Ten Pound Island Light, and as we stand over once more,

"Haul down the foresail!" shouts the captain. "Stand by your main and jib halyards! see your anchor all clear!"

"There's a good berth, skipper," says one of the old hands, "right alongside of that Chatham smack." (It is so dark that, do my best, I can not make out even the rig of the vessel to which my old friend so readily gives a local habitation and a name.)

"Here we are — down jib!" and down it rattles without any trouble, as her head swings into the wind. As her headway is deadened, "let go the anchor!" is the word, and a plash, and the rattle of a few fathoms of cable tell us we are fast for the night.

"Pay out cable, boys; a good scope, and let her ride easy!" and the rest of us go aft and haul down the enormous mainsail, the wet canvas of which feels as though made of stout wire. It is soon furled up, and a lantern fastened in the rigging, and then we make a general rush for the cabin. Here wet clothes and boots are flung off and thrown pell mell on deck, dry suits donned, and then one half crawl into their bunks, while the balance eat their suppers.

Meanwhile we hear an incessant rattling of sails and plashing of anchors on every side of us, while the wind whistles wildly through the rigging, and the rain dashes fiercely against the skylight and deck overhead, increasing our comfort by reminding us of the sufferings we have escaped.

It is not until after supper that we begin to think of the damages sustained in our persons during the past day's work. And now rags, salve, and liniment, and all the various preparations for ameliorating the condition of sore fingers, sore wrists, sore arms, sore feet, sore ankles, and sore shins, are brought into requisition; the cook is flattered and cajoled out of modicums of hot fresh water; and stockings are taken off, sleeves rolled up, bandages unrolled, and groans and growls resound from every corner of the cabin.

Before retiring to rest I take a peep on deck. The gale is roaring fiercely through the bare rigging, and a blinding storm of hail and sleet, a blast of which salutes my face as I put it out of the companion-way, adds to the inclemency of the night. The dark storm clouds scud wildly across the sky, and the wind fairly shrieks at times, as though glorying in the strength to bear down everything coming in its path. It is truly a wild night, and as I descend again to my comfortable place by the fire, I think anxiously of the poor souls who are tossed about in such weather — cold, wet, and suffering at the mercy of the winds and waters. I am not alone in my thoughts, for as I shake the sleet off my rough cap, I hear our grayheaded old skipper mutter softly to himself, "God pity poor sailors who are caught in Boston Bay in this storm."

We go to sleep early — get up late the next morning — get breakfast — the storm still raging — head up, and strike down the mackerel caught the preceding day; clear up decks, and then go ashore or visit some of the other vessels. . . .

Toward evening the wind hauls to the northward, the weather clears up, and great snow-white clouds, looking like gigantic puffs of steam from some engine in the other world, roll grandly across the sky, sure signs of good weather. We turn in early, and are called out at three o'clock to get under way. We find everybody around us in motion, some heaving up their anchors, others hoisting their sails, some with boats ahead, being towed out of the crowd, so as to enable them to shape a course, and a few already steering out of the harbor. We follow suit with all haste, and daylight finds us in Boston Bay, with the fleet around us, and the hills of Cape Ann blue in the distance.

Such is a fish-day, with its accompaniments. Of a series of such, with the intervening periods of idleness, our trip was composed. It would be tedious to enter into a narrative of the voyage, therefore. Sufficient understanding of the delights and discomforts of the business will be gained by what I have recounted. Our first trip lasted five weeks. In that time we filled up every barrel on board. Returning to Harwich, we landed our cargo. Here the fish were assorted, packed and weighed; and the barrels finally branded to show "200 lbs. mackerel," No. 1, 2, or 3, as the case may be. After four days detention, we set out upon another trip. This time we were four weeks in filling up our vessel. It was now getting cold. So upon our second return to port, I left the vessel, received the returns for my labor, and with about forty dollars in my pocket, took passage in a schooner bound to New York.

—From WHALING AND FISHING

෨෴

The story is told of two Cape Cod sisters who came home from boarding school in New York and complained to their father that he smelled fishy.

"Girls, I smell of money!" was his stern reply.

෨෴

A plain marble shaft on a brownstone base in the Snow Burial Ground in Truro bears this inscription:

Sacred
to the memory of
FIFTY-SEVEN CITIZENS OF TRURO
who were lost in seven
vessels, which
foundered at sea in
the memorable gale
of October 3, 1841.

Then shall the dust return to the earth as it was; and the spirit shall return to God who gave it.

Man goeth to his long home, and the mourners go about the streets.

The names, with ages in single columns, cover the other sides of the shaft. Of the lost citizens Henry Paine, Benjamin F. Bridgman, Reuben Snow, Henry Bradly, and Richard Atwood were fourteen years old; Joseph Wheat was thirteen; Andrew W. Cordes and Thomas C. White were twelve, and Charles W. B. Nott was eleven.

The Grand Bankers left home in the early spring and disappeared into oblivion for from three to five months. Fog and icebergs were

*constant perils off the banks. In the great days the fishing vessels
often carried small boats as whaleships did in which men went out
from the mother vessel to fish; many grim stories are told of them
being swept away in storm or fog never to be seen again. One had
a happy ending.*

☙

SAILORS' RETURN

BY DONALD G. TRAYSER

MAY 27 Provincetown mourned for three days in May, 1898.
Schooner Joseph E. Johnson had come in decked in black, with the sad
news that 16 of her crew, caught out in a fog in their dories on the
Grand Banks, had never been found. Then, this day, an incredible
thing happened. Around Long Point came the fleet of dories, with
every one of the lost 16 safe and sound! This was their story: lost
in the fog they hung together and started a 200-mile pull to LeHavre,
N.S.; hardtack gave out and they got down to a raw fish diet; then
by great good luck along came the Norwegian bark China, Hamburg
for New York, which took men and dories aboard; then she fell in with
the schooner Merritt, homeward bound to Boston; the Merritt this
day dropped fishermen and dories nine miles off Race Point, and
they triumphantly rowed into Provincetown. The lost were found.
— From ONCE UPON A TIME ON CAPE COD

*The Cape's trading activities were the natural outgrowth of the
fishing. It was the custom of many of the early Grand Bankers to
salt and dry their catch on the nearest beach and carry it directly to
the West Indies where they picked up a cargo of rum and molasses
for the journey home. Soon glut threatened this market and the
more ambitious fishermen began to salt their fish only enough to
keep them for the run back to the Cape; here they cured them
thoroughly in the fall, the fishing season over, packed them into their
round-bottomed, two-masted, seventy-ton schooners, and set sail for
France, Spain and Portugal, bringing home from the foreign ports
whatever adventure they could find. The master of one of these*

vessels was likely to be merchant, owner, captain, all in one, save for the shares that might be owned by members of his crew. To fit his vessel for fishing, to catch, to cure, to find the foreign market and to come home generally required about a year. It was a profitable, cosy, independent business while it lasted but early in the nineteenth century the tremendous maritime development of the whole eastern seaboard brought a demand for longer voyages still and for larger ships.

There are few harbors on Cape Cod capable of accommodating clipper ships and, although the Cape was thriving, there lacked the capital to build them or to finance them on their long voyages. But if the Cape didn't have the ships, it had the men. Cape Cod shipmasters were eagerly pressed into service by the great companies of Boston and New York and, although they sailed for others, the ships they drove and the records they hung up add lustre to the Cape's history.

Even the roll of the names of the great captains is too long to print here.

ᥫᩣ

CIRCUMNAVIGATOR

BY DONALD G. TRAYSER

DECEMBER 12 Died this day in 1794 in Hawaii, Captain John Kendrick, the Cape Cod shipmaster often called the first American commander to circumnavigate the world. He was born in Harwich in 1740, went early to sea, was whaling at 20, fought in the French and Indian wars, and was master of three privateers in the Revolution. He commanded the expedition of the Columbia and Lady Washington which sailed out of Boston in 1787 for the Northwest coast. After some trading there he transferred the Columbia to his associate Captain Robert Gray, and sailed in the Lady Washington for China. After more than a year trading he returned to the Northwest coast via Japan, where he was the first American to fly the Stars and Stripes. In 1793 Captain Kendrick voyaged again to China and then to the Northwest, stopping off at Hawaii. There he engaged in some inter-island troubles, and being on the prevailing side, requested a fellow trader in the harbor, Captain Brown of the Jackal, to salute him. By some negligence one of Brown's guns had not been unshotted. The ball pierced the hull of the Washington and killed Captain Kendrick at his table.

—From ONCE UPON A TIME ON CAPE COD

ↄ∾ↄ

ONE RECORD

In 1852 He Became Famous Making the Astonishing Passage in Clipper Ship North Light from 'Frisco to Boston in 76 days 6 hours, an Achievement Won by No Other Mortal Before or Since.

—Epitaph on grave of Captain Freeman Hatch in Eastham

ↄ∾ↄ

WOMEN WHO WENT TO SEA

BY ORA A. HINCKLEY

Sing praises all ye people to the men of the sea, from the
   lowest in rank to the greatest.
Sing praises to those of the humblest of sailing vessels;
   to those of the fishing fleet; to those of whaling vessels; to those of the great and beautiful clipper ships.
But this time the women of the sea are to be the theme
   and praises we sing in their honor.

ENVIRONMENT largely makes people what they are. Cape Cod boys watched the sea and whatever was doing on it, played by it, listened to tales of it. In many, many cases they went to sea before they were in their 'teens and were captains before they were out of them. Do you not think that something of the sea's strength and spirit was absorbed in the makeup of the Cape Cod girls? They, too, lived by it, listened to stories of it and answered its call. Women could not have done all that men have done, but they have, on occasion, performed gloriously. Then men went to sea to gain a livelihood. The women shared in the responsibilities of living. The wife at home, the husband at the ends of the earth perhaps, each doing a part. It is more difficult to work apart in keeping a home and bringing up a family, than working shoulder by shoulder. As far as the home and children were concerned, perhaps the wives of Cape Cod sailors carried the heavier load. And partings, the long separations — often voyages were years long — and the worry, taxed women's strength and nervous energy almost beyond endurance.

> This is the land where women mated
> And gave their men to the deep and waited,
> Bearing their babes alone,
> And by the bleak hearthstone
> Battling the awful dread
> Interminable absence bred.

At best, letters were infrequent. No telephone or radio, and one might be fearful of news when it should arrive. And many, many times it never came. One might hear reports of storms at sea, yet not learn particulars. And all the time the wife must go on with her household work. Nancy, wife of Captain Ezra Nye of Sandwich, wrote her sister in a time of anxiety: "I have learned to keep my anxious feelings to myself and hide an aching heart under a cheerful face . . . what good does it do to bare your troubles to the world? I say to you, Lucy, if I had my life to live over again and my choice between the bare necessities of existence and such anxious homes and bitter partings, I would be content with one meal a day."

There is the prayer of the fisherman's wife:

> When the storm breaks on the sea, God,
> Be kind to the fishing ships.

The New England Gazetteer for 1839 said that in Barnstable County lived nearly a thousand widows who had lost their husbands at sea. In two towns alone, Harwich and Wellfleet, there were 223 women who had thus lost their life's companions. Every history of Cape Cod records storms and shipwrecks. The gale of 1841 brought to Truro the loss of fifty-seven men, to Yarmouth ten, and to Dennis twenty. Think of the darkened homes. What did that storm do to women's hearts? What, when their little boys at the age of ten, eleven, twelve or fourteen left snug homes for the sea? Why are these things mentioned here? It is to tell of what Cape Cod women were made. Does not strength and fineness stand out? In the book, *Mary Peters,* by Mary Ellen Chase, it is said: "And now I see that the sea made women too."

But there is also a bright side to the picture. What joy of anticipation when father or husband or lover was expected home. What preparations — house cleaned, sewing put away, pantry shelves loaded. Everything possible must be set aside for entertainment. And then what a welcoming! How gay the house! What festivities! Everyone concerned must join the party. The silver and china that had reposed on spotless shelves, the fine table linen, all must be brought forth. How the silks rustled and the satins shone. The village news was told, this event and that rehearsed. And beaux and maids somehow found corners for little conversations. What joy the gift bringing was! "What did your father bring?" "What did Robert bring?" What a great opening and unloading of gifts. Perhaps there were furs from the great north, or china from England, or silks and shawls from India, or beautiful cabinets and lacquered boxes from China, or vases from Japan. Every port and every land must contribute something for the folks at home. The captain who had a wife and three or four daughters and perhaps a niece to whom he wished to bring some gift, what a task was his, to choose what each would best like. How about Captain Benjamin Hallett of Osterville, with ten daughters? One thing he did for them was to name one of his ships the Ten Sisters.

Bureau drawers, chests and attics held so much in those days. One woman recalls that sometimes, when she wanted a new dress, her mother would say: "Why don't you go upstairs and get some of that Pina cloth your father brought from India? There's a whole roll." No, she preferred to go to the store, and get a little new calico or muslin, something not half as nice or pretty. Pina cloth was common then among her friends.

Then there were the thrilling tales told by the returning captains and sailors, of other lands and other peoples. It was better than studying and reading books of geography, to hear them talk. Cape Cod folks lived ȯn a narrow bit of land, but they had contacts with the whole world, with wherever ships sailed. This peninsula is narrow, but the people were not. The women at home kept track of their men as best they could, through letters, and through the shipping lists in the newspapers. If one's husband was in Liverpool, whatever the newspapers remarked of that city caught the eye. If one's sailor was in South America, news from that country was of engrossing interest. If war or famine or cholera were reported in China, it was read with concern. Captain Crowell's wife could not "call up" Captain Baxter's wife and say "I see the Cap'n has arrived," but we may be sure of the conversation at afternoon calling, after church on Sunday, or when they went to spend the day. The main talk was not idle gossip; international affairs and great trade were involved; for did not Captain Crowell have in his chest many thousands of dollars in cash, and in his ship very valuable cargoes? These women sensed the vastness of responsibility, even if they had no direct part in shouldering it.

·   ·   ·   ·   ·

Cape Cod women generally were travelled. If they did not accompany their husbands on sea voyages, they were frequently going to this port or that, to welcome them when they arrived, to be with them when they were in port, or to say goodbye when they sailed again. To go to Boston, or New York, was simple; this or that Hyannis woman might be in San Francisco to watch the clipper ship of her heart as it came through the Golden Gate. . . . And now we must begin to tell about a few of these very real people, these women who went to sea.

Let us commence with Sylvia Baxter. . . . Sylvia Baxter Crowell Allyn was first the wife of Captain William Allen Crowell, son of Captain Allen Crowell, and she went to sea with him in the schooner Hattie Baker. Captain Joshua Baker had an interest in the vessel, and named her for his daughter. While the Hattie Baker lay at anchor in Mobile Bay one morning in November, 1874, Captain Crowell went out in a small boat, gunning. He never returned, and his body was not recovered until several months later. C. Howard Allyn, first mate of the Hattie Baker, brought her home. After Mrs. Crowell's return to Hyannis a son was born, and named William Allen, for his father. The son, who has since died, is remembered in Hyannis as "Willie Allen" Crowell. After several years, Mrs. Crowell married Captain Allyn, who as mate had brought her home on that sad voyage from Mobile. She accompanied Captain Allyn on all his voyages, perhaps seven or eight years in all. They journeyed far and wide, visiting ports in all the continents and sailing every ocean. They went to China, and Mrs. Allyn had a great interest in Japan. She was there in cherry time, in chrysanthemum time.

In the ship Importer, Captain Allyn made six consecutive voyages around the world. Their last voyage was in the ship Titan and it came to an end in a tropical hurricane in October, 1894. It was a frantic time. The Titan, loaded with phosphate from Navassa, bound for New York, was overtaken by the gale midway between Mobile Bay and Yucatan. The Norwegian bark Chrisolite saved everyone. A rope was tied about Mrs. Allyn and she was drawn from the wrecked vessel to the rescuer. In a dreadful state of mind, Mrs. Allyn hesitated at first, but encouraged by Captain Allyn, she consented and came through the experience safely. The Norwegian bark landed the Titan's crew and Mrs. Allyn at Mobile, the very port where her first husband was lost, and there she was received into the same family as before — a family of friends, indeed. The Allyns never went to sea again. The loss of the Titan was a great blow to them, for Captain Allyn had owned a share of her. Everything on the ship was arranged for their comfort and convenience. Mrs. Allyn had her own piano, and both had fine libraries, she of music and pleasurable reading, he of philosophy and the sciences. She was a fine musician and for many years, perhaps thirty in all, played the organ at the Universalist church. Mrs. Allyn died in 1923, Captain Allyn in 1932. In his last illness, realizing he could not recover, Captain Allyn remarked to his physician: "Doc, you may as well put me on a plank and shove me to Davy Jones' locker." He was Hyannis' last deep-water shipmaster.

Of Mary Gorham Baker, wife of Captain Ezekiel Baker, it is related that she did not enjoy going to sea, and that she was often seasick, but that her happiness in being with her husband outweighed all other feelings. It must have, for she went around Cape Horn with him eleven times! . . .

Captain Baker's commands were numerous, and many thousands were Mrs. Baker's miles of sea travel. She crossed the country overland to California numerous times to meet him. She could tell of parties and gaiety in many ports. She could tell of how, when the ship arrived in port for a stay, it was cleaned and painted, and there were always parties and grand dances and balls aboard her. Captain

Baker was a big man, a handsome one, and a dandy. He always had a span of horses to take them about, and they lived like lords. She told of wonderful balls in London and Liverpool, such as one to which she wore a yellow moire silk gown, and of which she remembered best that the Captain was the handsomest man there. On one trip she brought home four pieces of moire silk of four different colors, one white for her sister's wedding gown, another for her own dress for the wedding, and so on.

Charles R. Flint, a shipowner who had hired Captain Baker as "Grand Admiral" when he fitted out the "Dynamite Fleet" for Brazil in 1893, and who had previously placed Captain Baker in command of the clipper Young America, told this in his memoirs of Mrs. Baker:

"A striking example of courage and presence of mind was the case of the wife of Captain Baker, commanding an American bark that was transporting Negroes to work on the Panama Canal. The bark was at anchor off Colon. The Captain went ashore, leaving his wife alone in the cabin. There were five hundred Negroes on board. Just before dark they mutinied. Mrs. Baker from a cabin window saw the fight going on between the Negroes and the crew, but instead of being demoralized by the fact that the Negroes, owing to their greater numbers, would soon overpower the crew, rush aft and break down the cabin doors, she reached out of one of the cabin windows, took the signal halyards off the mizzen-pin band, bent on and hoisted from inside the cabin the signal: "Mutiny on Board." The American flagship Tennessee immediately responded and put down the mutiny just as the Negroes were entering the cabin."

· · · ·

How wonderful it must have been for another Mrs. Baker, Sophia Lovell Baker, to go on her honeymoon trip, with her captain-husband, to the West Indies! Seth was captain and part owner of the topsail schooner Pequot. They were married in 1822, and he took her with him on a voyage to Jamaica. It was a red letter event in her life and she never tired telling of it, particularly of their dinner with the governor general. The governor general, Edourd Arojah, lived in a fine residence outside Kingston, on a mountain side, and he sent a palanquin to convey Captain Baker and his bride to the mansion. When they departed after a royal dinner, Governor Arojah presented his young guests with a small mahogany case containing four bottles

of Jamaica rum. Two of these gold-engraved bottles have been preserved in the family. Walter D. Baker, a grandson, speaks with sad-
ness in recalling them; they have now degenerated to receptacles for
rubbing alcohol! . . . After that honeymoon voyage of 1822 Sophia
Lovell Baker did little seafaring; she was busy at home raising eight
children. The first was named Edward Arojah for the gracious governor general. . . .

Hersilia Basset, wife of Zenas D. Basset, Jr., sailed to Africa once,
and there a chief wanted to buy her, which was not strange, for she
was a handsome woman. But as Captain Basset remarked, American
women are not sold . . . Mrs. Basset went on several voyages to Brazil
about 1843-4 and one little incident she used to relate was that
Emperor Don Pedro, when married, cried. He was only eighteen and
didn't like his bride. . . .

Captain Zenas Marston of Hyannis Port, according to a niece, had a
clean shirt and shaved every day during his voyages. Going away
on a long one, he would take enough shirts for a year, more than three
hundred in all, and all hand-made by his wife. Does this sound
like a tall story? Well, Captain Sumner Pierce of Barnstable wore
a clean boiled shirt every day, and sometimes returned from a voyage
with seven hundred to be laundered. It is somewhat amazing, this
matter of sea captains' shirts. One wife recalled: "There were rafts of
them." Another: "There were stacks of them, literally, when the
Captain set forth on a voyage." The heart of the story is that in
those days of long and distant voyages, shirts were made at home because not only were they difficult to buy, but more difficult to get
washed and starched, away from home. A daughter of a sea captain
remarked: "I was so proud when I could iron a shirt." James Percival of Barnstable wrote home from San Francisco in 1851 — he was
on the ship Gamecock — "I suppose this is one of the worst places
in the world for gambling, murders and robbery . . . everything is extremely dear. . . . Washing is six dollars per dozen. It is cheaper to buy
new shirts at auction than to get dirty ones washed."

The shirt problem of these sea captains was but part of another —
their careful attention to dress in general. In Mary Starbuck's book
on Nantucket she refers to her father, as, like many seafaring men,
of great personal fastidiousness. His shirts had to be of the finest
linen and of perfect fit; his shoe ribbons were always perfectly tied
and the bows flattened out perfectly. When Captain Ezra Baker of

Hyannis returned from an expedition to Brazil and put up at a New York hotel, the very first thing he did was to send his suit out to be pressed and cleaned. He sent it so hastily that the astounded tailor found in a vest pocket a roll of bills containing $10,000!

. . . . .

To China on a voyage with her husband, Captain Richard Bearse, went Bethia Bearse. She always remembered that first visit and well she might. With a party of friends she went "up country" and was almost mobbed by the Chinese. It was 1856, not long after the country had been opened to foreigners. The Chinese threw themselves on the ground to gaze at her feet which, to those used to seeing only tiny, bound feet, seemed so large. . . .

Seafaring Halletts were as numerous as seafaring Bearses in Hyannis during the last century. Captain Alvin Hallett was another noted shipmaster, and his wife Lydia often accompanied him on foreign voyages. Once in London, with their son Alvin, they had a beautiful family portrait painted. . . . Speaking of the Hallett portrait reminds one that many a sea captain sat for his picture in a foreign land. And many times they would take photographs of wives or sweethearts to foreign lands, to be enlarged and copied. Many a captain, too, had his ship painted in Canton or Hong Kong, and these were those stiff, formal pictures one often sees. Family portraits and ship's pictures done in foreign lands hang on the walls of many Cape Cod houses today.

. . . . .

Rose Scudder, who married Captain Henry Parker, could tell of a Calcutta voyage so rough that the captain tied her in bed to keep her from rolling about. . . . Mostly in our village we remember Captain Parker for the wreck of the Bark Santee in a hurricane off Bermuda when he clung to the overturned hull for three days, suffered a broken leg, and didn't have it set until he reached Hyannis, just thirty days after he lost his fine bark. But the Parkers are also remembered for "Spanish Teresa." Returning from a voyage to Spain, they brought home a bright, alert little Spanish girl of twelve years. This was "Spanish Teresa." Many Hyannis people remember her. She afterwards married a Cahoon, and her descendants are the Washington family, living in and near Hyannis Port. Her daughter, who is Mrs. George Washington, tells that this happened: Her mother and sister were down on the wharves in the Spanish port and Teresa went aboard Captain Parker's ship to sell flowers and fruits; then the ship set sail and she couldn't get back to shore; and she never got back to Spain to see her mother; and that to her dying day — she lived to be ninety-nine years old — she never ceased to cry for her mother and her home in far-off Spain. . . .

The list of Hyannis women who sailed on foreign voyages seems, indeed, almost endless. But we must not forget that these were not the only Hyannis women who went to sea. We must not forget those who sailed on the coasting vessels, on the steamers, and on the barges.

Adeline Brown accompanied her husband, Captain Allen H. Brown, on coasting voyages from Maine to the West Indies, for perhaps fifteen summers. As Captain Brown remarked, the cabins were nice and comfortable and made a good summer home. Sometimes the cargo was ice, and the coolness and dampness caused by two thousand tons of ice could be felt in the cabin quarters, and a good fire was necessary for comfort. Can you picture that — sailing along in midsummer, with the weather hot outside, and a fire to keep one warm? Captain Brown died in 1936, one of the last of our old coasting captains. . . .

Sally Allen Hallett often joined her husband, Captain George H. Hallett, on his steamer trips between New York and Baltimore. Sometimes in good weather he would take Sally and their three daughters. Ella, Mrs. Frederick L. Lothrop, one of the daughters, remembers that her father insisted that on the steamer they always be dressed at night, thus that they "sleep with their clothes on." He would say, before they started, "bring along an old dress for nights." They might loosen their clothes, but must be fully dressed for an emergency. And, woman-like, Ella never took an old dress; she made a new one for nights at sea. That was part of the pleasant preparations. She chose inexpensive material, usually a pretty calico. Someone else who went on foreign voyages made a similar remark: that she always wore a nightgown other than white, of material more like a day dress. It may have been the common thing. . . .

Barges are no trim ships; they are made for carrying cargo only, and plenty of that. Yet a few Hyannis women enjoyed pleasant voyages on them. Captain Horace F. Hallett owned a line running out of New York to Jersey and Connecticut ports which employed several Hyannis men, and sometimes they took their wives along in summer. Cora Baxter went with Edwin Baxter several voyages, and Eunice Ring went with William D. Ring two seasons. "Going barging" she enjoyed every minute, Mrs. Ring said. "It was almost like living out of doors." She remarked upon the little cabin, the little stove on which meals were cooked, and the lines stretched on the barge for hanging out clothes. Life was leisurely and pleasant on those summer cruises. She missed seeing her neighbors going to work, or to the stores, and running in and out to see the folks next door; but there were other barges and ships to watch, skies to gaze upon, and though she wouldn't like it for all time, there was always home ahead, so both could be enjoyed. . . .

— From BARNSTABLE: THREE CENTURIES OF A CAPE COD TOWN

BARNSTABLE: THREE CENTURIES OF A CAPE COD TOWN, by Donald G. Trayser, was published by F. B. & F. P. Goss in Hyannis in 1939. The volume contains a number of articles by distinguished contributors and was sponsored by the Barnstable Tercentenary Committee, appointed by the Town of Barnstable to arrange for suitable observance of the town's tercentenary year in 1939. Ora A. Hinckley's long, careful, loving piece mentions many other sea-going Hyannis ladies whose stories the editors of SAND IN THEIR SHOES have reluctantly been obliged to omit for reasons of space.

☙

Cape Cod was never a shipbuilding center but early in the nineteenth century Asa Shiverick was building sloops, schooners and brigs in his shipyard at East Dennis. In 1848 his three sons, David, Asa, Jr., and Paul closed that yard and constructed a larger one from which were launched eight deep-water, square-rig ships averaging 1000 tons register, the only such vessels ever built upon the Cape. In 1924 a monument was erected in Dennis to mark the site of their achievement.

☙

1848–1863

SHIPBUILDING AT EAST DENNIS

BY THOMAS F. HALL

ON LAUNCHING DAYS, neighbors from surrounding towns flocked to the shipyard to witness a completed vessel take her first plunge. Many of the men visitors took positions on the ship's deck, ready to man the capstans and ropes as soon as the ship reached the water, in order to hurry her down the stream during the brief time she was afloat

It required several days of tugging and hauling to get a ship out of the creek safely into the bay. The sharp bend in the creek, just below the present cold storage building (which was then midway the wharf), caused some delay in getting the ships around it, delaying them usually over a tide, or a day. But, strangely enough, it so happens that the "Webfoot," the largest ship of them all, was the easiest to get around that corner.

The first two ships built, "Revenue" and "Hippogriffe," were provided with jury masts, yards and sails; and sailed to Boston under their own rig. In Boston they were permanently sparred and rigged for sea.

None of the other ships had a full jury rig. Instead a tug boat came down from Boston, backed up into the creek as far as the wharf, took the ship in tow, and returned with her to Boston.

The launchings always occurred during the high course tides in the early spring or fall. Even then there was not a great surplus of water, only enough really to float the larger ships for about one-half to three-quarters of an hour at each tide.

The captains of the ships were appointed to their positions long before the ships were launched; sometimes before the keel was laid. It was, therefore, customary to say that the ship was built for the designated captain. These captains assumed command as soon as the ship reached the water.

In May (1857) my father died. The ship that was being built at the time of his death was launched on Sept. 1 of that year and named for him, "Christopher Hall."

No ship was built after his death for five years. Then only one more.

Every ship that was built while my father lived was commanded by an East Dennis man. Every one was officered and apprenticed, on every voyage, largely by East Dennis men and boys. The boys usually started on their seafaring career at about the age of 15. It will be seen, therefore, even across this long distance in time, that such an enterprise, located in such a small village, naturally conferred unnumbered blessings on every one of its inhabitants.

I can write about the joint enterprise of the shipyard, wharf and maritime commerce, with perhaps a pardonable pride, and with some sentiment, because my father was the capitalist, the promoter and prime mover in it all. He was the sole owner of the first ship, the "Revenue," and he determined the location of the shipyard.

I can write about the ships themselves from individual experience. Six years of my youth, commencing at the age of 15, were spent at sea on two of those beautiful ships, the "Wild Hunter" and the "Belle of the West," circumnavigating the globe in each.

To understand clearly the high standard reached in developing those shipyards, it should be remembered that they were built during the years when the American Mercantile Marine itself was in the very zenith of its fame and glory. The merchant ships of the United States eclipsed those of all nations in the world, in swiftness, in beauty, in seaworthiness, in stability, and in the standing of their builders and commanders. This fact is not an overdrawn statement; it is universally acknowledged history. When, therefore, it is realized that ships from the Shiverick yard were not only equal, but in some technical respects, superior to any in the American fleet, it is more than gratifying to local pride; it is touching very closely the immortal, to truthfully say that no loftier pitch of the shipbuilder's art has ever been attained than that which was reached through the skill of the Shivericks, made manifest in the ships they launched from that very yard, in the memorable years between 1849 and 1863.

The world has seen no finer ships. None ever floated on the sea that were more staunch, more lovely, swift, or more beautiful; none that made a grander sight when their transient beauties blended with the eternal beauty of the sea.

Those were great years; great events; great men.

It is to be hoped that the original drawings of the "Belle of the

West" may yet be found among the papers left by her brilliant designer, Samuel Hartt Pooke of Boston. She was, in my opinion, the finest specimen of naval architecture ever seen. Every line in her hull was grace and beauty.

It was my good fortune, at one time, in a foreign port, to see that beautiful ship, full rigged, hauled out of the water, to be recoppered.

I still suffer the regret I then felt, on observing for a week or two that beautiful picture, silhouetted against a fleecy Indian sky, in a grand panoramic view, that it could not at that time have been wrought in marble, to vie in artistic beauty through the ages with the choicest Phidian statues, and to immortalize the name of her designer, the youthful Samuel Hartt Pooke of Boston, the Praxiteles of his time.

The cabin of the "Belle of the West" was my home for four and one-half years. She at last became my sweetheart, my idol. She was a graven image before which, for years, I daily bowed and worshipped, and although she has been lying in her grave at the bottom of the sea in the Bay of Bengal for sixty years, I would delight, if it were possible, to erect a marble shaft over the spot where her sacred bones are resting.

> "I know what master laid her keel,
> What workmen wrought her ribs of steel,
> Who made each mast, and sail, and rope,
> What anvils rang, what hammers beat
> In what a forge, in what a heat
> Were shaped the anchors of her hope."

It was a beautiful sight, in New York and Boston harbors in those days, to see the laden vessels almost daily unfold their wings, to furl them in a foreign clime. But change is the order of the universe.

The perilous task of doubling Cape Horn to westward; or "running down the easting in the roaring forties," will hereafter gradually become a memory and a legend, to be known only in song and story, by the Masefields and Conrads of the future.

It will, therefore, be seen that in a brief quarter of a century, the glory of sail has passed away. Sailing ships that at one time were the pride and wonder of their age, have become a reverie and a dream. The sound of foaming waters tumbling beneath their advancing prows; the winds of the trades and westerlies, whistling and singing through their standing rigging, have died into the silence of eternity.

The ships, the owners, the builders, the seamen, are gone. The queens of sail, in all their splendor, that contributed for so many years to such glorious ocean scenes, whitening every sea, are gone.

The monument, of which I write to dedicate, has been erected in the hope that it may be a reminder of greater days and greater men; that it may halt, even though temporarily, the vanishing memory of noble deeds; that its tablet may tell to future passerby some part of the story of a great local industry that has passed away.

Thomas F. Hall wrote this memoir which he calls "a fragmentary statement from a defective memory" *in his eighty-third year in 1924 and it was published in 1925 by C. W. Swift in his* LIBRARY OF CAPE COD HISTORY & GENEALOGY *at the Register Press in Yarmouthport. Only a part of it is reprinted here. The names of the eight vessels launched from the Shiverick shipyard are* Revenue, Hippogriffe, Belle of the West, Kit Carson, Wild Hunter, Webfoot, Christopher Hall and Ellen Sears.

౽∾౺

Worldly advice to Cape Cod girls: If you can dance with the captain, never dance with the mate.

౽∾౺

THE COAST GUARD

BY NANCY W. PAINE SMITH

THE COAST GUARD was organized by the United States Government in 1872. It was called at first the Life-Saving Service. No shore more dangerous than the shore of Cape Cod faces the Atlantic Ocean. It has been called the "Graveyard of Ships." Hundreds of wrecks are scattered on the bottom from Long Point to Monomoy. From 1907 to 1917 there were a hundred and fifty-six wrecks on the

Backside. Few early charts were reliable. The shifting bars compel yearly a new survey and a new chart. The first lighthouse, that at the Highland, was built in 1797, Race Point in 1816, Long Point in 1826, Wood End in 1873. Each year now sees fewer disasters. Improvements in the charts and in the lights, in the fog-bells and horns, better appliances for rescue, entrance examinations, and regular drill for the men, and a pension for the men retiring, better models in building vessels, use of power against the wind, the Canal, all combine to defeat the hungry sea and the treacherous sand.

Wrecks

Nevertheless, every winter has its wrecks. The horror of those who stand and see it marks the date more sharply than do the figures of the calendar. "My son was born the day the *Caledonia* came ashore, the first day of January, 1863." The *Caledonia* was an English ship with broadcloth, linen, cotton cloth and thread, which next morning were washing up in the tide. The last of that cargo is scarcely used up now. The Italian bark *Giovanni* with wine, white grapes, nuts and raisins will be recalled when 1872 has little significance.

Men on the shore stand helpless as they see a ship break in pieces on the bar, and dead men washed up with the flotsam and jetsam. They see the men on the wreck launch a boat and they shudder as it overturns in the breakers, just beyond their reach. They see men drop one by one from the rigging. They calculate the chances of a man swimming on a plank. They find the frozen body of one who reached the shore in the darkness and then wandered about till he died. Scenes like this fix the years for the life-savers.

Wreckers

In the early days, wrecking companies were organized to save ship, cargo and men. They had ready boats, oars and sails, cables and anchors, ropes, barrels, tackles, crowbars and axes, life-preservers, bandages, medicines, stimulants, dry clothes, dry wood and matches, everything needed. At news of a wreck they were early on the scene, prepared to help and not afraid to try. The story is told of how a company of wreckers floated a vessel at high tide and at dark in a howling southeast snowstorm. What then? She would ground again on the ebb, the wind was ahead to take her into the harbor but fair for Boston. Therefore, "To Boston we go. It will not take long to get there in this breeze. Nobody else will be out to-night, so we shall have a clear road. She will likely keep afloat till morning." Two men took the leaky old craft to Boston and she was beside the wharf before daylight. Word was sent to the waiting wife in town, "Don't you worry about Joshua. He has gone to Boston on the wreck. We think it will moderate, bye-and-bye." Gone to Boston on a wreck!

The Humane Society

More than a hundred years ago, the Humane Society built on the beach huts for shelter. In 1802, Rev. James Freeman wrote a pamphlet on the work of the Humane Society and located the huts. He described them as a rude charity house with fireplace, wood and matches and a signal pole. Which things, public-spirited citizens promised to keep supplied.

The Seaman's Aid Society

The Seaman's Aid Society for the care of shipwrecked sailors was organized in 1882, with a dollar a year membership and an annual public meeting. At one of these public meetings, Mr. James Gifford read a detailed account of the wreck on the Backside of three East India ships from Salem, owned by the Crowninshields, the *Volusia*, the *Ulysses*, the *Brutus*, February 22, 1802. The Commonwealth has now made provision that the towns shall furnish money to shipwrecked persons and be reimbursed by the State. Therefore the treasury of the Seamen's Aid Society, about two thousand dollars, has been given to the Helping Hand, and the Seamen's Aid is disbanded.

Mooncussing

Since the Lloyds now have representatives in every town, the romantic days of "mooncussing" are done. How much was snatched from the maw of the sea and made useful will never be known, because only the audacious and the funny stories are told. To get ahead of Eben Smith, the underwriters' agent, was a laudable ambition, and to outwit another beachcomber was worth while. Once upon a time a man stood in the evening on the beach where during the day a vessel had gone to pieces. A rope washed up at his feet and he hauled it in and threw it behind him as he hauled. When he came to the end of the rope and turned to coil it, there was in his hand a piece only ten feet long. Somebody behind him in the darkness had coiled the rope as he hauled, and had cut it and disappeared.

The Life-saving Service on Cape Cod

This was established in 1872. Positions in the service are eagerly sought, for the men feel that life-saving is as much better than going to sea, as the life-savers in a storm are better off than the men on the wreck. Patrol along the beach in a northeast gale would be impossible for most people. Sometimes the cutting wind and sand compel men to crawl on their hands and knees. But these men are young and strong, they are dressed for the weather, they know the beach, and they leave the station dry and warm. A vessel ashore in a bad time, however, taxes even their vitality. But there are many days of leisure and comfort. One of their number goes into town every day to market and for the mail. More books than they can read are sent to them. More visitors than they can entertain come to see them. They take turns at cooking, they keep hens and set lobster-pots, they build boats and braid rugs and have a pension bye-and-bye.

· · · · ·

When the Life Saving Service was first established, The Government furnished all the stations with flat-bottomed boats, such as were used on the New Jersey coast. These our men could not use on this shore. At the wreck of the *Annie J. Fort* the life-crew at Peaked Hill Bars tried in vain, all day long, to launch the Government life-boat. When they were exhausted, Captain Isaac Mayo, a spectator on the shore, sent into town for a whaleboat, and called for a volunteer crew. The boat was carted across the beach and manned by a fresh crew. They knew a whale-boat. They knew that a boat, with a keel, narrow, sharp at both ends, and deep, could be launched through the breakers and could be safely beached on its return. They watched their chance, they ran her off beyond the breakers, they saved the men on the wreck. A picture of this crew launching their boat hangs in the Public Library. After this experience the Government had the boats for the Cape Cod service built on Cape Cod, by Cape Cod men. They are a little smaller than a whale-boat, and they have airtight compartments.

— From THE PROVINCETOWN BOOK, privately printed, 1922

ᴓᴥᴑ

THE WADENA

BY DONALD G. TRAYSER

MARCH 17 The worst disaster in the history of the life-saving service on Cape Cod occurred this day in 1902 when seven men of the crew of the Monomoy station and five men from the stranded coal barge Wadena, were drowned. The barge had stranded on Shovelful shoal a few days previously, and five men remained on board for salvage operations. A storm blew up this day, and in response to a distress signal, Monomoy lifesavers launched their surfboat and battled the elements an hour to reach the wrecked barge. Seas were breaking heavily, but the lifesavers skillfully got the five into the surfboat, one by one, and shoved off for shore. While it was backing around, a big wave struck the crowded boat causing panic among the rescued crew and greatly handicapping the lifesavers. Then another wave struck, and over she went. Most of the rescued men, and the life-savers, clung to the overturned boat, but one by one they were swept into the icy waters. Finally only Seth Ellis, No. 1 man, was left. A brave Chatham fisherman, who was aboard a second stranded barge, rescued him in a 14-foot dory — for which heroism Elmer Mayo was later rewarded both by the Federal Government and Massachusetts Humane Society.

— From ONCE UPON A TIME ON CAPE COD

ख∾ॐ

The official motto of the Coast Guard is "Semper Paratus." The unofficial one runs: "The Book says you got to go out. It don't say you got to come back."

The Cape Itself

ICE, SAND AND SEA

BY KATHARINE DOS PASSOS

CAPE COD is a geological oddity. It does not look like any other
section of the American continent, even to an amateur physiographer
who doesn't know a terminal moraine from a trilobite. What is the
secret of this curious and attractive topography that strikes you at
first glance when you cross the high steel arch over the Canal at
Buzzards Bay?

In the first place, the scale of the Cape is small. It is only a little
over twenty miles wide at its widest point, at Barnstable it is six miles
across, two from sea to sea at Truro, and less than a mile at Provincetown, where you can see two oceans as you drive. Here the whole
gigantic process of geology is visible on a diminished scale, just as by
a reverse process cell structure can be seen through a microscope.

From the monument at Provincetown, from Signal Hill in Bourne,
from the high sweet-smelling moors of Truro you can see nearly the
whole circuit of the Cape and draw a pretty good map of it just from
the view.

Cape Cod is a narrow glacial peninsula, running 40 miles out to
sea, its frail and perishable coast of sand cliffs and earth continually
crumbled and torn down by the wind and the pounding ocean, but
it is anchored to the bottom of the world by rock and a preglacial
clay foundation that is one of the "ancient drainage divides of the
country." Over this the glaciers piled hills and dug valleys, spread
and raked a top-dressing of soil and debris that in time became the
"fat and lustie soil" that Brereton speaks of.

Fingerprinting glaciers is still not an exact science, but roughly
speaking, it was 35,000 years ago that the great ice floe from the
north poured thickly over New England, thrusting a hundred miles
out into the ocean. At the southeastern end the ice field split into
huge thumb-shaped projections called lobes. One of these lobes, the

Buzzards Bay glacier, lay along the eastern shore of Buzzards Bay and north along the Massachusetts coast. Next to it on the east the Cape Cod glacier filled Cape Cod Bay. Geologists hypothecate a third glacier called the South Channel glacier, part of a vast ice field reaching down from Maine to Nova Scotia. The wicked shoals of Nantucket and Georges Banks may be submerged terminal moraines of this glacier. Its pack pushing west helped to block out the land between Chatham and Highland Light, and there are about a dozen parallel valleys in Eastham, Truro and Wellfleet whose floors run from east to west. The simplest explanation of them is that ice rivers flowed out from the South Channel glacier on the west scoring these valleys that are now so sunny and green.

Together the glaciers moved southward, spreading out right and left as they crawled on. They scraped and pushed ahead of them huge heaps of debris, piled it up in front of and between their edges, finally melted away and left it there in the form of moraine hills that run from Buzzards Bay down to Woods Hole and Falmouth, and bending eastward through Sandwich along the bay shore, continue through the northern parts of the coast villages through Orleans to the sea.

These ridges of high ground are true terminal moraines, and nice ones too. Pine woods cover them, their sides slope gently down to a great plain. This, the whole South Shore, meadows, little valleys, green marshes cut by blue strips of sea, is an outwash plain, made by glacier rivers flowing out from under the ice, spreading and leveling the surface like frosting on a cake. The plain is starred with shining lakes and ponds (270 of them) and pitted with countless deep hollows called kettle holes. These are glacial, too, the marks of huge ice blocks which were left by old glaciers in depressions, buried under earth by new glaciers, but finally melted and sank, caving into pockets which were sometimes filled with the seepage of ground water, or merely made deep dimples in the ground. There are thousands of them from Woods Hole to Truro, and they are found by sounding under the water. One, near Woods Hole, is 120 feet deep.

Scattered like nuts in the frosting are occasional great chunks of rock. These are not part of the backbone of Cape Cod, but are "drift boulders" dragged by glaciers from northern New England or New Hampshire or Canada. Even Plymouth Rock is not a native, but comes from Boston.

The most notable examples of these are Enos Rock on the Nauset moraine in Eastham, 34 feet long, the Indian Prayer Rock at West Brewster, Great Rock, 400 tons, at Bourne, and a 12-foot boulder near Highland Light. There is a foreign settlement or rocks called "Bear's Den" in Falmouth, west of Falmouth village, and also "Devil's Den" in Pocasset.

There are no very sensational heights on the Cape, but there are some respectable summits. Bourne Hill in Sandwich is the highest, nearly three hundred feet, but there is no driving road to the top and no real view. A road leads up to Pine, or Signal Hill in Bourne, however, with a fine prospect at the top. Scargo Hill in Dennis has a tower with an eighty-mile glance around the Bay. Shoot-Flying Hill in Barnstable is so called because it is said to be a vantage point for shooting wild fowl. Manomet Hill in Plymouth is the highest landmark of them all. In colonial days these hills were used to signal from, fires by night and smudges by day.

He who walks may read all this glacial history of the Cape, and it is pleasant summer reading, but there is a more dramatic story along the shore.

No man saw the paralyzed earth stir slowly to life when the glaciers weakened. For only three hundred years has history checked this coast and three hundred years is a short time for observation when the sea has been working away for centuries, leveling and smoothing the rough shore, tearing down cliffs, wrecking old harbors and cutting out new. The waves have completely washed away Nauset Island, where Leif Ericsson is thought to have landed about 1003. It lay between Chatham and Eastham, and a long point ran out into the Atlantic. There was a shoal rip on the northeast side which gave Gosnold in 1602 such a scare that he called it "Tucker's Terror," and the point which took very tricky sailing to round he called Point Care.

All this is gone now, the sea works fast, and Cape Cod people have seen great changes in their own time. The shore line is continually shifting, shoals and harbors come and go, and the United States Coast Guard Survey must revise its maps every few years. The waves sweep north and south, slanting into the shore, and this carpenter work has cut back the head of the Cape and added regular Cape Cod additions or lean-tos right and left. The sand "walks," the bones of ancient ships are buried for years and dug up again, the whole coast moves and shudders with the endless stir of the sea.

It was this "variable and inconstant" shore that made our ancestors think the whole of Cape Cod was perhaps only a hieroglyphic of sand, written by the sea, doomed to be rubbed out by the sea.

Only ten miles of this is true. The old glacial Cape ends at High Head at Truro. From there to Long Point at Provincetown is made land, made out of the wreckage of the old cliffs and shore material torn away from the coast of Truro and Wellfleet and Eastham.

The Cape is constantly narrowing as the sea pulls down the shore and sweeps its winnings north and south. The piled-up shoals grow and rise above the water, winds blow the top into dunes, beach grass springs up and ties the sand down. So the line of shoals beyond Truro finally joined the mainland. Peaked Hill Bar is now in the making and will some day rise from the ocean and join the dunes of the Back Shore. Only a hundred years ago Race Run was a free salt river, splitting the Race off from the mainland; now it is silted up and built solid into the land.

This process of destruction and repair goes on forever. If you stand on the Clay Pounds at Highland Light in a northeast gale and watch the surf bite out the base of the cliff, you wonder how long before the waves will eat clear across the mild hills at Truro and make an island of Provincetown. Geologists say the shore recedes on an average about three feet a year. Peaked Hill Life Saving Station has been moved twice in the last few years, its old brick foundations are now part of the beach. Chatham had lost four hundred feet of ground and two lighthouses by 1879. At Nauset Light four lighthouses have been built to avoid the encroachment of the waves.

But the sea is freakish and unpredictable and it builds up new beaches and harbors out of the ruins of the old. Instead of destroying the old glacial shore of Eastham, it has thrown up the fifteen-mile barricade of Nauset Beach and given Eastham a small harbor, though the harbor will not stay put and has now moved over to Orleans. Southward this clear reach of sand goes on to make the magnificent stretches of Monomoy which extend miles south of Chatham and this is all young land robbed from Chatham and Orleans. Monomoy Point is growing and its shoals push out toward Great Point, the northeast end of Nantucket. But a great scour of current will probably always keep this entrance to Nantucket Sound open.

So on the Bay Shore. The high dunes of Sandy Neck are an extension of Spring Hill beach and protect the old inner shore of Barnstable, also giving it a harbor. True, the neck is stretching across the harbor toward Dennis, and the channel of Barnstable Harbor is filling up, but the tide rushes in more powerfully as it contracts and may keep it clear. On the Bay Shore, too, the waves have cut back the cliffs of Truro and Wellfleet and leveled and polished the fine beaches that run clear to Provincetown. But at Pamet River, which was once a good harbor with even a lighthouse, the channel is filling up with marsh and is a harbor no more.

Bound Brook Island at Wellfleet, Great Island and Griffith's Island were once real islands lying free in Cape Cod Bay. Now they have been puttied together with sand and marsh till they are one — but just to be different the sea has cut away Billingsgate from its logical chain, and left it a sand bar with a run of shallow water between it and the end of what used to be Great Island.

As for the delicate and perishable hooked spit that makes Provincetown Harbor one of the best in the world, it is more sturdy than it looks. This also was built of stolen material, loose masses of earth and gravel torn from the old shore, driven northward and washed westward by winds and currents. These same forces feed and reinforce it continually, making the thin whiplash of land that swings round from the dunes and seems to lie so lightly on the surface of the sea that it looks like a mirage. But notice that its tip points northeast. Throw a bottle out on the Back Shore. You may find it at Long Point.

East Harbor — it does not look like a harbor now but merely a largish pond — which you pass on the Beach Point road to Provincetown was once open salt water, a long spit running far back with only a strip of marsh between it and the ocean beach. At one point it was only five rods wide at high water and the sea threatened to break through in any gale and shovel a tidal wave of sand into Provincetown Harbor. Provincetowners, already fighting sand which was blowing over their houses, were alarmed by this into several makeshifts — beach grass, a bridge, a fence — finally, in 1869 an expensive dike which was 1,400 feet long. It destroyed East Harbor, but it saved Provincetown Harbor and the town.

At Long Point, too, sand washed around from Race Point into the harbor, where it set to work building flats, but the government stopped this with wooden bulwarks. In 1911 the great breakwater was thrown across from the west end to Long Point and now Provincetown Harbor stands firm.

— From DOWN CAPE COD, by Katharine Dos Passos and Edith Shay, 1947

❧

1849
"CAPE COD BEACH"

BY HENRY D. THOREAU

IT HAS AT PRESENT no name any more than fame. That portion south of Nauset Harbor is commonly called Chatham Beach. The part in Eastham is called Nauset Beach, and off Wellfleet and Truro the Backside, or sometimes, perhaps Cape Cod Beach. I think that part which extends without interruption from Nauset Harbor to Race Point should be called Cape Cod Beach, and do so speak of it.

I
The Beach

At length we reached the seemingly retreating boundary of the plain,[1] and entered what had appeared at a distance an upland marsh, but proved to be dry sand covered with beach-grass, the bearberry, bayberry, shrub-oaks, and beach-plum, slightly ascending as we approached the shore; then, crossing over a belt of sand on which nothing grew, though the roar of the sea sounded scarcely louder than before, and we were prepared to go half a mile farther, we suddenly stood on the edge of a bluff overlooking the Atlantic. Far below us was the beach, from half a dozen to a dozen rods in width, with a long line of breakers rushing to the strand. The sea was exceedingly dark and stormy, the sky completely overcast, the clouds still dropping rain, and the wind seemed to blow not so much as the exciting cause, as from sympathy with the already agitated ocean.

[1] At Nauset.

The waves broke on bars at some distance from the shore, and curving green or yellow as if over so many unseen dams, ten or twelve feet high, like a thousand waterfalls, rolled in foam to the sand. There was nothing but that savage ocean between us and Europe.

. . . . .

There was not a sail in sight, and we saw none that day, — for they had all sought harbors in the late storm, and had not been able to get out again; and the only human beings whom we saw on the beach for several days were one or two wreckers looking for drift-wood, and fragments of wrecked vessels. After an easterly storm in the spring, this beach is sometimes strewn with eastern wood from one end to the other, which, as it belongs to him who saves it, and the Cape is nearly destitute of wood, is a godsend to the inhabitants. We soon met one of those wreckers, — a regular Cape Cod man, with whom we parleyed, with a bleached and weather-beaten face, within whose wrinkles I distinguished no particular feature. It was like an old sail endowed with life, — a hanging-cliff of weather-beaten flesh, — like one of the clay boulders which occurred in that sand-bank. He had on a hat which had seen salt water, and a coat of many pieces and colors, though it was mainly the color of the beach, as if it had been sanded. His variegated back — for his coat had many patches, even between the shoulders — was a rich study to us when we had passed him and looked round. It might have been dishonorable for him to have so many scars behind, it is true, if he had not had many more and more serious ones in front. He looked as if he sometimes saw a doughnut, but never descended to comfort; too grave to laugh, too tough to cry; as indifferent as a clam, — like a sea-clam with hat on and legs, that was out walking the strand. He may have been one of the Pilgrims, — Peregrine White, at least, — who has kept on the back side of the Cape, and let the centuries go by.[2] He was looking for wrecks, old logs, water-logged and covered with barnacles, or bits of boards and joists, even chips which he drew out of the reach of the tide, and stacked up to dry. When the log was too large to carry far, he cut it up where the last wave had left it, or rolling it a few feet, appropriated it by sticking two sticks in the ground crosswise above

[2] This description of "a regular Cape Cod man," and others like it, vastly offended the people of Cape Cod. It was years before they could find a good word for Thoreau or his book.

it. Some rotten trunk, which in Maine cumbers the ground, and is, perchance, thrown into the water on purpose, is here thus carefully picked up, split and dried, and husbanded. Before winter the wrecker painfully carries these things up the bank on his shoulders by a long diagonal slanting path made with a hoe in the sand, if there is no hollow at hand. You may see his hooked pike-staff always lying on the bank, ready for use. He is the true monarch of the beach, whose "right there is none to dispute," and he is as much identified with it as a beach-bird.

. . . The wrecker directed us to a slight depression, called Snow's Hollow, by which we ascended the bank, — for elsewhere, if not difficult, it was inconvenient to climb it on account of the sliding sand which filled our shoes.

This sand-bank — the backbone of the Cape — rose directly from the beach to the height of a hundred feet or more above the ocean. It was with singular emotions that we first stood upon it and discovered what a place we had chosen to walk on. On our right, beneath us, was the beach of smooth and gently-sloping sand, a dozen rods in width; next, the endless series of white breakers; further still, the light green water over the bar, which runs the whole length of the fore-arm of the Cape, and beyond this stretched the unwearied and illimitable ocean. On our left, extending back from the very edge of the bank, was a perfect desert of shining sand, from thirty to eighty rods in width, skirted in the distance by small sand-hills fifteen or twenty feet high; between which, however, in some places, the sand penetrated as much farther. Next commenced the region of vegetation, — a succession of small hills and valleys covered with shrubbery, now glowing with the brightest imaginable autumnal tints; and beyond this were seen, here and there, the waters of the bay. Here, in Wellfleet, this pure sand plateau, known to sailors as the Table Lands of Eastham, on account of its appearance, as seen from the ocean, and because it once made a part of that town, — full fifty rods in width, and in many places much more, and sometimes full one hundred and fifty feet above the ocean, — stretched away northward from the southern boundary of the town, without a particle of vegetation, — as level almost as a table, — for two and a half or three miles, as far as the eye could reach; slightly rising towards the ocean, then stooping to the beach, by as steep a slope as sand could lie on, and as regular as a military engineer could desire. It was like the escarped rampart of a stupendous fortress, whose glacis was the beach, and whose champaign the ocean. From its surface we overlooked the greater part of the Cape. In short, we were traversing a desert, with the view of an autumnal landscape of extraordinary brilliancy, a sort of Promised Land, on the one hand, and the ocean on the other. Yet, though the prospect was so extensive, and the country for the most part destitute of trees, a house was rarely visible, — we never saw one from the beach, — and the solitude was that of the ocean and the desert combined. A thousand men could not have seriously interrupted it, but would have been lost in the vastness of the scenery as their footsteps in the sand.

· · · · ·

For sixteen miles, commencing at the Nauset Lights, the bank held its height, though farther north it was not so level as here, but interrupted by slight hollows, and the patches of beach-grass and bayberry frequently crept into the sand to its edge. There are some pages entitled "A Description of the Eastern Coast of the County of Barnstable," printed in 1802, pointing out the spots on which the Trustees of the Humane Society have erected huts called Charity or Humane Houses, "and other places where shipwrecked seamen may look for shelter." Two thousand copies of this were dispersed, that every vessel which frequented this coast might be provided with one. I have read this Shipwrecked Seaman's Manual with a melancholy kind of interest, — for the sound of the surf, or, you might say, the moaning of the sea, is heard all through it, as if its author were the sole survivor of a shipwreck himself. Of this part of the coast he says: "This highland approaches the ocean with steep and lofty banks, which it is extremely difficult to climb, especially in a storm. In violent tempests, during very high tides, the sea breaks against the foot of them, rendering it then unsafe to walk on the strand which lies between them and the ocean. Should the seaman succeed in his attempt to ascend them, he must forbear to penetrate into the country, as houses are generally so remote that they would escape his research during the night; he must pass on to the valleys by which the banks are intersected. These valleys, which the inhabitants call Hollows, run at right angles with the shore, and in the middle or lower part of them a road leads from the dwelling-houses to the sea." By the word *road* must not always be understood a visible cart-track.

There were these two roads for us, — an upper and a lower one, — the bank and the beach; both stretching twenty-eight miles north-west, from Nauset Harbor to Race Point, without a single opening into the beach, and with hardly a serious interruption of the desert. If you were to ford the narrow and shallow inlet at Nauset Harbor, where there is no more than eight feet of water on the bar at full sea, you might walk ten or twelve miles farther, which would make a beach forty miles long, — and the bank and beach, on the east side of Nantucket, are but a continuation of these. I was comparatively satisfied. There I had got the Cape under me, as much as if I were riding it bare-backed. It was not as on the map, or seen from the stage-coach; but there I found it all out of doors, huge and real, Cape Cod! as it cannot be represented on a map, color it as you will, the thing itself, than which there is nothing more like it, no truer picture or account; which you cannot go farther and see. I cannot remember what I thought before that it was. They commonly celebrate those beaches only which have a hotel on them, not those which have a humane house alone. But I wished to see that seashore where man's works are wrecks; to put up at the true Atlantic House, where the ocean is land-lord as well as sea-lord, and comes ashore without a wharf for the landing; where the crumbling land is the only invalid, or at best is but dry land, and that is all you can say of it.

· · · · ·

Though for some time I have not spoken of the roaring of the breakers, and the ceaseless flux and reflux of the waves, yet they did not for a moment cease to dash and roar, with such a tumult that, if you had been there, you could scarcely have heard my voice the while; and they are dashing and roaring this very moment, though it may be with less din and violence, for there the sea never rests. We were wholly absorbed by this spectacle and tumult, and like Chryses, though in a different mood from him, we walked silent along the shore of the resounding sea.

· · · · ·

There was but little weed cast up here, and that kelp chiefly, there being scarcely a rock for rock-weed to adhere to. Who has not had a vision from some vessel's deck, when he had still his land legs on, of this great brown apron, drifting half upright, and quite submerged through the green water, clasping a stone or a deep-sea mussel in its unearthly fingers? I have seen it carrying a stone half as large as my head. We sometimes watched a mass of this cable-like weed, as it was tossed up on the crest of a breaker, waiting with interest to see it come in, as if there was some treasure buoyed up by it; but we were always surprised and disappointed at the insignificance of the mass which had attracted us. As we looked out over the water, the smallest objects floating on it appeared indefinitely large, we were so impressed by the vastness of the ocean, and each one bore so large a proportion to the whole ocean, which we saw. We were so often disappointed in the size of such things as came ashore, the ridiculous bits of wood or weed, with which the ocean labored, that we began to doubt whether the Atlantic itself would bear a still closer inspection, and would not turn out to be but a small pond, if it should come ashore to us. This kelp, oar-weed, tangle, devil's apron, sole-leather, or ribbon-weed, — as various species are called, — appeared to us a singularly marine and fabulous product, a fit invention for Neptune to adorn his car with, or a freak of Proteus. All that is told of the sea has a fabulous sound to an inhabitant of the land, and all its products have a certain fabulous quality, as if they belonged to another planet, from seaweed to a sailor's yarn, or a fish story. In this element the animal and vegetable kingdoms meet and are strangely mingled. One species of kelp, according to Bory St. Vincent, has a stem fifteen hundred feet long, and hence is the longest vegetable known, and a brig's crew spent two days to no purpose collecting the trunks of another kind cast ashore on the Falkland Islands, mistaking it for driftwood.[3] This species looked almost edible; at least, I thought that if I were starving, I would try it. One sailor told me that the cows ate it. It cut like cheese; for I took the earliest opportunity to sit down and deliberately whittle up a fathom or two of it, that I might become more intimately acquainted with it, see how it cut, and if it were hollow all the way through. The blade looked like a broad belt, whose edges had been quilled, or as if stretched by hammering, and it was also twisted spirally. The extremity was generally worn and ragged from the lashing of the waves. A piece of the stem which I carried home shrunk to one quarter of its size a week afterward, and was completely covered with crystals of salt like frost. The reader will excuse my greenness, — though it is not sea-greenness, like his,

[3] See Harvey on *Algae*. H.D.T.

perchance, — for I live by a river shore, where this weed does not wash up. When we consider in what meadows it grew, and how it was raked, and in what kind of weather got in or out, we may well be curious about it. One who is weather-wise has given the following account of the matter: —

> "When descends on the Atlantic
>   The gigantic
> Storm-wind of the equinox,
> Landward in his wrath he scourges
>   The toiling surges,
> Laden with sea-weed from the rocks.
>
> "From Bermuda's reefs, from edges
>   Of sunken ledges,
> In some far-off bright Azore;
> From Bahama and the dashing,
>   Silver-flashing
> Surges of San Salvador:
>
> "From the tumbling surf that buries
>   The Orkneyan Skerries,
> Answering the hoarse Hebrides;
> And from wrecks of ships and drifting
>   Spars, uplifting
> On the desolate rainy seas;
>
> "Ever drifting, drifting, drifting
>   On the shifting
> Currents of the restless main."

But he was not thinking of this shore, when he added, —

> "Till, in sheltered coves and reaches
>   Of sandy beaches,
> All have found repose again."

These weeds were the symbols of those grotesque and fabulous thoughts which have not yet got into the sheltered coves of literature.

"Ever drifting, drifting, drifting
On the shifting
Currents of the restless heart;"
And not yet "in books recorded
They, like hoarded
Household words, no more depart."

The beach was also strewn with beautiful sea-jellies, which the
wreckers call Sun-squall, one of the lowest forms of animal life,
some white, some wine-colored, and a foot in diameter. I at first
thought that they were a tender part of some marine monster, which
the storm or some other foe had mangled. What right has the sea to
bear in its bosom such tender things as sea-jellies and mosses, when
it has such a boisterous shore, that the stoutest fabrics are wrecked
against it? Strange that it should undertake to dandle such delicate
children in its arms. I did not at first recognize these for the same
which I had formerly seen in myriads in Boston Harbor, rising, with
a waving motion, to the surface, as if to meet the sun, and discoloring
the waters far and wide, so that I seemed to be sailing through a
mere sun-fish soup. They say that when you endeavor to take one up,
it will spill out the other side of your hand like quicksilver. Before
the land rose out of the ocean, and became *dry* land, chaos reigned;
and between high and low water mark, where she is partially disrobed
and rising, a sort of chaos reigns still, which only anomalous creatures can inhabit. Mackerel gulls were all the while flying over our
heads and amid the breakers, sometimes two white ones pursuing a
black one; quite at home in the storm, though they are as delicate
organizations as sea-jellies and mosses; and we saw that they were
adapted to their circumstances rather by their spirits than their bodies.
Theirs must be an essentially wilder, that is less human, nature, than
that of larks and robins. Their note was like the sound of some
vibrating metal, and harmonized well with the scenery and the roar
of the surf, as if one had rudely touched the strings of the lyre, which
ever lies on the shore; a ragged shred of ocean music tossed aloft on
the spray. But if I were required to name a sound, the remembrance
of which most perfectly revives the impression which the beach has
made, it would be the dreary peep of the piping plover (*Charadrius
melodus*) which haunts there. Their voices, too, are heard as a
fugacious part in the dirge which is ever played along the shore for

those mariners who have been lost in the deep since first it was created. But through all this dreariness we seemed to have a pure and unqualified strain of eternal melody, for always the same strain which is a dirge to one household is a morning song of rejoicing to another.

·   ·   ·   ·   ·

We found some large clams, of the species *Mactra solidissima,* which the storm had torn up from the bottom, and cast ashore. I selected one of the largest, about six inches in length, and carried it along, thinking to try an experiment on it. We soon after met a wrecker, with a grapple and a rope, who said he was looking for tow cloth, which had made part of the cargo of the ship Franklin, which was wrecked here in the spring, at which time nine or ten lives were lost. The reader may remember this wreck, from the circumstance that a letter was found in the captain's valise, which washed ashore, directing him to wreck the vessel before he got to America, and from the trial which took place in consequence. The wrecker said that tow cloth was still cast up in such storms as this. He also told us that the clam which I had was the sea-clam, or hen, and was good to eat. We took our nooning under a sand-hill, covered with beach-grass, in a dreary little hollow, on the top of the bank, while it alternately rained and shined. There, having reduced some damp drift-wood, which I had picked up on the shore, to shavings with my knife, I kindled a fire with a match and some paper, and cooked my clam on the embers for my dinner; for breakfast was commonly the only meal which I took in a house on this excursion. When the clam was done, one valve held the meat, and the other the liquor. Though it was very tough, I found it sweet and savory, and ate *the whole* with relish. Indeed, with the addition of a cracker or two, it would have been a bountiful dinner.[4] I noticed that the shells were such as I had seen in the sugar-kit at home. Tied to a stick, they formerly made the Indian's hoe hereabouts.

At length, by mid-afternoon, after we had two or three rainbows over the sea, the showers ceased, and the heavens gradually cleared up, though the wind still blowed as hard and the breakers ran as high as before. Keeping on, we soon after came to a Charity-house,

[4] Elsewhere in the book, the writer tells us that later that day the clam made him violently though briefly ill. It was the same clam that caused the Pilgrim Fathers "to cast and scour." These newcomers to Cape Cod made their mistake in eating *the whole.* Parts of this clam are wholesome and delicious, but certain other parts are poisonous.

which we looked into to see how the shipwrecked mariner might fare. Far away in some desolate hollow by the seaside, just within the bank, stands a lonely building on piles driven into the sand, with a slight nail put through the staple, which a freezing man can bend, with some straw, perchance, on the floor on which he may lie, or which he may burn in the fire-place to keep him alive. Perhaps this hut has never been required to shelter a shipwrecked man, and the benevolent person who promised to inspect it annually, to see that the straw and matches are here, and that the boards will keep off the wind, has now grown remiss and thinks that storms and shipwrecks are over; and this very night a perishing crew may pry open its door with their numbed fingers and leave half their number dead here by morning. When I thought what must be the condition of the families which alone would ever occupy or had occupied them, what must have been the tragedy of the winter evenings spent by human beings around their hearths, these houses, though they were meant for human dwellings, did not look cheerful to me. They appeared but a stage to the grave. The gulls flew around and screamed over them; the roar of the ocean in storms, and the lapse of its waves in calms, alone resounds through them, all dark and empty within, year in, year out, except, perchance, on one memorable night. Houses of entertainment for shipwrecked men! What kind of sailor's homes were they?

"Each hut," says the author of the "Description of the Eastern Coast of the County of Barnstable," "stands on piles, is eight feet long, eight feet wide, and seven feet high; a sliding door is on the south, a sliding shutter on the west, and a pole, rising fifteen feet above the top of the building, on the east. Within it is supplied either with straw or hay, and is further accommodated with a bench." They have varied little from this model now. There are similar huts at the Isle of Sable and Anticosti, on the north, and how far south along the coast I know not. It is pathetic to read the minute and faithful directions which he gives to seamen who may be wrecked on this coast, to guide them to the nearest Charity-house, or other shelter, for, as is said of Eastham, though there are a few houses within a mile of the shore, yet "in a snow-storm, which rages here with excessive fury, it would be almost impossible to discover them either by night or by day." You hear their imaginary guide thus marshalling, cheering, directing the dripping, shivering, freezing troop along: "At the entrance of this valley the sand has gathered, so that at present a little climbing is necessary. Passing over several fences and taking heed not to enter the wood on the right hand, at the distance of three quarters of a mile a house is to be found. This house stands on the south side of the road, and not far from it on the south is Pamet River, which runs from east to west through a body of salt marsh." To him cast ashore in Eastham, he says, "The meeting-house is without a steeple, but it may be distinguished from the dwelling-houses near it by its situation, which is between two small groves of locusts, one on the south and one on the north, — that on the south being three times as long as the other. About a mile and a quarter from the hut, west by north, appear the top and arms of a windmill." And so on for many pages.

We did not learn whether these houses had been the means of saving any lives, though this writer says, of one erected at the head of Stout's Creek, in Truro, that "it was built in an improper manner, having a chimney in it; and was placed on a spot where no beach-grass grew. The strong winds blew the sand from its foundation, and the weight of the chimney brought it to the ground; so that in January of the present year (1802) it was entirely demolished. This event took place about six weeks before the Brutus was cast away. If it had remained, it is probable that the whole of the unfortunate crew of that ship would have been saved, as they gained the shore a few rods only from the spot where the hut had stood."

II
The Beach Again

Today the air was beautifully clear, and the sea no longer dark and stormy, though the waves still broke with foam along the beach, but sparkling and full of life.[5] Already that morning I had seen the day break over the sea as if it came out of its bosom: —

"The saffron-robed Dawn rose in haste from the streams
Of Ocean, that she might bring light to immortals and to mortals."

The sun rose visibly at such a distance over the sea, that the cloud-bank in the horizon, which at first concealed him, was not per-

[5] The writer and his companion have resumed their walk after a night spent at the house of the Wellfleet Oysterman.

ceptible until he had risen high behind it, and plainly broke and dispersed it, like an arrow. But as yet I looked at him as rising over land, and could not, without an effort, realize that he was rising over the sea. . . .

There were many vessels, like gulls, skimming over the surface of the sea, now half concealed in its trough, their dolphin-strikers ploughing the water, now tossed on the top of the billows. One, a barque standing down parallel with the coast, suddenly furled her sails, came to anchor, and swung round in the wind, near us, only half a mile from the shore. At first we thought that her captain wished to communicate with us, and perhaps we did not regard the signal of distress, which a mariner would have understood, and he cursed us for cold-hearted wreckers who turned our backs on him. For hours we could still see her anchored there behind us, and we wondered how she could afford to loiter so long in her course. Or was she a smuggler who had chosen that wild beach to land her cargo on? Or did they wish to catch fish, or paint their vessel? Erelong other barques, and brigs, and schooners, which had in the meanwhile doubled the Cape, sailed by her in the smacking breeze, and our consciences were relieved. Some of the vessels lagged behind, while others steadily went ahead. We narrowly watched their rig and the cut of their jibs, and how they walked the water, for there was all the difference between them that there is between living creatures. But we wondered that they should be remembering Boston and New York and Liverpool, steering for them, out there; as if the sailor might forget his peddling business on such a grand highway. They had perchance brought oranges from the Western Isles; and were they carrying back the peel? We might as well transport our old traps across the ocean of eternity. Is *that* but another "trading flood," with its blessed isles? Is Heaven such a harbor as the Liverpool docks?

Still held on without a break the inland barrens and shrubbery, the desert and the high sand-bank with its even slope, the broad white beach, the breakers, the green water on the bar, and the Atlantic Ocean; and we traversed with delight new reaches of the shore; we took another lesson in sea-horses' manes and sea-cows' tails, in sea-jellies and sea-clams, with our new-gained experience. The sea ran less hardly than the day before. It seemed with every wave to be subsiding, because such was our expectation, and yet when hours had elapsed we could see no difference. But there it was, balancing itself, the restless ocean by our side, lurching in its gait. Each wave left the sand all braided or woven, as it were with a coarse woof and warp, and a distinct raised edge to its rapid work. We made no haste, since we wished to see the ocean at our leisure, and indeed that soft sand was no place in which to be in a hurry, for one mile there was as good as two elsewhere. Besides, we were obliged frequently to empty our shoes of the sand which one took in in climbing or descending the bank. . . .

The plants which I noticed here and there on the pure sandy shelf, between the ordinary high-water mark and the foot of the bank, were Sea Rocket (*Cakile Americana*), Saltwort (*Salsola kali*), Sea Sandwort (*Honkenya peploides*), Sea Burdock (*Xanthium echinatum*), Sea-side Spurge (Euphorbia polygonifolia); also, Beach Grass (Arundo, Psamma, or Calamagrostis arenaria), Sea-side Goldenrod (*Solidago sempervirens*), and the Beach Pea (*Lathyrus maritimus*).

Sometimes we helped a wrecker turn over a larger log than usual, or we amused ourselves with rolling stones down the bank, but we rarely could make one reach the water, the beach was so soft and wide; or we bathed in some shallow within a bar, where the sea covered us with sand at every flux, though it was quite cold and windy. The ocean here is commonly but a tantalizing prospect in hot weather, for with all that water before you, there is, as we were afterward told, no bathing on the Atlantic side, on account of the undertow and the rumor of sharks. At the light-house both in Eastham and Truro, the only houses quite on the shore, they declared, the next year, that they would not bathe there "for any sum," for they sometimes saw the sharks tossed up and quiver for a moment on the sand. Others laughed at these stories, but perhaps they could afford to because they never bathed anywhere. One old wrecker told us that he killed a regular man-eating shark fourteen feet long, and hauled him out with his oxen, where we had bathed; and another, that his father caught a smaller one of the same kind that was stranded there, by standing him up on his snout so that the waves could not take him. They will tell you tough stories of sharks all over the Cape, which I do not presume to doubt utterly, — how they will sometimes upset a boat, or tear it pieces, to get at the man in it. I can easily believe in the undertow, but I have no doubt that one shark in a dozen years is enough to keep up the reputation of a beach a hundred miles long. I should add, however, that in July we walked on the bank here a quarter of a mile parallel with a fish about six feet in length, possibly a shark, which was prowling slowly along within two rods of the shore. It was of a pale brown color, singularly film-like and indistinct in the water, as if all nature abetted this child of ocean, and showed many darker transverse bars or rings whenever it came to the surface. It is well known that different fishes of the same species are colored by the water they inhabit. We saw it go into a little cove or bathing-tub, where we had just been bathing, where the water was only four or five feet deep at that time, and after exploring it go slowly out again; but we continued to bathe there, only observing first from the bank if the cove was preoccupied. We thought that the water was fuller of life, more aerated perhaps than that of the Bay, like soda-water, for we were as particular as young salmon, and the expectation of encountering a shark did not subtract anything from its life-giving qualities.

Sometimes we sat on the wet beach and watched the beach birds, sandpipers, and others, trotting along close to each wave, and waiting for the sea to cast up their breakfast. The former (*Charadrius melodus*) ran with great rapidity, and then stood stock still, remarkably erect, and hardly to be distinguished from the beach. The wet sand was covered with small skipping Sea Fleas, which apparently made a part of their food. These last are the little scavengers of the beach, and are so numerous that they will devour large fishes, which have been cast up, in a very short time. One little bird not larger than a sparrow — it may have been a Phalarope — would alight on the turbulent surface where the breakers were five or six feet high, and float buoyantly there like a duck, cunningly taking to its wings and lifting itself a few feet through the air over the foaming crest of each breaker, but sometimes outriding safely a considerable billow which hid it some seconds, when its instinct told it that it would not break. It was a little creature thus to sport with the ocean, but it was as perfect a success in its way as the breakers in theirs. There was also an almost uninterrupted line of coots rising and falling with the waves, a few rods from the shore, the whole length of the Cape. They made as constant a part of the ocean's border as the pads or pickerel-weed do of that of a pond. We read the following as to the Storm Petrel (*Thalassidroma Wilsonii*), which is seen in the Bay as well as on the outside. "The feathers on the breast of the Storm Petrel are, like those of all swimming-birds, water-proof; but substances not susceptible of being wetted with water are, for that very reason, the best fitted for collecting oil from its surface. That function is performed by the feathers on the breast of the Storm Petrels as they touch on the surface; and though that may not be the only way in which they procure their food, it is certainly that in which they obtain great part of it. They dash along until they have loaded their feathers and then they pause upon the waves and remove the oil with their bills."

.   .   .   .   .

To-day it was the Purple Sea, an epithet which I should not before have accepted. There were distinct patches of the color of a purple grape with the bloom rubbed off. But first and last the sea is of all colors. Well writes Gilpin concerning "the brilliant hues which are continually playing on the surface of a quiet ocean," and this was not too turbulent at a distance from the shore. "Beautiful," says he, "no doubt in a high degree are those glimmering tints which often invest the tops of mountains; but they are mere coruscations compared with these marine colors, which are continually varying and shifting into each other in all the vivid splendor of the rainbow, through the space often of several leagues." Commonly, in calm weather, for half a mile from the shore, where the bottom tinges it, the sea is green, or greenish, as are some ponds; then blue for many miles, often with purple tinges, bounded in the distance by a light, almost silvery stripe; beyond which there is generally a dark blue rim, like a mountain ridge in the horizon, as if, like that, it owed its color to the intervening atmosphere. On another day, it will be marked with long streaks, alternately smooth and rippled, light-colored and dark, even like our inland meadows in a freshet, and showing which way the wind sets.

.   .   .   .   .

We discerned vessels so far off, when once we began to look, that only the tops of their masts in the horizon were visible, and it took a strong intention of the eye, and its most favorable side, to see them at all, and sometimes we doubted if we were not counting our eyelashes. . . .

Though there were numerous vessels at this great distance in the horizon on every side, yet the vast spaces between them, like the spaces between the stars, — far as they were distant from us, so were they from one another — nay, some were twice as far from each other as from us, — impressed us with a sense of the immensity of the ocean, the "unfruitful ocean," as it has been called, and we could see what proportion man and his works bear to the globe. As we looked off, and saw the water growing darker and darker and deeper and deeper the farther we looked, till it was awful to consider, and it appeared to have no relation to the friendly land, either as shore or bottom, — of what use is a bottom if it is out of sight, if it is two or three miles from the surface, and you are to be drowned so long before you get to it, though it were made of the same stuff with your native soil? — over that ocean where, as the Veda says, "there is nothing to give support, nothing to rest upon, nothing to cling to," I felt that I was a land animal. The man in a balloon even may commonly alight on the earth in a few moments, but the sailor's only hope is that he may reach the distant shore. I could then appreciate the heroism of the old navigator, Sir Humphrey Gilbert, of whom it is related, that being overtaken by a storm on his return from America, in the year 1583, far northeastward from where we were, sitting abaft with a book in his hand, just before he was swallowed up in the deep, he cried out to his comrades in the Hind, as they came within hearing, "We are as near to Heaven by sea as by land." I saw that it would not be easy to realize.

On Cape Cod the next most eastern land you hear of is St. George's Bank (the fishermen tell of "Georges," "Cashus," and other sunken lands which they frequent). Every Cape man has a theory about George's Bank having been an island once, and in their accounts they gradually reduce the shallowness from six, five, four, two fathoms, to somebody's confident assertion that he has seen a mackerel-gull sitting on a piece of dry land there. It reminded me, when I thought of the shipwrecks which had taken place there, of the Isle of Demons, laid down off this coast in old charts of the New World. There must be something monstrous, methinks, in a vision of the sea bottom from over some bank a thousand miles from the shore, more awful than its imagined bottomlessness; a drowned continent, all livid and frothing at the nostrils, like the body of a drowned man, which is better sunk deep than near the surface.

Yet this same placid Ocean, as civil now as a city's harbor, a place for ships and commerce, will erelong be lashed into sudden fury, and all its caves and cliffs will resound with tumult. It will ruthlessly heave these vessels to and fro, break them in pieces in its sandy or stony jaws, and deliver their crews to sea-monsters. It will play with them like seaweed, distend them like dead frogs, and carry them about, now high, now low, to show to the fishes, giving them a nibble. This gentle Ocean will toss and tear the rag of a man's body like the father of mad bulls, and his relatives may be seen seeking the remnants for weeks along the strand. From some quiet inland hamlet they have rushed weeping to the unheard-of shore, and now stand uncertain where a sailor has recently been buried among the sand-hills.

· · · · ·

The Greeks would not have called the ocean ἀτρύγετος, or unfruitful, though it does not produce wheat, if they had viewed it by the light of modern science, for naturalists now assert that "the sea, and not the land, is the principal seat of life," — though not of vegetable life. Darwin affirms that "our most thickly inhabited forests appear almost as deserts when we come to compare them with the corresponding regions of the ocean." Agassiz and Gould tell us that "the sea teems with animals of all classes, far beyond the extreme point of flowering plants"; but they add, that "experiments of dredging in very deep water have also taught us that the abyss of the ocean is nearly a desert;" — "so that modern investigations," to quote the words of Desor, "merely go to confirm the great idea which was vaguely anticipated by the ancient poets and philosophers, that the Ocean is the origin of all things." Yet marine animals and plants hold a lower rank in the scale of being than land animals and plants. "There is no instance known," says Desor, "of an animal becoming aquatic in its perfect state, after having lived in its lower stage on dry land," but as in the case of the tadpole, "the progress invariably points towards the dry land." In short, the dry land itself came through and out of the water in its way to the heavens, for, "in going back through the geological ages, we come to an epoch when, according to all appearances, the dry land did not exist, and when the surface of our globe was entirely covered with water." We looked on the sea, then, once more, not as ἀτρύγετος, or unfruitful, but as it has been more truly called, the "laboratory of continents."

Though we have indulged in some placid reflections of late, the reader must not forget that the dash and roar of the waves were incessant. Indeed, it would be well if he were to read with a large conch-shell at his ear. But notwithstanding that it was very cold and windy today, it was such cold as we thought would not cause one to take cold who was exposed to it, owing to the saltness of the air and the dryness of the soil. Yet the author of the old "Description of Wellfleet" says, "The atmosphere is very much impregnated with saline particles, which, perhaps, with the great use of fish, and the neglect of cider and spruce-beer, may be a reason why the people are more subject to sore mouths and throats than in other places."

III
The Sea and the Desert

The light-house lamps were still burning,[6] though now with a silvery lustre, when I rose to see the sun come out of the Ocean; for he still rose to the eastward of us; but I was convinced that he must have come out of a dry bed beyond that stream, though he seemed to come out of the water.

> "The sun once more touched the fields,
> Mounting to heaven from the fair flowing
> Deep-running Ocean."

Now we saw countless sails of mackerel fishers abroad on the deep, one fleet in the north just pouring round the Cape, another standing down toward Chatham, and our host's son went off to join some lagging member of the first which had not yet left the Bay.

Before we left the light-house we were obliged to anoint our shoes faithfully with tallow, for walking on the beach, in the salt water and the sand, had turned them red and crisp. To counterbalance this, I have remarked that the seashore, even where muddy, as it is not here, is singularly clean; for, notwithstanding the spattering of the water and mud and squirting of the clams, while walking to and from from the boat, your best black pants retain no stain or dirt, such as they might acquire from walking in the country.

. . . . .

Still one after another the mackerel schooners hove in sight round the head of the Cape, "whitening all the sea road," and we watched

6 Thoreau and his companion have spent the night at Highland Light in Truro.

each one for a moment with an undivided interest. It seemed a pretty sport. Here in the country it is only a few idle boys or loafers that go a-fishing on a rainy day; but there it appeared as if every able-bodied man and helpful boy in the Bay had gone out on a pleasure excursion in their yachts, and all would at last land and have a chowder on the Cape. The gazetteer tells you gravely how many of the men and boys of these towns are engaged in the whale, cod, and mackerel fishery, how many go to the banks of Newfoundland, or the coast of Labrador, the Straits of Belle Isle or the Bay of Chaleurs (Shalore, the sailors call it); as if I were to reckon up the number of boys in Concord who are engaged during the summer in the perch, pickerel, bream, horn-pout, and shiner fishery, of which no one keeps the statistics, — though I think that it is pursued with as much profit to the moral and intellectual man (or boy), and certainly with less danger to the physical one.

One of my playmates, who was apprenticed to a printer, and was somewhat of a wag, asked his master one afternoon if he might go a-fishing, and his master consented. He was gone three months. When he came back, he said that he had been to the Grand Banks, and went to setting type again as if only an afternoon had intervened.

. . . . .

Though once there were more whales cast up here, I think that it was never more wild than now. We do not associate the idea of antiquity with the ocean, nor wonder how it looked a thousand years ago, as we do of the land, for it was equally wild and unfathomable always. The Indians have left no traces on its surface, but it is the same to the civilized man and the savage. The aspect of the shore only has changed. The ocean is a wilderness reaching round the globe, wilder than a Bengal jungle, and fuller of monsters, washing the very wharves of our cities and the gardens of our seaside residences. Serpents, bears, hyenas, tigers, rapidly vanish as civilization advances, but the most populous and civilized city cannot scare a shark far from its wharves. It is no further advanced than Singapore, with its tigers, in this respect. The Boston papers had never told me that there were seals in the harbor. I had always associated these with the Esquimaux and other outlandish people. Yet from the parlor windows all along the coast you may see families of them sporting on the flats. They were as strange to me as the merman would be,

Ladies who never walk in the woods, sail over the sea. To go to sea! Why, it is to have the experience of Noah, — to realize the deluge. Every vessel is an ark.

We saw no fences as we walked the beach, no birchen riders, highest of rails, projecting into the sea to keep the cows from wading round, nothing to remind us that man was proprietor of the shore. Yet a Truro man did tell us that owners of land on the east side of that town were regarded as owning the beach, in order that they might have the control of it so far as to defend themselves against the encroachments of the sand and the beach-grass, — for even this friend is sometimes regarded as a foe; but he said that this was not the case on the Bay side. Also, I have seen in sheltered parts of the Bay, temporary fences running to low-water mark, the posts being set in sills or sleepers placed transversely.

After we had been walking many hours, the mackerel fleet still hovered in the northern horizon nearly in the same direction, but farther off, hull down. Though their sails were set they never sailed away, nor yet came to anchor, but stood on various tacks as close together as vessels in a haven, and we, in our ignorance, thought that they were contending patiently with adverse winds, beating eastward; but we learned afterward that they were even then on their fishing-ground, and that they caught mackerel without taking in their mainsails or coming to anchor, a "smart breeze" (thence called a mackerel breeze) "being," as one says, "considered most favorable" for this purpose. We counted about two hundred sail of mackerel fishers within one small arc of the horizon, and a nearly equal number had disappeared southward. Thus they hovered about the extremity of the Cape, like moths round a candle; the lights at Race Point and Long Point being bright candles for them at night, — and at this distance they looked fair and white, as if they had not yet flown into the light, but nearer at hand afterward, we saw how some had formerly singed their wings and bodies.

A village seems thus, where its able-bodied men are all ploughing the ocean together, as a common field. In North Truro the women and girls may sit at their doors, and see where their husbands and brothers are harvesting their mackerel fifteen or twenty miles off, on the sea, with hundreds of white harvest wagons, just as in the country the farmers' wives sometimes see their husbands working in a distant hillside field. But the sound of no dinner-horn can reach the fisher's ear.

· · · · ·

Before sunset, having already seen the mackerel fleet returning into the Bay, we left the seashore on the north of Provincetown, and made our way across the desert to the eastern extremity of the town. From the first high sand-hill, covered with beach-grass and bushes to its top, on the edge of the desert, we overlooked the shrubby hill and swamp country which surrounds Provincetown on the north, and protects it, in some measure, from the invading sand. Notwithstanding the universal barrenness, and the contiguity of the desert, I never saw an autumnal landscape so beautifully painted as this was. It was like the richest rug imaginable spread over an uneven surface; no damask nor velvet, nor the work of any loom, could ever match it. There was the incredibly bright red of the Huckleberry, and the reddish brown of the Bayberry, mingled with the bright and living green of small Pitch-Pines, and also the duller green of the Bayberry, Boxberry, and Plum, the yellowish green of the Shrub-Oaks, and the various golden and yellow and fawn-colored tints of the Birch and Maple and Aspen, — each making its own figure, and, in the midst, the few yellow sandslides on the sides of the hills looked like the white floor seen through rents in the rug. Coming from the country as I did, and many autumnal woods as I had seen, this was perhaps the most novel and remarkable sight that I saw on the Cape. Probably the brightness of the tints was enhanced by contrast with the sand which surrounded this tract. This was a part of the furniture of Cape Cod. We had for days walked up the long and bleak piazza which runs along her Atlantic side, then over the sanded floor of her halls, and now we were being introduced into her boudoir. The hundred white sails crowding round Long Point into Provincetown Harbor, seen over the painted hills in front, looked like toy ships upon a mantel-piece.

· · · · ·

The next morning, though it was still more cold and blustering than the day before, we took to the deserts again, for we spent our days wholly out of doors, in the sun when there was any, and in the wind which never failed. After threading the shrubby hill-country at the southwest end of the town, west of the Shank-Painter Swamp, whose expressive name — for we understood it at first as a landsman naturally would — gave it importance in our eyes, we crossed the sands to the shore south of Race Point and three miles distant, and thence roamed round eastward through the desert to where we had left the sea the evening before. We traveled five or six miles after we got there, on a curving line, and might have gone nine or ten, over vast platters of pure sand, from the midst of which we could not see a particle of vegetation, except the distant thin fields of beach-grass, which crowned and made the ridges toward which the sand sloped upward on each side; all the while in the face of a cutting wind as cold as January; indeed, we experienced no weather so cold as this for nearly two months afterward. . . .

The wind was not a Sirocco or Simoon, such as we associate with the desert, but a New England northeaster, — and we sought shelter in vain under the sand-hills, for it blew all about them, rounding them into cones, and was sure to find us out on whichever side we sat. From time to time we lay down and drank at little pools in the sand, filled with pure, fresh water, all that was left, probably, of a pond or swamp. The air was filled with dust like snow, and cutting sand which made the face tingle, and we saw what it must be to face it when the weather was drier, and, if possible, windier still, — to face a migrating sand-bar in the air, which has picked up its duds and is off, — to be whipped with a cat, not o' nine tails, but of a myriad of tails, and each one with a sting to it. A Mr. Whitman, a former minister of Wellfleet, used to write to his inland friends that the blowing sand scratched the windows so that he was obliged to have one new pane set every week, that he might see out.

· · · · ·

The attention of the general government was first attracted to the danger which threatened Cape Cod Harbor from the inroads of the sand about thirty years ago, and commissioners were at that time appointed by Massachusetts to examine the premises. They reported in June, 1825, that, owing to "the trees and brush having been cut down, and the beach-grass destroyed on the seaward side of the Cape, opposite the Harbor," the original surface of the ground had been broken up and removed by the wind toward the Harbor, — during the previous fourteen years, — over an extent of "one half mile in breadth, and about four and a half miles in length." — "The space where a few years since were some of the highest lands on the Cape, covered with trees and bushes," presenting "an extensive waste of undulating sand;" — and that, during the previous twelve months, the sand "had approached the Harbor an average distance of fifty rods, for an extent of four and a half miles!" and unless some measures were adopted to check its progress, it would in a few years destroy both the harbor and the town. They therefore recommended that beach-grass be set out on a curving line over a space ten rods wide and four and a half miles long, and that cattle, horses, and sheep be prohibited from going abroad, and the inhabitants from cutting the brush.

I was told that thirty thousand dollars in all had been appropriated to this object, though it was complained that a great part of it was spent foolishly, as the public money is wont to be. Some say that while the government is planting beach-grass behind the town for the protection of the harbor, the inhabitants are rolling the sand into the harbor in wheelbarrows in order to make house-lots. The Patent-Office has recently imported the seed of this grass from Holland, and distributed it over the country, but probably we have as much as the Hollanders.

Thus Cape Cod is anchored to the heavens, as it were, by a myriad little cables of beach-grass, and, if they should fail, would become a total wreck, and erelong go to the bottom. Formerly, the cows were permitted to go at large, and they ate many strands of the cable by which the Cape is moored, and well-nigh set it adrift, as the bull did the boat which was moored with a grass rope; but now they are not permitted to wander.

— From CAPE COD

CAPE COD, *published as a book in 1865, is the account of three visits Henry Thoreau made to the Cape, the first in October, 1849, the others in June, 1850, and July, 1855. He was here in all only about three weeks, but his book tells us more about the history of Cape Cod, its natural life, geology, economy and culture than most people know who have lived here all their lives. It is with great trepidation that the editors of* SAND IN THEIR SHOES *have ventured, for reasons of space, to make excisions in the three chapters presented here.* CAPE COD *should be read in its entirety. After a hundred years it remains the freshest and most perceptive book ever written about the Cape. Private and government planting to stay the walking sands have shrunk the desert Thoreau describes to a region around Provincetown and Truro, and even over this a tinge of green is creeping. Cape Cod is leafier and woodier than it was in 1849, but Cape Cod Beach, — except for the appearance of new bars and shoals, and the disappearance of some old ones, — and even most of the hollows leading inland from it look as they looked when Thoreau blown along beneath a great black umbrella set forth upon his famous walk.*

ତ∾ର

1928
NIGHT ON THE GREAT BEACH

BY HENRY BESTON

I

OUR FANTASTIC CIVILIZATION has fallen out of touch with many aspects of nature, and with none more completely than with night. Primitive folk, gathered at a cave mouth round a fire, do not fear night; they fear, rather, the energies and creatures to whom night gives power; we of the age of the machines, having delivered ourselves of nocturnal enemies, now have a dislike of night itself. With lights and ever more lights, we drive the holiness and beauty of night back to the forests and the sea; the little villages, the crossroads even, will have none of it. Are modern folk, perhaps, afraid of night? Do they fear that vast serenity, the mystery of infinite space, the austerity of stars? Having made themselves at home in a civilization obsessed with power, which explains its whole world in terms of energy, do they fear at night for their dull acquiescence and the pattern of their beliefs? Be the answer what it will, to-day's civilization is full of people who have not the slightest notion of the character or the poetry of night, who have never even seen night. Yet to live thus, to know only artificial night, is as absurd and evil as to know only artificial day.

Night is very beautiful on this great beach. It is the true other half of the day's tremendous wheel; no lights without meaning stab or trouble it; it is beauty, it is fulfilment, it is rest. Thin clouds float in these heavens, islands of obscurity in a splendour of space and stars: the Milky Way bridges earth and ocean; the beach resolves itself into a unity of form, its summer lagoons, its slopes and uplands merging; against the western sky and the falling bow of sun rise the silent and superb undulations of the dunes.

My nights are their darkest when a dense fog streams in from the sea under a black, unbroken floor of cloud. Such nights are rare, but are most to be expected when fog gathers off the coast in early summer; this last Wednesday night was the darkest I have known. Between ten o'clock and two in the morning three vessels stranded on the outer beach — a fisherman, a four-masted schooner, and a beam trawler. The fisherman and the schooner have been towed off, but the trawler, they say, is still ashore.

I went down to the beach that night just after ten o'clock. So utterly black, pitch dark it was, and so thick with moisture and trailing showers, that there was no sign whatever of the beam of Nauset; the sea was only a sound, and when I reached the edge of the surf the dunes themselves had disappeared behind. I stood as isolate in that immensity of rain and night as I might have stood in interplanetary space. The sea was troubled and noisy, and when I opened the darkness with an outlined cone of light from my electric torch I saw that the waves were washing up green coils of sea grass, all coldly wet and bright in the motionless and unnatural radiance. Far off a single ship was groaning its way along the shoals. The fog was compact of the finest moisture; passing by, it spun itself into my lens of light like a kind of strange, aërial, and liquid silk. Effin Chalke, the new coast guard, passed me going north, and told me that he had had news at the halfway house of the schooner at Cahoon's.

It was dark, pitch dark to my eye, yet complete darkness, I imagine, is exceedingly rare, perhaps unknown in outer nature. The nearest natural approximation to it is probably the gloom of forest country buried in night and cloud. Dark as the night was here, there was still light on the surface of the planet. Standing on the shelving beach, with the surf breaking at my feet, I could see the endless wild uprush, slide, and withdrawal of the sea's white rim of foam. The men at Nauset tell me that on such nights they follow along this vague crawl of whiteness, trusting to habit and a sixth sense to warn them of their approach to the halfway house.

Animals descend by starlight to the beach. North, beyond the dunes, muskrats forsake the cliff and nose about in the driftwood and weed, leaving intricate trails and figure eights to be obliterated by the day; the lesser folk — the mice, the occasional small sand-coloured toads, the burrowing moles — keep to the upper beach and leave their tiny footprints under the overhanging wall. In autumn skunks, beset by a shrinking larder, go beach combing early in the night. The animal is by preference a clean feeder and turns up his nose at rankness. I almost stepped on a big fellow one night as I was walking north to meet the first man south from Nauset. There was a scamper, and the creature ran up the beach from under my feet; alarmed he certainly was, yet he was contained and continent. Deer are frequently seen, especially north of the light. I find their tracks upon the summer dunes.

Years ago, while camping on this beach north of Nauset, I went for a stroll along the top of the cliff at break of dawn. Though the path followed close enough along the edge, the beach below was often hidden, and I looked directly from the height to the flush of sunrise at sea. Presently the path, turning, approached the brink of the earth precipice, and on the beach below, in the cool, wet rosiness of dawn, I saw three deer playing. They frolicked, rose on their hind legs, scampered off, and returned again, and were merry. Just before sunrise they trotted off north together down the beach toward a hollow in the cliff and the path that climbs it.

Occasionally a sea creature visits the shore at night. Lone coast guardsmen, trudging the sand at some deserted hour, have been startled by seals. One man fell flat on a creature's back, and it drew away from under him, flippering toward the sea, with a sound "Half-way between a squeal and a bark." I myself once had rather a start. It was long after sundown, the light dying and uncertain, and I was walking home on the top level of the beach and close along the slope descending to the ebbing tide. A little more than halfway to the Fo'castle a huge unexpected something suddenly writhed horribly in the darkness under my bare foot. I had stepped on a skate left stranded by some recent crest of surf, and my weight had momentarily annoyed it back to life.

Facing north, the beam of Nauset becomes part of the dune night. As I walk toward it, I see the lantern, now as a star of light which waxes and wanes three mathematic times, now as a lovely pale flare of light behind the rounded summits of the dunes. The changes in the atmosphere change the colour of the beam; it is now whitish, now flame golden, now golden red; it changes its form as well, from a star to a blare of light, from a blare of light to a cone of radiance sweeping a circumference of fog. To the west of Nauset I often see the apocalyptic flash of the great light at Highland reflected on the clouds or even in the moisture in the starlit air, and, seeing it, I often think of the pleasant hours I have spent there when George and Mary Smith were at the light and I had the good fortune to visit as their guest. Instead of going to sleep in the room under the eaves, I would lie awake, looking out of a window to the great spokes of light revolving as solemnly as part of the universe.

All night long the lights of coastwise vessels pass at sea, green lights going south, red lights moving north. Fishing schooners and flounder draggers anchor two or three miles out, and keep a bright riding light burning on the mast. I see them come to anchor at sundown, but I rarely see them go, for they are off at dawn. When busy at night, these fishermen illumine their decks with a scatter of oil flares. From shore, the ships might be thought afire. I have watched the scene through a night glass. I could see no smoke, only the waving flares, the reddish radiance on sail and rigging, an edge of reflection overside, and the enormous night and sea beyond.

One July night, as I returned at three o'clock from an expedition north, the whole night, in one strange, burning instant, turned into a phantom day. I stopped and, questioning, stared about. An enormous meteor, the largest I have ever seen, was consuming itself in an effulgence of light west of the zenith. Beach and dune and ocean appeared out of nothing, shadowless and motionless, a landscape whose every tremor and vibration were stilled, a landscape in a dream.

The beach at night has a voice all its own, a sound in fullest harmony with its spirit and mood — with its little, dry noise of sand forever moving, with its solemn, overspilling, rhythmic seas, with its eternity of stars that sometimes seem to hang down like lamps from the high heavens — and that sound the piping of a bird. As I walk the beach in early summer my solitary coming disturbs it on its nest, and it flies away, troubled, invisible, piping its sweet, plaintive cry. The bird I write of is the piping plover, *Charadrius melodus,* sometimes called the beach plover or the mourning bird. Its note is a whistled syllable, the loveliest musical note, I think, sounded by any North Atlantic bird.

Now that summer is here I often cook myself a camp supper on the beach. Beyond the crackling, salt-yellow driftwood flame, over the pyramid of barrel staves, broken boards, and old sticks all atwist with climbing fire, the unseen ocean thunders and booms, the breaker sounding hollow as it falls. The wall of the sand cliff behind, with its rim of grass and withering roots, its sandy crumbling and erosions, stands gilded with flame; wind cries over it; a covey of sandpipers pass between the ocean and the fire. There are stars, and to the south Scorpio hangs curving down the sky with ringed Saturn shining in his claw.

Learn to reverence night and to put away the vulgar fear of it, for, with the banishment of night from the experience of man, there vanishes as well a religious emotion, a poetic mood, which gives depth to the adventure of humanity. By day, space is one with the earth and with man — it is his sun that is shining, his clouds that are floating past; at night, space is his no more. When the great earth, abandoning day, rolls up the deeps of the heavens and the universe, a new door opens for the human spirit, and there are few so clownish that some awareness of the mystery of being does not touch them as they gaze. For a moment of night we have a glimpse of ourselves and of our world islanded in its stream of stars — pilgrims of mortality, voyaging between horizons across eternal seas of space and time. Fugitive though the instant be, the spirit of man is, during it, ennobled by a genuine moment of emotional dignity, and poetry makes its own both the human spirit and experience.

II

At intervals during the summer, often enough when the tides are high and the moon is near the full, the surf along the beach turns from a churn of empty moonlit water to a mass of panic life. Driven in by schools of larger fish, swarms of little fish enter the tumble of the surf, the eaters follow them, the surf catches them both up and throws them, mauled and confused, ashore.

Under a sailing moon, the whole churn of sea close off the beach vibrates with a primeval ferocity and intensity of life; yet is this war of rushing mouth and living food without a sound save for the breaking of the seas. But let me tell you of such a night.

I had spent an afternoon ashore with friends, and they had driven me to Nauset Station just after nine o'clock. The moon, two days from the full, was very lovely on the moors and on the channels and flat, moon-green isles of the lagoon; the wind was southerly and light. Moved by its own enormous rhythms, the surf that night was a stately incoming of high, serried waves, the last wave breaking alone. This inmost wave broke heavily in a smother and rebound of sandy foam, and thin sheets of seethe, racing before it up the beach, vanished endlessly into the endless thirst of the sands. As I neared the surf rim to begin my walk to the southward, I saw that the beach close along the breakers, as far as the eye would reach, was curiously atwinkle in the moonlight with the convulsive dance of myriads of tiny fish. The breakers were spilling them on the sands; the surf was aswarm with the creatures; it was indeed, for the time being, a surf of life. And this surf of life was breaking for miles along the Cape.

Little herring or mackerel? Sand eels? I picked a dancer out of the slide and held him up to the moon. It was the familiar sand eel or sand launce, *Ammodytes americanus*, of the waters between Hatteras and Labrador. This is no kin of the true eels, though he rather resembles one in general appearance, for his body is slender, eel-like, and round. Instead of ending bluntly, however, this "eel" has a large, well-forked tail. The fish in the surf were two and three inches long.

Homeward that night I walked barefooted in the surf, watching the convulsive, twinkling dance, now and then feeling the squirm of a fish across my toes. Presently something occurred which made me keep to the thinnest edge of the foam. Some ten feet ahead, an enormous dogfish was suddenly borne up the beach on the rim of a slide of foam; he moved with it unresisting while it carried him; the slide withdrawing and drying up, it rolled him twice over seaward; he then twisted heavily, and another minor slide carried him back again to the shore. The fish was about three feet long, a real junior shark, purplish black in the increasing light — for the moon was moving west across the long axis of the breakers — and his dark, important bulk seemed strange in the bright dance of the smaller fish about him.

It was then that I began to look carefully at the width of gathering seas. Here were the greater fish, the mouths, the eaters who had driven the "eels" ashore to the edge of their world and into ours. The surf was alive with dogfish, aswarm with them, with the rush, the cold bellies, the twist and tear of their wolfish violence of life. Yet there was but little sign of it in the waters — a rare fin slicing past, and once the odd and instant glimpse of a fish embedded like a fly in amber in the bright, overturning volute of a wave.

Too far in, the dogfish were now in the grip of the surf, and presently began to come ashore. As I walked the next half mile every other breaker seemed to leave behind its ebb a mauled and stranded sharklet feebly sculling with his tail. I kicked many back into the seas, risking a toe, perhaps; some I caught by the tails and flung, for I did not want them corrupting the beach. The next morning, in the mile and three quarters between the Fo'castle and the station, I counted seventy-one dogfish lying dead on the upper beach. There were also a dozen or two skates — the skate is really a kind of shark — which had stranded the same night. Skates follow in many things, and are forever being flung upon these strands.

I sat up late that night at the Fo'castle, often putting down the book I read to return to the beach.

A little after eleven came Bill Eldridge to the door, with a grin on his face, and one hand held behind his back. "Have you ordered tomorrow's dinner yet?" said he. "No." "Well, here it is," and Bill produced a fine cod from behind his back. "Just found him in front of your door, alive and flopping. Yes, yes, haddock and cod often chase those sand eels in with the bigger fish; often find them on the beach about this time of the year. Got any place to keep him? Let me have a piece of string and I'll hang him on your clothesline. He'll keep all right." With a deft unforking of two fingers, Bill drew the line through the gills, and as he did so the heavy fish flopped noisily. No fear about him being dead. Make a nice chowder. Bill stepped outside; I heard him at the clothesline. Afterward we talked about it till it was time for him to shoulder his clock and Coston case again, pick up his watch cap, whistle in his little black dog, and go down over the dune to the beach and Nauset Station.

There were nights in June when there was phosphorescence in the surf and on the beach, and one such night I think I shall remember as the most strange and beautiful of all the year.

Early this summer the middle beach moulded itself into a bar, and between it and the dunes are long, shallow runnels into which the ocean spills over at high tide. On the night I write of, the first quarter of the moon hung in the west, and its light on the sheets of incoming tide coursing thin across the bar was very beautiful to see. Just after sundown I walked to Nauset with friends who had been with me during the afternoon; the tide was still rising, and a current running in the pools. I lingered at the station with my friends till the last of sunset had died, and the light upon the planet, which had been moonlight mingled with sunset pink, had cleared to pure cold moon.

Southward, then, I turned, and because the flooded runnels were deep close by the station, I could not cross them and had to walk their inner shores. The tide had fallen half a foot, perhaps, but the breakers were still leaping up against the bar as against a wall, the greater ones still spilling over sheets of vanishing foam.

It grew darker with the westing of the moon. There was light on the western tops of the dunes, a fainter light on the lower beach and the breakers; the face of the dunes was a unity of dusk.

The tide had ebbed in the pools, and their edges were wet and dark. There was a strange contrast between the still levels of the pool and the seethe of the sea. I kept close to the land edge of the lagoons, and as I advanced my boots kicked wet spatters of sand ahead as they might have kicked particles of snow. Every spatter was a crumb of phosphorescence; I walked in a dust of stars. Behind me, in my footprints, luminous patches burned. With the double-ebb moonlight and tide, the deepening brims of the pools took shape in smouldering, wet fire. So strangely did the luminous speckles smoulder and die and glow that it seemed as if some wind were passing, by whose breath they were kindled and extinguished. Occasional whole breakers of phosphorescence rolled in out of the vague sea — the whole wave one ghostly motion, one creamy light — and, breaking against the bar, flung up pale sprays of fire.

A strange thing happens here during these luminous tides. The phosphorescence is itself a mass of life, sometimes protozoan its origin, sometimes bacterial, the phosphorescence I write of being probably the latter. Once this living light has seeped into the beach, colonies of it speedily invade the tissues of the ten thousand sand fleas that are forever hopping on this edge of the ocean. Within an hour the grey bodies of these swarming amphipods, these useful, ever hungry sea scavengers *(Orchestia agilis; Talorchestia megaloph-*

thalma), show phosphorescent pin points, and these points grow and unite till the whole creature is luminous. The attack is really a disease, an infection of light. The process had already begun when I arrived on the beach on the night of which I am writing, and the luminous fleas hopping off before my boots were an extraordinary sight. It was curious to see them hop from the pool rims to the upper beach, paling as they reached the width of peaceful moonlight lying landward of the strange, crawling beauty of the pools. This infection kills them, I think; at least, I have often found the larger creature lying dead on the fringe of the beach, his huge porcelain eyes and water-grey body one core of living fire. Round and about him, disregarding, ten thousand kinsmen, carrying on life and the plan of life, ate of the bounty of the tide.

III

All winter long I slept on a couch in my larger room, but with the coming of warm weather I have put my bedroom in order — I used it as a kind of storage space during the cold season — and returned to my old and rather rusty iron cot. Every once in a while, however, moved by some obscure mood, I lift off the bed-clothing and make up the couch again for a few nights. I like the seven windows of the larger room, and the sense one may have there of being almost out-of-doors. My couch stands alongside the two front windows, and from my pillow I can look out to sea and watch the passing lights, the stars rising over ocean, the swaying lanterns of the anchored fishermen, and the white spill of the surf whose long sound fills the quiet of the dunes.

Ever since my coming I have wanted to see a thunderstorm bear down upon this elemental coast. A thunderstorm is a "tempest" on the Cape. The quoted word, as Shakespeare used it, means lightning and thunder, and it is in this old and beautiful Elizabethan sense that the word is used in Eastham. When a schoolboy in the Orleans or Wellfleet High reads the Shakespearean play, its title means to him exactly what it meant to the man from Stratford; elsewhere in America, the term seems to mean anything from a tornado to a blizzard. I imagine that this old significance of the word is now to be found only in certain parts of England and Cape Cod.

On the night of the June tempest, I was sleeping in my larger room, the windows were open, and the first low roll of thunder opened my eyes. It had been very still when I went to bed, but now a wind from the west-nor'west was blowing through the windows in a strong and steady current, and as I closed them there was lightning to the west and far away. I looked at my watch; it was just after one o'clock. Then came a time of waiting in the darkness, long minutes broken by more thunder, and intervals of quiet in which I heard a faintest sound of light surf upon the beach. Suddenly the heavens cracked open in an immense instant of pinkish-violet lightning. My seven windows filled with the violent, inhuman light, and I had a glimpse of the great, solitary dunes staringly empty of familiar shadows; a tremendous crash then mingled with the withdrawal of the light, and echoes of thunder rumbled away and grew faint in a returning rush of darkness. A moment after, rain began to fall gently as if someone had just released its flow, a blessed sound on a roof of wooden shingles, and one I have loved ever since I was a child. From a gentle patter the sound of the rain grew swiftly to a drumming roar, and with the rain came the chuckling of water from the eaves. The tempest was crossing the Cape, striking at the ancient land on its way to the heavens above the sea.

Now came flash after flash amid a roaring of rain, and heavy thunder that rolled on till its last echoes were swallowed up in vast detonations which jarred the walls. Houses were struck that night in Eastham village. My lonely world, full of lightning and rain, was strange to look upon. I do not share the usual fear of lightning, but that night there came over me, for the first and last time of all my solitary year, a sense of isolation and remoteness from my kind. I remember that I stood up, watching, in the middle of the room. On the great marshes the lightning surfaced the winding channels with a metallic splendour and arrest of motion, all very strange through windows blurred by rain. Under the violences of light the great dunes took on a kind of elemental passivity, the quiet of earth enchanted into stone, and as I watched them appear and plunge back into a darkness that had an intensity of its own I felt, as never before, a sense of the vast time, of the thousands of cyclic and uncounted years which had passed since these giants had risen from the dark ocean at their feet and given themselves to the wind and the bright day.

Fantastic things were visible at sea. Beaten down by the rain, and sheltered by the Cape itself from the river of west wind, the offshore brim of ocean remained unusually calm. The tide was about halfway up the beach, and rising, and long parallels of low waves, forming close inshore, were curling over and breaking placidly along the lonely, rain-drenched miles. The intense crackling flares and quiverings of the storm, moving out to sea, illumined every inch of the beach and the plain of the Atlantic, all save the hollow bellies of the little breakers, which were shielded from the light by their overcurling crests. The effect was dramatic and strangely beautiful, for what one saw was a bright ocean rimmed with parallel bands of blackest advancing darkness, each one melting back into light as the wave toppled down upon the beach in foam.

Stars came out after the storm, and when I woke again before sunrise I found the heavens and the earth rainwashed, cool, and clear. Saturn and the Scorpion were setting, but Jupiter was riding the zenith and paling on his throne. The tide was low in the marsh channels; the gulls had scarcely stirred upon their gravel banks and bars. Suddenly, thus wandering about, I disturbed a song sparrow on her nest. She flew to the roof of my house, grasped the ridgepole, and turned about, apprehensive, inquiring . . . 'tsiped her monosyllable of alarm. Then back toward her nest she flew, alighted in a plum bush, and, reassured at last, trilled out a morning song.

— From THE OUTERMOST HOUSE

THE OUTERMOST HOUSE *is the record of a year of solitary life spent by the writer in the "Fo'castle," a small house built atop a dune on a remote stretch of Eastham Beach. The coast guards at Nauset two miles away were his nearest neighbors. There was no road to the "Fo'castle" across the dunes. To get supplies he was obliged to walk twice a week in every kind of weather along the beach to Nauset Station where a car met him to take him to Eastham or Orleans. "The world today is sick to its thin blood for lack of elemental things," Henry Beston wrote, explaining his decision to protract the few weeks in September he had intended to spend in the "Fo'castle" to a year. The book that came out of his experience is much loved on Cape Cod, even by Cape Cod people who are sometimes inclined to look askance upon what outsiders write about them and their land.*

ॐ

A HINT AT THE NATURAL HISTORY
OF PROVINCETOWN

BY J. HENRY BLAKE

THE WHOLE geographical position of the Cape is such that it catches the animals of the north and those of the south, and the hand with the index finger bent inward holds varied faunae. The Gulf Stream brings animals from the south, while the cold current from the north, which bathes the Maine coast to Massachusetts Bay, brings animals from that region. The Sperm Whale (*Physeter machocephalus*), and the Pygmy Sperm (*Kogia breviceps*), the only two kinds of Sperm Whales known, and the Bottle-nose Whale (*Hyperooden ampullatum*), all of them tropical whales, have been captured in Massachusetts Bay, and with the Right Whale (*Balaena glacialis*), a representative of the North Atlantic. Because of these favorable agencies Provincetown's fauna is varied, and most interesting. Shells have been found alive in Provincetown, the true habitat of which is Florida and the West Indies.

The flora of Provincetown deserves consideration because of the wholly sea formation of its soil. In its woods and on the margins of its ponds are found 500 or more different plants, some of them having beautiful flowers and fragrant perfume. . . . Only one of the plants of Provincetown lives wholly in salt water and that is the Eelgrass (*Zostera marina*), from the Greek meaning sea-ribbon, or belt, from its resemblance to the same. This Eelgrass has monoecious flowers arranged alternately in two rows on the spadix, and the ribbed seeds ¼ inch long, and looking much like a Chinese lantern, are found plentifully among the cast-up seaweeds on the shore. It is a beautiful sight to see Zostera waving its slender, green, ribbon-like leaves in the water, making a home for Hydroids, Bryozoa, and myriads of little creatures which live among its branches.

The algae, or seaweeds of Provincetown, are not numerous because of lack of rocks on the shores, but are very handsome, the rich brown, green and red making them objects of beauty when growing in the sunny pools or floating in the sea. There are about 50 species, some of which are found living in the waters all around the earth. They are attractive objects in albums, as they can be floated upon paper, pressed easily, and retain their natural colors.

The fishes consist of more than 125 species, none of them without interest, from the historic Cod to the little Stickleback (*Apeltes quadracus*) which makes its nest and rears its young in a homelike manner. Among the curious fish is the Pipe-fish (*Syngnathus fuscus*), which lives among the seaweeds, and has this peculiarity — that it is the male fish which takes care of the young by carrying them in a pouch on the ventral side, like the Kangaroo. The Horse-fish (*Hippocampushudsonius*) is a near relative, and with the same habits, the young swimming out and into this pouch at will. The Torpedo (*Tetronace occidentalis*), with its electric batteries; the Swell-fish (*Spheroides maculatus*), which has the power to inflate itself as large as a football, as a means of protection; and the Sunfish (*Mola mola*), which is curious in form, and pieces of which can be used like a rubber ball, is sometimes 7 feet from tip of dorsal to tip of ventral fins, are all found at Provincetown.

The Goose-fish, so named "because it does not know as much as a goose," is often found on the beach. It is known in the scientific world as *Lophius piscatorius,* and is noted for its large mouth, which is one-third as large as the fish. The gill openings are placed behind the pectoral fins, a feature possessed by no other Provincetown fish. Many instances are told of their swallowing large birds which were resting on the water, fish half as large as themselves, and even floating buoys.

The Flatfish are well represented, from the Halibut, weighing more than 300 lbs., to the small "Window-pane" Flounder. All Flatfish have their eyes on the two sides, like other fish, when young, but as they grow and swim on the side, right or left, one eye is forced over, so in all adults the two eyes are on one side. To compare a Flounder with an ordinary fish it should be placed on its edge, when all fins will be in place. The skull of the Flounder is twisted to accommodate the eyes. Many other fish could be enumerated, such as the gamey Pollock, Horse-mackerel, weighing 600 lbs., and others. Provincetown has sport for fisherman, food for the epicure, and abundant material for the student in natural history, all for the taking.

. . . The common clam, (*mya arenaria*), is the most conspicuous shell on the beach, and, although many are dug, few people know that the so-called snout or siphon of the clam is its tail, that the head and mouth are in the opposite end, and that the large, brown mass seen on the inside is the liver, the richest part of the clam, although often thrown away by cooks. This illustrates the saying that, "We often know the least about those things which are the most familiar to us."

Of the 300 or more different species of shells found on the shores of Provincetown there is a large number which resemble clams, but are not. Therefore the name is very misleading. The so-called "little-neck clam," is simply the young of the quahaug (*Venus mercenaria*). The quahaug is common in Provincetown, and it was from the blue part on the interior of the shell that the Indians made their "suckan-hock," or black money, which was twice the value of white money or "Wampum."

The common mussel (*Mytilus edulis*) is perhaps the next most familiar shell, and is of a beautiful blue, and edible, as the scientific name implies. . . . Unlike the clam, its habit is to live above ground, where, soon after its escape from the egg, it anchors itself by a strong byssus and spends its life near the spot. It has no foot that can be used to crawl with, but in the lower part of this corresponding organ is a long groove in which this strong anchor rope is prepared and extended to carry out this hair-like byssus and attach it to a stone or shell. This process repeated many times produces a hair-like bunch of threads, and if the shell dies, or is bitten away by some fish, this byssus is left attached to the stone or shell, and is often pulled up by fisherman who believe it is "growing hair."

Another interesting shell seen on our walk is *Astarte castanea,* found alive in only one place in the harbor, and on the Long Point alone. It is quite plentiful, one inch in diameter, chestnut color as the name shows, and the animal is bright orange. The shells are white when bleached in the sun, and washed by the sea, looking like white buttons minus the holes, and like the quahaug in shape. This shell is more interesting from the fact that it is a deep water shell, but with characteristics of those inhabiting island shores, and Prov-incetown, being almost an island, this shell thrives there.

Another little shell should not pass notice because of its beauty and great numbers. There is no common name, but the scientific name is *Gemma gemma.* It is shaped like the quahaug, but is seldom more than ⅛ inch long, and this little blue shell is found along the beach, and so plentiful in places that they make a blue streak as they lay upon the sand.

The "Ship-worm" (*Teredo navalis*), is not a worm, but a bivalve shell. The two valves are on the anterior end, within the wood bored by these little shells.

The few shells mentioned above are Bivalves (2 valves). I will now mention the Univalves, a group which contains the larger number. The two most conspicuous univalve shells on the beach are "Sweetmeats" or "Conchowinkles," local names of no special meaning. . . . The egg-cases of these shells are often seen on the flats and are called "sand-collars" because of their shape. These eggs are mixed with sand as they are layed around the anterior part of the shell and so moulded. If the shell is placed in this collar it fits perfectly, and if the collar or egg-case is held to the light the egg capsules containing the young are easily seen.

The most plentiful univalve shell seen at Provincetown is the "Periwinkle" (*Littorina littorea*), although not known here previous to 1869. It is a black shell, sometimes one inch in diameter, and was introduced from England, where it is used as food, to the Provinces, from which it has spread its way along the coast of Maine and Massachusetts, until today it is plentiful as far as New York.

·   ·   ·   ·   ·

The Cephalopods (head-foot) are the most highly developed of all shellfish, and include the Squid, which are found in Provincetown, at times, in great numbers. There are two kinds. One with big fins (*Loligo pealii*) and one with small fins (*Ommastrephes illecebrosa*). The Squid swim by ejecting a jet of water from the siphon which is under the head, and can dart through the water rapidly, always going tail foremost. When pursuing their prey, however, they can dart head foremost by reversing their siphons, and seize little fish with their two long tentacles, which have suckers on their tips only, then grasp it with the eight tentacles, which have suckers their whole length, thence to the mouth, situated between the tentacles, which is armed with beaks like a bird, except that the lower beak of the Squid laps over the upper, opposite to that of birds.

The shell consist of a thin, transparent "pen," just under the skin the whole length of the back, and the Squid also carries a sack of ink for clouding the water, similar to the smoke screens used during the war, to enable them to escape from their enemies. They can also change their color at will, from a deep red to a pale white, which aids them in capturing their prey. Both species possess these characteristics, and there is no "boneless Squid."

The Radiata, Starfish, etc., are represented by several interesting forms. The common Starfish is recognized in different varieties. Any one arm of the star is able to reproduce its kind, and the five points, if separated, will grow into five individuals, all having five points and an eye at the extremity of each.

The "Basket-fish (*Astrophyton agassizii*), named for the great naturalist, Prof. Louis Agassiz, is a common form, having the points of the star divided and subdivided until it has 81,920 terminal branches. The name "Basket-star" was given by John Winthrop, Governor of Connecticut, who sent one to London in 1670. One of its modes of feeding is to raise itself and rest on the tips of its many arms, like an inverted basket, whence the name "Basket-fish," and little fish etc., are easily caught in this trap. The "Basket-fish" is caught off Race Point on the "Spider Bottom," a bank named for this starfish, where it can be found in great numbers.

But I think that the "Sea-urchin" is the most wonderful animal of its class — Radiata. The common Sea-urchin (*Strongylocentrotus drobachiensis*) is very plentiful in some localities and is found along the coast northward, Provincetown being its southern limit. It is closely related to the Starfish, which is easily seen by bending the five arms of the Starfish upward to the dorsal center, the so-called legs corresponding to those of the Sea-urchin. It has no eyes, ears, feet, stomach, etc., yet has the power to substitute the functions of all these organs. It is covered with spines for protection, and these three kinds of spines are movable on little knobs which arise from calcareous plates which make up the test. The five ambulacra which radiate from the dorsal center have holes in the two rows of plates through which some 1800 long sucker-bearing tubes, used for locomotion, are protruded. The mouth, which is on the ventral side, is armed with five teeth, and this complicated structure (called Aristotle's lantern) requires 60 muscles to work the five jaws in masticating its seaweed food.

But the most interesting feature of the Sea-urchin is the fact that its body is covered with hundreds of pedicellariae whose purpose is to keep the body and spines clean. These little organs can easily be seen attached to the test at the base of the spines, and consist of a pointed stalk with a three-pointed pincer at the tip which can be seen picking up particles of dirt and sometimes handing them along to other pincers, until carried clear of the body. The mouth of the Sea-urchin is in the center of the ventral side, while the anus is in the center of the dorsal side.

The common Sand-dollar (*Echinarachnius parma*) is closely related to the Sea-urchin, and has most of its characteristics, the chief difference being that it has short spines instead of long.

There are many forms of Crustacea (from "custa" referring to the shell-like covering), or crabs, but the most familiar is the Hermit-crab which carries a borrowed shell on its back for protection. When very young it swims at the surface, after which it sinks to the bottom never more to rise. As it had no hard covering for its body, like other crabs, it looks about for a house to live in, and, finding a common shell handy, it backs in, thus protecting the soft part of its body which is a tempting morsel to some fish. From the Hermit-crab's early days instinct leads it to choose a house, and when the animal outgrows one shell it moves into a larger one without consulting a landlord.

The Fiddler-crab (*Gelasimus pugilator* or *Uca puligator*) lives in the marshes, in holes which they dig by rolling up and bringing out the sand in pellets, carrying it some distance away from their holes. Their food, or algae, they carry into their holes the same way. Only the male has one small, and one large claw like a fiddle, hence the name, while the female has two small claws.

The common "Beach-flea" (*Orchestia agilis*) is found in holes along the beach, even above the tide.

An interesting Crustacean is the common Horseshoe Crab (*Limulus polyphemus*), as it is the only living representative of a prehistoric race, the Trilobites, many of which are found in a fossil state. It has two sets of eyes, one compound eye on each side of the head, and a pair of simple eyes in the anterior middle of the head, a characteristic of the Spiders, to which it is more closely related than to the Crabs. As its hard, chitinous shell prevents growth, it is shed and a new one formed, thus allowing growth of the animal to take place. Not only is the outer covering shed, but all the chitinous internal structure also. The shedding takes place by the anterior edge of the shell splitting, allowing the newly-formed animal to work its way out of the old shell. Many of the cast-off shells are seen on the beaches. The female is four times larger than the male, but at a certain molting, not yet discovered, the front claws of the male change to a pair adapted to holding on to the shell of the female, as they go in pairs in the breeding season, and lay their eggs in the sand to hatch in a month. When the young are hatched from the eggs, they have no tail, this terminal spine developing later.

I have mentioned only a few of the marine animals found on the beaches of Provincetown, but I trust that enough have been mentioned to create some interest in the products which Nature has bestowed so abundantly. "Nature never yet betrayed the heart that loved her," and to the one seeking wisdom in the line of natural history there is no better place than Provincetown. For the summer visitor, like Whittier's "Barefoot Boy,"

> "Eschewing books and tasks,
> Nature answers all he asks."

— From an article contributed to Nancy W. Paine Smith's THE PROVINCETOWN BOOK

∽

1605

HORSESHOE CRAB

BY SAMUEL CHAMPLAIN

IN THIS PLACE and along the whole coast from Quinibequy, there are a great many *siguenocs,* which is a fish with a shell on its back like the tortoise, yet different, there being in the middle a row of little prickles, of the colour of a dead leaf, like the rest of the fish. At the end of this shell, there is another still smaller, bordered by very sharp points. The length of the tail varies according to their size. With the end of it, these people point their arrows, and it contains also a row of prickles like the large shell in which are the eyes. There are eight small feet like those of the crab, and two behind longer and flatter, which they used in swimming. There are also in front two other very small ones with which they eat. When walking, all the feet are concealed excepting the two hindermost, which are slightly visible. Under the small shell there are membranes which swell up, and beat like the throat of a frog, and rest upon each other like the folds of a waistcoat. The largest specimen of this fish that I ever saw was a foot broad, and a foot and a half long.

— From his VOYAGES

ACROSS THE CAPE

BY HENRY D. THOREAU

WHEN WE HAVE RETURNED from the seaside, we sometimes ask ourselves why we did not spend more time in gazing at the sea; but very soon the traveler does not look at the sea more than at the heavens. As for the interior, if the elevated sand-bar in the midst of the ocean can be said to have any interior, it was an exceedingly desolate landscape, with rarely a cultivated or cultivable field in sight. We saw no villages, and seldom a house, for these are generally on the Bay side. It was a succession of shrubby hills and valleys, now wearing an autumnal tint. You would frequently think, from the character of the surface, the dwarfish trees, and the bearberries around, that you were on the top of a mountain. The only wood in Eastham was on the edge of Wellfleet. The pitch-pines were not commonly more than fifteen or eighteen feet high. The larger ones were covered with lichens, — often hung with the long gray *Usnea*. There is scarcely a white-pine on the forearm of the Cape. Yet in the northwest part of Eastham, near the Camp Ground, we saw, the next summer, some quite rural and even sylvan retreats, for the Cape, where small rustling groves of oaks and locusts and whispering pines, on perfectly level ground, made a little paradise. The locusts, both transplanted and growing naturally about the houses there, appeared to flourish better than any other tree. There were thin belts of wood in Wellfleet and Truro, a mile or more from the Atlantic, but, for the most part, we could see the horizon through them, or, if extensive, the trees were not large. Both oaks and pines had often the same flat look with the apple-trees. Commonly, the oak woods twenty-five years old were a mere scraggy shrubbery nine or ten feet high, and we could frequently reach to their topmost leaf. Much that is called "woods" was about half as high as this, — only patches of shrub-oak, bayberry, beach-plum, and wild roses, overrun with woodbine. When the roses were in bloom, these patches in the midst of the sand displayed such a profusion of blossoms, mingled with the aroma of the bayberry, that no Italian or other artificial rose-garden could equal them. They were perfectly Elysian, and realized my idea of an oasis in the desert. Huckleberry bushes were very abundant, and the next summer they bore a remarkable quantity of that kind of gall called Huckleberry-apple, forming quite handsome though monstrous blossoms. But it must be added, that this shrubbery swarmed with wood-ticks, sometimes very troublesome parasites, and which it takes very horny fingers to crack.

The inhabitants of these towns have a great regard for a tree, though their standard for one is necessarily neither large nor high; and when they tell you of the large trees that once grew there, you must think of them, not as absolutely large, but large compared with the present generation. Their "brave old oaks," of which they speak with so much respect, and which they will point out to you as relics of the primitive forest, one hundred or one hundred and fifty, ay, for aught they know, two hundred years old, have a ridiculously dwarfish appearance, which excites a smile in the beholder. The largest and most venerable which they will show you in such a case are, perhaps, not more than twenty or twenty-five feet high. I was especially amused by the Liliputian old oaks in the south part of Truro. To the inexperienced eye, which appreciated their proportions only, they might appear vast as the trees which saved his royal majesty, but measured they were dwarfed at once almost into lichens which a deer might eat up in a morning. Yet they will tell you that large schooners were once built of timber which grew in Wellfleet. The old houses also are built of the timber of the Cape; but instead of the forests in the midst of which they originally stood, barren heaths, with poverty-grass for heather, now stretch away on every side. The modern houses are built of what is called "dimension timber," imported from Maine, all ready to be set up, so that commonly they do not touch it with an axe. Almost all the wood used for fuel is *imported* by vessels or currents, and of course all the coal. I was told that probably a quarter of the fuel and a considerable part of the lumber used in North Truro was drift-wood. Many get *all* their wood from the beach.

Of birds not found in the interior of the State, — at least in my neighborhood, — I heard, in the summer, the Black-throated Bunting (*Fringilla Americana*) amid the shrubbery, and in the open land the Upland Plover (*Totanus Bartramius*), whose quivering notes were ever and anon prolonged into a clear, somewhat plaintive yet hawk-like scream which sounded at a very indefinite distance. The bird may have been in the next field, though it sounded a mile off.

· · · · ·

The highest and sandiest portion next the Atlantic was thinly covered with beach-grass and indigo-weed. Next to this the surface of the upland generally consisted of white sand and gravel, like coarse salt, through which a scanty vegetation found its way up. It will give an ornithologist some idea of its barrenness if I mention that the next June, the month of grass, I found a night-hawk's eggs there, and that almost any square rod thereabouts, taken at random, would be an eligible site for such a deposit. The kildeer plover, which loves a similar locality, also drops its eggs there, and fills the air above with its din. This upland also produced *Cladonia* lichens, poverty-grass, savory-leaved aster (*Diplopappus linariifolius*), mouse-ear, bearberry, etc. On a few hillsides the savory-leaved aster and mouse-ear alone made quite a dense sward, said to be very pretty when the aster is in bloom. In some parts the two species of poverty-grass (*Hudsonia tomentosa* and *ericoides*), which deserve a better name, reign for miles in little hemispherical tufts or islets, like moss, scattered over the waste. They linger in bloom there till the middle of July. Occasionally near the beach these rounded beds, as also those of the sea-sandwort (*Honkenya peploides*), were filled with sand within an inch of their tops, and were hard, like large ant-hills, while the surrounding sand was soft. In summer, if the poverty-grass grows at the head of a Hollow looking toward the sea, in a bleak position when the wind rushes up, the northern or exposed half of the tuft is sometimes all black and dead like an oven-broom, while the opposite half is yellow with blossoms, the whole hillside thus presenting a remarkable contrast when seen from the poverty-stricken and the flourishing side. This plant, which in many places would be esteemed as an ornament, is here despised by many on account of its being associated with barrenness. It might well be adopted for the Barnstable coat-of-arms, in a field *sableux.* I should be proud of it. Here and there were tracts of beach-grass mingled with the seaside golden-rod and beach-pea, which reminded us still more forcibly of the ocean.

We read that there was not a brook in Truro. Yet there were deer here once,[1] which must often have panted in vain, but I am pretty

[1] There are many today.

sure that I afterward saw a small fresh-water brook emptying into the south side of Pamet River, though I was so heedless as not to taste it. At any rate, a little boy near by told me that he drank at it. There was not a tree as far as we could see, and that was many miles each way, the general level of the upland being about the same everywhere. Even from the Atlantic side we overlooked the Bay, and saw to Manomet Point in Plymouth, and better from that side because it was the highest. The almost universal bareness and smoothness of the landscape were as agreeable as novel, making it so much the more like the deck of a vessel. We saw vessels sailing south into the Bay, on the one hand, and north along the Atlantic shore, on the other, all with an aft wind.

·　　·　　·　　·　　·

In the north part of the town there is no house from shore to shore for several miles, and it is as wild and solitary as the Western Prairies — used to be. Indeed, one who has seen every house in Truro, will be surprised to hear of the number of the inhabitants but perhaps five hundred of the men and boys of this small town were then abroad on their fishing-grounds. Only a few men stay at home to till the sand or watch for blackfish. The farmers are fishermen-farmers and understand better ploughing the sea than the land. They do not disturb their sands much, though there is plenty of sea-weed in the creeks, to say nothing of blackfish occasionally rotting on the shore. Between the Pond and East Harbor Village there was an interesting plantation of pitch-pines, twenty or thirty acres in extent, like those which we had already seen from the stage. One who lived near said that the land was purchased by two men for a shilling or twenty-five cents an acre. Some is not considered worth writing a deed for. This soil or sand, which was partially covered with poverty and beach grass, sorrel, etc., was furrowed at intervals of about four feet and the seed dropped by a machine. The pines had come up admirably and grown the first year three or four inches, and the second six inches and more. Where the seed had been lately planted the white sand was freshly exposed in an endless furrow winding round and round the sides of the deep hollows in a vortical, spiral manner, which produced a very singular effect, as if you were looking into the reverse side of a vast banded shield. This experiment, so important to the Cape, appeared very successful, and perhaps the time will come when the greater part of this kind of land in Barnstable

County will be thus covered with an artificial pine-forest, as has been done in some parts of France. In that country 12,500 acres of downs had been thus covered in 1811 near Bayonne. They are called *pignadas,* and according to Loudon "constitute the principal riches of the inhabitants, where there was a drifting desert before." It seems a nobler kind of grain to raise than corn even.

.　　.　　.　　.　　.

To the fisherman, the Cape itself is a sort of store-ship laden with supplies, — a safer and larger craft which carries the women and children, the old men and the sick, and indeed sea-phrases are as common on it as on board a vessel. Thus it is ever with a sea-going people. The old Northmen used to speak of the "keel-ridge" of the country, that is, the ridge of the Doffrafield Mountains, as if the land were a boat turned bottom up. I was frequently reminded of the Northmen here. The inhabitants of the Cape are often at once farmers and sea-rovers; they are more than vikings or kings of the bays, for their sway extends over the open sea also. A farmer in Wellfleet, at whose house I afterward spent a night, who had raised fifty bushels of potatoes the previous year, which is a large crop for the Cape, and had extensive salt-works, pointed to his schooner, which lay in sight, in which he and his man and boy occasionally ran down the coast a-trading as far as the Capes of Virginia. This was his market-cart, and his hired man knew how to steer her. Thus he drove two teams a-field,

> "ere the high *seas* appeared
> Under the opening eyelids of the morn."

Though probably he would not hear much of the "gray-fly" on his way to Virginia.

.　　.　　.　　.　　.

On our way back to the light-house, by whose whitewashed tower we steered as securely 'as the mariner by its light at night, we passed through a graveyard, which apparently was saved from being blown away by its slates, for they had enabled a thick bed of huckleberry bushes to root themselves amid the graves. We thought it would be worth while to read the epitaphs where so many were lost at sea; however, as not only their lives, but commonly their bodies also, were lost or not identified, there were fewer epitaphs of this sort than we expected, though there were not a few. Near the eastern side we started up a fox in a hollow, the only kind of wild quadruped, if I except a skunk in a salt-marsh, that we saw in all our walk (unless painted and box tortoises may be called quadrupeds). He was a large, plump, shaggy fellow, like a yellow dog, with, as usual, a white tip to his tail, and looked as if he fared well on the Cape. He cantered away into the shrub-oaks and bayberry bushes which chanced to grow there, but were hardly high enough to conceal him. I saw another the next summer leaping over the top of a beach-plum a little farther north, a small arc of his course (which I trust is not yet run), from which I endeavored in vain to calculate his whole orbit; there were too many unknown attractions to be allowed for. I also saw the exuviae of a third fast sinking into the sand, and added the skull to my collection. Hence, I concluded that they must be plenty thereabouts; but a traveler may meet with more than an inhabitant, since he is more likely to take an unfrequented route across the country. They told me that in some years they died off in great numbers by a kind of madness, under the effect of which they were seen whirling round and round as if in pursuit of their tails. In Crantz's account of Greenland, he says, "They (the foxes) live upon birds and their eggs, and, when they can't get them, upon crow-berries, mussels, crabs and what the sea casts up."

— From CAPE COD

၄~၄

OLD HOUSES AND NEW AMERICA

BY KATHARINE DOS PASSOS

CAPE COD HOUSES are wooden witnesses of the idea of severe doctrine combined with a stiff-necked belief in the civil and political rights of the individual. They seem frail but are sturdy, look small but are larger than they look, they are plainly built out of plain materials, and their chief beauty is their proportion.

"Sober-looking houses" Thoreau calls them, "low and broad" — firmly planted on the land and seeming part of it. Cape Cod men have always been fishermen, seamen, farmers, millers, carpenters, shipmasters, close to the land and close to the sea. Their houses have about them a democratic equality which is part of their early American charm, and the virtues of thrift, neatness and independence are built up visibly in the solid frames of hewn oak, hand-split shingles, careful construction and detail. . . . The earliest builders usually followed two or three models — houses which derived from the simple English cottages of Cornwall and Devon.

There are several types of these houses, and these types have variations, for the builders were individualistic and suited their houses to their needs, but it is always noticeable that their individuality expresses itself not in a chaos of personal notions, but in the original treatment of an established form. This gives uniformity without monotony or dullness. It makes you think again of the early plan of the villages, where each community was organized as a self-governing body, deriving its powers from the voters. But a voter had to be eligible, and to be eligible he had to be regular, that is, a respectable citizen and an accepted church member. So we find the houses — all fundamentally alike — regular church members, but still exhibiting their own character and personality.

The Cape Cod Cottage

How can you recognize an original Cape Cod house? There are three types, which are very distinct, but they all follow the common Cape Cod pattern, a low, broad frame building, generally a story and a half high, with a steep, perfectly pitched roof without gables, "a short hoist and a long peak" this was called, low eaves, no cornices, and six-paneled door flush with the lintel. In the best period there was no porch. The door is the decorative high light of the house. Individual ornament centers in it, and it may be carved or fluted or set in beautifully molded pilasters with a line of glazing; it may have fan or side lights, or a small Greek pediment to keep off dripping snow. If it is a true Cape Cod door, it will be truly proportioned, and if the house is lucky, it may have a millstone for a doorstep.

There is generally an odd collection of windows in the gable ends — where they are genuinely old the panes are uneven in number — nine and six are the most common.

Thoreau liked these windows — "there were so many of odd sizes in the ends of the buildings — windows for grown folks and windows for the children, three or four apiece, as a certain man had a large hole in his barn door for the cat and another for the kitten." He also adds suspiciously that the windows must serve as "so many peep holes that a traveler has small chance with them."

Attached to the main house there is nearly always a lean-to or ell, set at the back or one side. It has a side door less formal than the front but more often used. The house may be entirely shingled, or the front clapboarded and the back and walls shingled. Often it is unpainted and has weathered to a beautiful silvery gray. In very old houses there is a slight pleasing sag in the line of the roof and gable ends that gives the house a handmade look.

The "half-house" is of this same sort, but it had only one front room, and the door at the side.

There is also the two-story house, but where there are two stories the foundation is wide enough to keep the house looking low.

The roofs are one of the most notable things about Cape houses. There are several distinct types:

The plain cottage roof — sliced down steeply on a slant from a short ridgepole.

The gambrel roof — the arch broken in the middle on a two-story house.

The salt-box roof — called after the old salt boxes that used to hang on our grandmother's kitchen wall, and called so because from the two floors in front the roof slants down almost to the ground on the other side.

The ship's-bottom roof — also called whaleback, hogback and rainbow roof. It is really a roof shaped like a ship's bottom, and it is rare on the Cape, though new houses occasionally have it for fun. It was an idea taken from boats. They say the timbers for these roofs were cut green and laid over an 18-inch rock with the ends weighed down to give the right curve. It took four years from the time the trees were cut till the house was finished.

Inside, these houses are as uniform as on the outside and here the house plays the trick of being more spacious than it looks. The front door opens into a tiny hall, the stairway running steeply up, like a ship's companionway. A room opens on either side — these rooms are small and square, often paneled with pine; there are fireplaces with simple classic wooden mantels; wooden cupboards beside the fireplace, with small old glass panes. The floors are of wide pine boards — the kind you can't buy today. One of these rooms was generally used as a bedroom, the other as a parlor. Behind them, running the full width of the house, is the middle room — this too often paneled, and the

central chimney opens into a big central fireplace often with a brick
oven at one side. A side door opens into the side yard, closed in by a
picket fence. There's a buttery at one end, and a kitchen bedroom,
hardly big enough to swing a cat, but the warmer for that in winter.
The life of the house went on in this middle room, full of warmth,
enticing smells of baking and cooking, activity, children, pets, and the
gossip of neighbors who always stopped in at the side door. There are
few pleasanter rooms now than one of these old kitchens with
geraniums in the window and jellies on the shelves and a Cape Cod
view outdoors.

Upstairs are three bedrooms and the attic. The best bedroom is
plastered and paneled in white pine — it has a fireplace; the two
smaller rooms may be paneled, but were more often left unfinished.
The old hand-hewn beams, aged to a nut brown, often show the
honest structure of the house. If there are timbers from saltworks, you
can tell them by their rough furry surface, and the way they take up
paint.

Captains' Houses

It is these little houses that people think of as typically Cape Cod,
but there are mansions too, built after the Revolution when trade
picked up fast and ships sailed fast and money came in fast with every
rich voyage to London or China or the West Indies. Deepwater captains built square Georgian houses with big rooms and fine woodwork
and beautiful mantels and paneling. But even the great houses on the
Cape are on a smaller scale than those of Salem or Newburyport.
They are handsome, but "careful" — never swanky or show-off. This
may be partly because Cape Cod did not pile up such big fortunes as
the great seaports, and partly because the Cape was always country-
fied and did not have the metropolitan competitive spirit of the rich
coast towns.

Captains' houses are two and a half stories as a rule — they have a
hip roof, some have one huge chimney, some two, some four. Four
chimneys mean a fireplace upstairs and down in each one of the large
square rooms. Brick side walls are not frequent, but there are some.
The decoration is never elaborate, but is centered in doors, with Doric
or Corinthian pilasters, front and side fanlights, and hand-carved
woodwork. Labor was fifty cents a day then, and craftsmen were
skilled, and for six or seven thousand dollars a man could build himself

a local manor with fifteen or twenty rooms, and "everything hand-some about him."

Inside you may still see English china and Revere silver, and maple and walnut furniture. And among these purely Colonial fittings are foreign fads and treasures, both beautiful and awful, that struck a seafaring man's fancy. There are old black-and-gold lacquer boxes from China, Japanese silks, sandalwood, rare shells, bits of ivory and alabaster. Outside may be a pair of huge pink seashells from the West Indies. And there may be a poll parrot surviving, still shivering in his feathers in the wintertime. I remember one bird in Brewster which had been brought back to his wife by a sea captain. He had never learned to like the Cape Cod winter and if he was asked how he felt he always made the same reply: "Mighty cold here, captain."

These Georgian houses have suffered less from improvements than the small cottages, and more of them have kept their original appearance. It is depressing to see how many good old dwellings have been ruined with clumsy additions, dormers like false noses, wild arty shutters, dismal little porches and enlargements badly planned. They look sad, too, with shapeless bungalows as neighbors, or among the dreary huddle of boards and brick that often passes for a summer cottage. The grace of these houses is in the just line and true proportion of roof, doors, windows and ells, their beauty is in workmanship, the simple molding, the window sills and paneling, the mantelpiece and cupboards so purely designed. Fortunately, now people have taken an interest in the old houses, there is an increasing amount of good new building on the Cape in harmony with the old. And when it is well done, a new Cape Cod house will settle down indistinguishably from its neighbors, and grace the landscape instead of defacing it. There is nothing more shipshape or taking in the way of a small house than a real Cape Codder, with a fresh spring coat of paint and a clipped lawn, a flower garden tucked in be-hind a picket fence. White and green are the favorite colors, but some are painted lemon yellow, pink, gray pumpkin yellow, and even plain barn red. Sometimes the chimneys are painted in two colors, giving a gay steamboat effect. This is noticeable particularly in Truro.

Churches and Meetinghouses

The churches and meetinghouses show this early blend of austerity and culture. They are severe, but pleasing; they had their practical use, for they were often set on hills to serve as landmarks, they are not large but they dominate the landscape with their naive wooden classicism. Many of them are empty now, but their influence is not gone. As an old man in Truro, who was considered a freethinker, once said about them, "I ain't been inside of one of 'em for fifty year — but I like to know the God-damned things are there."

Windmills

Windmills on the Cape deserve a few remarks of their own. They are queer birds, half-ship, half-house, and they once meant a great deal in Cape economy. Corn was the most important crop to the settlers; it was almost money, and the mills which ground the corn were worth their weight in it. So were millwrights and millers. It was hard to find men who could build mills — they were skilled craftsmen, and the mills they did build were so valuable that they were constantly being bought up and moved from town to town.

Thomas Paine of Eastham was a famous millwright. He built mills in Eastham, Barnstable, Yarmouth and Truro. The Baxters of West Yarmouth were celebrated too. Kittredge quotes a verse about them.

> The Baxter boys they built a mill
> Sometimes it ran, somes stood still
> And when it ran it made no noise
> Because it was built by the Baxter boys.

Along with the millwright the miller was also a big shot. He was paid in corn — "the miller's pottle"; he was specially privileged in being exempt from military duty, and his social rating was secure.

The mills were probably copied from those of Holland. They were circular or hexagonal and built of heavy oak timbers. Strips of canvas for sails were fastened to the arms. In a forty-mile gale you would have a twelve-horsepower engine and running them was a difficult, almost nautical job. Many of the millers were retired seamen.

Daniel Wing of South Yarmouth tells, in an entertaining article on windmills, that he remembered how boys of the windmill period used to risk their lives by braiding themselves between the slats of a mill arm and going around with their heads down — fifty feet above the ground at its highest point. The trick was in jumping down at just the right moment. The mills used to frighten horses, and were set off from the highroad.

The oldest mill in America once stood in West Yarmouth. It is the Farris mill, and is thought to be about three hundred years of age. It was brought from Sandwich to Bass River by a yoke of twenty oxen, moved later again to South, then next to West Yarmouth. In 1935 it was bought for Henry Ford, and this was its fifth and longest journey. We miss it on the Cape.

About 1800 there were 39 mills still forming part of the landscape — they were moved and retired and torn down until now there are only a few. The last working mill was in Orleans in 1892.

> — From DOWN CAPE COD by Katharine Dos Passos and Edith Shay

ॐ

THE MILLER

BY SHEBNAH RICH

HE IT WAS who climbed the slender latticed arms and set the sails; he it was who hitched the oxen to the little wheel to turn the white wings into the wind's eye; he it was who touched the magic lever and presto! the long wings beat the air, the great shaft began to creak and turn, cog played on its fellow cog, and the mammoth stones began to revolve; he it was who mounted like Jove upon his Olympian seat, and with one hand on the little regulator that, better than the mills of the gods that grind only slow, could grind fast or slow, coarse or fine, and with the other hand caught the first golden meal.

> — From TRURO — CAPE COD

ॐ

PROVINCETOWN HOUSES

BY MARY HEATON VORSE

THE FIRST TIME I saw Provincetown it rose in magic fashion from the sea. We came down by boat from Boston and skirted a remote shore inhabited only by colonies of seagulls. Then, suddenly we turned a corner and the town was before us. It was a long town with gray wharves jutting out to sea, a town shaded by huge willow trees, and over it a lovely church spire built after the designs of Christopher Wren. In those old days the "standpipe" back on the dunes was our landmark. It stood out as unpretentious as a slate pencil against the skyline for incoming vessels to lay their course by.

Presently I was walking down Provincetown streets, and right there at the first moment I knew that this was my home. Maybe it was because of the low-lying houses spread out three miles along the waterfront. I saw one house after another that beckoned to me as a likely place in which to spend my days. There were houses with beautiful old Colonial doorways, a few stately houses with pillared porticos, all of them rather near together as though crowded on one another, neighborly fashion, in fear of storms. I like the crowded streets and having a bay for a front yard. This was fifteen years ago,[1] and within that time I have seen many other places, and still this town of all others seems to me a place for living.

Let me describe the kind of house I like best to live in. It is a wide, low-lying house, a story and a half high. The pitch of the roof is almost a right angle, and unless it has been tampered with, a great square chimney arises from the center. Dormer windows, like as not, give light and air to the upper chambers. The doorway of this house had a half oval above the door. The spaces and adornments about it hark back to the nobler traditions of house building, for all its un-pretentiousness. It is a shingled house, and if you look closely you will see that the shingles were riven by hand, that the door shows the mark of gouges, and that the nails are hand wrought.

This house is a deceptive house — seen from the street it looks small; in reality it is ample, it rambles on room after room. Its wide fireplaces can hold big logs. Its best rooms are wainscoted, and the woodwork, though plain, has been fitted with the nice workmanship of older days. The proportions of its rooms have a satisfying quality. The rooms have a comfortable dignity for all their low ceilings and their modest size. Plenty of cupboards and closets there are. And most of all, it is a house very comfortable to work in.

It is, of course, a matter of individual taste, but personally I like to live in an old house. I like the careful, leisurely workmanship of a former day. I like the quiet patina which is purchased only with time,

[1] The author was writing in 1921.

the golden dimness that the years lay across a well-constructed dwelling. I do not like a house glittering with highlights, floors and furniture too shiny, and the spaces all too open. For, above all, give me a house with doors, rooms and not enlarged hallways. Give me a house whose work I can do myself if need be — then I am no man's debtor. In a house of a shape and size where I can do my own work I am insured against fate. No home means home to me that is shaped so that it cries for paid service, a house where you must necessarily be overworked and uncomfortable if you cannot find some one to do your work for you.

Now this brings me to wny Provincetown seemed like home to me. One of the things that cried out so eloquently on the first day, though at the time I had not analyzed it, was that the houses in Provincetown one and all are built exclusively to live in. They were built for the convenience and the comfort of the dwellers. They were built, too, for a generation which knew nothing of paid service. There was no "servant problem" in Provincetown when its comfortable houses were put up.

In the old days the first houses faced the sea. The kitchens looked out upon the encroaching dunes. There was no street at that time. Ox teams dragged low-hung wagons with wide tires through the sand, and they said up Cape that you could tell a Provincetown girl by the dexterous way in which she could flip the sand from her slipper by a twist of her ankle.

· · · · ·

In most places when a man builds a house he builds it and there it stands, practically unchanged, almost invariably in the same place. This is not true in Provincetown. Houses here do not remain upon their foundations. Every summer you may see houses of all sizes solemnly waddle down the front street. People here do not regard houses as stationary objects. A man will buy a piece of dune land above the town and a cottage on the front shore, and presently up the hill toils the little house. Or he buys a piece of shore front and a cottage on the back street, and presently the little house is wabbling along to take its place on the water view.

It had always been so since the old days. Provincetown houses got the habit of moving some generations ago when the original colony was built on the outward hook over by Long Point. This is a sickle of sand which encloses one of the finest harbors on the North Atlantic. But so narrow is this sickle that encroaching storms played havoc with it and threatened at one time to sweep the narrow point away. It was too valuable a harbor to be so destroyed, and the Government bought it and the houses on it. But the thrifty Province-towners asked the Government:

"What are you going to do with these houses?"

"Nothing," responded the Government.

"Well, can we take them?"

"If you take them away," answered the Government. The Province-town fathers consulted together. And next, houses supported on wrecking barrels bobbed solemnly across the bay.

. . . . . .

If you walk up and down Provincetown streets in spring or fall you will see a prodigious carpentry going on. As sure as spring comes, houses cut bay windows and dormers with the regularity of a baby cutting teeth. Some houses sprout ells, while others build on a "Cape Cod cellar," for our cellars are mostly above ground, it being considered difficult to build a cellar in sand.

As you walk down the street you will notice that in many of the yards there is a little flock of outhouses, of "shops," or two-room dwellings. Houses expand or diminish according as people's folks come or go away. The mother of a neighbor of mine came to live with him in her old age, and he moved down a two-room cottage which he attached to the main house, so that his mother needn't be bothered with the children and could have her privacy. After a time the old lady died, and he moved the house away again, because he said it made him feel lonely. Next his sister's husband died, and home she came with her children. Well and good. He moved down the cottage from the back lot. So the progress of a house can be marked by additions in the family.

Why this carpentry is never done and why every one brings out hammer and saw and goes to work remodeling his house to his heart's desire when spring comes I did not at first understand. I didn't understand this peculiar flexibility of Provincetown houses or why they did not stay upon their foundations after the fashion of houses in other towns, but picked up their skirts in their old age and went wandering up roadways or sandy dunes — not until some out-of-town people bought a piece of property near me and wanted to build on it. What to do with the old house? The carpenter was a Provincetown man and he was not for a moment perplexed. He shoved the house out into the bay and there he anchored it. Unfortunately a storm came up and for two days the distracted house rocked and curtseyed. Its shutters and door blew open. The blank windows and the yawning door looked like frightened eyes and a doleful, screaming mouth. Then I realized why it was that our houses are more flexible than other houses in other towns. Provincetown men are not landsmen at all. Almost without exception they have at one time or another followed the sea. Certainly their forbears have. The life of their race has spent so much of its time on the sea in ships that they look upon houses as a sort of land-ship, or a species of houseboat, and therefore not subject to the laws of houses.

Now every man who owns a boat or a vessel overhauls it, alters it, tinkers with it. So that is why all Provincetown people tinker with their houses ashore and add to them perpetually. Once you understand that the people here are seafaring folk and you will understand why it is that every good housewife takes her can of varnish out in the spring and varnishes all her mahogany furniture over again, for do you not varnish down the bright work on your boat and do you not varnish down your spars? Therefore it follows you should varnish the bright work in your house. This likeness of Provincetown houses to ships explains some of their architectural peculiarities. In many an old house the front door opens on a narrow entry. The stairs mount sheer. They are not truly stairs but a companionway. I have seen upstairs chambers where the small windows had the air of portholes, as though built for security against the weather rather than for light.

In the old days, after the first upheaval and when the first road was building, almost every house had attached to it a building known as a shop or a store. This did not mean a store where you bought and sold things, but a place where you stored things. These shops or "fish houses" had one wide room with doors that opened on the sea, and a loft where tackle, net, and all sorts of gear were stowed. The greater number of these shops have now been turned into houses for summer visitors.

·　·　·　·　·

Legends linger around many of the old houses. This tall, white house on the hill was the home of a whaling captain who drove his men to death in the northern seas. In a cemetery a stone with "Lost at Sea" marks his memory, but old people say that he has been seen walking around his old house to which he never returned, trying to get in. Way "Up Along" a comfortable Colonial house sits far back from the road, yet when you pass it strikes you in the eye with its strangeness: a fence occupies the middle of the front path right up to the front door. This fence has been there so long that a big tree has grown alongside it, encroaching on some of the pickets. Here until recently two brothers lived in the house which had been left them jointly by an injudicious father. Because of some quarrel they divided the house in two and put the fence up, and throughout their lives they never spoke to one another again. When one of the brothers died it was found he had left his will in such a fashion that his share of the house could never fall into the hands of his surviving house-mate. One could fill a book with Provincetown legends and Province-town customs. But slowly the old are dying.

When I first came to Provincetown it was considered not quite the thing to have the front yard that was not ornamented with a few whale's vertebrae or a whale's jaw. Garden beds were bedecked with large shells, disabled dories were turned into flower beds, and morning glories climbed up the great bleaching whale jaws. I learned that I was vaguely criticized for my failure to conform. I remember very well the day when Mr. Berry beckoned to me in the friendly way he had when he had a new treasure to show me. Mr. Berry was for years an institution in Provincetown. In summer a proud sign in front of his store read "Antiques." When fall came and the conches of the schooners had whistled a loud goodby to the departing boat, and the last of summer folks had flitted back to town; when the storm signals were beginning to fly on Town Hill and the town took on its autumnal aspect, its streets filled with men in oil-skins and hip boots instead of girls in bright summer dresses, a new sign better suited to a Provincetown audience appeared before Mr. Berry's store. It read "OLD JUNK."

"Come inside," said Mr. Berry to me, "come here, I' got something to show you; I' got something you need. Your yard don't look stylish. You ain't got any whale's vertebrees; you ain't got a whale's jaw in your front yard with morning glories twining on it. You ain't got a figger head. Why, you ain't got nothing in your yard. It ain't right for a woman like you. What you need is this ship's bill." He pointed to a huge bronze bell almost as tall as I. "That'll give tone to your yard, that'll give style to you, that'll shut folks' mouths when they start talking how plain your yard is. Why, the other day I went past and I see you down on the waterfront hollering out to sea like any common woman, hollering for your kids to come home to dinner. Now you buy this ship's bill. Come noon, you can ring eight bells stylish and you won't have to holler on the end of a wharf any more. Won't be any other house around there that's got a ship's bill. Come noon, you ring eight bells and your kids come right in."

By this kindly advice I saw that I had not lived up to what was expected of me, but fifteen years have seen a change. Some of the old customs are passing along with the boardwalk. We always have bright flower gardens and the encroaching flowers have driven out the whale's vertebrae. A yard can be stylish without them.

Every year sees another of the old houses passing into the hands of "summer people." The newcomers have treated the old houses tenderly. . . . But the old days are passing . . . Berry is dead, and for years the monument to the memory of the Pilgrims has loomed above the town.[2] There are more flowers and more trees than there used to be when I first came. There are fewer sailing dories.

It looks as if the old days were on the wane. But whatever happens, nothing can change the wild back country and nothing can tame the outside shore. Nothing can happen that will make Provincetown anything for me but the pleasantest place in all the world in which to live.

— From TIME AND THE TOWN

❧

CAPE COD BIRD LIFE

BY OLIVER L. AUSTIN, JR.

EVER SINCE Gosnold arrived here in 1602 and christened Buzzards Bay from its conspicuous population of what were probably ospreys, birds have been a significant part of the Cape Cod scene. Bird names are sprinkled over the Cape's topography as commonly as

[2] Dedicated August 5, 1910.

those of fishes and plants. Almost every township has its Gull Pond as well as its Herring Brook and Bayberry Hill. The presence on the Cape map of Goose Pond, Duck Pond, Duck Harbor, Duck Island, Swan Pond, Owl Pond, Hawknest Pond, Bluebill Hole, Tern Island, Bird Island and Egg Island, to mention only a few, attests the one time importance in the Cape Codder's daily life of the species for which they were named.

In colonial days wild birds were an important source of food, a welcome addition to an otherwise monotonous and unbalanced diet. As recently as post-revolutionary times, long after many Cape Cod houses still standing were built, more wildfowl were cooked in Cape kitchens than domestic varieties. Birds have contributed their mite to the Cape's economy in other ways, as sources of feathers and fertilizer, as guides to schooling fish, and as scavengers keeping the beaches and harbors clean. But the days of direct revenue from wildlife have long been over in this part of the world. We now value the birds because they control insects and otherwise help maintain the "balance of nature," but their main contribution to civilization today is the aesthetic and intellectual pleasure they afford mankind.

The ranks of those who delight in observing and studying birds are increasing constantly. More and more of them are visiting the Cape in pursuit of their hobby, and finding it one of the best birding grounds on the eastern seaboard. Its diversity of distinctive natural habitats, its mild, ocean-controlled climate, and its fortunate geographical position give Cape Cod a richer, more varied avifauna than any other area of similar size in New England. This ornithological opulence now attracts bird lovers and scientists from far and wide.

Very few other places in North America offer wildlife so many different types of natural surroundings in so limited and sharply defined a compass. Being a land of waters, the Cape has always been particularly rich in water birds, and it is the water birds that the bird-minded visitors from inland come here primarily to see. Whatever time of year they come, whichever of the Cape's shores they visit, they find birds of interest. On the outer beaches in summer they can see the dainty least terns and the plaintive piping plovers, and if they are sharp-eyed and patient enough they may even find the well-camouflaged eggs or young. If they keep their glasses pointed seaward they may catch a glimpse of a shearwater or a petrel, those true pelagic species which spend their lives at sea and come ashore only to breed. Here in winter are found the rafts of lumbering eiders, the hardy old-squaws playing unconcernedly in the icy surf, and the little dovekies, the "pine-knots" of the fishermen, down from their fabulous breeding cliffs in Greenland. In spring the scoter flight still marches past the "back shore," its ranks sadly reduced however, from the days just a century ago when Thoreau wrote: "There was also an almost uninterrupted line of coots rising and falling with the waves, a few rods from shore, the whole length of the Cape. They made as constant a part of the ocean's border as the pads or pickerel-weed do of that of a pond."

In the milder salt waters of the more sheltered bays and inlets are the mergansers, the golden-eyes, buffle-heads, scaup, and other bay ducks in season. The salt marshes and the bay flats exposed at low tide support geese and brant in the cold months, and a wave of waders in August and September. The latter are the despair of the inland amateur bird student. Having mastered the somewhat involved identification of the various sparrows and warblers, he now finds a real challenge in learning to differentiate between the least, the semipalmated, and the western sandpipers. But the more distinctive of the Cape's twenty-odd beach birds give him little trouble, and he recognizes the black-breasted and semipalmated plovers, the knot, the dowitcher, the sanderling, the greater and the lesser yellow-legs, and a dozen others with ease. He may even be fortunate enough to glimpse a marbled godwit, a Hudsonian curlew, a red phalarope, or even a Baird's sandpiper.

In summer before the returning shorebirds arrive, he may be able to visit one of the Cape's famous tern colonies. But he had better clear with the authorities first. These species, barely saved from the guns of the plume hunters fifty years ago, now have to be protected from the ravages of unthinking picnickers, and careless visitors to the rookeries are not welcome.

In the surprising plethora of fresh ponds filling the kettle-holes the glaciers left behind is still another association of water birds, the fresh water ducks in winter; loons and grebes on migration, true coots, kingfishers, and always occasional gulls, terns, and other salt water species coming in for a sip of fresh water or a cleansing bath. In the inland fresh swamps the little green heron and the bittern breed. And if the visitor be a true zealot, he will put on his oldest clothes and visit one of the many "quawk swamps," to be christened properly with guano and half-digested fish disgorged by the young black-crowned night-herons. If he examines the herons carefully, especially in late summer or early fall, he may find a yellow-crowned night-heron that has strayed north as do the egrets and little blue herons after their breeding season south of the Mason-Dixon line.

More surprising to the uninitiate is the abundance and variety of land birds the Cape supports, which equals in numbers of individuals and exceeds in number of species that of any area of similar size on the adjoining mainland. Varied habitat is again responsible, for the Cape has even more distinct upland ecological associations than it has water and shore communities. The dominant cover of the Cape today is the pitch pine forest, and there are miles and miles of pure stands of it, where the thin song of the pine warbler is heard, and the broad-winged hawk finds a safe eyrie for its crude nest. Between the pines and the back shore, beyond the huckleberry and blueberry copses of the burned-over areas, are acre upon acre of impenetrable pin oak scrub, where the handsome chewink holds forth and the hermit thrush pipes his arpeggios at dawn and dusk. These give way to the bayberry barrens, the mainstay of large flocks of wintering myrtle warblers, so named because of their fondness for the fruits of this aromatic shrub which the colonists called the wax myrtle. The terrain here is carpeted with glossy mats of bearberry, known more prosaicly as the hog-cranberry to the Cape Codders who formerly harvested it, so they say, and sold it to the makers of some long forgotten patent nostrum. It is of more interest to the ornithologist as a frequent nesting site of the savannah sparrow.

Finally we come to the rolling dunes, anchored insecurely against the moving easterlies by the sparse, rough-edged beach-grass. Their ever-shifting sands offer neither food nor cover enough to attract many species. The savannah sparrow forages occasionally in the flat patches of grey, lichenous poverty-grass, which bursts so startlingly into vivid yellow in June. And in late fall, long after the lavender beach peas have faded, sharp eyes may find the savannah's rare and vanishing relative, the larger, paler, sand-colored Ipswich sparrow, skulking here en route southward from its dwindling summer home on Sable Island. Where the dunes meet the salt marshes is more fertile ground, where the high-voiced meadow lark still finds sustenance where he found it before the white man's cultivation gave him lusher pastures. Among the sedums and marsh grasses of this narrow belt is the spot to hunt for the seaside and the sharp-tailed sparrows, retiring little birds, and hard to identify, but a "must" for the inland birder if he can find them.

In addition to these and other specialties the Cape supports the same land birds, with very few exceptions, one finds along the mainland. In February and March the fresh marshes burgeon with red-winged blackbirds, the earliest harbingers of warmer times to come, joining their reedy chorus to the "spring-soon" and "sweet-weather" prophecies of the hardy, optimistic chickadees. They are soon followed by the harsh-voiced grackles, and by roving flocks of meddlesome cowbirds, waiting patiently to deposit their unwelcome eggs in their neighbors' nests. Now the mournful, owl-like cooing of the doves dusting themselves along the roadsides is punctuated by the kiu-kiuing and the hammering of the mating flickers, whose depredations to the shingles of vacant buildings are not appreciated by returning cottagers. Song and vesper sparrows pipe their vernal melodies from prominent vantage points to encourage and lighten the labor of their incubating mates, and the tame little chipping sparrows forage at your feet on the greening lawn. In the dry, sandy fields, once planted to asparagus but now abandoned and gone to grass, the assiduous birder will find the unobtrusive grasshopper sparrow, a common breeding species here but known to few because of its modest and diffident nature. The only notable absentee is the friendly house wren, which, though common elsewhere in Massachusetts, has yet to be found nesting on the Cape.

The autumn migration of land birds is one of the birders' busiest and most interesting seasons. The prevailing westerlies frequently veer the heavy coastal flight seaward, and fill the Cape covers with juncos, white-throated, white-crowned, Lincoln, field, and fox sparrows, yellow-palm, Cape May, magnolia, and black-poll warblers, various vireos, flycatchers, wrens, kinglets, and their brethren on their routine southward journey. With them come inland rarities, more easily observed here where the available terrain is limited, such unusual visitors as the clay-colored sparrow, seldom seen east of the Mississippi Valley, the lark sparrow, the blue grosbeak, and the black-throated bunting or dickcissel which so delighted Thoreau when he heard it for the first time singing in Truro.

The winter winds bring hardy northern visitors the inland birder seldom sees, puffins, murres, and razor-billed auks from the St. Lawrence rookeries, and occasional snowy owls and errant evening grosbeaks. Among the crowds of herring gulls tending the fish wharves in Provincetown are always a glaucus or an Iceland gull or two, and once in a while the rare Kumlein's gull from the shores of Baffin Land.

The Cape is especially attractive to the bird enthusiast because of its high percentage of off-season stragglers. These are sought particularly by the rising coterie of "bird-golfers," a hardy, inquisitive, and indefatigable clan who invade the privacy of every copse and woodland, beach and waterway with binoculars and high-powered telescopes. Their aim is to make lists of as many different species as possible in a day, a trip, a season, or a year. These sportsmen without guns delight in swelling their note-book game-bags with species which, by all the natural laws governing the presence and absence of birds, should be elsewhere at the time.

The Cape violates all the rules which regulate bird distribution on the mainland, for its temperate climate, kept equable by the waters surrounding it, makes it cooler in summer, and what is more important to the birds and birders, warmer in winter. This allows many summer residents to remain and prosper here after their kinsfolk have been forced to leave the snow-covered mainland. Hermit thrushes, catbirds, and even an occasional mockingbird find sustenance throughout the winter in the cat-briar tangles. Flickers share the tree trunks with the downies and hairies which usually monopolize the woodpecker niche at this season. Flocks of goldfinches and a random song and chipping sparrow keep the conventionally wintering tree sparrows, redpolls, and snow buntings company in the snow-free weed fields. Little bands of bluebirds wander aimlessly through the bare locust groves, lending a brightening patch of unseasonable color to the drab landscape. Robins can always be found wintering in the cedar swamps, where somehow the laity never seems to notice them until time for the newspapers' perennial space-filling "first robin" story in March.

The converse is also true, but to a lesser degree. All summer a scattering of eiders, scoters, and mergansers remains to sport idly in the cool waters of the bay while their kin are nesting far to the northward. The annual presence in June and July of dowitchers, least sandpipers, and other boreal breeding waders offers another riddle to the ornithologist. He cannot determine whether they are late stragglers still moving northward, the vanguard of the southward flight, or, what is more likely, non-breeding individuals who, lacking the migratory urge to carry them to the northern tundras, are waiting here patiently for their more vigorous relatives to return.

These extra-seasonal tarriers are always a pleasure to find, but what really thrills the true bird-golfer anywhere is to encounter the "accidentals" or "vagrants," the strays wandering outside their normal orbits. Thanks to its geographical position the Cape has more than its share of them. The long arm of land projecting thirty miles out into the Atlantic is not only a land barrier which all water birds moving along the coast must by-pass or surmount. It is a welcome haven for terrestrial species lost or driven off their course to sea, a providential carrier-deck where they can alight and find shelter from the unfriendly elements while they rest and refuel. Here they remain long enough to be spotted by the keen observer before they wander on. Spring gales drive up purple gallinules, Wilson's plovers, worm-eating warblers, and hepatic tanagers, which normally never venture north of the Virginia capes. An ivory gull taken off Monomoy is one of the few recorded occurrences of this high arctic dweller south of Labrador. A surprising number of European species wander or are blown across the Atlantic, and make their first landfall on the Cape. The barnacle goose collected from a flock of four that appeared in North Eastham in 1885 was one of the first North-American records of a transatlantic bird visitor, and the forerunner of an astonishing series. The Eurasian turnstone, the dunlin, the bar-tailed godwit, the curlew sandpiper, and that Elizabethan dandy among shorebirds, the ruff, all find a place on the American list from specimens taken on Cape Cod.

Rich and varied as the Cape's bird life is today, only a pitiful fragment now remains of what our forefathers found here. Our knowledge of the Cape's early fauna comes from the Indian kitchen middens excavated in Wellfleet and Eastham. The Indians usually camped where potable fresh water was nearest their most easily procured food, the shellfish of the bay flats. Into their camp refuse piles of oyster and clam shells they tossed broken pottery and other artifacts, and the bones of the birds and animals they ate. Digging them up now, four centuries later, we identify among them many species still present on the Cape. We find the Indians ate deer, rabbits, red and grey squirrels, muskrats and raccoons, mallards, black ducks, scoters, geese, brant, loons, dovekies, and a score of other species still not uncommon here.

We also find tantalizing fragments of forms that have long since disappeared from the Cape, and some of them from the earth. The timber wolf, the moose, and the bear of the Indians' day were driven to distant wilderness fastnesses in earliest colonial times. The wild turkey, which the Pilgrim Fathers made into the most famous of our national holiday dishes, has not occurred on the Cape since before the Revolution. The great auk, the passenger pigeon, the heath hen, and the Labrador duck were not fortunate enough to find even distant sanctuary, and are now extinct. Several leg bones of the great auk unearthed from shell heaps in South Wellfleet are the only indisputable evidence that this flightless bird, extinct for more than a century, once swam in Cape Cod waters, although J. Freeman lists the "penguin" as one of the sea-fowl that were "plenty on the shores and in the bay" off Truro in 1794.

The phenomenally abundant passenger pigeons, now only a memory and an almost legendary one at that, were not an unmixed blessing. John Winthrop records how they threatened the Plymouth colony with famine when great flocks of them appeared and beat down the ripening corn and ate "a very great quantity of all sorts of English grain" in 1643. The same authority also tells how they came again in 1648, but after the harvest was gathered so they proved a great blessing, "it being incredible what multitudes of them were killed daily." The pigeons lasted two more centuries, but were apparently no longer of importance on the Cape after colonial times, as almost no mention of them here is made in subsequent literature.

That garrulous octogenarian, the old Wellfleet Oysterman, told Thoreau in 1849 how in his youth he had killed "wild hens" after they had gone to roost in the woods. He was referring, of course, to the heath hen, which was wide-spread along the Atlantic seaboard before the Revolution, but which by Thoreau's time was already restricted to its last stronghold on the Elizabeth Islands and Martha's Vineyard, where it finally died out only a score of years ago.

So far we have been unable to unearth any evidence that the

mysterious and little-known Labrador duck ever occurred on Cape
Cod. That it did so there can be little doubt, for it wintered along
the Atlantic coast from Maine to New Jersey. The only nearby
records are the two specimens Daniel Webster shot at Martha's
Vineyard, and which Audubon, who never saw the bird alive, used
as models for his drawings of this species. However, Cape Cod
probably played a major and shameful part in its extermination.
Barnstable was one of the main home ports of the "feather boats"
that cruised to southern Labrador for eider down in the early 1700's.
The crews so slaughtered the myriads of ducks nesting on the islands
there, of which the Labrador duck is believed to have been one,
that by 1760 the trade was no longer profitable and the voyages were
abandoned.

This was not the Cape's last contact with the feather trade. A
century later a temporary bonanza was found right at home when
Paris fashions decreed the use of white sea-bird feathers for trimming
milady's millinery. Hitherto the graceful terns had nested on many
of the Cape's isolated points and islets in large numbers, undisturbed
except by some desultory egging. But when the demand for their
skins at about five cents each was thus created, their breeding grounds
were invaded mercilessly. They were almost sent to join the great
auk and the Labrador duck in oblivion before the bloody, heartless,
needless slaughter was stopped by Massachusetts law in 1897. This
radical legislation, which was contested bitterly in the courts at the
time, was one of the first of many necessary hunting reforms to come,
and it came barely in time to save the terns. The larger, hardier
species, the common, the roseate, and the arctic terns, made swift
recoveries under protection and a decade later were almost as plentiful as ever. But the fairy-like least tern which had borne the brunt of
the persecution has only recently become common again on our
beaches.

The development of rail transportation down the Cape immediately after the Civil War gave added impetus to the decline of the
Cape's game birds by bringing the city markets within easy reach
of the pot shooters. For a short time game was plentiful enough
to allow a good shot a fair livelihood, and the local gunners were
able to ship out waterfowl and beachbirds by the barrel in season.
But the uncontrolled slaughter decimated the supply of birds so rapidly that by the time Massachusetts legislated the sale of game out

of existence (again one of the first states to do so, and almost two decades before corresponding action was taken by the federal government) there were too few birds left to afford the most skillful hunter a living. Sport hunting then took the place of market hunting, and the former pot-hunting bayman found a new source of income guiding city sportsmen to the remaining covers. But the damage had already been done, and at least two more fine species, the golden plover and the Eskimo curlew which the Cape had known for so long as "pale bellies" and "dough birds," disappeared. A lonesome golden plover is still reported occasionally, but it is a rare bird indeed. The last Eskimo curlew taken in New England was shot in East Orleans in 1913.

The days of exploitation of wildlife for economic purpose are rapidly disappearing of necessity. Birds simply cannot withstand the increasing pressure of more hunters and improved weapons combined with dwindling habitats. Most commercial utilization of game has now been stopped in North America, and even sport hunting is being progressively curtailed. Beach-bird shooting, a fine sport which once brought hundreds of gunners to the Cape in August and September, had to be abolished to save these vanishing species in 1926. Shortly thereafter the Cape's famous and over-efficient goose blinds were forced to close when the use of live decoys on which their success depended was outlawed. Duck hunting has attracted fewer and fewer of its former devotees since the shrinking supply of waterfowl necessitated the banning of night shooting and baiting. As the open seasons grow shorter and the bag limits smaller, the sport is becoming ever more difficult to enjoy, and the results therefrom less rewarding. Nevertheless these reforms are beginning to show results of benefit to a wider circle than the hunting fraternity alone. The downward trend that wildlife populations have suffered for centuries is now beginning to be halted. But more careful management, backed by an aroused public opinion, will be necessary to start it upward again.

The chief remaining danger to the Cape's birds is the rapid over-development of the remaining wild lands for and by vacationists. Both upland and water areas are being made less and less attractive to wildlife as they are altered to meet the needs and desires of the ever-increasing crowds of visitors. The marshes are ditched for mosquito-control, and the ducks and rails that once nested in them vanish as the water table lowers. Planes blanket the countryside with DDT to destroy the gypsy moths and tent caterpillars that disfigure our woodlands and reduce our crops. All other insects, good and bad, are wiped out too, and the tree swallows, bluebirds, chickadees, and flycatchers decline in numbers accordingly. The piping plovers and the least terns that have so recently revived from the plume-hunters' attentions, now face a new menace. Broad-tired beach wagons of sight-seers, picnickers, and bass fishermen, plow unseeing and un-thinking through their once pristine nesting grounds on the outer beaches. In their rutty wakes parent birds flutter disconsolately over crushed eggs and chicks until the cleansing wind-blown sand merci-fully hides the remains from view.

The Cape has not escaped the doubtful blessings of modern pro-gress, and it can never again be the wildlife paradise it once was. Where the overnight cabins and roadside stands now line Route 6 the heath hen will never again strut his nuptial dance and tootle his weird love song. The penetrating cry of the upland plover that greeted Thoreau in Truro may never be heard here again, though the bank swallows he found under the cliff at Highland Light still dig their holes in the same place year after year.

Inexorable as is the advance of human civilization, hope still re-mains for the birds. Some of them do eventually adapt themselves to changing conditions, and in some cases even profit by them. Lighthouses no longer take the toll of birds of passage they did when first erected. Birds have learned to avoid them, even as they now elude the automobiles which killed so many more of them a decade or two ago. Perhaps the terns and plovers may learn to lay their eggs in sections of the beaches unfrequented by beach buggies. The prairies horned lark was unknown on the Cape fifty years ago. It has only recently pushed its way eastward, seemingly following the development of golf courses, whose fairways offer it the type of nest-ing site it prefers.

Above all in the birds' favor is mankind's increasing thoughtfulness of them, his growing appreciation of the pleasure they can give him as neighbors. We no longer shoot robins and blackbirds, although they are just as difficult a target as a quail, and equally good eating, as our great-grandfathers were well aware. We value them alive in the fields around us more than we do in the pot. With this steady change in public thought, call it softening if you wish, the birds will be preserved for posterity as a living memorial that this and suc-ceeding generations cared enough to save them.

Dr. Oliver L. Austin, Jr., is director of the Austin Ornithological Research Station at South Wellfleet. He served as Lt. Cdr. in the Navy and was later Chief, Wild Life Branch, Natural Resources Section SCAP, Tokyo, 1946–50. He is the author of BIRDS OF NEW-FOUNDLAND LABRADOR; BIRDS OF KOREA; WATERFOWL OF JAPAN; *and* JAPANESE FUR SEALING.

☙❧

DAWN — CAPE COD

BY HARRY KEMP

Before the day's creation is begun
I must go forth to meet the unseen sun —
Out to the hushed, expectant dunes I love,
More lone because of the still sky above.
The village houses lie like herds asleep.
The tide, black-burnished, spreads out, flat and deep.
There walks a wind of coming change abroad. . . .
The sun shows like a traveller down a road. . . .
Then — what the dark reserved unseen before —
I see long, dancing, golden slopes of shore. . . .
Then, as I walk back, close to left and right,
I find young summer in full tides of green;
Where flickering branches thwart the morning lean
Leaves touch my face, leaves brush against my hand,
And beach plums bloom in little banks of white
Up slopes of infinite, immaculate sand.
                    — From THE SEA AND THE DUNES

The Captain's Table

THE CAPTAIN'S TABLE

*T*HE CAPTAIN, *and for that matter, all of his crew, live comfortably and eat very well. His food, for the most part locally produced, is on the solid and substantial side; it is traditional and still prepared from recipes in use since the eighteenth century. He is pardonably proud of his table and his invariable greeting after asking grace is, "Now, eat hearty and give the ship a good name!"*

The Captain demands the old-fashioned strawberry shortcake, and the shorter the better, capped with Falmouth berries; he likes his blueberry pie made of the Cape swamp berries, which are smaller and tangier than other blueberries. His jelly is of the beachplum and he likes it sharp and his favorite compote is cranberry sauce. He grows excellent tomatoes in his garden but will have none of them in his chowder and he seldom has oyster stew because he had already eaten the oysters raw.

The foregoing with fish, and what a variety! lobsters, clams and quahaugs, are the main items of his diet and after three centuries of sailing all the world's seas he has little or no desire for more exotic dishes. Indeed, common to his table, are the little bay scallops that are high up among the exotic blue chips in the gourmet's cuisine.

৩৵৩

CLAMS AND QUAHAUGS

BY JOSEPH C. LINCOLN

A NEW YORKER will tell you that there are two kinds of clams — hard and soft. The variety with the long, thin shell is a soft clam and that with the round, thick shell is a hard clam. The Cape Codder, however, will tell you nothing of the kind.

To him a clam is a clam and a quahaug is a quahaug. They are both shellfish — yes; but that does not prove anything. A hen and a canary are both feathered, but if you expect a hen to sing like a canary, you will be disappointed. And if you expect a quahaug soup with tomatoes in it to taste like a Cape Cod clam chowder, you will be even more so. Each of them may be good of its kind, but they are different kinds, that's all. You may call a clam a "sedge" or a "sea clam" or a "rundown," but he is a clam, just the same. And calling a quahaug a "Little Neck" or a "cherry-stone" does not make him any the less a quahaug.

Yes, and there are other differences. For example, you dig clams and you rake quahaugs.

The distinction between the two is something the Cape Cod child learns at his mother's knee — or at her table. He knows and therefore to him the carelessness of the outlander is surprising. Even more surprising is the indisputable fact that, in this world of ours, there are people who never saw a clam — would not recognize one if they met him on the flat at low tide.

The dictionary — we infer that it was not compiled by a Cape Codder — says there are countless varieties of clams. It even mentions the "razor clam" among them. Now, every boy of our generation in our town knew that a "razor fish" was not a clam at all. He was not shaped like a clam. He was long and thin — he did look something like an old-fashioned razor with the blade closed into the handle — and he lived buried in the wet sand on the flats, a quarter of a mile or more from high-tide mark. He marked his home by a tiny ring, with a hole in the middle of it, in the sand above his head. He had made that ring by squirting water up through the hole. In that respect he was like a clam, for clams squirt too — real clams, we mean, not quahaugs.

The Cape Cod boy's procedure with a razor fish was, and perhaps still is, simple and primitive. Having located him, he thrust his fingers into the sand and dug as rapidly as possible. Rapidity was essential for, unless one was very quick, the razor fish slid out from between his shells and downward; in which case, when the two shells were resurrected, their former occupant was no longer at home; he was at large and seeking lower levels.

But, if we were quick enough, we got him while at least a third of him was still in residence. After that — well, if you don't mind, we won't go into details.

I have known people who said that razor fish made a wonderful stew, as sweet and flavorsome as a scallop stew. I never tasted a stew made from the razor fish, but I do remember what he used to taste like. And, after all, everyone eats oysters and Little Necks *au naturel*.

Our wide stretches of flats were habited by clams, thousands and thousands of them. At the inner edge, bordering the clumps of coarse beach grass, were the "sedge clams," the little fellows, tender and just right for a bake or a boil. Farther out were the "rundowns," the big chaps with their shells snowy white. Rundowns were best in a chowder. And, away out, along the outer bar, almost two miles from shore and only get-at-able when the tide was at full ebb, were the large "sea clams." Sea clams made the best clam pie.

To dig clams, as they should be dug, a clam hoe and a "dreener" are the proper equipment. The clam hoe, as of course almost everyone knows, differs from the garden hoe. To dig clams with a garden hoe is a rash and unprofitable adventure. The sharp edge of the blade cuts through the tender shells and, although you may get your clam, you are all too likely to get him in sections. I remember a neighborhood clam bake, presided over and superintended by a veteran Codder, where one of the guests, a city visitor, insisted on digging his own share and, as the clam hoes were all in use, he dug with an ordinary hoe. When he brought in his spoil, the veteran looked into the half-filled pail and sniffed.

"Say, Mr. Jones," he observed sadly, "it's too bad, but you've made a mistake in your figurin'. We wasn't cal'latin' to have clam hash."

The Cape Cod clam hoe has three or four narrow and deep prongs instead of one shallow blade. Its handle, too, is short, no more than two or three feet long. You set the prongs into the sand at their full depth and then pull. The wet sand is heaped between your feet as you dig and, between hoefuls, you stoop and pick up the clams you have uncovered. By "stoop" I mean, of course, stoop lower, for you have been stooping all the time. Clam digging is a back-breaking business — for a greenhorn. An hour of it is enough to take the starch out of the most dignified backbone and helps to add to a pious vocabulary.

The "dreener" is a sort of a lath crate with a handle to carry it by. The clams, as they are dug, are deposited in it and, after digging, are washed by dipping the dreener and its contents into a pool of clean water. Moving the dreener up and down in the water rinses away the sand, or is supposed to.

The dreener was a drainer once, probably, but it has not been one for a century or more down on the Cape. It is a dreener, just as a Cape fisherman's barrel is a — a — I declare I don't know exactly how to tell you what it is. Something between a barrel and a "beerill" and a "burrill," but not precisely either. I could pronounce it for you but to save my life I cannot spell it adequately. There is a "b-r-r-r" in the middle of it that defies orthography.

Digging the rundowns is like digging for sedge clams, except that the digger works faster. And he gets fewer clams at a time. The results are worth the effort, however, for they — the clams are often from three to four inches in length, fat — and, oh, so white and clean.

There is little real digging in a sea clam hunt. These big, three-cornered fellows lie with their backs exposed or just beneath a clearly visible mound of sand. I never heard that sea clams were good for anything, as an edible, except, as stated before, in a clam pie. They are tough. The fish like them and they are gathered principally for bait.

The quahaug — please give him the local pronunciation "Ko-hog" — is not brought to the surface with a clam hoe. He must be raked for. If you are a casual, an amateur quahauger, you may use a garden rake and go after him at low tide. He lies at the bottom, usually under a layer of seaweed and in at least a few inches of water. You rake the seaweed just as you would rake a lawn, lifting the rake after each stroke to pick the quahaugs from between its teeth. Then you would put them in a bucket or dreener. Raking for quahaugs in this way is not as hard as clam digging.

But if you are a professional — if you "go quahauging" regularly, to earn a living — you do work hard. Indeed you do. You may do it in two ways, the first a trifle easier than the second. The first way is to put on fisherman's boots, high rubber boots reaching above the hips and secured to your belt, and wade the submerged flats at the edges of the channels, raking as you go. And you use a regulation quahaug rake. Its teeth are much longer than those of an ordinary rake and are turned up at the ends, making the implement a sort of scoop. And, because a dreener would be a hindrance rather than an aid to this sort of work, you fasten a canvas or burlap bag, open end up, to your belt, and put your quahaugs into that. The bag is heavy and growing heavier all the time, the boots are heavy, the rake anything but light, and the wading through seaweed not easy. Does sound like hard work, doesn't it? Yes, but wait a moment. You have not been "deep quahauging" yet.

Deep quahauging is a comparatively recent innovation on the Cape — at least, I believe it is. Cape Codders have always raked quahaugs; no doubt the first settlers raked for them along the flats. But when we were youngsters, we never heard of anyone seeking them in deep water. To go quahauging in a boat would have been a town joke in our youth. But scores do that very thing now and do it daily.

There is a yarn to the effect that the idea originated like this: Someone was out in the bay — we were never told which bay — dredging for flounders. And, at one spot, the dredges brought up hundreds and hundreds of quahaugs, big ones. Flounders were scarce at the time and there was always a market for quahaugs. So this particular dredger marked the spot and returned to it the next day and the days succeeding. Others, of course, followed his example and "deep quahauging" became a regular and profitable profession.

The deep quahauger goes out to the grounds in a motor-boat or skiff. There he anchors and begins to work. His rake is a toothed scoop, somewhat like that used by the wader, but bigger and heavier; sometimes it is weighted to make it heavier still. Its wooden handle is forty feet long and flexible. He throws the scooped end as far from the boat as he can, lets it sink to the bottom, and then draws it toward him and up to the boat, working the long handle backward over his shoulder in a series of jerks. When he gets it into the boat, he paws over the half bushel or so of mud and sand and seaweed, picks out his quahaugs, dumps the trash — "culch" he would call it — over the side and makes another cast. And he keeps on casting and jerking and sorting and dumping all day long, with a brief rest while he eats his lunch. He makes, so they say, a pretty fair wage, and I think he earns it.

If, in the summer, you are motoring by — well, let us say the upper end of Pleasant Bay, between Orleans and Chatham, and look out over the water toward the east, you will see a dozen or more boats anchored a mile or so out. The occupants of those boats are quahaugers, every one of them.

— From CAPE COD YESTERDAYS, 1935

⁊≈⁊

CAPTAIN'S CLAM CHOWDER

1 pint of clams, with their juice
3 oz. salt pork, diced
1 chopped onion
2 medium potatoes, sliced
2 cups boiling water
3 cups milk
1 cup cream
1 teaspoon salt
2 tablespoons butter
black pepper
4 common crackers

Try out the salt pork, add chopped onions, and sauté till golden. Drain the clams, setting aside the juice. Clean, chop and add to pork and onions. Parboil the potatoes for five minutes and add to the clams. Cover with the boiling water and simmer until the potatoes are done. Scald the milk and cream together. Heat clam juice and add it slowly to the hot milk. Now pour the hot milk over the clam and potato mixture and don't cook any more. Add butter and black pepper.

Put in each soup plate a split commons which has been soaked for a few minutes in cold milk. Or use crumbled pilot crackers — but not salty crackers of any kind.

Aye, it's good enough to set a bone!

SEA CLAM PIE

10 medium sea clams, cleaned, or,
2 pints quahaugs
3 oz. salt pork, diced
⅔ cup onion, chopped
1 cup bread or cracker crumbs
1 recipe plain pastry
½ pint cream

Chop or grind the clams. Try out salt pork and fry onion lightly. Add clams and cook a few minutes, till the clams shrink a little. Remove from fire and add crumbs, add salt and pepper and cream. Line a pie plate with pastry and put in the clam filling. Dot with butter and put on top crust. Brush with milk and bake. (Some prefer not to include the onion.)

Life giving, we call it!

BAY SCALLOPS

These are one of the many compensations for spending the entire year on the Cape. They come in after Thanksgiving and go away before St. Patrick's Day. The process is simple: wash, drain and dry thoroughly, roll lightly in flour or very fine cracker crumbs and sauté in melted butter, keeping the scallops rolling about the pan.

FRIED EELS

Clean and skin two pounds of salt-water eels and cut in short lengths and boil them for about five minutes. Drain and cool. Dip the pieces in beaten egg and corn meal and fry in bacon fat.

CLAM CAKES

1 cup quahaugs, chopped	4 tablespoons flour
2 eggs, well beaten	salt and pepper

Shape into cakes and fry in a well-greased frying pan. Turn once and brown on the other side. Serve with lemon butter or quartered lemons.

— From THE BEST MEN ARE COOKS

CAPE COD TURKEY

1 codfish	1 hard boiled egg, chopped
2 tablespoons butter	1 slice salt pork, or
1 cup breadcrumbs, coarse	2 slices bacon
2 tablespoons celery, chopped	Salt and pepper
½ teaspoon marjoram, or summer savory, or a pinch of sage.	

Brush fish inside and out with melted butter or olive oil. Melt butter; add chopped onions and bread crumbs and brown a little. Moisten with a little water or with stock, if you have it, and add celery, herb, salt and pepper and chopped egg. Stuff and sew up the fish. Lay slices of salt pork in the pan and put the fish on them. Dredge with salt and pepper. Bake in a moderate oven and baste with the drippings. It's the chopped hardboiled egg that makes this special. Serve with an egg sauce.

— From DOWN CAPE COD

PUNKHORN STEW

BY GENEVA A. ELDREDGE

MY FATHER when a young man taught school in Punkhorn, and "boarded round" as was the custom, a week in the home of each child attending his school. . . . "Punkhorn" stew was served in all the families for everyone had plenty of winter vegetables from their gardens, and most everyone had raised a hog or two during the summer.

Towards spring when all the fresh meat had been consumed, Punkhorn Stew came into its own, and Father said he ate it once or twice a week at every house where he stayed, and enjoyed it to the last morsel.

So he brought home the recipe to Mother, and when I was growing up, many years later, (being the 11th child) Punkhorn was still a family favorite. I can see that huge white ironstone china platter now, as Mother set it on the table. And hear the whoops of joy from the hungry boys, my older brothers, who came up at noontime from clearing the cedar swamp, preparatory to making a cranberry bog. What appetites they had and how the food vanished once they got at it!

Here's what went into the stew:

At hog killing time, Father salted spare ribs and odd pieces of pork not too heavily, in a big stone crock and put it down cellar on purpose for use in this stew. And the morning of the day Mother was to make one, he would go down cellar, fish out perhaps enough to weigh a couple of pounds. Mother always said, "enough to scent the stew, anyway." And cutting it into fairly small pieces, Mother would put it in a basin, cover it with scalding water and leave it to simmer on the middle of the old wood stove.

About ten o'clock she would get out the old iron kettle, slice an onion or two in the bottom, lay the spare ribs and lean pieces of pork over them, add water to cover well, salt and pepper to taste, and sometimes a little of the water it had simmered in, if not too salty, fill the stove with oak and pine wood sticks, set the kettle directly over the fire and let it cook.

About 11 o'clock, the vegetables peeled and ready, she would put thick slices of white turnip, parsnips, carrots, small onions and large size potatoes, cut lengthwise, add a bit more water, pepper and salt if needed and set it back over the fire, watching carefully after that to keep enough water in it to prevent its "catching on."

At quarter of twelve, the vegetables all cooked, she would lift the kettle from the fire, remove the cover and lay thick chunks of brown bread crust over the top of it all, cover it tightly to steam until noontime on the back of the stove.

Then she heaped the big platter full, set the brownbread on one side of it, and a dish of stewed squash on the other, with a low bowl of "pickalilly" in between, and dinner was ready. Plum duff, with sweet sour vinegar sauce followed for dessert, and there was never a snitch of anything left when those boys had filled those "bottomless pits" known as stomachs.

Cape cooks cook by dead reckoning.

— From THE CAPE CODDER

∽

A *PRETTY* KETTLE OF FISH

MANY YEARS AGO, legend tells us, a fishmonger returned to his Marseilles home pushing his little cart before him. "Hey, mama," he called from the street, "I didn't sell all my stock and tomorrow's a feast day!"

Mama told papa off in good fishwife terms. She didn't want fish on a feast day any more than the customers.

"Give it here!" she ordered, and in a fine frenzy threw the entire stock — fish, bivalves and crustaceans — into pot with whatever else came to her angry hands. Covering the kettle she pushed it to the back of the stove and went on with her pre-feast visiting. When she returned in the evening she found her old man sniffing the celestial aroma that emanated from the pot.

"That's a fine kettle of fish, mama. What did you put in it?"

Mama, now calm, could not recall. All she could mutter was "bouillabaisse," a word that seems to mean different things to different Frenchmen; but in Provençal means over a low fire. The dish was so good that all who shared in it forgot the festival meat.

Bouillabaisse entered what is now the United States at New Orleans or New England. The Deep South's claim is valid and is based upon the fact that Southerners have made more of the dish. Over the years several tidy little fortunes have been rolled up by those who excelled in its preparation. New England's pretensions are not to be dismissed lightly.

When the Pilgrims were bumped on the cold and lonely shore they quickly learned they would have to eat fish or starve while they were learning to fire their blunderbusses with enough accuracy to bring down red meat. And what were they trying to make when they cooked a mess of fish and shellfish in a big pot called a *chaudière?* Were they clumsily trying to put together a bouillabaisse? Whatever they were cooking up they, or their descendants, called it a chowder, after the kettle in which it was cooked — a dish entirely unknown to the rest of the world. And let it be added that the best damn' chowder ever made is only a pale, feeble imitation of a bouillabaisse.

The Provençal fishwife never could recall all she had put into her pot and French cooks have been guessing ever since. They call for rascasse, chapon, fielas, cabillaud, boudreuil and whiting, with langouste and huitres added. In America we have plenty of whiting and the cabillaud is our old friend the cod.

Down in New Orleans they begin by tearing up the French recipes and coming forth with a very nice one of their own calling for redfish, red snapper, green trout, sheepshead and blackfish, with handfuls of crabs, crayfish and lake shrimps added. The working recipe they guard as though it were the formula for the atomic bomb.

Cape Cod cooks, with deep bows to Mme. Foyot, of Marseilles, and to Mme. Begue and MM. Antoine and Gallatoire, of New Orleans, assemble their fishes, the cod, hake and haddock, striped bass and yellow-tail flounders, omitting the oily fishes. They have also the fine North Atlantic lobsters, those grown in cold shallow waters with paper-thin shells, excellent oysters, scallops, clams, quahaugs, mussels and a few crabs. "If it's variety we have it, and if it's freshness we have that too."

To be a veritable bouillabaisse the pot should contain at least one fish, one bivalve and one crustacean, in addition to other indispensable ingredients. Nevertheless variety enriches the dish.

The service varies. In France it comes to the table with glassy-eyed head of a fish bobbing about and many a hungry diner has decided at that point he could never care for a bouillabaisse. New World cooks are prone to leave shrimps, crabs or lobster halves, still in their original jackets, floating about presumably to please the eye. The Cape Cod bouley is edible down to the last morsel.

A resident native observing the preparation sniffed appreciatively and sighed. "You know, mister, during the war I ate so much fish my stomach still rises and falls with the tides."

BOUILLABAISSE CAPE COD
(Makes four servings)

2 pounds firm fish	1 lemon, juice only
6 oysters and/or	1 bay leaf
6 clams and/or	1 clove garlic, crunched
6 mussels	2 tblsp. parsley, minced
1 cup crabmeat and/or	½ cup pimientoes, chopped
1 cup lobster and/or	½ cup white wine
1 cup shrimps	Heavy pinch of saffron
2 tomatoes, peeled	Light pinch of thyme
2 onions, sliced	4 slices garlic bread, toasted.
½ cup olive oil	

Routine: cut heads tails and fins from fish and place in one quart of water and boil until liquid is reduced to a pint, drain and save liquid. Cut fish into pieces for serving, brush with olive oil, sprinkle with salt, pepper, crumbled bay leaf and thyme, and let stand a while. Put the olive oil and fish stock into a large pot, adding onions, garlic, tomatoes, parsley and lemon juice and let the whole simmer for about an hour. Wet the saffron in a small part of the wine and add with fish and shellfish, pimientoes, and continue simmering until fish is done, rolling the pot to distribute the saffron. Just before removing from the fire add the balance of the wine and serve over the garlic toast.

— From THE BOSTON TRANSCRIPT

A true Cape Cod man or woman is hard to define. "A Cape Cod man? Not him!" a Truro man said of his neighbor. "He was born here, true enough. He went to school here, and got married here, and belonged to the church, like his parents before him. And he's living now in the house where he was born. But he went to Brockton to work when he was a young man and he stayed away thirty years. No, we don't call him a Cape Cod man."

After Three Centuries

1872–1873
PENIKESE

BY ELIZABETH CARY AGASSIZ

IN OCTOBER, 1872, Agassiz returned to Cambridge. To arrange the collections he had brought back, to write a report of his journey and its results, to pass the next summer quietly at his Nahant laboratory, continuing his work on the Sharks and Skates, for which he had brought home new and valuable material, seemed the natural sequence of his year of travel.[1] But he found a new scheme of education on foot; one for which he had himself given the first impulse, but which some of his younger friends had carefully considered and discussed in his absence, being confident that with his help it might be accomplished. The plan was to establish a summer school of natural history somewhere on the coast of Massachusetts, where teachers from our schools and colleges could make their vacations serviceable, both for work and recreation, by the direct study of nature. No sooner was Agassiz once more at home than he was confronted by this scheme, and he took it up with characteristic ardor. Means there were none, nor apparatus, nor building, nor even a site for one. There was only the ideal, and to that he brought the undying fervor of his intellectual faith. The prospectus was soon sketched, and, once before the public, it awakened a strong interest. In March, when the Legislature of Massachusetts made their annual visit to the Museum of Comparative Zoology, Agassiz laid this new project before them as one of deep interest for science in general, and especially for schools and colleges throughout the land. He considered it also an educational branch of the Museum, having, as such, a claim on their sympathy, since it was in the line of the direct growth and continuance of the same work. Never did he plead more eloquently for the cause of education. His gift as a speaker cannot easily be described. It was born of conviction, and was as simple as it was impassioned. It kept the freshness of youth, because the things of

[1] The famed voyage of the *Hassler*.

which he spoke never grew old to him, but moved him to the last hour of his life as forcibly as in his earlier years.

This appeal to the Legislature, spoken in the morning, chanced to be read in the evening papers of the same day by Mr. John Anderson, a rich merchant of New York. It at once enlisted his sympathy both for the work and for the man. Within the week he offered to Agassiz, as a site for the school, the island of Penikese, in Buzzard's Bay, with the buildings upon it, consisting of a furnished dwelling-house and barn. Scarcely was this gift accepted than he added to it an endowment of $50,000 for the equipment of the school. Adjectives belittle deeds like these. The bare statement says more than the most laudatory epithets.

Agassiz was no less surprised than touched at the aid thus unexpectedly offered. In his letter of acknowledgment he says: "You do not know what it is suddenly and unexpectedly to find a friend at your side, full of sympathy, and offering support to a scheme which you have been trying to carry out under difficulties and with very scanty means. I feel grateful to you for making the road so easy, and I believe you will have the permanent gratitude of scientific men here and elsewhere, for I have the utmost confidence that this summer school will give valuable opportunities for original work, as well as for instruction." At Agassiz's suggestion the school was to bear the name of "The Anderson School of Natural History." Mr. Anderson wished to substitute the name of Agassiz for his own. This Agassiz absolutely refused to permit, saying that he was but one of many scientific men who had already offered their services to the school for the coming summer, some of whom would, no doubt, continue to work for it in the future, and all of whom would be equally indebted to Mr. Anderson. It was, therefore, most suitable that it should bear his name, and so it was agreed.

Thus the material problem was solved. Name and habitation were found; it remained only to organize the work for which so fitting a home had been provided. Mr. Anderson's gift was received toward the close of March, and, in the course of the following month, the preliminaries were concluded, and the property was transferred to the trustees of the Anderson School.

Few men would have thought it feasible to build dormitories and laboratories, and provide working apparatus for fifty pupils as well as for a large corps of teachers, between May and July. But to Agassiz no obstacles seemed insurmountable where great aims were involved, and the opening of the school was announced for the 8th of July. He left Boston on Friday, the 4th of July, for the island. At New Bedford he was met by a warning from the architect that it would be simply impossible to open the school at the appointed date. With characteristic disregard of practical difficulties, he answered that it must be possible, for postponement was out of the question. He reached the island on Saturday, the 5th, in the afternoon. The aspect was certainly discouraging. The dormitory was up, but only the frame completed; there were no floors, nor was the roof shingled. The next day was Sunday. Agassiz called the carpenters together. He told them that the scheme was neither for money, nor for the making of money; no personal gain was involved in it. It was for the best interests of education, and for that alone. Having explained the object, and stated the emergency, he asked, whether, under the circumstances, the next day was properly for rest or for work. They all answered "for work." They accordingly worked the following day from dawn till dark, and by night-fall the floors were laid. On Monday, the 7th, the partitions were put up, dividing the upper story into two large dormitories; the lower into sufficiently convenient working-rooms. On Tuesday morning (the 8th), with the help of a few volunteers, chiefly ladies connected with the school, who had arrived a day or two in advance, the dormitories, still encumbered by shavings, sawdust, etc., were swept, and presently transformed into not unattractive sleeping-halls. They were divided by neat sets of furniture into equal spaces, above each of which was placed the name of the person to whom it was appropriated. When all was done, the large open rooms, with their fresh pine walls, floors, and ceilings, the rows of white beds down the sides, and the many windows looking to the sea, were pretty and inviting enough. If they somewhat resembled hospital wards, they were too airy and cheerful to suggest sickness either of body or mind.

Next, a large barn belonging to Mr. Anderson's former establishment was cleared, and a new floor laid there also. This was hardly finished (the last nails were just driven) when the steamer, with its large company, touched the wharf. There was barely time to arrange the seats and to place a table with flowers where the guests of honor were to sit, and Agassiz himself was to stand, when all arrived. The barn was, on the whole not a bad lecture-room on a beautiful summer day. The swallows, who had their nests without number in the rafters, flew in and out, and twittered softly overhead; and the wide doors, standing broadly open to the blue sky and the fresh fields, let in the sea-breeze, and gave a view of the little domain. Agassiz had arranged no programme of exercises, trusting to the interest of the occasion to suggest what might best be said or done. But, as he looked upon his pupils gathered there to study nature with him, by an impulse as natural as it was unpremeditated, he called upon them to join in silently asking God's blessing on their work together. The pause was broken by the first words of an address no less fervent than its unspoken prelude.[2]

Thus the day, which had been anticipated with so much anxiety, passed off, unclouded by any untoward accident, and at evening the guests had departed. Students and teachers, a company of some fifty or sixty persons, were left to share the island with the sea-gulls whose haunt it was.

We will not enter into the daily details of the school. It was a new phase of teaching, even for Agassiz, old as he was in the work. Most of his pupils were mature men and women, some of whom had been teachers themselves for many years. He had, therefore, trained minds to deal with, and the experience was at that time as novel as it was interesting. The novelty has worn off now.[3] Summer schools for advanced students, and especially for teachers, have taken their place in the general system of education; and, though the Penikese school may be said to have died with its master, it lives anew in many a seaside laboratory organized on the same plan, in summer schools of Botany and field classes of Geology. The impetus it gave was not, and cannot be, lost, since it refreshed and vitalized methods of teaching.

Beside the young men who formed his corps of teachers, among whom the resident professors were Dr. Burt G. Wilder, of Cornell University, and Professor Alpheus S. Packard, now of Brown University, Agassiz had with him some of his oldest friends and colleagues. Count de Pourtalès was there, superintending the dredging, for which there were special conveniences, Mr. Charles G. Galloupe having presented the school with a yacht for the express purpose. Professor Arnold Guyot, also, — Agassiz's comrade in younger years, — his companion in many an Alpine excursion, — came to the island to give a course of lectures, and remained for some time. The lectures

[2] This whole scene is fitly told in Whittier's poem, "The Prayer of Agassiz." E. C. A.
[3] 1885.

of the morning and afternoon would sometimes be followed by an informal meeting held on a little hill, which was a favorite resort at sunset. There the whole community gathered around the two old friends, to hear them talk of their glacial explorations, one recalling what the other had forgotten, till the scenes lived again for themselves, and became almost equally vivid for their listeners. The subject came up naturally, for, strange to say, this island in a New England bay was very suggestive of glacial phenomena. Erratic materials and boulders transported from the north were scattered over its surface, and Agassiz found the illustrations for his lectures on this topic ready to his hand. Indeed, some of his finest lectures on the ice-period were given at Penikese.

Nothing could be less artificial, more free from constraint or formality, than the intercourse between him and his companions of this summer. He was at home with every member of the settlement. Ill-health did not check the readiness of his sympathy; languor did not chill the glow of his enthusiasm. All turned to him for help and inspiration. Walking over their little sovereignty together, hunting for specimens on its beaches, dredging from the boats, in the laboratory, or the lecture-room, the instruction had always the character of the freest discussion. Yet the work, although combined with out-of-door pleasures, and not without a certain holiday element, was no play. On the part of the students, the application was close and unremitting; on the part of the teachers, the instructions, though untrammeled by routine, was sustained and systematic.

Agassiz himself frequently gave two lectures a day. In the morning session he would prepare his class for the work of the day; in the afternoon he would draw out their own observations by questions, and lead them by comparison and combination of the facts they had observed, to understand the significance of their results. Every lecture from him at this time was a lesson in teaching as well as in natural history, and to many of his hearers this gave his lectures a twofold value, as bearing directly upon their own occupation. In his opening address he had said to them: "You will find the same elements of instruction all about you wherever you may be teaching. You can take your classes out, and give them the same lessons, and lead them up to the same subjects you are yourselves studying here. And this mode of teaching children is so natural, so suggestive, so true. That is the charm of teaching from Nature herself. No one can warp her to suit his own views. She brings us back to absolute truth as often as we wander."

This was the bright side of the picture. Those who stood nearest to Agassiz, however, felt that the strain not only of work, but of the anxiety and responsibility attendant upon a new and important undertaking, was perilous for him. There were moments when this became apparent, and he himself felt the danger. He persevered, nevertheless, to the end of the summer, and only left Penikese when the school broke up.

—From LOUIS AGASSIZ, HIS LIFE AND CORRESPONDENCE, 1885

The sunny nineteenth-century American idyll of the summer of 1873, all mixed up with clambakes and classes, lovemaking and learning, was never wholly repeated, for Louis Agassiz died before the end of the year. His son opened and conducted the school the next summer, but not again. The immense importance of the short-lived adventure can be read between the lines of the inscription on a bronze tablet which was set in a granite boulder on the highest point of Penikese on August 13, 1923:—

In Commemoration of the Anderson School of Natural History Established Fifty Years Ago on the Island of Penikese by Jean Louis Rodolphe Agassiz: The Marine Biological Laboratory the Direct Descendant of the Penikese School Erects This Tablet.

A replica of this tablet may be seen in the Wood's Hole Marine Biological Laboratory. This institution is actually more the spiritual than the lineal descendant of Agassiz's school. There is no real connection between the two, but the one would probably never have existed without the other. Founded in 1888, the Wood's Hole laboratory is one of the greatest marine biological laboratories in the world. Its sister establishment, the Wood's Hole Oceanographic Institution, erected and endowed by the Rockefeller Foundation, goes back to 1930. In 1885 a United States Bureau of Fisheries Station was established at Wood's hole.

Penikese, a great tern-breeding ground, is today the haunt of serious ornithologists.

FULL FATHOM FIVE

BY ALEXANDER WOOLLCOTT

THIS IS THE STORY just as I heard it the other evening — a ghost story told me as true. It seems that one chilly October night in the first decade of the present century, two sisters were motoring along a Cape Cod road, when their car broke down just before midnight and would go no further. This was in an era when such mishaps were both commoner and more hopeless than they are today. For these two, there was no chance of help until another car might chance to come by in the morning and give them a tow. Of a lodging for the night there was no hope, except a gaunt, unlighted, frame house which, with a clump of pine trees beside it, stood black in the moonlight, across a neglected stretch of frost-hardened lawn.

They yanked at its ancient bell-pull, but only a faint tinkle within made answer. They banged despairingly on the door panel, only to awaken what they first thought was an echo, and then identified as a shutter responding antiphonally with the help of a nipping wind. This shutter was around the corner, and the ground-floor window behind it was broken and unfastened. There was enough moonlight to show that the room within was a deserted library, with a few books left on the sagging shelves and a few pieces of dilapidated furniture still standing where some departing family had left them, long before. At least the sweep of the electric flash which one of the women had brought with her showed them that on the uncarpeted floor the dust lay thick and trackless, as if no one had trod there in many a day.

They decided to bring their blankets in from the car and stretch out there on the floor until daylight, none too comfortable, perhaps, but at least sheltered from that salt and cutting wind. It was while they were lying there, trying to get to sleep, while, indeed, they had drifted halfway across the borderland, that they saw — each confirming the other's fear by a convulsing grip of the hand — saw standing at the empty fireplace, as if trying to dry himself by a fire that was not there, the wraithlike figure of a sailor, come dripping from the sea.

After an endless moment, in which neither woman breathed, one of them somehow found the strength to call out, "Who's there?" The challenge shattered the intolerable silence, and at the sound, muttering a little — they said afterwards that it was something between a groan and a whimper — the misty figure seemed to dissolve. They strained their eyes, but could see nothing between themselves and the battered mantelpiece.

Then, telling themselves (and, as one does, half believing it) that they had been dreaming, they tried again to sleep, and, indeed, did sleep until a patch of shuttered sunlight striped the morning floor. As they sat up and blinked at the gritty realism of the forsaken room, they would, I think, have laughed at the shared illusion of the night before, had it not been for something at which one of the sisters pointed with a kind of a gasp. There, in the still undisturbed dust, on the spot in front of the fireplace where the apparition had seemed to stand, was a patch of water, a little, circular pool that had issued from no crack in the floor nor, as far as they could see, fallen from any point in the innocent ceiling. Near it in the surrounding dust was no footprint — their own or any other's — and in it was a piece of green that looked like seaweed. One of the women bent down and put her finger to the water, then lifted it to her tongue. The water was salty.

After that the sisters scuttled out and sat in their car, until a passerby gave them a tow to the nearest village. In its tavern at breakfast they gossiped with the proprietress about the empty house among the pine trees down the road. Oh, yes, it had been just that way for a score of years or more. Folks did say the place was spooky, haunted by a son of the family who, driven out by his father, had shipped before the mast and been drowned at sea. Some said the family had moved away because they could not stand the things they heard and saw at night.

A year later, one of the sisters told the story at a dinner party in New York. In the pause that followed a man across the table leaned forward.

"My dear lady," he said, with a smile, "I happen to be the curator of a museum where they are doing a good deal of work on submarine vegetation. In your place, I never would have left that house without taking the bit of seaweed with me."

"Of course you wouldn't," she answered tartly, "and neither did I."

It seems that she had lifted it out of the water and dried it a little by pressing it against a window pane. Then she had carried it off in her pocketbook, as a souvenir. As far as she knew, it was still in an envelope in a little drawer of her desk at home. If she could find it, would he like to see it? He would. Next morning she sent it around by messenger, and a few days later it came back with a note.

"You were right," the note said, "this is seaweed. Furthermore, it may interest you to learn that it is of a rare variety which, as far as we know, grows only on dead bodies."

And that, my dears, is the story as I heard it the other evening, heard it from Alice Duer Miller who, in turn, had heard it five-and-twenty years before from Mrs. George Haven Putnam, sometime dean of Barnard College and author of that Admirable work, *The Lady*. To her I must go if — as I certainly did — I wanted more precise details. So to Mrs. Putnam I went, hat in hand and, as an inveterate reporter, showered her with questions. I wanted the names of the seaweed, of the curator, of the museum, of the two sisters, of the dead sailor, and of the nearby village on Cape Cod. I wanted a roadmap marked with a cross to show the house in the grove of pines. I wanted — but the examination came to a dead stop at the sight of her obvious embarrassment. She was most graciously apologetic, but, really, what with this and with that, she had forgotten the whole story. She could not even remember — and thus it is ever with my life in science — who it was that had told it to her.

FOOTNOTE: More recently, the Curator of the Botanical Museum in St. Louis has assured me that this tale, whispered from neighbor to neighbor across the country, has become distorted in a manner offensive to students of submarine vegetation. According to him, the visitor from the sea was seen in a house in Woods Hole, Mass. He was a son of the house who had been drowned during his honeymoon off the coast of Australia. The seaweed picked up off the dusty floor of that New England mansion was of a variety which grows only off the Australia coast. The Curator even presented me with the actual seaweed. I regard it with mingled affection and skepticism, and keep it pressed between the pages of Bullfinch's Mythology.   A.W.

— From WHILE ROME BURNS

☙❧

On Cape Cod it is believed that a sick man can not die until the ebb tide begins to run. Watchers by beds of sickness anxiously note the change of tides, and if the patient lives until the flood begins to set in again he will live until the next ebb.

☙❧

1906
"A SUPREME QUEERNESS"

BY HENRY JAMES

CLEARLY, none the less, there were puzzles and puzzles, and I had almost immediately the amusement of waking up to another — this one of a different order altogether. The point was that if the bewilderments I have just mentioned had dropped, most other things had dropped too: the challenge to curiosity here was in the extreme simplification of the picture, a simplification on original lines. Not that there was not still much to think of — if only because one had to stare at the very wonder of a picture so simplified. The thing now was to catch this note, to keep it in the ear and see, really, how far and how long it would sound. The simplification, for that immediate vision, was to a broad band of deep and clear blue sea, a blue of the deepest and clearest conceivable, limited in one quarter by its far and sharp horizon of sky, and in the other by its near and sharp horizon of yellow sand overfringed with a low woody shore; the whole seen through the contorted cross-pieces of stunted, wind-twisted, far-spreading, quite fantastic old pines and cedars, whose bunched bristles, at the ends of long limbs, produced, against the light, the most vivid of all reminders. Cape Cod, on this showing, was exactly a pendent, pictured Japanese screen or banner; a delightful little triumph of "impressionism," which, during my short visit at least, never departed, under any provocation, from its type. Its type, so easily formulated, so completely filled, was there the last thing at night and the first thing in the morning; there was rest for the mind — for that, certainly, of the restless analyst — in having it so exactly under one's hand. After that one could read into it other meanings without straining or disturbing it. There was a couchant promontory in particular, half bosky with the evergreen boskage of the elegant kakemono, half bare with the bareness of refined, the *most* refined, New England decoration, a low, hospital headland projected, as by some water-colorist master of the trick, into a mere brave wash of cobalt. It interfered, the sweet promontory, with its generous Boston bungalow, its verandas still haunted with old summer-times, and so wide that the present could elbow and yet not jostle the past — it interfered no whit, for all its purity of style, with the human, the social question always dogging the steps of the ancient contemplative person and making him, before each scene, wish really to get *into* the picture, to cross, as it were, the threshold of the frame. It never lifts, verily, this obsession of the story-seeker, however often it may flutter its wings, it may bruise its breast, against surfaces either too hard or too blank. "The *manners,* the manners: where and what are they, and what have they to tell?" — that haunting curiosity, essential to the honor of his office, yet making it much of a burden, fairly buzzes about his head the more pressingly in proportion as the social mystery, the lurking human secret, seems more shy.

Then it is that, as he says to himself, the secret must be most queer — and it might therefore well have had, so insidiously sounded, a supreme queerness on Cape Cod. For not the faintest echo of it trembled out of the blankness; there were always the little white houses of the village, there were always the elegant elms, feebler and more feathery here than farther inland; but the life of the little community was practically locked up as tight as if it had *all* been a question of painted Japanese silk. And that was doubtless, for the story-seeker, absolutely the little story: the constituted blankness was the whole business, and one's opportunity was all, thereby, for a study of exquisite emptiness. This was stuff, in its own way, of a beautiful quality; that impression came to me with a special sweetness that I have not forgotten. The help in the matter was that I had not forgotten, either, a small pilgrimage or two of far-away earlier years — the sense as of absent things in other summer-times, golden afternoons that referred themselves for their character simply to sandy roads and primitive "farms," crooked inlets of mild sea and, at the richest, large possibilities of worked cranberry-swamp. I remembered, in fine, Mattapoisett, I remembered Marion, as admirable examples of that frequent New England phenomenon, the case the consummate example of which I was soon again to recognize in Newport — the presence of an *unreasoned* appeal, in nature, to the sense of beauty, the appeal on a basis of items that failed somehow, count and recount them as one would, to justify the effect and make up the precious sum. The sum, at Newport above all, as I was soon again to see, is the exquisite, the irresistible; but you falter before beginning to name the parts of the explanation, conscious how short the list may appear. Thus everything, in the whole range of imagery, affirms itself and interposes; you will, you inwardly determine, arrive at some notation of manners even if you perish in the attempt. Thus, as I jogged southward, from Boston, in a train that stopped and stopped again, for my fuller enlightenment, and that insisted, the good old promiscuous American car itself, on having as much of its native character as possible for my benefit, I already knew I must fall back on old props of association, some revival of the process of seeing the land grow mild and vague and interchangeably familiar with the sea, all under the spell of the reported "gulf stream," those mystic words that breathe a softness wherever they sound.

It was imperative here that they should do what they could for me, and they must have been in full operation when, on my arrival at the small station from which I was to drive across to Cotuit — "across the Cape," as who should say, romantic thought, though I strain a point geographically for the romance — I found initiation awaiting me in the form of minimized horse-and-buggy and mini-mized man. The man was a little boy in tight knickerbockers, the horse barely an animal at all, a mere ambling spirit in shafts on the scale of a hair-pin, the buggy disembodied save for its wheels, the whole thing the barest infraction of the road, of the void: circumstances, altogether, that struck the note, the right, the persistent one — that my baffled endeavor, while in the neighborhood, to catch life in the fact, and of my then having to recognize it as present *without* facts, or with only the few (the little white houses, the feath-ery elms, the band of ocean blue, the stripe of sandy yellow, the tufted pines in angular silhouette, the cranberry-swamps stringed across, for the picking, like the ruled pages of ledgers), that fell, incorruptibly silent, into the picture. We were still far from our goal, that first hour, when I had recognized the full pictorial and other "value" of my little boy and his little accessories; had seen, in the amiable waste that we continued to plough till we struck, almost with a shock, the inconsistency of a long stretch of new "stone" road, that, socially, economically, every contributive scrap of this detail was required. I drained my small companion, by gentle pres-sure, of such side-lights as he could project, consisting almost wholly, as they did, of a prompt and shrill, an oddly-emphasized "Yes, *sir!*" to each interrogative attempt to break ground. The summer people had already departed — with, as it seemed to me, undue precipita-tion; the very hotel offered, in its many-windowed bulk, the semblance of a mere huge brittle sea-shell that children tired of playing with it have cast again upon the beach; the alignments of white cottages were, once more, as if the children had taken, for a change, to building houses of cards and then had deserted *them*. I remember the sense that something *must* be done for penetration, for discovery; I remember an earnest stroll, undertaken for a view of waterside life, which resulted in the perception of a young man, in a spacious but otherwise unpeopled nook, a clear, straightforward young man to converse with, for a grand opportunity, across the water, waist-high in the quiet tide and prodding the sea-bottom for oysters; also in the discovery of an animated centre of industry of which oysters again were the motive: a mute citizen or two packing them in boxes, on the beach, for the Boston market, the hammer of some vague carpentry hard by, and, filling the air more than anything else, the unabashed discourse of three or four school-children at leisure, visibly "prominent" and apparently in charge of the life of the place. I remember not less a longish walk, and a longer drive, into low extensions of woody, piney, pondy landscape, veined with blue inlets and trimmed, on opportunity, with blond beaches — through all of which I pursued in vain the shy spectre of a revelation. The only revelation seemed really to be that, quite as in New Hampshire, so many people had "left" that the remaining characters, on the sketchy page, were too few to form a word. With this, accordingly, of what, in the bright air, for the charmed visitor, were the softness and sweetness of impression *made?* I had again to take it for a mystery.

— From THE AMERICAN SCENE

❧

There was a week when the noon whistle in Provincetown failed to sound off. It was seldom accurate, but it did announce the coming of lunch time and had its value. A visitor asked his neighbor what had happened and was told that the man who blew the whistle was sick.

"Is he the only man in town who can pull the lanyard?"

"O, it's not that. He's pretty sick and it would break his heart if he thought someone else had got his job."

1915–1916
THE PROVINCETOWN PLAYERS

BY SUSAN GLASPELL

WE WANTED our play put on, as who doesn't, but even the little theatres thought "Suppressed Desires" "too special." Now it has been given by every little theater, and almost every Methodist church; golf clubs in Honolulu, colleges in Constantinople; in Paris and China and every rural route in America. I wish I had the records of how many thousands of times Step-hen has been asked to be rooster. He had been far from special.

Well, if no one else was going to put on our play, we would put it on ourselves. Neith Boyce had a play — "Constancy." We gave the two in her house one evening. Bobby Jones was there and helped us with the sets. He liked doing it, because we had no lighting equipment, but just put a candle here and a lamp there.

A few minutes before it was time to give our play, Jig[1] and I took a walk up the shore. We held each other's cold hands and said, "Never mind, it will be over soon."

But when it was over we were sorry. People liked it, and we liked doing it.

Neighbors who had not been asked were hurt, so we gave the plays again. Margaret Steele had taken for studio the old fish-house out at the end of the Mary Heaton Vorse wharf, across from our house. She let us have this, so more people could come. Jig became so interested he wrote another comedy, "Change Your Style," having to do with Provincetown art schools, a jolly little play. Wilbur Steele had written "Contemporaries," and those two we gave together. Thus ended the first season of the Provincetown Players, who closed without knowing they were the Provincetown Players.

It might have ended there — people giving plays in the summer, if it hadn't been — Do you remember Jig's dream city, how there was to be a theater and "why not write our own plays, and put them on ourselves, giving writer, actor, designer, a chance to work together without the commercial thing imposed from without? A whole community working together, developing unsuspected talents. . . .

[1] George Cram Cook.

We were back early in the spring, after seeing more Broadway plays. Jack Reed came home from Mexico, where he saw a medieval miracle play which has survived in unbroken tradition among the natives of a certain village, as the poems of Homer existed for some centuries in the Ionian villages of Asia Minor.

Students of dreams tell us our dreams use the things of the moment as vehicle, pattern, symbol, for the deep-lying thing. In our activities, as in our dreams, the accidental is seized to be shared by our deep necessities.

"One man cannot produce drama. True drama is born only of one feeling animating all the members of a clan — a spirit shared by all and expressed by the few for the all. If there is nothing to take the place of the common religious purpose and passion of the primitive group, out of which the Dionysian dance was born, no new vital drama can arise in any people."

He and Neith Boyce said it together. He came home and wrote it down as an affirmation of faith.

The people who came back that summer had little chance of escaping. Purpose had grown in him, he was going to take whom he wanted and use them for the creation of his Beloved Community.

We hauled out the old boat, took oars and nets and anchors to various owners, bought lumber at the second wharf "up-along," and Jig, Nordfeldt, Ballantine, Joe O'Brien, others helping, converted the fish-house into the Wharf Theater, a place where ninety people could see a play, if they didn't mind sitting close together on wooden benches with no backs. The stage, ten feet by twelve, was in four sections, so we could have different levels, could run it through the big sliding-door at the back, a variety of set surprising in quarters so small.

We gave our first bill, then met at our house to read plays for a second. Two Irishmen, one old and one young, had arrived and taken a shack just up the street. "Terry," I said to the one not young, "haven't you a play to read to us?"

"No," said Terry Carlin, "I don't write, I just think, and sometimes talk. But Mr. O'Neill has got a whole trunk full of plays," he smiled.

That didn't sound too promising, but I said: "Well, tell Mr.

O'Neill to come to our house at eight o'clock tonight, and bring some of his plays."

So Gene took "Bound East for Cardiff" from his trunk, and Freddie Burt read it to us, Gene staying out in the dining-room while the reading went on.

He was not left alone in the dining-room when the reading had finished.

Then we knew what we were for. We began in faith, and perhaps it is true when you do that "all these things shall be added unto you."

I may see it through memories too emotional, but it seems to me I have never sat before a more moving production than our "Bound East for Cardiff," when Eugene O'Neill was produced for the first time on any stage. Jig was Yank. As he lay in his bunk dying, he talked of life as one who knew he must leave it.

The sea has been good to Eugene O'Neill. It was there for his opening. There was a fog, just as the script demanded, fog bell in the harbor. The tide was in, and it washed under us and around, spraying through the holes in the floor, giving us the rhythm and the flavor of the sea while the big dying sailor talked to his friend Drisc of the life he had always wanted deep in the land, where you'd never see a ship or smell the sea.

It is not merely figurative language to say the old wharf shook with applause.

The people who had seen the plays, and the people who gave them, were adventurers together. The spectators were part of the Players, for how could it have been done without the feeling that came from them, without that sense of them there, waiting, ready to share, giving — finding the deep level where audience and writer and player are one. The last month of his life he wrote:

> I who am audience insofar as the author is one with me,
> And author insofar as the audience is one with me,
> More than any person's name and fame
> I will to hear
> The music of the identity of men.

People sometimes said, "Jig is not a business man," when it seemed opportunities were passed by. But those opportunities were not things wanted from deep. He had the unique power to see just how the thing he wanted done could be done. He could finance for the spirit, and seldom confused, or betrayed, by extending the financing beyond the span he saw ahead, not weighing his adventure down with schemes that would become things in themselves.

He wrote a letter to the people who had seen the plays, asking if they cared to become associate members of the Provincetown Players. The purpose was to give American playwrights of sincere purpose a chance to work out their ideas in freedom, to give all who worked with the plays their opportunity as artists. Were they interested in this? One dollar for the three remaining bills.

The response paid for seats and stage, and for sets. A production need not cost a lot of money, Jig would say. The most expensive set at the Wharf Theater cost thirteen dollars. There were sets at the Provincetown Playhouse which cost little more. He liked to remember "The Knight of the Burning Pestle" they gave at Leland Stanford, where a book could indicate one house and a bottle another. Sometimes the audience liked to make its own set.

"Now, Susan," he said to me, briskly, "I have announced a play of yours for the next bill."

"But I have no play!"

"Then you will have to sit down tomorrow and begin one."

I protested. I did not know how to write a play. I had never "studied it."

"Nonsense," said Jig. "You've got a stage, haven't you?"

So I went out on the wharf, sat alone on one of our wooden benches without a back, and looked for a long time at that bare little stage. After a time the stage became a kitchen — a kitchen there all by itself. I saw just where the stove was, the table, and the steps going upstairs. Then the door at the back opened, and people all bundled up came in — two or three men, I wasn't sure which, but sure enough about the two women, who hung back, reluctant to enter that kitchen. When I was a newspaper reporter out in Iowa, I was sent down-state to do a murder trial, and I never forgot going into the kitchen of a woman locked up in town. I had meant to do it as a short story, but the stage took it for its own, so I hurried in from the wharf to write down what I had seen. Whenever I got stuck, I would run across the street to the old wharf, sit in that leaning little theater under which the sea sounded, until the play was ready to continue. Sometimes things written in my room would not form on the stage, and I must go home and cross them out. "What playwrights need is a stage," said Jig, "their own stage."

Ten days after the director said he had announced my play, there was a reading at Mary Heaton Vorse's. I was late to the meeting, home revising the play. But when I got there the crowd liked "Trifles," and voted to put it in rehearsal next day.

It was a great summer; we swam from the wharf as well as rehearsed there; we would lie on the beach and talk about plays — every one writing, or acting, or producing. Life was all of a piece, work not separated from play.

I like to remember certain times late at night. The audience had gone home, the big door had been drawn shut; the last actor who wanted a drink had the last drop there was at our house, and Jig and I might stroll out on the wharf before going to bed. The sea had taken it all again — the wharf was the old wharf and the theater the fish-house that had been there while so many tides came and went. Fishermen, people from deep in the land who wanted to write plays about both sea and land that — Why? At such times one wondered. It seemed now, on the wharf that jutted out from a sleeping town, as if we had not been at all; and before many more tides came in, it would indeed be as if we had not been at all. And yet, would it? Perhaps we wanted to write plays and put them on just because we knew, more intensely than the fishermen, that the tide comes, the tide goes. You cannot know that and leave things just as they were before.

One night I was lonely in the house, suspected where Jig was and went out to find him. The theater a dark bulk behind him, he was sitting at the end of the wharf, feet hanging over. "Thinking about the theater?" I asked after a little — things hadn't gone so well that night.

He shook ashes from his pipe. "No," he said, "I was thinking about raft boats on the Mississippi."

I was appalled the day Jig said, "When we go to New York for the winter, we will take our theater with us." That, I thought, was a very different thing. I was afraid for him. I knew how it had been through the summer. Many had been interested, and some of them had worked hard, but after all the others worked when they

wanted to. "What is Jig going to do about this?" they would say
when a real difficulty presented itself. There were people who would
be animated when they were with him, and then next day — "But
really, I haven't time for it, you know," and they would have to be
captured anew, or let go, and some one else captured. He was the
center; for the most part, he made the others want to do it, as well
as persuaded them it could be done. I felt the energy must go into
keeping that fire of enthusiasm, or belief, from which all drew.
It was hard to see Jig hurt — he always seemed so surprised it should
be like that. He had so much trust, valuing people by the finest
moment they showed him — sometimes largely a radiation from his
own glow. And I was afraid people would laugh at him, starting
a theater in New York — new playwrights, amateur acting, somewhere in an old house or stable. He himself never thought of this,
too concentrated on the thing to be done. . . .

"Where will we get the money?" I asked.

"Our associate members will subscribe for the New York season.
That will be our nucleus."

It was one of Jig's warmest satisfactions that members of our
audience that summer of nineteen-sixteen were members every year
thereafter. There was our strength, he said; we did not need to take
money that would threaten what we were; our audience was part
of us.

We were going to call ourselves the Provincetown Players, but
Gene proposed we also be the Playwrights' Theater.

Two hundred and forty-five dollars in his pockets, in the glow
of vision, energetic with belief, Jig boarded the train to look for a
place for the Provincetown Players in New York. He stood alone
on the back platform, waving to me. "Don't worry!" he called, as
the train was starting. Then something I couldn't hear, and I went
running after him. He cupped his mouth with his hands to call
back: "Write — another — play!"

— From THE ROAD TO THE TEMPLE, 1927

☙

1911

THE CAPE COD CANAL

BY AUGUST BELMONT

TO ME, AND NATURALLY to New Englanders, the idea of a canal cut across Cape Cod was always an interesting fairy tale. The hope that it might some day become a reality served as a solace for the pain given to one by the accounts of wreck and suffering while rounding the Cape. A short synopsis of the story is worth the recital.

It began in 1623, and for four years the Plymouth Colony endeavored to establish connection by water with the Dutch at New Amsterdam, and for the remainder of the seventeenth century attempts were made at intervals to cut a connection between the Scusset River, a little stream emptying into Barnstable Bay, and the Herring River, a distance of three miles, a stream which emptied into the Monument River and which in turn found Buzzard's Bay. For the small trading vessels of those days this very limited undertaking was perfectly feasible, but the Colony was too poor to spend the necessary money.

From then to 1776 the Colony of Massachusetts made examinations of the same locality for a canal, and individuals as well flirted with the subject.

On May 1, 1776, General Washington sent Thomas Machin, a noted engineer of the time, to the Cape, to see if it could be made possible for him to carry his army by water from Boston to New York across the Cape, and by this maneuver gain a march on Lord Howe.

The General Court of Massachusetts went so far as to recommend to the Continental Congress the construction of a canal through much the same route as today. This was an interesting first step to the control by the United States over the proposed channel. The Congress took no action, although the report stated the "canal practicable as giving greater security to navigation and against the enemy." Nothing further transpired until 1780 when General Knox used his influence toward having the Government build the canal.

In 1808, on April 4th, Albert Gallatin, the Secretary of the Treasury, advocated the construction of the canal as being highly useful in time of war, as well as for commerce.

During the War of 1812, the Canal Isthmus was frequently used for the transit of merchandise to avoid capture by the enemy's cruisers on the coast. Here is a distinct forecast of a security demanded for a vast commerce plying in the same directions today.

In 1818 the United States Senate caused a survey to be made on Cape Cod for a canal of a size to admit vessels of war to pass: January 5, 1824, Senator Lloyd, of Massachusetts, introduced a resolution in the United States Senate, instructing the Government to make a survey for a canal, reciting as a reason that (I quote from the Resolution) "after the completion of the Chesapeake, Delaware and Raritan canals, inland water communication would extend from Albemarle Sound to Massachusetts Bay, passing in its progress through the territory or along the borders of ten states."

From 1825 to 1827 further surveys were made under Government orders.

The Erie Canal had been opened on November 14, 1825, and it is a moot question whether Massachusetts, had she pushed her canal, would not have retained her commercial marine importance. Pennsylvania, as well as Massachusetts, lost its former supremacy to New York from that time.

During the period following, up to 1844, Government surveys and reports on the subject continued, but nothing came of them, for railroads were then growing as transportation agencies.

As the Civil War was casting its shadow over the country in 1860, the interest in a canal in Massachusetts was revived by the United States Government. Surveys were made by distinguished army and navy officers.

Special stress was laid upon the advantage to the country in time of war possessed by the proposed canal. The war broke out and nothing further was done at that time.

In 1870 private enterprise revived the project. The Cape Cod Ship Canal Company obtained a charter, and the Government made a survey under General J. G. Foster. General Foster wrote: "Its military value in time of war equals its commercial value in time of peace." He stated among other points "the breakwater can be properly classed as a national work," and cited as a kindred work the Delaware Breakwater, upon which the Government has expended over $2,000,000. General Humphries, in forwarding General Foster's report on May 19, 1870, stated: "the canal would also be advantageous in time of war, and that the breakwater required would cost not less than $3,000,000."

On June 16th of the same year, Senator Chandler reported favorably from the Committee on Commerce a bill authorizing the expenditure by the Government for a breakwater and harbor of refuge at Barnstable Bay. This passed to a second reading.

In 1871, March 9th, Senator Wilson introduced a bill which also passed its second reading, authorizing the construction of a breakwater and harbor of refuge at Barnstable Bay during the construction of the canal by the Cape Cod Ship Canal Company, provided the canal should be forever free and without toll or charges to the ships, vessels and property of the United States. The Ship Canal Company, however, failed, and nothing came of this very significant move.

Not until 1882 do we hear again of the project, and then only in the form of a report in February by General Warren to the Chief of Engineers, U.S.A. He stated that the Buzzard's Bay approach would cost $350,000; and the Barnstable Bay approach, including jetties and preliminary work, $1,131,000; a total of $1,481,000, and that the approaches were susceptible of easy defense.

In 1891 another private effort was made and a charter granted by the State of Massachusetts to the Massachusetts Maritime Canal Company, but this charter was allowed to lapse without results.

With this ended the fairy tale.

In 1899 a charter was granted to the Boston, Cape Cod & New York Canal Company. Mr. DeWitt C. Flanagan was the moving spirit of this beginning. He and his associates clung with pertinacity to the project for five years, when he brought the enterprise to me.

We worked together, and after securing suitable amendments, my firm undertook the task of providing the organization and means for carrying out the work of construction.

On May 8, 1907, the Joint Board of Railroad and Harbor and Land Commissioners approved the present location of the canal, and under the supervision of William Barclay Parsons, as chief engineer, and Commodore J. W. Miller, as vice-president and manager, we began work June 22, 1909, and have been steadily at work ever since.

. . . . .

During our life as a company, working at this undertaking on the Cape, phantom after phantom, conjured by long years of waiting and failure, colored by the croakings of retired seafarers and other loquacious wiseacres, have vanished.

The exaggerated floes of ice, the unmanageable shifting sands and hopelessly destructive winds, and finally the bugaboo of the insurmountable obstacle of a six-foot difference of tides at the two proposed ends of the cut, have faded into commonplace. It is to be a perfectly workable sea-level canal.

A terribly severe and boisterous winter a year ago did not dislodge a dozen stones on the breakwater, not then quite finished, nor shift the sands at the mouth of the canal, nor did ice form sufficiently in the existing cut to be an impediment to either work or navigation, and this, too, with water less mobile than will be the case when the canal is open and in operation.

. . . . .

The Cape Cod Canal is now on the road to rapid and positive completion. The breakwater, three thousand feet in length, is built. About three miles of the Canal at the Barnstable end are cut. The Buzzard's Bay channel dredging is well advanced; the railroad location has been changed, and the Old Colony Railroad is now in operation over a magnificent new drawbridge crossing the Monument River, which is rapidly losing its name to the Cape Cod Canal. A fine passenger bridge at Bourne over the canal location is finished. The highways along and adjacent to the canal are mapped out and being rapidly developed and changed to a perfect system of well macadamized roads serving the canal zone. Another bridge will shortly be begun at Sagamore. Thus the Cape Cod Canal is already a fact, and its opening for traffic cannot in the ordinary course of events be deferred beyond 1913, or at latest, the Spring of 1914. I am wedded to the first date.

— From CAPE COD CANAL AND ATLANTIC COAST WATERWAYS

This review of the history of the Canal is taken from an address delivered December 7, 1911 before the National Rivers and Harbors Congress at Washington, D.C.

The Canal was opened to traffic July 29, 1914, eight vessels sailing through with August Belmont on the first. It cost $16,000,000 to build. Operated as a toll waterway at first, it passed into Federal ownership in 1926 and the tolls were abolished the following year. In 1935 two bridges with a clearance of 135 feet at high tide, the same as that of Brooklyn Bridge, replaced the jackknife bridges that had spanned the Canal at Sagamore and Buzzard's Bay. Shortly before World War II the Canal was lengthened, widened, and deepened by the Government. It is now 17 miles long, 540 wide, and 32 feet deep at low tide: the widest artificial waterway in the world. It has been a lifesaver from the start, invaluable to New England commerce, and, as we learned after Pearl Harbor, invaluable in war. Convoys passed through in numbers in the years while German submarines prowled this coast. On endless lines of men-of-war, freighters, tankers, barges you could see the flags of all our Allies and most of our friends. Cape Cod people were proud of the war work of the Canal but much relieved when normal peacetime traffic was resumed. The sea's for fishing in and trading on, to Cape Cod minds.

Old-timers will tell you winters are milder now that the Canal has made an island of Cape Cod. Maybe so.

༶

CAPE COD MEN *are still farming, still fishing, still going to sea when they get a chance, going to church, minding their own business, saving money, taking a hard life and hard work easy, living to a ripe old age. There can be few places in America except in some parts of the South where a man's great-great-great-grandson is so likely to resemble him physically and spiritually as on Cape Cod. The glory years are gone but Cape Cod people who looked the gale in the eye during the French and Indian Wars and the Revolution and the War of the Embargo and the Civil War and World Wars I and II, are still the navigators of their destiny, making do as always with what they have or can find.*

Their feeling towards summer visitors has changed since the days

364 · AFTER THREE CENTURIES

of the first invasion back in the last century when a Harwich man complained that "those city boys just come down here to trample all over your cranberry bogs and make free with your daughters." But Cape Cod to the world today is far more than what advertising writers call a "vacationland." In proportion to its size it has become an extraordinarily important center for science and the arts. Cape Cod people, always respectful of learning and sometimes very learned, take pride in this.

They go their own way. Cranky, honest, independent, kind, unsentimental, holding fast to traditions and superstitions bred by the sea, they haven't changed much in the last three hundred years. It's not likely they'll ever change.